The Ecoregions of Saskatchewan

The Ecoregions of Saskatchewan

Prepared and edited by

Saskatchewan Environment and Resource Management

Principal Authors

D.F. Acton, G.A. Padbury, C.T. Stushnoff

Contributing Authors

L. Gallagher, D. Gauthier, L. Kelly, T. Radenbaugh, J. Thorpe

Canadian Plains Research Center

University of Regina

March 1998

Canadian Plains Research Center
University of Regina
Regina, Saskatchewan S4S 0A2
Canada

Canadian Cataloguing in Publication Data

Ecoregions of Saskatchewan

ISBN 0-88977-097-2

1. Ecology--Saskatchewan. 2. Biotic communities--Saskatchewan. I. Acton, D.F. (Donald F.) II. Stushnoff, C.T. (Colette T.) III. Padbury, G.A. IV. University of Regina. Canadian Plains Research Center. V. Saskatchewan. Saskatchewan Environment and Resource Management.

QH106.2.S38 E36 1998 577'.097124 C98-920054-X

Cover Design: Bruce Weild

Printed and bound in Canada by
Hignell Printing Limited, Winnipeg, Manitoba
Printed on recycled and acid-free paper.

Contents

List of Figures

Index to Landscape Areas

Taiga Shield Ecozone

Boreal Shield Ecozone

Boreal Plain Ecozone

Foreword

This book is one of a set of materials that has been prepared to act as information guides and learning tools to better understand our human partnership with the environment. That partnership requires that we think, plan and act in terms of ecosystems. The material topics range from a North American perspective on continental ecological regions, through a Canadian national framework on terrestrial ecozones and ecoregions, to the ecoregions of Saskatchewan. The NAFTA Commission for Environmental Cooperation's (CEC) 1997 *Ecological Regions of North America* provides the integrated, continental perspective. The Canadian Council on Ecological Area's (CCEA) 1996 *A Perspective on Canada's Ecosystems* and Environment Canada and Agriculture and Agri-food Canada's 1996 *A National Ecological Framework for Canada* provide a complementary country-wide framework. They are accompanied by Environment Canada's 1997 "Ecozone Poster Set," each unit focussing on ecological, physical, biological, and human characteristics of each of Canada's ecozones. The Saskatchewan perspective is provided through four products: the 1994 "Ecoregions of Saskatchewan" poster map; the 1998 "Ecoregions of Saskatchewan CD-ROM"; the 1998 *Ecoregions of Saskatchewan Teachers Guide*; and, fourthly, this book. Each product provides differing levels of detail. This book is intended to provide the most complete, detailed source of information about Saskatchewan's ecoregions in support of the poster map, CD-ROM, and teachers guide.

Beginnings

The process of developing a standardized classification of the Ecoregions of Saskatchewan began in 1991 with the creation of Saskatchewan's Protected Areas Task Force. The task force was created with the goal of "establishing a system of protected areas in order to protect or enhance life support systems, in situ biological diversity including wildlife habitat, cultural and heritage resources and natural landscapes providing ecological, economic and social benefits." Saskatchewan Environment and Resource Management (SERM) led the initiative and numerous agencies and organizations were represented on the task force over its four years of operation.

A number of subcommittees were created to facilitate the work of the task force. For example, subcommittees were created to develop a statistical summary of characteristics of protected areas in the province and to develop a geographical information system database of protected area boundaries. The task force members recognized Saskatchewan's need for a protected areas systems plan. They recognized that the identification of areas for protection and their distribution throughout the province should be based on their value in maintaining the ecological integrity of the province. To make such assessments, the province needed to be viewed in terms of its ecological characteristics.

The task force created the Ecological Land Classification (ELC) Committee with the mandate to produce a standardized classification of the ecoregions of the province. There were at that time, however, at least five different types of land classification systems used within the province by various agencies and organizations. To display and interpret information about protected areas, task force members required a standardized ecological land classification (ELC) system for the province at coarse to moderate scales. The ELC Committee was formed to develop that classification for the province. Ecological land classification provided the means by which to group ecosystems based on their ecological similarities and differences.

The ELC initiative reflected the thinking about an ecosystem perspective that underlay Canada's Green Plan and Saskatchewan's Conservation Strategy. The release of Canada's Green Plan (Government of Canada 1990) in December of 1990 outlined the federal government's commitment to new policy thrusts to manage Canadian resources prudently and to encourage sensitive environmental decision-making. One cornerstone of the Green Plan was the direction to think, act and plan in terms of ecosystems; to move away from an emphasis on individual elements towards a more comprehensive approach that helps each of us to better understand ecological systems and manage our natural resources. Saskatchewan's Round Table on the Environment and Economy released its *Conservation Strategy for Sustainable Development in Saskatchewan* in 1992. That report emphasized the sustainable use of Saskatchewan's ecosystems and called for an ecological management approach to sustaining resources.

In addition to the ideas presented in the Green Plan and Conservation Strategy, Saskatchewan also benefited from the Canadian Council on Ecological Area's two part report entitled *Framework for Developing a Nation-wide System of Protected Areas*. They provided a conceptual basis and methodology for the use of standardized ecological classification for assessing the representation of protected areas based on enduring landscape features.

The formation of the ELC committee was timely since, also in 1991, a collaborative project was coordinated by federal government agencies (Environment Canada, Agriculture and Agri-Food Canada) with a wide range of stakeholders to revise Canada's terrestrial ecological framework. The revisions were to meet the specific needs of each jurisdiction and yet provide a common framework across the country, i.e., methodology to develop the classification was identical, boundaries of each ecological unit matched across jurisdiction boundaries regardless of scale, names of ecoregions were standardized. In 1996, that work was published as *A National Ecological Framework for Canada*.

In 1994, the ELC committee published its work as the "Ecoregions of Saskatchewan" poster map. That map was distributed to all schools and selected agencies and organizations within the province, as well as to agencies and organizations nationally and internationally. In 1996, the Canadian Council on Ecological Areas presented the ELC Committee with a national award for the excellence of its work in developing the poster map. In addition, the map has been used as a template by some U.S. states to develop their own jurisdictional maps of ecoregions. During this period, at the international level, the NAFTA Commission for Environmental Cooperation was facilitating a project to develop a standardized ecological classification of North America that would be used to help achieve its mandate. They formed a North American Ecological Regions Working Group that included federal and provincial Canadian representatives, as well as Mexican and U.S. representatives. A number of the individuals involved in the development of the Canadian and Saskatchewan ecoregion products were members of that working group. The development of Saskatchewan's poster map was an important example to the NAFTA Working Group since it was based on the same methodology to be employed by that group. In 1997, the CEC published its work as the *Ecological Regions of North America*.

Some members of the ELC committee recognized that there was further work to be done in providing more detailed information about the ecoregions of Saskatchewan to the public. With the support of the ELC, SERM undertook the preparation of a technical document to describe characteristics of each of the ecoregions. That technical document evolved into this book. In addition, some former members of the ELC joined with other interested partners to form the Ecoregions of Saskatchewan CD-ROM Committee, which developed the 1998 Ecoregions of Saskatchewan CD-ROM, a learning tool for high schools. Saskatchewan Education recognized the value of the material being produced about Saskatchewan's ecoregions and undertook the production of a teachers guide for Saskatchewan schools.

With this book there is now an integrated set of information on ecoregions that range from the continental level of North America through to the regional level in Saskatchewan.

Dr. David Gauthier
Canadian Plains Research Center
University of Regina

Acknowledgements

Saskatchewan Environment and Resource Management extends its appreciation to the many persons who shared their knowledge, ideas, and time in the preparation of this publication, *The Ecoregions of Saskatchewan*. In particular, we are indebted to the authors and to the Interprovincial Ecological Classification Steering Committee.

Interprovincial Ecological Land Classification Committee (IELC):
Agriculture and Agri-Food Canada
Canadian Plains Research Center, University of Regina
Environment Canada
Natural Resources Canada
Prairie Farm Rehabilitation Administration
Saskatchewan Agriculture and Food
Saskatchewan Conservation Data Centre
Saskatchewan Energy and Mines
Saskatchewan Environment and Resource Management
Saskatchewan Municipal Government
Saskatchewan Research Council
Sask Geomatics Division, Saskatchewan Property Management Corporation
University of Saskatchewan

Lynda Langford (current Chair, IELC) and Joseph Hnatuik (past Chair, IELC) of SERM were instrumental in guiding the committee through the successful completion of its work. In addition, numerous SERM employees provided a great deal of time and effort in the preparation of this book. We also thank Ed Wiken, Chair, Canadian Council on Ecological Areas, for his contribution of material on ecological classification and ecosystem perspective concepts. To all of those who contributed, your assistance and dedication is much appreciated.

This book is based on and expands upon the "Ecoregions of Saskatchewan" poster map produced in 1994. We wish to thank the authors and contributors to the development of that map for their support and encouragement.

INTRODUCTION

Saskatchewan has a bounty of beautiful landscapes, from the big-sky vistas and charming valleys and coulees on the prairies to the green forests, white-water rivers and clear lakes of the north. Many of them are highly altered by human activity while others exist in relatively pristine conditions.

In Saskatchewan, as well as in many places around the world, humans have depleted and threatened the existence of many native ecosystems. Ensuring a healthy environment while at the same time ensuring economic prosperity for people is an ongoing challenge. Decisions regarding the environment must be made on a broader and more inclusive basis than has been done in the past, recognizing that, in one way or another, everything is linked. We must recognize the relationships between people and the environment, including the short and long term implications of human activities, the varied components and functions of ecosystems, as well as the carrying capacity and transformations of ecosystems.

Fostering an ecological perspective begins with a more integrated view of ecosystems. This book describes the ecoregions of Saskatchewan, following a hierarchial framework for terrestrial ecosystems in Canada. The framework is part of a three level hierarchy of ecological units of the province, first published in the 1994 "Ecoregions of Saskatchewan" poster map. It addresses many of the processes that are responsible for the formation of Saskatchewan ecological systems. It explains how landscapes form, how various physical and biological factors act together to determine the character of the regions, and how these regions have been altered by human activity.

The main body of the book describes Saskatchewan within the context of the four ecozones and 11 ecoregions that were identified on the poster map. This involves a description of the physical setting, such as geology and climate, as well as the biological features that have developed in response to this physical environment. The impact of human activities on the ecology of the area concludes each of these descriptions.

Ecological Land Classification

An ecosystem is a community of organisms (including people), interacting with one another, plus the physical environment in which they live and with which they interact. The ecosystem concept states that the earth operates as a series of interrelated systems within which all components are linked so that a change in one component brings about a corresponding change in other components. Ecosystems are holistic in the sense that the full range of biophysical characteristics are considered, including the land which is an important and integral component of the environment.

Ecological land classification is a process of classifying and delineating ecologically distinctive areas of land, so that we can better understand their similarities and relationships. Each land area is viewed as a discrete system resulting from the interaction of geology, climate, soils, landforms, vegetation and, at times, human factors. Ecological land classification stresses the interrelationships among components rather than treating each one as a separate characteristic of the landscape, and because of the linkages among systems, modification of one system may affect the operation of surrounding systems. The underlying basis for delineation of ecological units is to capture the major ecological composition and the linkages between the various components, as opposed to dealing with resources as singular and independent items.

It is important to recognize that while ecological land classification is science based, it is also an art in the sense that ecological cycles, interactions and characteristics are not always readily apparent and therefore need to be interpreted. The relationships between an ecosystem at one scale and ecosystems at smaller or larger scales must be examined to predict the effects of management. Also because management deals at various levels from regional to site specific, one of the prerequisites of ecological land classification is to delineate ecosystems at a level, scale, and intensity appropriate to management levels.

Ecosystems not only vary tremendously, but they also exist at multiple scales in a hierarchy, from local to regional. A hierarchal system permits the choice of detail that suits management objectives and the proposed use. Ecosystems are considered to be nested or reside within each other. Smaller ecosystems are encompassed within larger ecosystems.

Key points in ecological land classification

- **it incorporates all major components of ecosystems: air, water, land, and biota, including humans;**
- **it is holistic — "the sum is greater than the whole";**
- **the number and relative importance of factors helpful in delineating ecological units varies from one area to another area, regardless of the level of generalization;**
- **it is based on a hierarchy with ecosystems nested within ecosystems and involves integration of knowledge;**
- **it is not simply an overlay process;**
- **it recognizes that ecosystems are interactive;**
- **it recognizes that characteristics of one ecosystem blend with those of another; and**
- **it recognizes that map lines generally depict the location of zones of transition.**

Although the ecosystem concept implies equality among components (soils, climate, vegetation, etc.), all components may not be equally significant throughout the hierarchy. The dominance or importance of any one factor may vary considerably in defining the spatial expression of an ecosystem at every scale.

Classification of ecosystems usually begins with the largest units. At the upper levels of the hierarchy differentiating criteria are generally broad and general in importance with the greatest control, whereas those at the lower levels are narrow and more specific in importance. Ideally, criteria are based on enduring components of the ecosystem, components that do not change appreciably over time, such as soil, landform, or major vegetation types. The dominance or importance of any factor may vary considerably from place to place. For instance, in northern Saskatchewan, ecosystems are controlled by a different suite of factors than those in the south. Bedrock, shallow soils and lakes are prominent occurrences in the north, whereas, in the south, deep soils and fewer lakes occur. These factors influence other conditions such as habitat, vegetation growth and productivity.

Establishing ecosystem boundaries on a map involves distinguishing those systems in which structures exhibit a consistent or significant degree of change when compared to adjacent systems. Since land classification is based on multiple factors, the key to placing boundaries on an ecological map is an understanding of genetic processes (how it originated) and an understanding of the causes of class differences as opposed to the effects. Ecosystem boundaries should be based on factors that control ecosystem distribution at various scales such that ecosystems can be recognized, compared and worked with regardless of present land use or other disturbance.

Climate, which is the composite of the generally prevailing weather of a region over the long term, offers the logical basis for delineating large ecosystems. As the primary source of energy and water, it is the primary control for ecosystem distribution. As climate changes, other components of the system change in response, and as a result, ecosystems of different climates often differ significantly. Macro-scale areas (ecoregions, ecozones) have an essentially homogenous macro-climate.

Landform is one important criterion for recognizing smaller divisions within macro-ecosystems. Landform, with its geologic substrate and surface shape and relief, often modifies climatic regimes both regionally (e.g., Cypress Upland) and locally. At the meso-scale (Ecodistricts), the landform and landform pattern often form natural ecological boundaries.

The National Ecological Land Classification System and the Ecoregions of Saskatchewan

In 1991 a collaborative project involving federal, provincial and territorial agencies, all under the aegis of the Ecological Stratification Working Group, was established to develop a national ecological framework. The national framework comprised three levels of stratification, namely, ecozone, ecoregion, and ecodistrict.

The development of an ecological land classification framework for Saskatchewan was part of the national effort and culminated with the publication of the "Ecoregions of Saskatchewan" poster map in 1994.

The building blocks for the national ecological classification framework was the Soil Landscapes of Canada map series, which is a standard series of 1:1 million scale maps published on a provincial basis by Agriculture and Argifood Canada. These maps, as the name implies, provide an inventory of the country's land resources in terms of major soil (e.g., texture, soil profile) and landscape characteristics (e.g., surficial geologic materials, slope, landform).

In the agricultural and southern forest regions of Saskatchewan, the soil landscape map was compiled by generalizing detailed soil maps. Since these maps were compiled using a standard classification and mapping system combined with intensive ground-truthing, they provide a consistent database on which to base ecosystem boundaries. Surficial geology maps were used in the far northern regions of the province where soil maps are not available.

In Saskatchewan, ecosystems at the macro-scale (ecozones and ecoregions) are largely climatic zones, reflecting the effect of latitude and the diminishing energy gradient from the southwest to the northeast. In fact, in no other part of the country are the zonal relationships between climate, soils and the distribution of native species, so clearly displayed, from the warm, dry native grasslands of the southwest through the cool, moist parkland area, to the cold, dry lichen woodlands in the northeast. The exception

Terminology

ECOZONES: the ecozone lies at the top of the ecological hierarchy, and as such, it defines, on a subcontinental scale, the major physiographic features of the country (e.g., Canadian Shield, Great Plains, Rocky Mountains).

ECOREGIONS: subdivisions of the ecozone, characterized by distinctive climatic zones or regional landforms, and constitute the major bridge between the subcontinental scale ecozones and the more localized ecodistricts.

ECODISTRICTS: subdivisions of ecoregions, characterized by distinctive assemblages of landform, relief, surficial geological material, soil, water bodies, vegetation and land uses. ***Also referred to as Landscape Areas in Saskatchewan.***

is the boundary between the Boreal Shield and Boreal Plain ecozones, which is a geologic boundary corresponding to the Canadian Shield. Delineation of the Athabasca Plain Ecoregion with the Boreal Shield Ecozone was also based on bedrock geology.

At the landscape area level, ecosystems correspond roughly to physiographic areas and were defined specifically by generalizing information from the soil landscapes map and merging it with independent topographic and geologic data sources. The soil landscape units themselves were maintained as the smallest unit in the stratification to capture the capability of its associated database as a basis for further characterization of these larger ecological units.

Four ecozones are recognized in the province, corresponding roughly to the prairie (Prairie Ecozone), southern boreal forest (Boreal Plain Ecozone), Shield (Boreal Shield Ecozone) and northern subarctic (Taiga Shield Ecozone) regions.

Eleven ecoregions are identified as subsets of the four ecozones. The Mixed Grassland, Moist Mixed Grassland, and Aspen Parkland ecoregions are recognized within the Prairie Ecozone. In addition, the unique geology and vegetation of the Cypress Hills Upland helped to separate it as a fourth ecoregion within the Prairie Ecozone. Three ecoregions, the Boreal Transition, the Mid-Boreal Upland, and the Mid-Boreal Lowland occur within the Boreal Plains Ecozone. The Churchill River Uplands Ecoregion and the Athabasca Plains Ecoregion comprise the Boreal Shield Ecozone. The Taiga Shield Ecozone also consists of two ecoregions, namely the Selwyn Lake Uplands and the Tazin Lake Uplands.

Ecosystem Development

Saskatchewan's great diversity of terrestrial and aquatic ecosystems reflects the nature and interaction of many physical, biological, and human factors. This chapter describes the nature and role of the physical landscape, climate, vegetation, soils, and wildlife, as well as the activities of humans in the development of terrestrial ecosystems. A greater appreciation of the nature of the various ecosystems comes from an appreciation of their origin; hence, we describe the various interrelated factors that are involved in the development of these ecosystems.

Geology

The shape of the Saskatchewan landscape is determined primarily by its bedrock geology and glacial history and, to a lesser extent, by geologic processes since glaciation. Human activity has modified this natural landscape in many ways.

Saskatchewan has two main geologic regions, each underlain by a different suite of rock types. The Precambrian Shield, exposed in northern Saskatchewan, comprises crystalline basement rocks and sedimentary rocks that represent more than two billion years of earth's history. Younger sedimentary rocks cover the crystalline basement rocks in the Phanerozoic Basin, which occupies the southern part of the province. Continental glaciers have significantly influenced Saskatchewan's landscape, eroding and redepositing vast quantities of sediment. This glacial landscape has undergone further modification since glaciation, primarily by the action of wind and water, but also through the forces of gravity.

Bedrock geology

In many parts of Saskatchewan today, landscapes reflect, and are strongly controlled by, bedrock geology. Some ecoregion boundaries even coincide with geologic boundaries.

The oldest rocks in Saskatchewan are the crystalline basement rocks, the metamorphosed volcanic, plutonic, and sedimentary rocks of the Precambrian Shield. These rocks, which were formed 3.6 to 1.8 billion years ago, underlie the entire Taiga Shield Ecozone and the Churchill River Upland Ecoregion of the Boreal Shield Ecozone. These ancient rocks are host to important deposits of copper, zinc, and gold.

In the northwestern part of the province, south of Lake Athabasca, the ancient basement rocks are covered by younger (deposited 1.7 to 1.6 billion years ago) sandstones, which fill the Athabasca Basin to a depth of some 1,400 m. The boundary of the Athabasca Plain Ecoregion corresponds to the erosional edge of the Athabasca Basin. The flat-lying, non-metamorphosed sandstone of the Athabasca Basin is softer and more easily eroded than the crystalline basement rocks. This imparts a less rugged topography to the Athabasca Plain, and the dominance of depositional glacial landforms, compared to the portions of the Shield where basement rocks are at, or near, the surface. The richest uranium deposits in the world occur at, or near, the base of the Athabasca Basin sandstone sequence, near the erosional unconformity with the underlying basement rocks.

Paleozoic and younger sedimentary rocks overlie the Precambrian rocks in the Phanerozoic Basin, which coincides with the Boreal Plain and Prairie ecozones in the southern part of the province. The older (Cambrian through Cretaceous) sedimentary rocks were formed

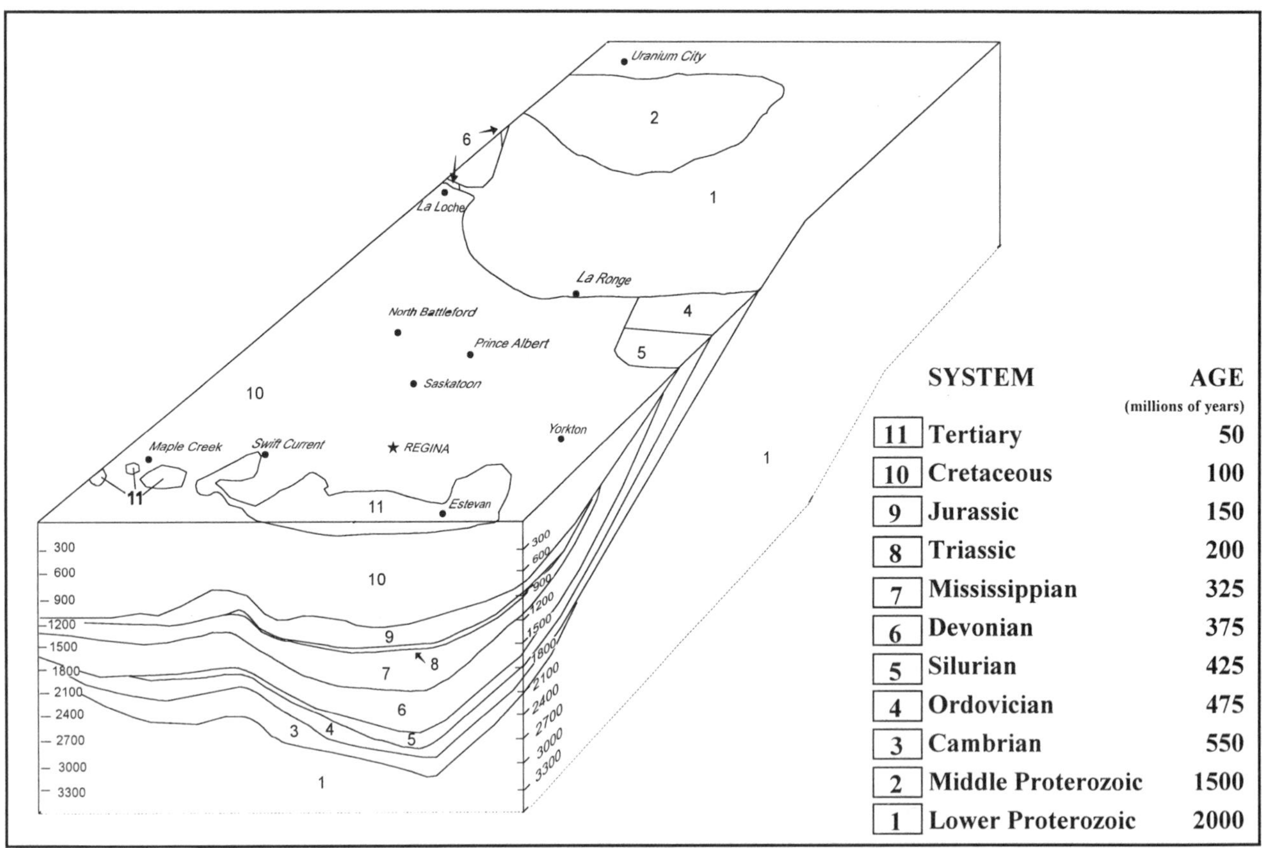

Figure 1. A block diagram depicting the bedrock geology of Saskatchewan (modified from Paterson, 1973).

from material deposited from 500 to 65 million years ago in shallow seas that intermittently covered western Canada. These marine rocks are host to the province's vast resources of potash, oil, and natural gas.

Tertiary rocks cover older Phanerozoic rocks in southern Saskatchewan. The Tertiary rocks were formed mainly in river and lake environments. They host Saskatchewan's coal reserves and important deposits of clay minerals. Geologists believe that a thickness of about one kilometre of Tertiary rocks has been eroded from Saskatchewan's landscape and that, before erosion, the extent of the Tertiary deposits may have been much greater than presently known. The Tertiary rocks are generally soft and easily eroded, but in southwestern Saskatchewan, deposits of coarse gravels protected the softer underlying rocks from erosion. This has resulted in the formation of the Cypress Hills, which stand as erosional, gravel-capped remnants above the surrounding prairie.

Saskatchewan's glacial history

At least five continental ice sheets covered the province during the last two million years, eroding older rocks and depositing a younger series of materials collectively referred to as glacial drift. These glacial deposits form much of the present-day landscape of Saskatchewan.

Glaciers have covered most of the continents at various times throughout the earth's history. Continental glaciation begins with the building of a snow field — an area where snow that falls in winter does not completely melt during the summer. As the snow pack thickens, the weight of accumulated snow turns the lower layers of the snow pack to ice. As the ice thickens, it begins to flow and slide away from the snow field in all directions. Additional ice continues to build at the snow field. The ice sheet continues to advance to a point where the rate of melting is equal to the rate of ice advance. The ice sheet may be thousands of metres thick. The weight of the accumulated ice and snow depresses the land surface.

Each glacial advance erodes and redeposits near-surface sediment so that, in general, only the effects of the most recent glacial advance and retreat are evident at the surface. The last glacial event to affect Saskatchewan, known as the Wisconsinan, began retreating from its maximum extent south of the Saskatchewan-Montana border about 17,000 years ago. The retreat of the ice sheet reached the southern margin of the Precambrian Shield about 10,000 years ago and had retreated beyond the northeast corner of the province by about 8,000 years ago.

In the Precambrian Shield, ice flow directions indicated by striations, grooves, flutings, and drumlins record south-southwest movement. The ice flow and features produced are to a large extent influenced by the nature of the underlying bedrock. Some areas, such as north of Lake Athabasca, were essentially stripped of their overburden, resulting in rugged, rocky terrain. The relatively soft sandstone of the Athabasca Basin eroded more easily, producing thick ground moraines (also called till plains) and ridged moraines of sandy glacial till, extensive drumlin fields, eskers (see Figure 2), and outwash plains. Upon reaching the Phanerozoic Basin, the crystalline materials encountered by the ice changed to limestones, sandstones and shales. Shales, in particular, were easily eroded by the ice, the materials being mixed with material incorporated earlier and transported southward. As the ice moved over this soft bedrock, a nearly level surface, called a ground moraine, or till plain, was formed by the erosion of these soft sediments combined with lodgement of eroded material at the base of the ice. Eventually, however, some of this eroded material was thrust to the frontal position of the ice and deposited as linear or curvilinear features termed ridged moraines.

Figure 2. The origin of eskers (from Rowe, 1983).

1. Meltwater forms a tunnel within the glacier following fractures and weak zones. Sand and gravel accumulate on stream bed.

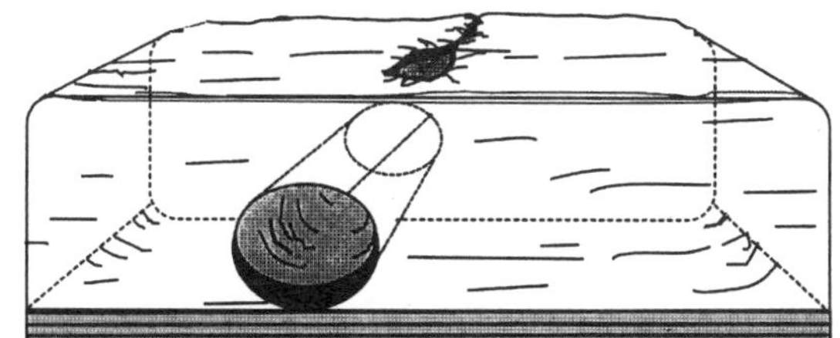

2. Melting eventually results in open, ice-walled channels.

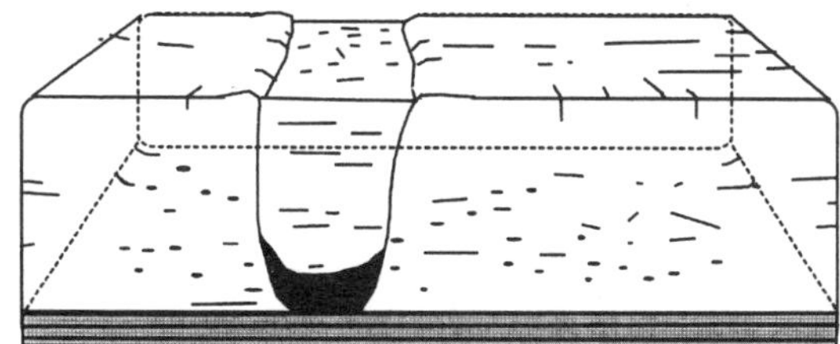

3. When ice melts totally, stream-bed sediments are left as a snake-like ridge.

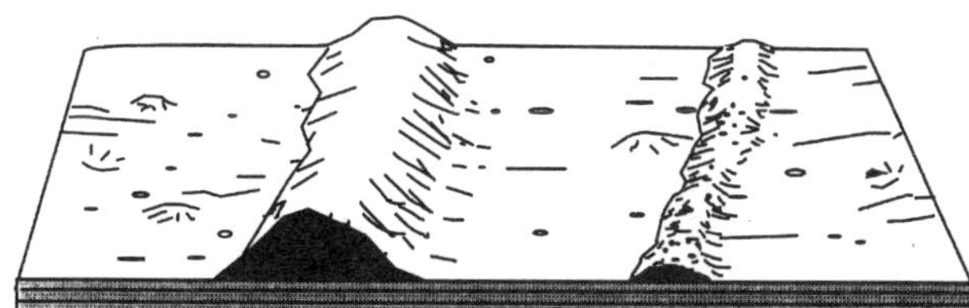

For reasons just as obscure as those that caused glaciation, all glacial epochs came to an end. In many parts, this meant mass stagnation. The ice ceased to flow. It is believed that upland areas became free of ice first, to be followed later by lower lands. The hummocky moraines and associated glacial till deposits that characterize much of southern Saskatchewan today represent landforms created during ice stagnation. The mechanics of the formation of these hummocky landscapes are illustrated in Figure 3.

An integral part of stagnation of the glacier was the creation of glacial lakes in areas where drainage of meltwater from the ice was restricted by higher land elevations in front of the ice. These glacial lake (glaciolacustrine) deposits formed nearly level landforms in some parts (such as the Regina Plains) where the underlying surface was bevelled by the

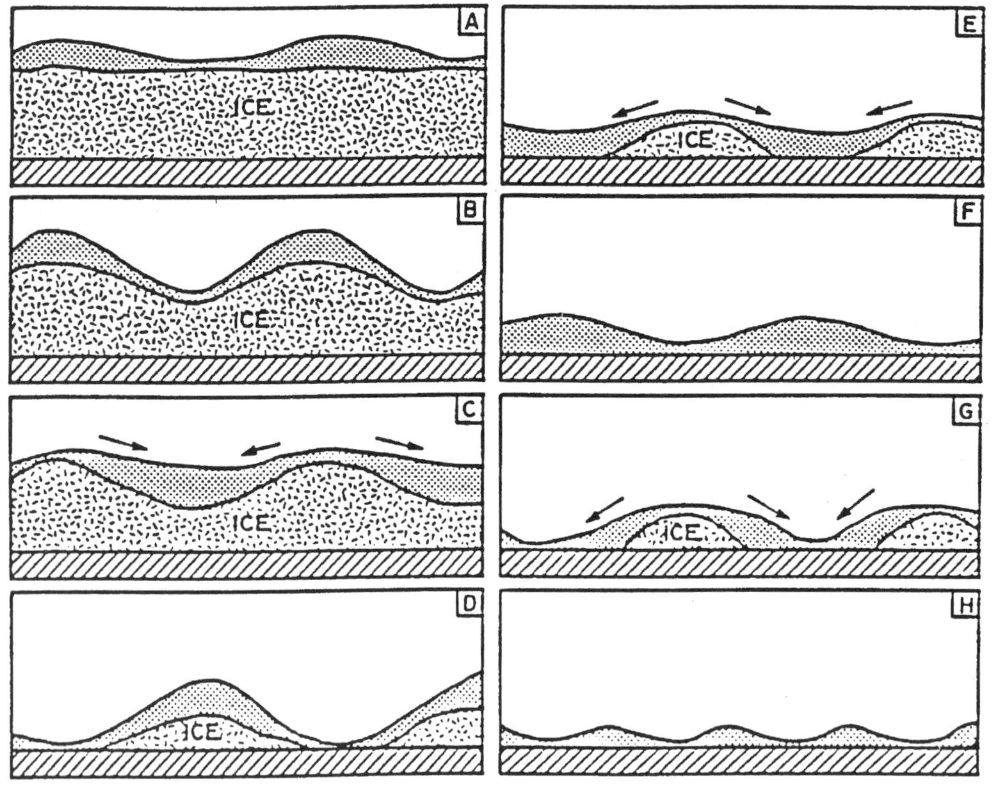

A Non-uniform thickness of sediment underlain by ice.

B Non-uniformity of insulation and melting of the ice.

C Movement of sediment from topographic highs to lows.

B, C, D Topographic highs become topographic lows.

E, F Only isolated blocks of ice remain. Hummocks are formed.

G, H Melting of the isolated blocks of ice results in the formation of circular ridges.

Figure 3. The formation of hummocky landscapes in glacial terrain. (Adapted from Clayton and Moran, 1974).

advancing glacier, but they also may be encountered on undulating or rolling landforms in accordance with the underlying topography. Also, it was not uncommon for glacial lakes to form on top of the ice, forming hummocky glaciolacustrine landforms, such as those in the Allan and Bear hills.

Meltwater channels flowing from the melting ice and spillways that drained glacial lakes have created many of the valleys and coulees that characterize the area. Stony, gravelly, and sandy sediments are typical of these glaciofluvial deposits.

There were glacier centres in the Rocky Mountains as well as in the Keewatin. Meltwater from these mountain glaciers also emptied into glacial lakes on the plains. The present-day North and South Saskatchewan rivers were formed to carry these meltwaters, as they do to the present. During glacial times, deltas formed at the point where the rivers entered glacial lakes. The sediments in the delta graded from sands to silts to clays with classic examples of these sediments prevailing south and west of Saskatoon, as far as Elbow and Rosetown.

Unglaciated and postglacial landscapes

Although the surface geological deposits that shape the surface of Saskatchewan are largely of glacial origin, there are areas of the province, such as the Cypress Hills, that were not glaciated and still other areas where the glacial deposits have been removed by erosion, exposing the bedrock. There also are deposits that have formed since glaciation. Wind has redistributed some of the sandy deltaic sediments to form dunes. The finer, wind-blown sediments called loess have mantled downwind areas. Rivers and lakes have also been responsible for the development of alluvial deposits and, in some areas, peat has formed in wet, low-lying environments. Slumps, landslides, and other forms of mass movement are common features on steep valley sides and scarpments.

Glacial and postglacial processes have had a significant economic impact on the province. They created vast resources of sand and gravel. Near-surface sources provide valuable aggregate for construction, while those at depth are a source of water for local and municipal use. Clay-rich glacial lake beds have become our most valued farmland, and rich deposits of sodium sulphate have formed in isolated lake basins.

Water

Water is a renewable resource that is essential for the survival of all living things. It occurs in an endless circulation between oceans, atmosphere, and land. Our interest centres on the land component. It includes the water that lies on the surface of the earth in lakes and rivers and other bodies. It also includes water below the earth's surface, the groundwater, where soils and geologic formations are saturated.

Surface water

Saskatchewan has an estimated 81,632 km^2 of surface water, or approximately 12% of the total area of the province. This water is found in rivers, streams, lakes, ponds, and man-made reservoirs.

Nearly all surface water originates from precipitation that falls within the confines of the provincial boundaries, with much smaller amounts entering the province in rivers and streams from the west. Local runoff of snowmelt and rainfall is the major contributor to water in natural ponds and lakes, but inter-provincial flow contributes to the water supply in major reservoirs. More than 90% of the precipitation returns to the atmosphere through evaporation and transpiration, with the balance returning to the oceans as stream-flow or becoming part of groundwater flow systems. Seepage and other forms of discharge from groundwater contribute to flows of most rivers, and may contribute to water levels in lakes and ponds.

Figure 4. Drainage basins in Saskatchewan.

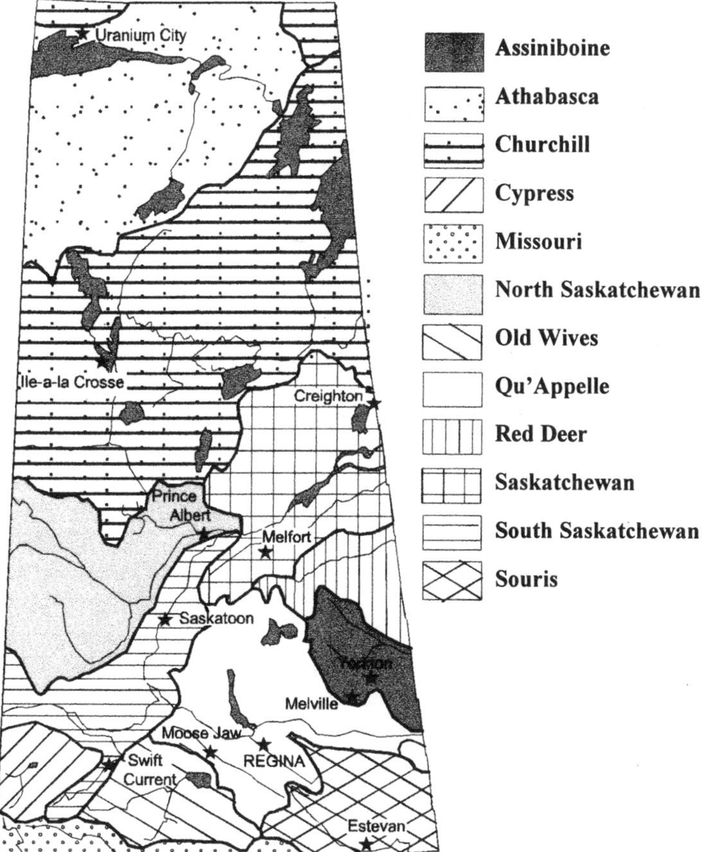

The distribution of surface water is often related to drainage basins or watersheds. In some parts of the world, virtually all of the land surface drains into a major river within the basin. In Saskatchewan, only about one-half of the area of most basins drains directly to such rivers, with the remaining area being occupied by land that drains to local lakes and ponds that are not connected to rivers. By assessing drainage divides between major rivers, Saskatchewan can be conveniently divided into four major drainage basins: Saskatchewan-Nelson, Churchill,

Athabasca, and Missouri. The Saskatchewan-Nelson basin occupies such a large portion of southern Saskatchewan that it is convenient to consider its many sub-basins: the North Saskatchewan, South Saskatchewan, Saskatchewan, Red Deer, Assiniboine, Qu'Appelle, and Souris river basins.

Much of the water in the North Saskatchewan, South Saskatchewan, and Saskatchewan rivers originates from melting ice and snow and rainfall on the eastern slopes of the Rocky Mountains and the foothills in Alberta, while the remaining rivers in the Saskatchewan-Nelson basin rely primarily on runoff from local precipitation for their flow.

There are relatively few lakes in the Saskatchewan-Nelson basin compared to the Churchill and Athabasca basins in the north; Manitou, Jackfish, Redberry, the Quill Lakes, Good Spirit, and Last Mountain lakes are the larger ones. The area does, however, possess a considerable number of smaller lakes and innumerable small ponds or sloughs. Although most of the lakes are natural, lakes such as Diefenbaker and Tobin are reservoirs created by dams on major rivers.

A small area in the extreme southwestern part of the province drains southward into the Missouri River in Montana, which is a part of the Mississippi River drainage system. Unlike the Saskatchewan-Nelson basin, there is no contribution from the Rocky Mountains in this basin, and drainage to the Frenchman River is well developed, resulting in a large proportion of the basin having significant outward flow of surface water. The Old Wives Lake basin in southwestern Saskatchewan is unique in that there is major flow from the Wood River and Notukue Creek to Old Wives Lake, but only at times of extremely high water levels does Old Wives Lake drain externally to the Missouri River system.

Most of northern Saskatchewan drains through the Churchill and Athabasca river systems to Hudson Bay and the Arctic, respectively. The Rocky Mountains do not contribute to flows in this system; however, there is some contribution from Alberta through the Beaver River. Most of the drainage of this vast land mass leads to the many local lakes and ponds that characterize this area, with a relatively small amount contributing to the flow of the Churchill River.

Northwestern Saskatchewan drains into the Mackenzie River system, mostly through the Fond du Lac, which empties into Lake Athabasca, and the Clearwater rivers. Virtually all of this water originates within the provincial boundaries and, like the Churchill River system, most of the drainage of this land mass leads to the many local lakes and ponds that prevail in the area.

The natural quality of surface water in Saskatchewan varies spatially and temporally. Rivers that flow into the province from the west carry a lot of bicarbonates, reflecting the carbonate rocks in their headwaters in the Rocky Mountains. However, as they cross the plains region of eastern Alberta and throughout Saskatchewan, they become more highly mineralized as they pick up additional calcium and magnesium, as well as sulphates and other ions from erosion of, and groundwater flow through, the glacial drift within the watershed. As a result, waters in the Saskatchewan-Nelson basin, in general, are hard and turbid. Water in sub-basins, such as the Red Deer, Assiniboine, and Souris, as well as those in the Missouri and Old Wives Lake basins, which all have local headwaters, are particularly hard and turbid.

The Churchill River basin receives some hard, high-sulphate waters from the plains region through the Beaver and Waterhen rivers; however, waters throughout most of the contributing area are very low in minerals and lacking turbidity, reflecting the mineralogy of the crystalline basement rocks.

Waters in the Mackenzie Basin vary from very soft to very hard, depending upon whether they rise on the Canadian Shield or the plains to the south.

The natural quality of surface water has been affected by the activities of humans through the release of industrial, agricultural, and municipal waste into the water supply. Many water bodies in southern Saskatchewan are eutrophic, with nuisance growths of algae and aquatic weeds commonplace during the summer. Such conditions reflect high nutrient levels in these lakes and high nutrient loadings in rivers and streams leading to them.

Natural water quality varies seasonally and from year to year. Long periods of drought on the southern prairies, snowfall in the Rockies, and storms on the prairies that impact on the quantity of water also impact on its quality.

Groundwater

Soils and geological deposits may or may not be saturated with water. Saturated conditions, when all of the voids between the sedimentary particles are filled with water, are referred to as groundwater. When water flows freely from these materials, especially when it is easily extracted for domestic or industrial use, the soils or deposits are called aquifers. When water moves slowly and is difficult to extract even though the materials are saturated, the deposits are called aquitards.

Topographic expression and composition of surface materials, climate, and geology are the major factors determining the presence, quality, and dynamic nature of groundwater resources. This section focusses on the hydrogeology of Saskatchewan, that is, the geological conditions and processes that determine the extent and magnitude of our groundwater resources.

Groundwater recharge, the amount of water that extends beyond the depth of most plant roots, is dependent upon the climate (precipitation, evaporation, and transpiration) as well as the topography and the texture or permeability of the materials along the flow path.

In Saskatchewan's semiarid to subhumid climate, groundwater recharge occurs during snowmelt in the spring and in the several months to follow when rains are heaviest. Annual recharge may reach some tens of millimetres where aquifers occur in the surficial materials. It drops to several millimetres in shallow aquifers within the glacial drift or bedrock and tenths of millimetres when these aquifers are deep. The amount of recharge is also dependent upon the topography at the surface as well as the permeability of the surface and subsurface materials.

The Precambrian Shield consists of metamorphic and igneous basement rocks that are overlain in places by sedimentary rocks. The basement rocks are permeable only along faults and fractures, which are not necessarily connected, and hence water supply is most likely to be limited. The Athabasca basin is the major sedimentary basin. Being a sandstone, it is much more permeable than the basement rocks; hence, it provides a major groundwater resource. Most areas of the Shield are covered by thin glacial deposits, which in turn are often covered with organic (peat) deposits. The sandy and gravelly glacial deposits should provide good domestic water supplies; however, permafrost in the organic soils may limit water supply, at least during part of the year.

The hydrogeology of the southern two-thirds of Saskatchewan is in sharp contrast to that in the Precambrian Shield region to the north. Simply stated, the hydrological setting of southern Saskatchewan consists of, in ascending order: i) an impermeable base formed by the top of the Precambrian basement rocks; ii) a basal aquifer system consisting of carbonates, evaporites, and sandstone; and iii) a thick aquitard, which confines the basal aquifer system. This latter aquitard also contains sands, providing additional and very important sources of potable water.

The deeper permeable formations of the basal aquifer system contain mostly brackish or saline water that is generally more saline than seawater. They are used for enhanced oil recovery and disposal of liquid wastes. Upper portions of this basal aquifer, rocks of Lower Cretaceous age, form an aquifer that occurs throughout southern Saskatchewan, but it provides potable water only in the Mannville aquifer, in a fringe along the southern edge of the Precambrian Shield. Supplies of potable groundwater are also thought to exist in the Cumberland aquifer, which is comprised of limestone and dolomite rocks that outcrop near the edge of the Precambrian Shield, close to the Manitoba border.

Cretaceous aquitards extend across southern Saskatchewan, except for a fringe along the southern edge of the Shield. They play an important role in separating the freshwater aquifers that occur within and above it from the saline-water yielding aquifers below. The Upper Cretaceous Judith River Formation forms a major aquifer in west-central and southwestern Saskatchewan. It is underlain and overlain by Cretaceous silts and clays, and it is locally overlain by glacial deposits. It is a major water supply for municipal, industrial, and domestic users. The Eastend and Ravenscrag formations are composed of sands and silts and include sandstone and coal layers. They form a single but complex aquifer unit, called the Eastend Ravenscrag aquifer, in southern Saskatchewan along the international border. Various sand members of the Upper Cretaceous Bearpaw Formation form aquifers that are locally important as a source of water.

Aquifers within Quaternary deposits also provide a major water supply for municipal, industrial, and domestic users. The Quaternary stratigraphy, in ascending order, may include the Empress Group, the Sutherland Group, and the Saskatoon Group. Sands and gravels of the Empress Group occur between bedrock and till, where they form buried valley and blanket aquifers. The Hatfield Valley aquifer is the most extensive of the buried valley aquifers, cutting diagonally across the province from Cold Lake to the Manitoba border. Blanket aquifers typically occur on the flanks of the Hatfield Valley aquifer. The Sutherland and Saskatoon groups consist mainly of tills, with minor occurrences of sands and gravels. Sands and gravels between these till units, called inter-till aquifers, are important source of potable groundwater.

Surficial aquifers are found throughout southern Saskatchewan. They are composed of sands and gravels deposited in glacial lakes, rivers, and deltas during the final deglaciation of Saskatchewan. Extensive surficial aquifers occur along the North and South Saskatchewan rivers and in the Great Sand Hills area of southwestern Saskatchewan.

Except for groundwater in surficial aquifers, virtually all groundwater in the Prairie and Boreal Plain ecozones is of marginal quality, that is, it fails to meet Canadian drinking water guidelines of 500 mg/L for total dissolved solids and 500 mg/L for sulphate. Chloride concentrations of most aquifers used for municipal and domestic use are less than the recommended guideline of 250 mg/L; however, iron and manganese levels quite often exceed the recommended guidelines.

As mentioned above, the freshest water is found in surficial aquifers. The quality in inter-till, buried valley, and blanket aquifers is variable (total dissolved solids in the 1500-3000 mg/L range), hard, and sulphate-rich. Also, treatment may be required for iron and manganese.

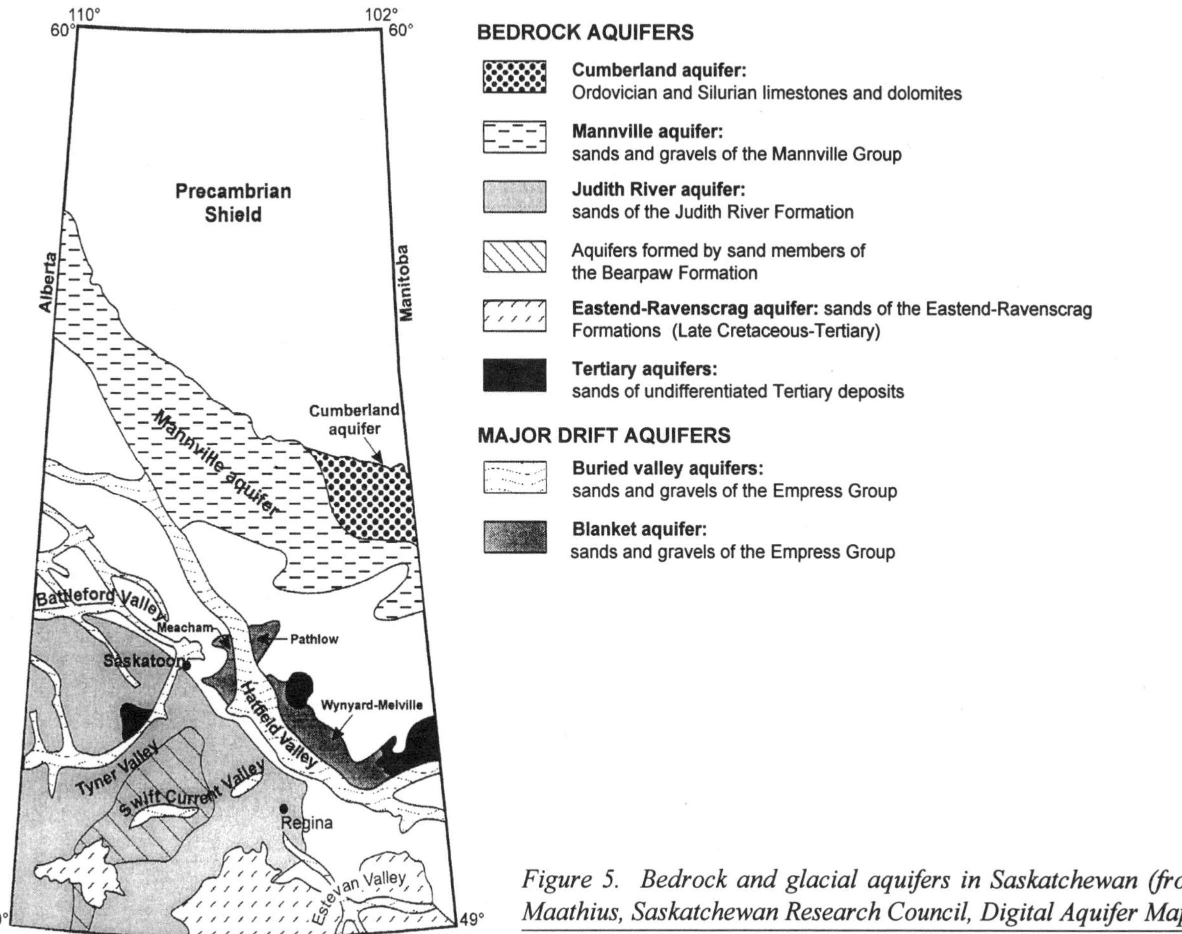

Figure 5. Bedrock and glacial aquifers in Saskatchewan (from H. Maathius, Saskatchewan Research Council, Digital Aquifer Map).

Groundwater in bedrock aquifers is of marginal quality. Total dissolved solids in groundwater from the Judith River Formation range from 1,300 to 8,000 mg/L. Levels tend to be lower in the Ravenscrag Formation. Groundwater in deeper bedrock aquifers may contain as much as 300,000 mg/L of total dissolved solids, and is only suitable for such industrial use as enhanced oil recovery. The best quality of water in bedrock is found in the Cypress Hills and Wood Mountain formations.

Groundwater quality in the Boreal Shield and Taiga Shield ecozones is generally good or very good in both surficial deposits and bedrock (except at extreme depths). Most water will be the calcium-magnesium-bicarbonate type. High concentrations of iron and manganese may also be found.

Climate

Weather, through the agencies of sun, wind, and rain, acts on the geological material to produce a suitable medium for terrestrial plants. Soils and plants, in turn, affect the atmosphere through the reflection and emission of radiation and the exchange of matter and energy. In this way, the physical environment of a region is determined by a combination of physical and biological processes.

Radiation exchange and air-mass frequency are two of the most important meteorological processes that determine the climate of an area; hence, they strongly influence ecosystem development in Saskatchewan.

The average annual flux of solar radiation reaching the earth's surface varies from high values in the tropics to low values in polar regions. In the middle latitudes of the northern hemisphere, where Saskatchewan lies, the average mean temperature decreases about 0.75°C for each degree of latitude toward the north pole. There is also an altitudinal effect on temperature, with a usual decrease of 0.5°C with each rise of 100 m. As a consequence of these relationships, at a given altitude, climate is warmest in the south and cools gradually northward. An area such as the Cypress Hills at 50° north latitude and at an elevation of approximately 1,300 m theoretically has the same temperature as an area at 54° north latitude and at an elevation of 600 m. This is a partial explanation for the "islands" of forests surrounded by grasslands in southern Saskatchewan.

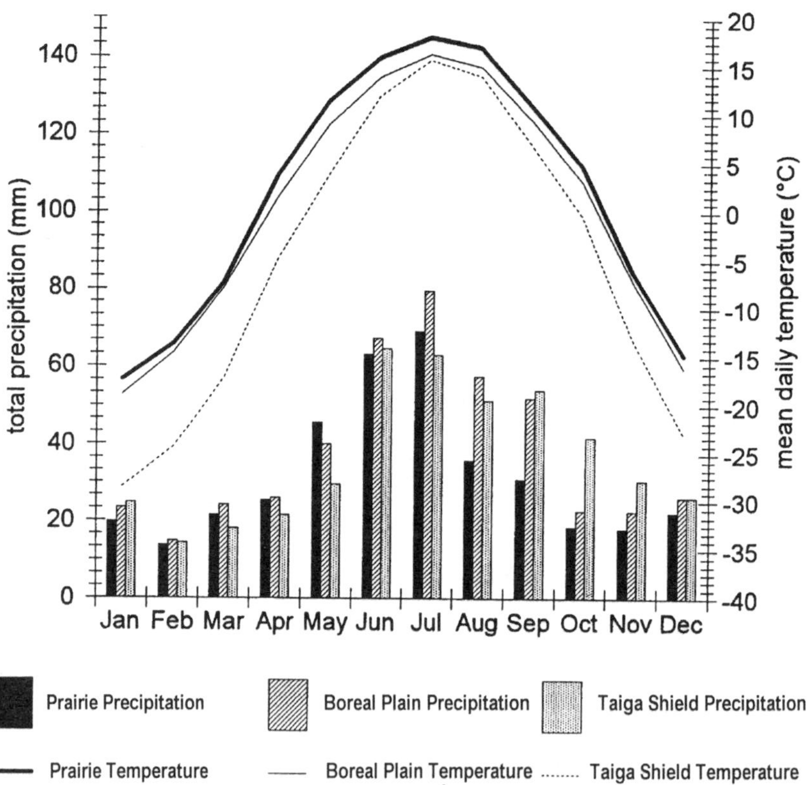

Figure 6. Mean monthly temperature and precipitation values for meteorological stations representing the grassland (Harris), boreal forest (Waskesiu Lake) and taiga regions (Brochet) in Saskatchewan.

The net effect of incoming radiation is tempered by greater reflectance of grasslands than forests, dry soils than wet soils, and bare soils than those with a vegetative cover. Snow and ice are very reflective, while open water is highly absorptive of incoming radiation. These land attributes have an ameliorating effect on total energy flux in a broad regional and a local context.

Net radiation is roughly indicated by air temperature. Various methods have been proposed for recording regional temperature characteristics. The number of frost-free days between the last spring frost and the first fall frost can be counted and averaged over the years. Another index, growing degree days, can be calculated by adding up the daily temperatures in excess of 5°C throughout the growing season and averaging for a number of years.

The amount of moisture that is available for ecosystem processes is the difference between what comes to the surface in rain or snow and what is evaporated and transpired back to the atmosphere. In Saskatchewan's dry climate this value averages zero over the year. A more useful measure of available moisture is potential evapotranspiration, that is, the total that could be evaporated if water was readily available. The difference between precipitation and potential evapotranspiration is termed "moisture or water deficit." It is often expressed in terms of aridity. In the semiarid southern part of the province, the water deficit during the

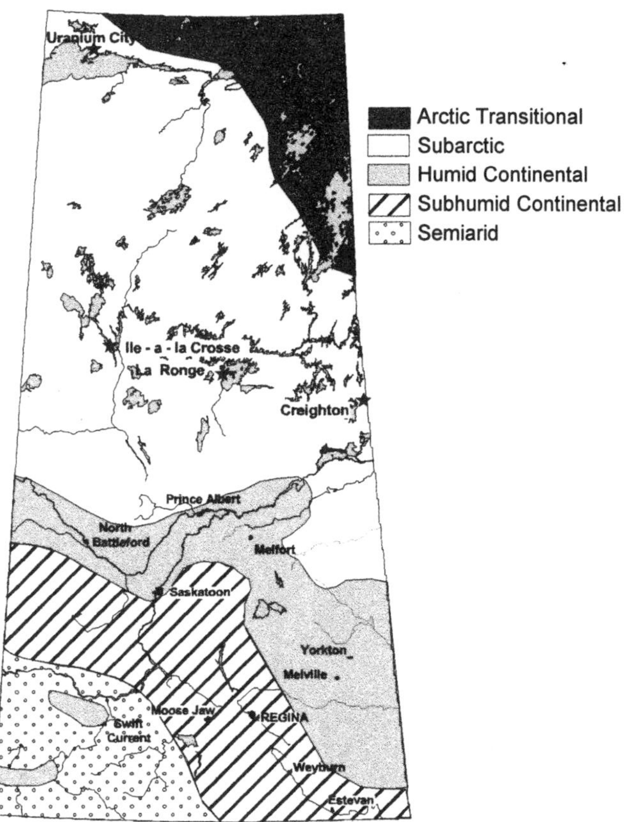

Figure 7. Climatic regions of Saskatchewan.

growing season is in excess of 450 mm. Deficits and aridity decrease northward, mainly because a decrease in the net radiative energy results in lower evaporation. As such, the taiga is less arid than the boreal forest and it, in turn, is less arid than grassland.

Saskatchewan's climate is also influenced by air pressure and wind fields. The western cordillera forms a significant obstacle to the mild, moist air currents from the Pacific. The region is readily accessible to cold Arctic high pressure systems in the winter and to frequent incursions of warm, moist tropical air from the southeast, particularly in the summer. This in turn results in higher precipitation in the summer than in the winter months. It is a region subject to extremes in temperature, but usually having low humidity.

The outcomes of the many factors described above can be better appreciated by comparing empirical values for mean monthly temperature and precipitation for meteorological stations representing the grassland, boreal forest, and taiga regions in Saskatchewan (Figure 6).

Temperatures are warmer throughout the year in the grassland than in the forest, and warmer in the forest than in the taiga. Although there is little difference in the late winter and spring, precipitation throughout the remainder of the year is higher in the boreal than the taiga, and higher in the taiga than in the grassland region.

Vegetation

Vegetation patterns seen in Saskatchewan's ecoregions are a result of a complex and dynamic set of physical and biological factors and, in some regions, have been heavily influenced by human activity. It has long been recognized that large-scale vegetation patterns mimic weather patterns by trending northwest to southeast across the province. Major stresses and disturbances also impact on vegetation patterns and diversity. Stress and disturbances can be of two sources: biotic (living) or abiotic (non-living).

The amount and distribution of water available to plants dramatically affects species associations. This is determined within a climatic framework but is also related to soil type, slope position, and direction of slope.

The size, frequency, and intensity of fires shape the landscape by making the species associations patchy. In forests the fire cycle is usually less than the life span of most tree species, as seen in the abundance of even-age stands. Fire generally burns the organic layer of forest soils, which can encourage the regrowth of species that sucker (e.g., trembling aspen) or sprout (e.g., white birch). The burning of surface organic material also exposes mineral soils that are more rich in nutrients.

Plants have adapted to frequent burning events. Jack and lodgepole pine, for example, have developed serotinous cones that require the heat of fire to open. Other species, such as pin cherry, have evolved as seed-banking species that can store their seeds in the soil for periods in excess of 50 years and will germinate following the favourable conditions created by fire. Also, many prairie grasses have their growing tips at soil level, allowing for rapid reproduction through vegetative propagation after fire.

In forested areas, human efforts to control fire have favoured the production of shrubs in the understory that compete with canopy trees. In addition to changing understory composition, the absence of fire can also result in a decrease in species associations and species richness diversity. It also has led to increases in insect infestations and disease, and changes in forest composition towards late successional species (e.g., balsam fir).

The effects of wind on species associations are much more variable than those of fire. This is partly a reflection of the frequency of reoccurrence of a severe wind event being much longer than the replacement time of most species associations in Saskatchewan.

The effects of wind-throw are more apparent in the boreal forest than in open grasslands. They include an increase in insect and fungi populations, a local buildup of nutrients stored in boles and branches, and the development of unique spatial patterns of plant associations due to succession.

Soil composition varies from place to place in Saskatchewan, and this impacts on the diversity and richness of the vegetation. Soils in the Precambrian Shield, which are generally sandy and stony, nutrient poor, acidic, and low in salts, are more conducive to the development of such species associations as a scattered jack pine canopy with lichen and Canada blueberry ground cover that can tolerate drought, a poor supply of plant nutrients, and acidity. Where the soils are shallow to bedrock or in more moist topographic positions, black spruce provides competition for the tap-rooted jack pine. In contrast, soils in the Phanerozoic Basin to the south generally have more clay and plant nutrients and are more alkaline and sometimes saline. These soils favour more highly productive stands of black or white spruce and trembling aspen, for example, with a diverse understory of broad-leaved herbs and shrubs in the forested region and luxurious stands encompassing a variety of grasses and herbs in the grassland region. These grasses and herbs diminish and may be completely replaced by red samphire, alkali grass, and other salt-tolerant species in saline and alkaline areas.

The gradient, position, and aspect of the land surface influence the microclimate (e.g., moisture and temperature regimes) and, consequently, the plant associations that are present along a slope. Little variability in microclimate occurs on level topography, and single plant associations may cover large flat areas. Where the topography is steeper, the south- and west-facing slopes tend to be warmer and drier than north- and east-facing slopes, and upper portions of slopes are drier than lower slopes. A series of plant associations, each best-suited to the specific moisture and temperature conditions of its site, are therefore found on slopes and contribute to a high species diversity across the slope.

Interactions between plants or animals, such as succession, herbivory, predation, disease, competition, and human habitat alteration, play a role in the organization of species assemblages. However, they are not as important as the abiotic ones described above, since severe abiotic forces put many species at their physiological limits.

For each of the fundamental abiotic factors, every plant species has an optimum range of physical conditions where physiological functions perform at their best and a tolerance range outside of which the species will die. When multiple species are considered, biotic factors come into play and species must use strategies developed for these interactions. An individual species, therefore, acquires a whole range of survival strategies and tolerances for its environment. This range helps the species to emerge into a specific niche where it can survive in the environment. When a collection of plant species lives in the same environment, it forms plant associations through sharing and competing for space and resources.

Descriptions of Saskatchewan plant associations are presented below. These descriptions identify only the most commonly occurring associations and species within these associations; many other species are usually present at a particular location. The plant associations have been grouped into: forests and woodlands, sparsely treed rock, grasslands, sand dunes, peatlands, and wetlands.

Forests and woodlands

Forests and woodlands occur primarily in the boreal forest and taiga regions and, to a lesser extent, in the prairie region. Typically, canopy cover for both woodlands and forests is greater than 10%. An open-crowned stand of trees is considered a woodland. When the crown is closed it is deemed to be a forest. Nine kinds of forests or woodlands have been recognized for the purposes of this report.

White spruce forests are usually found within the mixedwood region, although their range does extend to the northern coniferous forest. They are found on a variety of habitats. They most commonly occur on well to moderately well-drained soils developed from glacial till and glaciolacustrine deposits. In the classical example of forest succession, trembling aspen will dominate former mixedwoods following fire. As the canopy opens when the trembling aspen become over-mature, white spruce will increase in dominance.

Feather mosses are the dominant ground cover and occur with short shrubs and low herbs on well-drained sites and under mature stands. Horsetails are a common component of the understory on poorly drained sites. Patchy white spruce stands on rapidly drained soils have an understory of grasses and low shrubs including slender and awned wheatgrass and bearberry.

Black spruce-jack pine forests are found throughout the forest region, but they most commonly occur in the northern coniferous forest. They generally occur on moderately well to well-drained sites associated with medium-textured glacial till and glaciolacustrine deposits as well as on sandy glacial till and glaciofluvial deposits.

An understory that includes a profusion of ericaceous shrubs, such as Canada blueberry and bearberry and a cover of lichens occurs on rapidly drained sites in association with sandy deposits. Under improved moisture conditions, feather mosses and shrubs, such as Labrador tea, become more common. Tall shrubs such as green alder, sometimes in association with feather mosses, are widespread under relatively dense canopies.

Black spruce forests occur throughout the forest region and extend into the taiga region. They most commonly occur in the northern coniferous forest region, especially on the Precambrian Shield, where they are better adapted than many other trees to the harsh climate. Pure stands of black spruce often occur under moderately well to imperfectly drained conditions. Under poor drainage, there may be equal amounts of black spruce and tamarack, often with an understory dominated by Labrador tea and sedges. Under very poorly drained conditions, black spruce occurs as pure stands with an understory dominated by Labrador tea and sedges. Tamarack is the first tree species to grow on organic soils; however, it is a poor competitor as it cannot tolerate shade and usually is displaced by black spruce. Consequently, black spruce is commonly associated with wooded fens and horizontal and raised bogs.

Jack pine forests occur throughout the forested area of the province. Although they occur on a variety of habitats they are most common on rapidly drained, sandy glaciofluvial, glacial till and eolian deposits, as well as on outcrops of Precambrian basement rock. Usually, the water table occurs below the root zone, and an open stand with an open crown of ascending and arching branches prevails. Where the water table extends into the root zone, the trees are well formed and the stands are more uniform. Prominent lichen carpets of reindeer moss and a short shrub-short herb layer typified by Canada blueberry, bearberry and bunchberry represent the most common understory. A green alder shrub layer with a ground cover of hairy wild rye and other tall herbs is also a common occurrence under mature and open canopies.

Jack pine forests also occur under moist upland habitats associated with medium-textured glacial till and glaciolacustrine deposits. An understory of feather and club mosses are common under pure stands with moderately dense canopies, as well as when white spruce or green alder appear in the canopy or shrub layer. Ericaceous shrubs such as Labrador tea and Canada blueberry may replace the feather mosses under less dense canopies.

Mixedwood (spruce-aspen) forests, where trembling aspen is the main broadleaf species, occur most commonly on well-drained soils developed on glacial till in the mixedwood forest region. These forests develop following fires, either as even-aged stands or as uneven-aged stands where the white spruce becomes established after the trembling aspen. They often contain balsam fir, white birch, or jack pine. Balsam poplar-black spruce forests are common in imperfectly drained areas.

There is a diverse forest floor in mixedwood forests, with many herbs, forbs, and grasses. In moderately dense stands, tall and short herbs such as wild sarsaparilla and bunchberry and various mosses may occur alone or under a tall shrub cover of green alder and balsam fir. Hairy wild rye and giant reed grass often occur on drier sites or under over-mature stands.

Aspen forests, where trembling aspen is the dominant tree, most commonly occur in the mixedwood forest area, but extend throughout the forest region. Trembling aspen most commonly occur on rapidly to well-drained sites. Balsam poplar is more common under imperfect drainage.

An understory that includes hairy wild rye and prickly rose is associated with dry, rapidly drained sites. Reed grasses, beaked hazelnut, and wild sarsaparilla are usually associated with relatively open trembling aspen stands on well-drained sites. Most trembling aspen stands are established following fire and are relatively even-aged.

Aspen groves are most common in the prairies and often occur surrounding wet depressions. In natural conditions, these groves appear within a sea of grasslands, but these grasslands have largely been replaced with croplands. They also are widespread on sandy soils and along moist creek beds. They are more extensive in the aspen parkland, where they extend upslope from wet depressions and cover north-facing valley sides and escarpments. Trembling aspen, the predominant species, is found in pure stands or mixed with other broadleaf trees such as balsam poplar, Manitoba maple, and cottonwoods. Common woody species include balsam poplar, saskatoon, choke cherry, red-osier dogwood, pin cherry and wild red raspberry. Common forbs as ground cover include western Canada violet and

American wild strawberry and grasses that include brome and blue grass.

Lodgepole pine forests occur in the Cypress Upland Ecoregion. The lodgepole pine association has members from a remnant montane flora that include the lodgepole pine, bluebunch fescue, alpine bistort, white hawkweed, and many others. This association is adapted to fire. It is a mid-successional association and grows in dense stands shading out many other understory species. Because of this shading, the shrub and herb growth of the understory is limited.

Lichen woodlands are common on dry and somewhat exposed sites in the harsh subarctic climate of the taiga region. Black spruce, which is stunted, is the dominant tree but jack pine frequently occur on more sandy soils. Lichens provide a distinctive and highly reflective ground cover. Shrub-heath woodlands are common on very dry, somewhat sheltered sites in the harsh subarctic climate of the taiga region. Scattered dwarf black spruce among shrubs, including white birch, ground juniper, and bearberry, represent the typical cover. Lichens and herbs are not abundant and purple reed grass is the only significant grass. Bare ground can occupy as much as one-third of the surface area.

Sparsely treed rock

Precambrian basement rocks are frequently exposed at the surface throughout the taiga and much of the boreal area of the Shield. These rock outcrops most commonly occur on topographic rises; hence, they are very dry and exposed to wind.

Rock lichens prevail on bedrock outcrops and other extremely arid sites where there is no tree cover. These areas support lichens in cracks and fissures in the rock; where moisture levels are higher, sphagnum and feather mosses survive.

Rock lichen woodlands have a very open canopy of stunted jack pine. Stunted black spruce and small white birch may also be found in local, more moist areas. Similar to the canopy, understory vegetation is also not well developed but consists of Canada blueberry and bearberry. Additionally, shield areas that have recently experienced severe fire (where the canopy and understory have been removed) exhibit similar species associations to those described above. These burned areas illustrate the earliest successional stage in shield regions.

Grasslands

A *fescue prairie grassland* prevails in west-central Saskatchewan in association with aspen grove vegetation. It is associated with a more moist environment than the mixed-grass prairie. The bunch grass known as plains rough fescue is the dominant plant of this association, but porcupine grass, June grass, and various sedges are also common. These grasslands also have significant inclusions of shrubs such as prairie rose, western snowberry, thorny buffaloberry and wolf-willow, and forbs such as pasture sage, crocus anenome, and low goldenrod.

Plains rough fescue loses its dominance to porcupine, needle-and-thread, and blue grama grass in the eastern part of the aspen grove area.

The *mixed-grass prairie* is characteristic of drier, southwestern Saskatchewan. It was given its name due to the presence of short and midsize grass and sedge species. These shorter plants grow in this region due to the dryness of the area. This association is composed of the short plants blue grama grass, low sedge, and pasture sage as well as the somewhat taller northern and western wheatgrass, needle-and-thread, and June grass. Long-term heavy grazing pressure on these associations can cause significant changes in vegetation cover.

Saline flats occur in close association with grasslands in the Prairie Ecozone. Little vegetation survives on the extremely saline sites but red samphire, western sea-blite, and greasewood survive in low densities where the salt concentration is lower. Surrounding the saline flat, alkali grass, Nuttall's salt-meadow grass, foxtail barley, and seaside arrow-grass may also be found.

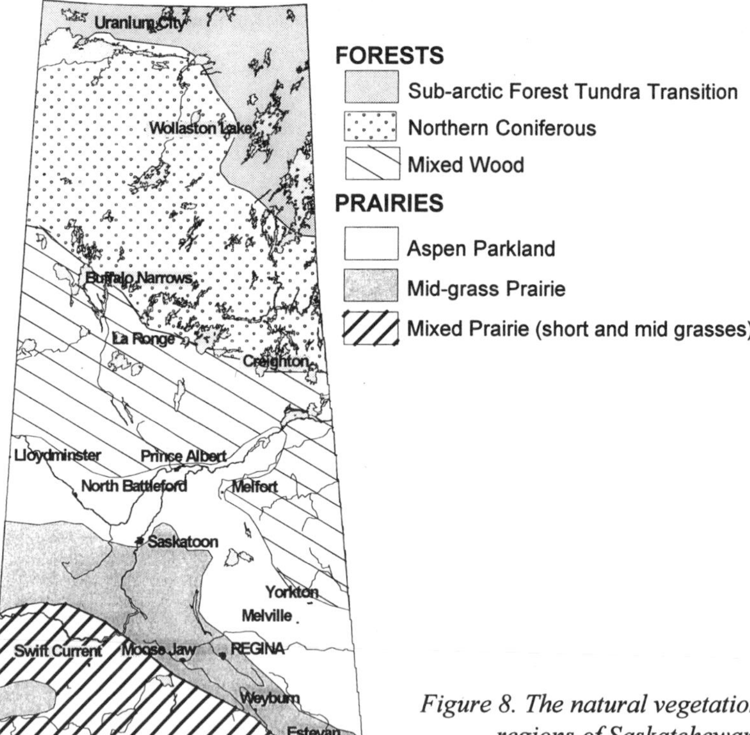

Figure 8. The natural vegetation regions of Saskatchewan.

Sand dunes

Sand dunes includes the Great Sand Hills, the Athabasca Sand Dunes, and other sand dune complexes in the prairie and forest region. Aridity and instability exclude the development of all but the most adapted plants.

Dune grass associations occur on active eolian ridges and to a degree on semistable dune ridges. Vegetation cover is sparse, and species composition is variable depending on moisture and latitude. In the northern dunes a few shrubs such as sand heather and willow may be found, but most plants are grasses such as northern awnless brome and hairy wild rye. In the southern sand area, active dunes are colonized by northern wheatgrass, Indian rice grass, sand grass, and sand dropseed. As a dune becomes stabilized, more typical prairie species are found such as needle-and-thread grass, June grass, sun-loving sedge, and creeping juniper.

Peatlands

Peatlands are relatively wet areas found throughout the forest region where, as their name implies, peat has accumulated. Peatlands form from a series of plant successional stages. The first stage typically is an open depression filled with water. As organic matter accumulates, a fen is created. As peat continues to develop, along with trapped sediments, drier conditions emerge that allow establishment of tree species. This stage is called a closed fen or a treed fen. Sphagnum mosses become established under this treed environment, raising the surface above the water table. This is the bog stage of development. Under cold environments, some of the bogs are sparsely treed, and the underlying materials are permanently frozen. These conditions are referred to as palsas.

Fens occur in areas where the water table is near the surface and where slow but effective drainage leads to a steady nutrient supply and, hence, to a less acid condition than prevails in bogs. They are characterized by a dense cover of sedge and cottongrass on mats of sphagnum or other mosses. These sedge mats may float, so they are often found in shallow areas of lakes and encroaching on the edges of small ponds. Characteristic grassy species include water sedge, beaked sedge, two-stamened sedge, hairy-fruited sedge, mud sedge, tall cotton-grass, close-sheathed cotton-grass, bluejoint, narrow reed grass, and spike-rush. Common herbs include buck-bean, bedstraw, marsh cinquefoil, and flat-leaved bladderwort.

The drier the sedge meadow, the higher the shrub component. Common shrubs include sweet gale and leather-leaf, and a number of willow species may often be present.

Bogs commonly occur in poorly drained depressions and along small streams, in areas where moisture is derived mainly from rainwater rather than runoff, causing the nutrient supply and the pH to be low. The interrupted tree canopy consists of small, thin-limbed, scattered black spruce with some tamarack and an occasional jack pine. Characteristic shrubs are Labrador tea, dwarf birch, bog laurel, willow, and leather-leaf. Deep mounds of sphagnum and feather mosses are characteristic. Common grassy species are water sedge, northern bog sedge, tall cotton-grass, and close-sheathed cotton-grass. Common broad-leaved herbs include three-leaved Solomon's-seal, cloudberry, leather-leaf, bog laurel, bog cranberry, and marsh cinquefoil.

Open bogs lack the tree species of closed bogs, but in respect to secondary flora, they do not differ except that they are often wetter with more open water in depressions between the sphagnum mounds.

A *palsa* is an irregular to sub-rounded peat dome that can rise 2.5 m or more above the surrounding organic terrain. It is formed when accumulating peat and developed plant cover insulate the frozen layer and allow it to increase in volume. The vegetation on the palsa is usually black spruce, but the surrounding area is dominated by sedges and grasses. An open "lead" of water is often found at the base of the palsa. As the frozen layer thickens, and the height of the palsa increases, it becomes unstable and cracks form in the top of the dome. The sides slump, breaking the insulating layer, changing the energy balance, and causing the frozen lens to melt and eventually collapse completely, leaving a small pool of water. A sedge meadow forms initially, and trees invade very slowly. This results in a nearly circular, treeless patch of meadow in the treed bog, known as a "palsa scar." A palsa scar indicates relatively recent disappearance of discontinuous permafrost from organic terrain.

Wetlands

In *boreal wetlands* the most abundant and varied aquatic flora occurs on muck-bottomed lakes and ponds with characteristic submerged or floating-leaved plants such as common floating pondweed, Richardson's pondweed, arum-leaved arrowhead, spike-leaved water-milfoil, and greater bladderwort. Characteristic emergent plants of muck bottoms include horsetail, mare's-tail, and western water-hemlock. Locally, common cattail, northern reed grass, great bulrush, and giant bur-reed may be abundant, often dominating the community. Sandy bottoms have a much reduced diversity because shifting sands make establishment of roots more difficult. They are dominated by submerged plants such as Richardson's pondweed, arum-leaved arrowhead, and spike-leaved water-milfoil, as well as such emergents as horsetails, tall manna grass, water sedge, green-fruited bur-reed, and water-parsnip.

There is a natural progression of three or four vegetation zones, based on moisture regime, along the edges of streams, ponds, and lakes. Near the edge of the water is found a grassy zone dominated by sedges, reed grasses, great bulrush, marshmarigold, wild mint, and buttercups. Above this is found a shrub zone characterized by willow and red-osier dogwood; a balsam poplar zone then occurs. Often a white spruce zone will be found on the moderately well to imperfectly drained areas adjacent to the well-drained uplands.

There are millions of small, freshwater wetlands and sloughs in the Prairie Ecozone. They range in size from small sloughs covering one-tenth hectare to larger wetlands covering many square kilometres. However, most *prairie wetlands* are less than one-half hectare.

Many of these wetlands are permanent but others are temporary, drying up in the dry years or the drier times in the spring and fall. Wetlands can form in any depression such as glacial spillways and meltwater channels but are most numerous in kettle depressions in till plains and hummocky moraines. Vegetation in prairie wetlands can change with water height, climate, soil, and age. Depending upon moisture and wetland size, there can be up to five generalized vegetation zones that form rings around the depression and change with the water depth. In the deepest area, a permanent open-water zone exists where water depth is over a metre and submerged and floating plants like duckweed and water crowfoot survive. Closer to shore's edge, the deep-marsh zone is found and supports common cattails and bulrushes. On the wetland margin lies the densely vegetated shallow-marsh zone consisting of bur-reeds, water plantains, tall manna grass, and sedges. Higher up, there may be a wet-meadow zone that is characterized by foxtail barley, reed grasses, prairie cord grass, and Baltic rush. Along the wetland's edge a low prairie zone exists with plants similar to the surrounding grassland association. This zone is inundated only during unusually high water.

Saline marshes are abundant in southern Saskatchewan. Freshwater vegetation patterns exist at lower salt concentrations, but as the salinity increases, different plant species enter according to their salt tolerances. In the brackish marshes, species richness is low but widgeon-grass and horned pondweed occupy open water areas while foxtail barley and alkali grass live along the wetland margin.

Freshwater lakes occur throughout Saskatchewan but are especially common in the north. Cold northern lakes have less dense plant life and lower nutrient levels and tend to be larger than southern lakes.

Plant life in lake systems is seasonally cyclic. During most of the year, lakes have little plant life. In the winter, extreme weather and ice cause plants to lie dormant until the spring melt. As summer approaches, floating plants such as algae, duckweed, and water crowfoot usually grow near the lake margins. As fall arrives, plant densities can become high, especially in the southern lakes.

Saline lakes in Saskatchewan are restricted to the Prairie Ecozone. They form in large closed basins in drier regions where evaporation exceeds precipitation. Salt concentrations are caused by one or more of the ions sodium, magnesium, and sulphate.

The most important factor controlling the vegetation and wildlife in saline lakes is salinity. Lakes with low salinity usually have vegetation patterns similar to freshwater lakes. Species richness and density is reduced in medium salinity lakes with the only common vascular vegetation being widgeon-grass and sago pondweed. As salinity increases, these species become less abundant and eventually no vascular vegetation is normally found.

Phytoplankton live in all but the most highly saline lakes. Saline wetland associations may also be found along the margins of lakes with low to medium salinity.

Agricultural land

Cropland is land used for the production of annual or perennial food or forage crops. It includes land in fallow. *Improved pasture* includes land planted to perennial grasses for livestock grazing. *Rangeland* is an extensive area of native grassland used for livestock grazing, but it may include some improved pasture.

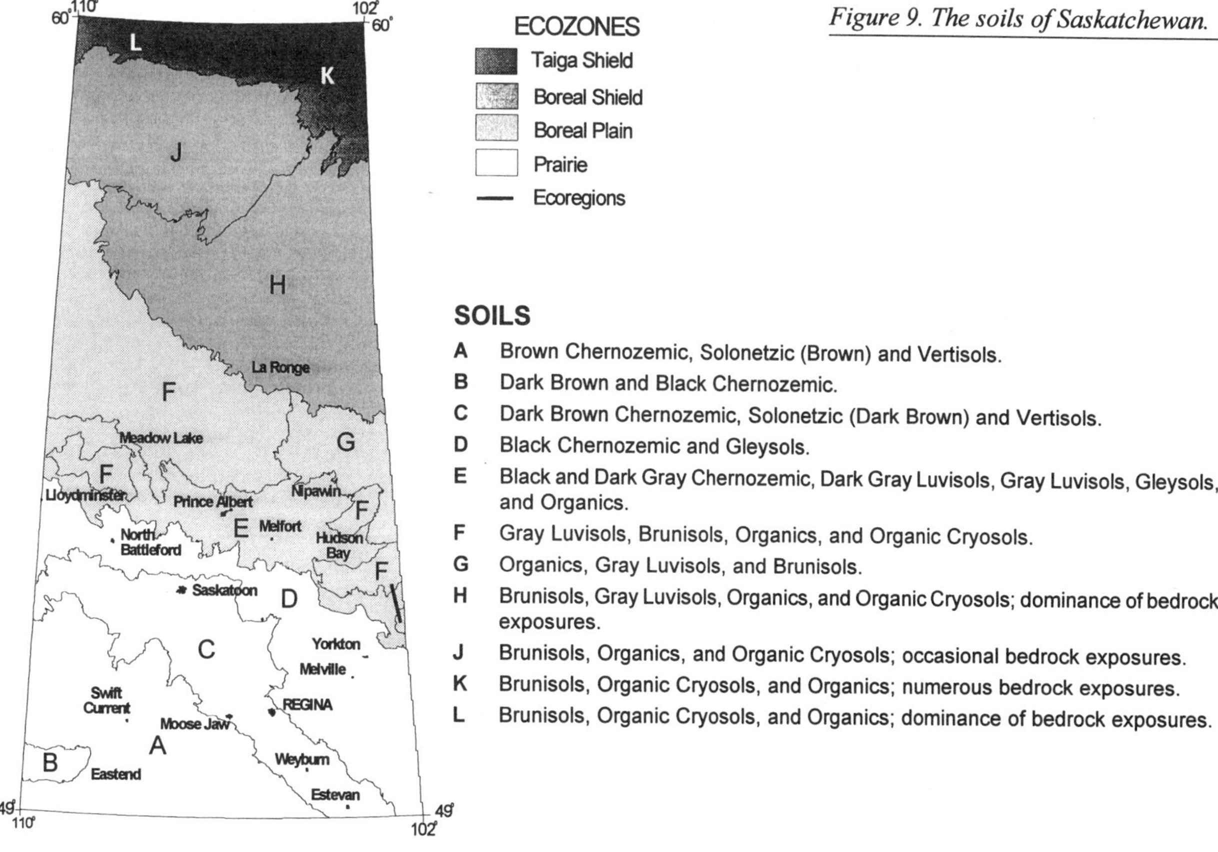

Figure 9. The soils of Saskatchewan.

Soils

Soils in Saskatchewan reflect the environment in which they have formed, including the environment created by human activity. These environments include passive elements, such as the composition and relief of the surficial deposits, and active elements, such as climate, vegetation, and the activities of humans.

A series of soil zones based on the colour of the surface soil have been recognized in Saskatchewan. These colours reflect the amount of organic matter in the upper part of the soil, which is related to the climatic regions described earlier. Brown Chernozemic soils prevail at low latitudes, in the semiarid mixed-grass prairie, where the amount of plant biomass produced is relatively low. Most of the soil organic matter in these grasslands originates from the decomposition of roots, and the products of decomposition are held in place by the mineral components of the soil. Dark Brown Chernozemic soils occur in the more moist grassland regions to the north and east and they, in turn, give way to Black Chernozemic soils in the fescue-dominated aspen parkland, where the biomass, in general, and the below-ground biomass, in particular, is higher than in the brown and dark brown soils. Dark Gray Chernozemic and Dark Gray and Gray Luvisolic soils prevail farther north, in the areas transitional to the forest and in the forest region, respectively. Gray-coloured layers near the surface indicate a greater proportion of total organic matter produced above ground in forests and the greater potential for organic matter in forest soils to be leached from the surface and carried to greater depths in the soil.

Within any of the zones, the soil colour may vary. Dark Brown, and even Black or Dark Gray soils, can be found at higher elevations or on the more moist north- and east-facing regional slopes within the brown soil zone. Similarly, Black and Dark Gray soils can be found at higher elevations within the dark brown soil zone, and Brown soils may be found at lower elevations or on south- and west-facing regional slopes, and so on for the other zones.

NAME OF SIZE CLASS	DIAMETER (mm)
Very coarse sand	2.0 – 1.0
Coarse sand	1.0 – 0.5
Medium sand	0.5 – 0.25
Fine sand	0.25 – 0.10
Very fine sand	0.10 – 0.05
Silt	0.05 – 0.002
Clay	<0.002

Table 1. Size classes of primary particles and their dimensions.

In the Prairie Ecozone, soils are usually thinner on upper slopes than they are further downslope. This is often reflected in lighter soil colours on these upper slopes, especially on steeper topography. In extreme cases, Regosolic soils prevail where all of the soil has been removed as a consequence of cultivation. Soils on upper slopes in the Boreal Plain Ecozone are also lighter colored but thicker than in lower slopes due to greater potential for leaching of organic and mineral materials from the upper slope positions. Bottoms of slopes, especially where glacial kettles prevail, are dominated by wet Gleysolic soils. In the Prairie Ecozone, these soils are dark colored where marshy vegetation prevails. They may be light coloured and saline where groundwater is discharging at the surface. In the Aspen Parkland, in particular, they may also be light coloured, especially after cultivation, where recharging groundwater has leached organic and mineral materials from the surface. In the Boreal Plain and Boreal Shield ecozones, lower temperatures favour accumulation rather than decomposition of organic matter, and lower topographic positions are covered by fens and bogs and associated Organic soils. In the northern extremities of the Boreal Shield and throughout the Taiga Shield ecozones, these peat deposits are often frozen permanently, and are termed Cryosols.

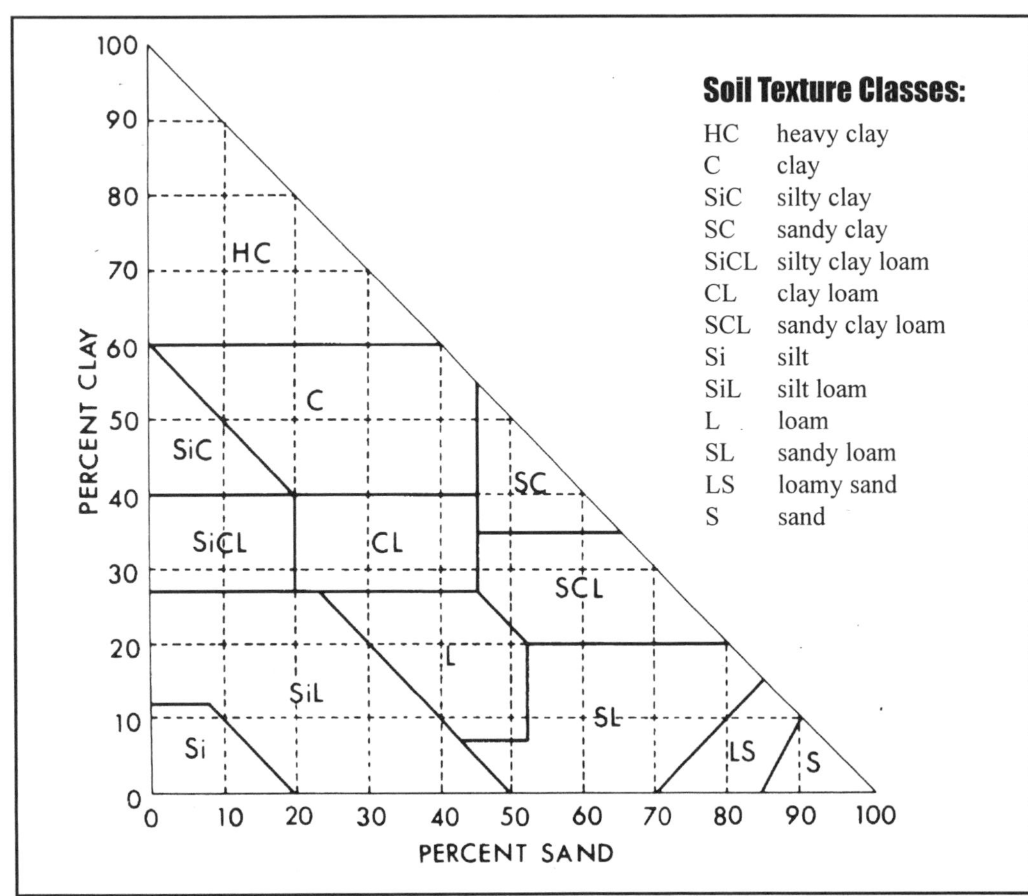

Figure 10. Particle size distribution in soil texture classes. Percentages of clay and sand in the main textural classes of soil; the remainder of each class is silt.

A list of the soil orders and great groups used in this report is presented in the glossary (see "soil classification").

Soil texture

Soil texture indicates the proportion of different sized particles present in a soil. The range in size of the mineral particles is given in Table 1 and the distribution of these size classes in the textural classes in Figure 10.

Soil drainage classes

Soil drainage classes are defined in terms of the actual moisture content in excess of field moisture capacity and the extent of the period during which such excess water is present in the plant root zone. It is affected by the permeability of the soil and subsoil materials, level of groundwater, and seepage. Six drainage classes are recognized and defined in the glossary (see "soil drainage classes").

Wildlife

Each animal species has a unique requirement for food, shelter, and breeding; each animal is said to occupy its own ecological niche. Hence, areas with a large number and variety of unique niches, or habitats, can be expected to contain a large number of species. The number of species, or species richness, of an area is also determined by climate and faunal history.

Generally in Saskatchewan, the number of plant and animal species declines with increasing latitude (see Figure 11). As many as 62 species of mammals have been reported at 49° latitude, while only 37 species occur at 60° latitude, thus reflecting the cooling climate gradient toward the north. The resulting vegetation shift forms a natural boundary for some species. For example, 25 mammal species are confined to the boreal regions, while 33 species range south of the boreal forest, and 18 extend their range over both distinct regions.

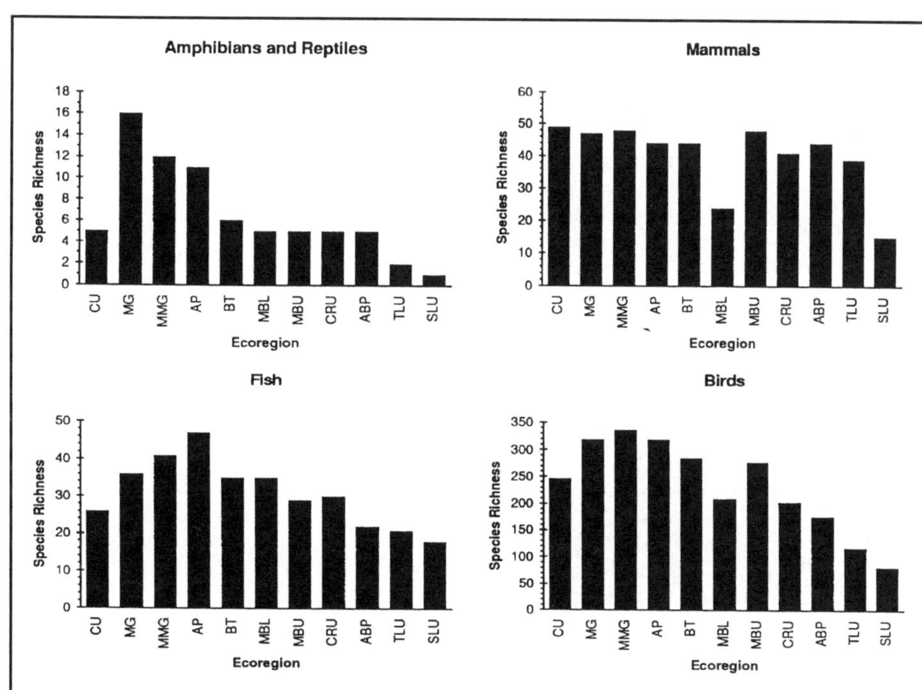

LEGEND

CU - Cypress Upland
MG - Mixed Grassland
MMG - Moist Mixed Grassland
AP- Aspen Parkland
BT - Boreal Transition
MBL - Mid-Boreal Lowland
MBU - Mid-Boreal Upland
CRU - Churchill River Upland
ABP - Athabasca Plain
TLU - Tazin Lake Upland
SLU - Selwyn Lake Upland

Figure 11. Vertebrate species richness for the ecoregions in Saskatchewan.

Habitat variety is greatly influenced by diversified topography; the greater the physical contrasts, the greater the variety of plants, resulting in more food and shelter choices.

Competition for food and shelter between closely related species also limits distribution of many species. For example, if a number of different mouse species occur in an area, one can assume that their food habits and lifestyles differ greatly. An animal often restricts itself to a "home range," which is proportional to the size of the species. For example, a meadow vole uses about 0.1 ha, a snowshoe hare ranges within 3 to 7 ha, while a lynx roams over 18 km^2. In general, males have a larger range than females, and carnivores have a larger range than herbivores. Some mammals (bats, caribou, pronghorn) and many birds are migratory, requiring different types of habitat in different seasons.

Populations vary irregularly due to natural fluctuations in their environment. Climatic extremes such as drought and excess precipitation can reduce numbers or accelerate them. Factors involved in population control include food availability, predation, and disease. All these affect breeding success, but it is the variation in mortality that ultimately controls animal numbers. Some species do fluctuate in a regular cycle. The cycle usually involves a herbivore and its predators. For example, snowshoe hare and lynx cycle through a population high and low over 10 years and, to a lesser extent, red fox, marten and fisher cycle within it.

Seventy-eight species of wild animals occur or have occurred in Saskatchewan in historic times. Rodents are the most abundant order, followed by carnivores, bats, ungulates, shrews and rabbits. The Norway rat and house mouse were introduced through European settlement.

Nesting requirements are often very specific and are a critical factor determining the presence of birds in an area. Birds prey on insects and mammals, and act as scavengers; grasshoppers and Richardson's ground squirrels form the diet of many birds. Birds, in turn, are a significant food source for many predators. The most common birds nesting in Saskatchewan are Brewer's and red-winged blackbirds, brown-headed cowbird, horned lark, western meadowlark, and house, clay-colored, savannah, and vesper sparrows. However, Saskatchewan is better known for three groups of more conspicuous birds: shorebirds, hawks, and waterfowl. The high density of waterfowl is due to the occurrence of numerous, shallow potholes, which are highly productive food factories. Poor nesting success for all bird species is the result of widespread destruction of nest site habitat.

Fish are more abundant in the north where water occupies nearly 30% of the area. Small streams and lakes generally support fewer (5-10) and smaller species than a large water body (20-25 species). Some species are temperature dependent. Lake trout, for example, do not thrive in water over 15°C and need deep lakes to access cooler water. For species such as smallmouth bass, the water may be too cold for successful spawning. Turbidity caused by excess siltation can inhibit some species. Water pollution and eutrophication can alter fish populations. This is a greater concern in southern Saskatchewan, where it is associated with runoff from snowmelt and major rainfall. Excessive algae growth due to an abundance of nutrients can deplete a lake of oxygen, killing many inhabitants.

Amphibians, with the exception of the wood frog, are not found in the extreme north, and reptiles are almost entirely associated with the prairie. Both need protection from winter, as their body temperature rises or falls according to external temperature. Snakes retreat below the frost line into rodent burrows and cracks in the ground. Amphibians bury into mud bottoms of rivers and sloughs. During the summer, reptiles travel far overland and many prefer the warm, dry mixed grassland; as a result, only the red-sided garter snake ranges into the northern part of the province.

Species richness for mammals, amphibians and reptiles, birds, and fish have been estimated for each ecoregion in Saskatchewan. Species richness of mammals was determined by overlaying data such as that from Abouguendia (1981), Banfield (1974), and Hart and Stewart (1981) onto the "Ecoregions of Saskatchewan" poster map. The same approach was used for amphibians and reptiles, using reference material by Secoy and Vincent (1976) combined with personal communication with Andrew Didiuk. Smith (1996) was the sole source for birds, while Scott and Crossman (1973) and personal communication with W.W. Sawchyn provided the data sources for fish. Species richness for these groups of vertebrates for the ecoregions in the province are presented in Figure 11.

Human impacts

This concluding section on ecosystem development examines the nature and extent of human activities within the province and outlines the impact of these activities on ecosystem composition and structure.

Farming and ranching are the most common and best known human land uses in Saskatchewan. Virtually all of the Prairie Ecozone is cropland or pasture (relatively small areas of grazing land where the farm enterprize is dominated by the production of cultivated crops), with most of the remaining land used for ranching (extensive areas of grazing land where the main enterprize is livestock production). Exceptions are urban development, roads and rail lines, mine sites, oil and gas production, parks, and lakes and rivers.

Despite the dominance of agricultural activities on the landscape, the majority of the population in the Prairie Ecozone is found in urban communities. These communities occupy less than one-half of one percent of the total area of the ecozone.

Agriculture, and, to a much lesser degree, urbanization have transformed more than 80% of the native prairie landscape. All landscape areas within this ecozone have been cultivated or grazed for at least 20% of their area, and many show 100% cultivation or grazing levels. Severe soil degradation by wind and water erosion has been experienced since European settlement over 100 years ago as farmers attempted to thrive, and at times simply survive, on a wheat-dominated farming system. Crop production has become much more diversified in recent years, from the traditional grain crops to more oilseed crops, such as canola, flax, and sunflowers. Producers have increasingly adopted more sustainable farming practices, including conservation tillage and reduced summerfallow, reducing the risk of water and wind erosion. The Prairie Ecozone has also been experiencing a trend towards increased and intensive livestock production.

Canada contains one-quarter of the world's wetland resource, and 17% of this is in Saskatchewan. Just under 2 million hectares of wetlands occur in the Prairie Ecozone. Most of the water systems in the ecozone have been modified and developed. Reservoirs have been constructed on many major river systems to supply water, prevent flooding, and generate power. Eutrophication of water bodies, caused to a large measure by the addition of phosphorus and nitrogen from farm sources and municipal sewage, is possibly the single most important issue concerning water quality in the Prairie Ecozone.

Over the past 100 years, the Prairie Ecozone has also undergone development by oil and gas extraction and refining, hydroelectric power generation, fisheries, and mining. Although these industries have fostered a thriving economy and high standard of living, they have also greatly modified the original ecosystems, diminishing wildlife and plant populations.

In summary, both national and global demand for agricultural products from the Prairie

Ecozone have led to the loss of habitat and wildlife, degradation of land, air, and water quality, urban sprawl, stream-flow regulation, and floods. More recent issues that have emerged include the inadvertent introduction of foreign species, impacts on riparian systems or riverside vegetation, and loss of biological diversity.

Forested lands are widely scattered in the Prairie Ecozone. There is relatively limited commercial fishing activity; however, it is a popular destination for anglers. Nearly one-quarter of the provincial trapping harvest, over one-half of the provincial total of hunting of big game, and more than three-quarters of the hunting for bird species occurs in the Prairie Ecozone. Just under 9% of this ecozone is in some form of park or protected area. Canada's only national park dedicated to the protection of grasslands, Grasslands National Park, is located in this zone.

Farming is a major land use in the southern part of the Boreal Plain Ecozone, but forestry dominates further north. Other land uses include forestry, mining, oil and gas exploration and production, hunting and trapping, outdoor recreation, and tourism. Roughly one-half of the zone is actually productive commercial forest land. Forestry operations focus on harvesting large volumes of wood fibre for pulp and paper.

Saskatchewan has embraced the concept of ecosystem management to address the sustainability of forests and wood supply and of the natural resources of water and soils, while accounting for and considering the interaction with wildlife, tourism, and aesthetic values.

Agriculture has also become a more widespread land use. The clearing of woodlands for agricultural expansion has affected local drainage flow patterns, watercourses, and wetlands. Agricultural practices that affect water quality alluded to in the Prairie Ecozone section also prevail here. As in the Prairie Ecozone, sustainable agricultural practices such as conservation tillage and reduced summerfallow have recently been adopted.

Water resources are abundant in the Boreal Plain Ecozone. The local residential impact on water quality is low compared with that of more populated areas.

Commercial and sport fishing and trapping are more prevalent here than in other ecozones in the province. The Boreal Plain Ecozone has very little mining development, but it has two hydroelectric dam operations.

Approximately 8% of the Boreal Plain Ecozone is managed within parks and protected areas, principally national and provincial parks and Wildlife Habitat Protection Act lands.

The direct measurable footprint of human activity is small in the Boreal Shield Ecozone compared to the ecozones to the south. Uranium mining is the major industrial activity. Today, the overall trend in the ecozone is probably towards greater sustainability, owing to changes in regulations and standards, corporate practices, and public and professional attitudes and goals, plus the gradual evolution of management practices. Approximately 3% of the ecozone is contained within a park or protected area.

By southern Canadian standards, the Taiga Shield is characterized by a generally low level of internal human activity. On the other hand, human activities external to the Taiga Shield, such as mineral exploration, are affecting, or have the potential to affect, the region. The impact of human activities, both within and outside this ecozone, will affect the future sustainability of its ecosystems. There are no parks or protected areas within this ecozone.

TAIGA SHIELD ECOZONE

The taiga shield, the land of the "little sticks" and innumerable lakes, is part of the general tundra and boreal forest transition that extends from Labrador to Alaska. More specifically, the taiga shield is a vast, broadly rolling plain that lies on either side of Hudson Bay. The western part of this plain extends from Hudson Bay to the Mackenzie Valley, between the boreal shield and the southern arctic. A lichen woodland typifies the vegetation that occurs under a subarctic climate. It is the smallest ecozone in Saskatchewan, occupying only 4.7 million hectares or approximately 7% of the provincial land mass.

PHYSIOGRAPHY. Precambrian basement rocks, the remnants of former mountains that have been eroded to a peneplain, are reflected in a series of broad, smooth uplands and intervening lowlands with very irregular local relief. Elevations on this peneplain range from 350 m to nearly 600 m. A veneer of glacial drift masks the bedrock surface in some areas, sometimes providing distinctive landscape features such as drumlins and eskers. The area straddles the divide between drainage to Hudson Bay and the Beaufort Sea.

GEOLOGY. The entire Taiga Shield Ecozone and the Churchill River Upland Ecoregion of the Boreal Shield Ecozone are underlain by crystalline basement rocks of the Precambrian Shield. The region is glacially sculpted, but the landscape strongly reflects bedrock geology. Over much of the region, bedrock is exposed or covered by relatively thin soil.

The metamorphosed rocks that make up the Precambrian Shield are the roots of ancient mountains, which were formed through the collision of continents. The collision folded, uplifted, and metamorphosed pre-existing sedimentary and volcanic rocks in a fashion similar to the formation of the Himalayas. The mountain building ended about 1.76 billion years ago, and over the next 100 million years or so, the mountain belt was eroded to become a low relief area of a new continental mass formed by the collision.

The collision of continental plates, located southeast and northwest of present day Saskatchewan, imparted a fabric perpendicular to the force of the continental collision, namely northeast-southwest. This is also the predominant orientation of the most recent glacial advance and retreat. Glacial erosion and deposition were strongly affected by the bedrock. Topographic relief is generally low, but can be rugged in areas where the glacier preferentially eroded low-lying areas underlain by softer (e.g., schistose) rocks or fault zones and polished resistant bedrock knobs. Many of the lakes and intervening bedrock ridges in the region are elongated about a northeast-southwest axis. This results in a trellis-like drainage network, with many rivers flowing parallel to one another in a northeast-southwest direction. Connecting these are short streams, generally at right angles to the major rivers, which follow faults, regional joint sets, or other weaknesses in the bedrock.

Boulder fields, or felsenmere, are common landscape features in the Taiga Shield Ecozone.

CLIMATE. The climate of the Taiga Shield Ecozone is transitional from the subarctic climate to the south and the arctic climate to the north. It is characterized by cold temperatures and low precipitation. The long, very cold winters last seven to eight months. The short, cool summers have periods of daylight greater than 18 hours per day, offsetting to some degree the shorter growing season and the less intensive solar radiation as compared to other ecozones in the south. Temperatures tend to decrease slightly from west to east across the ecoregion, due mainly to a stronger continental effect in the eastern part of the area. Total precipitation is variable and low, and tends to decrease toward the northern boundary of Saskatchewan. Maximum precipitation occurs from July through September.

LANDFORMS AND SOILS. The taiga shield is dominated by Precambrian bedrock outcrops and discontinuous glaciofluvial and morainal deposits. Brunisolic soils prevail in well-drained positions in the landscape, with Gleysolics in some poorly drained areas. Peat occurs in numerous bogs and fens. For the most part, these are not frozen permanently and are classified as Organic soils. They are often frozen under black spruce, however, where they are classified as Cryosolics. There is virtually no soil development on the numerous exposures of crystalline basement rocks.

GROUNDWATER. Groundwater in the Taiga Shield Ecozone is essentially limited to surficial aquifers formed in the thin and discontinuous, highly permeable glacial deposits. Groundwater is present in cracks and along faults in the basal Precambrian basement rocks, but these materials essentially represent an aquitard, restricting the downward movement of groundwater from the surficial sediments.

VEGETATION. As a result of the severe climate and short growing season, species diversity is low in the taiga shield. A type of subarctic vegetation cover known as lichen woodland, characterized by open black spruce stands underlain by a carpet of lichens dominates the area. In very dry locales, such as south-facing slopes on eskers, vegetation is sparse, and 30% of the ground surface is bare. The lowland areas are composed primarily of bogs, which may be wooded or treeless, and fens. Generally, this type of vegetation is typical of the Selwyn Lake Upland and its subarctic climate; these open coniferous forests are transitional to tundra communities characteristic of arctic climates to the north beyond

Willow ptarmigan often winter in the Tazin Lake upland of the Taiga Shield Ecozone.

Saskatchewan. The area near Uranium City tends to be slightly warmer; consequently, a transition occurs between the Selwyn Lake and Tazin Lake uplands, where the vegetation reflects that of a high boreal climate. Here, closed-crown coniferous forest occurs on upland areas, while treed bog covers lowland areas.

WILDLIFE. The taiga shield has the least productive and lowest number of wildlife species of any ecozone in the province, reflecting the harsh climate and lack of diversity in vegetation. The eastern part is particularly low, with somewhat higher productivity and species richness associated with the slightly warmer climate and more diverse vegetation to the west.

Approximately 50 mammal species have been reported to occur in the ecozone, reflecting a moderately low species richness. Representative species of the various orders include black bear, moose, barren-ground caribou (winter range), snowshoe hare, gray wolf, arctic fox, beaver, lynx, masked shrew, least chipmunk, and red squirrel.

Richness of bird species is also low, with 120 species reported to occur in this ecozone. Representative birds include spruce grouse, gray jay, boreal chickadee, pine grosbeak, ruby-crowned kinglet, gray-cheeked thrush, Harris' sparrow, American tree sparrow, white-crowned sparrow, blackpoll warbler, and golden eagle.

Representative fish include lake trout, northern pike, walleye, lake whitefish, cisco, burbot, white sucker, and arctic grayling. Only two amphibians occur in the ecoregion and the richness of fish species is also low, with approximately 20 species being recorded.

Rugged terrain along the north shore of Lake Athabasca.

HUMAN ACTIVITY. Approximately 1,300 people live in this zone, or 0.1% of the Saskatchewan population. In comparison with more southerly ecozones, taiga ecosystems are less biologically productive and diverse, the human population is smaller, and the ecozone is not characterized by high levels of natural resource development and use. Agriculture is virtually impossible owing to the short growing season and poor soil conditions. Commercial forestry is also limited in potential. Nonetheless, the economy of the taiga shield combines a number of industrial activities that spring from the vital resources found in this area: gold, base metals, and uranium. Small, local business support mineral exploration work in this zone. The network of roads is sparse compared with that in areas to the south. Consequently, there is a landing strip in almost every village. Most communities are accessible only by boat or air or by winter roads. Subsistence hunting, trapping, and fishing are still traditional and necessary activities for those who inhabit this land.

In the past, uranium was mined at a number of taiga sites in northern Saskatchewan. Since 1980, however, all uranium mining in the province has been south of the taiga. The environmental effects of mining activity in the taiga are generally localized. In northern Saskatchewan, low-level radioactive tailings remain following the closure of several uranium mines.

By southern Canadian standards, the taiga is characterized by a generally low level of internal human activity. On the other hand, human activities external to the taiga are affecting, or have the potential to affect, the region. The impact of human activities, both within and outside the taiga, will affect the future sustainability of its ecosystems. There are no parks or protected areas within this ecozone.

Selwyn Lake Upland Ecoregion

The Selwyn Lake Upland Ecoregion occurs in the extreme northeast corner of the province. It is part of a larger region that extends from Churchill River in Manitoba to the eastern end of Great Slave Lake. It is one of the smallest ecoregions in Saskatchewan, occupying 2.9 million hectares or 4% of the province.

PHYSIOGRAPHY. Ridged to hummocky crystalline bedrock forms broad, gently sloping terrain. Local relief rarely exceeds 50 m and elevations are typically in the order of 350 m to 420 m, reflecting a more subdued relief than in the Tazin Lake Upland. Most of the Selwyn Lake Upland drains to Hudson Bay by way of the Churchill and Nelson rivers.

GEOLOGY. The western portion of this ecoregion comprises the metamorphic rocks of the Rae Province. Two major northeast-trending units of granite gneiss and a linear belt of metamorphosed volcanic and metamorphosed sedimentary rocks interfolded with older granite rocks make up the Hearne Province in the eastern part of the region.

The ground moraine is thicker and more continuous in this ecoregion than in the Tazin Lake Ecoregion. Morainal or till plains and drumlinoid moraines are the dominant morphologies.

CLIMATE. The arctic transitional climate in the Selwyn Lake upland is characterized by cool summers and very cold winters. The mean annual daily temperature is -4.9°C. The mean July temperature is 15.7°C and the mean January temperature is -28.5°C. The mean annual precipitation is 369 mm, with 241 mm of rainfall occurring from May to September. The summers are short

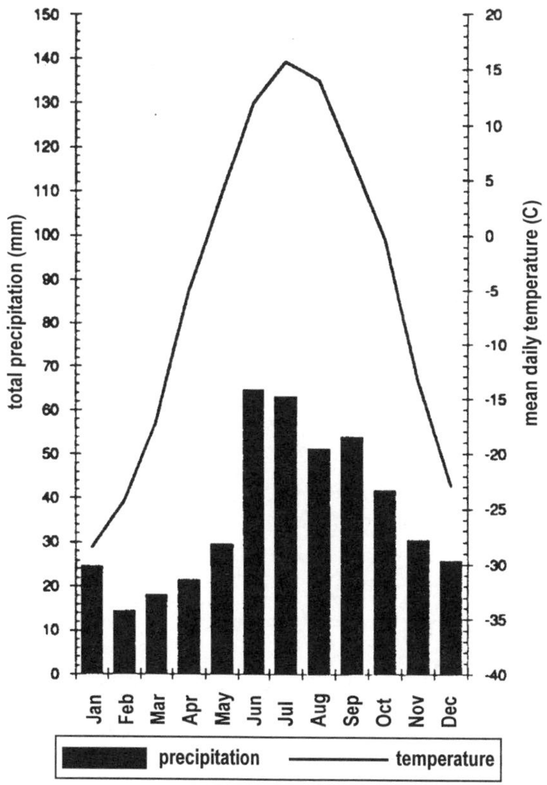

Figure 12. Mean monthly temperature and precipitation for the Selwyn Lake upland as represented by the meteorological record from Brochet.

and cool, having a frost-free period of 96 days and only 965 growing degree days above 5°C.

Water dominates the landscape throughout this ecoregion.

LANDFORMS AND SOILS. Bedrock outcrops dominate the rises and Brunisols are scattered throughout the intervening intermediate slopes, where they are associated with sandy and frequently stony glacial deposits, prominent, sinuous esker ridges, and cigar-shaped drumlins. Permafrost is sporadic along the southern edge but extensive and discontinuous further north. Organic soils dominate fens, especially along the southern border, with Cryosolics dominating the poorly drained fens and bogs farther north. As much as 3 m of peat has accumulated in some areas. This suggests a warmer climate prevailed in the past, with more recent, cooler climates leading to the development of permafrost within these deposits.

GROUNDWATER. The crystalline basement rocks that dominate the bedrock in this ecoregion are generally massive and dense. Permeability is usually determined by fractures and faults, which are not necessarily interconnected. There are no known wells drilled in this kind of rock in Saskatchewan, and any wells in materials such as this are likely to provide very limited water supply. The shallow depth of the glacial drift minimizes the opportunity for inter-till aquifers; however, the sandy nature of the glacial drift provides for extensive surficial aquifers. Bogs have permafrost, diminishing the opportunity for shallow groundwater.

VEGETATION. The vegetation of the Selwyn Lake Upland Ecoregion is fairly uniform and simple compared to that of other ecoregions. This is due to the limiting nature of the subarctic climate. Lichen woodland, rock lichen, peatlands (peat plateaus, palsas, and sedge fens), and boreal wetlands are the major vegetation associations that occur in this ecoregion.

The ecoregion is typically characterized by open lichen woodland. Stunted black spruce are scattered in an open, park-like setting, with a ground cover of yellowish- to whitish-coloured lichens, with dwarf shrubs interspersed. On more moist slopes, the trees are much closer together, and vascular plants and mosses become a significant component in the groundcover. The trees found in the Selwyn Lake upland are small for their age compared to those in the boreal shield farther south, a result of the harsh climate and short growing season.

The ubiquitous black spruce is the climax species and is by far the most prevalent tree. Jack pine, the second most common tree, dominates where the glacial drift veneer is thin, and on sandy and gravelly outwash plains where conditions are drier. White spruce is confined to warmer, protected areas such as alluvial plains and water margins, and the slopes of eskers and kames. Fire brings white birch into temporary prominence on sites not dominated by jack pine; white birch normally exist as scattered individuals throughout the coniferous forest. Tamarack pioneers on lowland areas after a fire. Lichen woodland tends to experience a burning rate of one fire every 150 to 200 years. Stands older than 200 years are quite common.

Fungi growing on a lichen-covered forest floor.

Rock lichen vegetation is commonly interspersed within lichen woodlands, occupying the upper, dry slopes of prominent bedrock outcrops. As the name implies, a range of lichens covers the rock surfaces. Only the occasional black spruce or jack pine, growing in the bedrock fissures, is present. After a fire, most successional change is confined to lichens, mosses, and herbs, as they invade and respond to shading that accompanies regeneration and growth of the dominant trees.

The typical peatlands are peat plateaus, which are raised permafrost bog. It is bordered by open water or fen on the wet lowland side and by a narrow strip of forested shallow peat that abruptly changes into lichen woodland on the dry upland mineral soils. The spaghnum moss that forms the peat tends to grow in mounds; hence, the peatland surfaces are hummocky. When mosses die, due to fire or climatic extremes, a dense mat of lichens sometimes covers the entire surface.

On level landscapes, the peat plateau surfaces are usually pitted with melt-out hollows where pools support various sedges. On sloping terrain, water drains downslope, forming "fen tracks" that give a rilled appearance to the plateau. Tamarack borders these fen tracks, and sedge, bulrush, and cotton-grass grow within them.

Barren-ground caribou migrate into this ecoregion during winter months.

Black spruce and dwarf birch may occur on the peat plateau, or it may be treeless. Lack of trees may be due to fire or to harsh climate. The treeless condition, termed palsas, becomes common as the climate becomes more severe toward the northeast. Treeless plateaus are lichen-covered and polygonally patterned by ice-wedge fissures. The lichen cover indicates a current lull in peat building, possibly due to surface drying as the ice-wedge fissures deepen in response to climate change.

Sedge fens, composed of sedge, cotton-grass, and bulrush, occupy very poorly-drained depressions.

Lake shores are characterized by narrow, marginal mats of aquatic vegetation composed of large sedges and bur-reeds. Shrubs such as green alder, willow, and dwarf birch encroach along the water edge.

Several arctic plants can be found in the northeast corner of the province, namely alpine azalea, false asphodel, and northern grass-of-Parnassus.

WILDLIFE. Wildlife populations are low due to the severe climate and resulting low diversity of vegetation. Fifteen mammal species have been reported to occur in the ecoregion. The density of large mammals such as black bear and moose is estimated to be one animal in 25 km^2. Barren-ground caribou can be found wintering in this ecoregion during most years. Other mammals include snowshoe hare and red-backed vole. Predator species are numerous and include red fox, arctic fox, wolverine, marten, gray wolf, and mink.

Dog sled teams are sometimes used as transportation in the north.

Bird diversity is also low, with an estimated 82 species occurring in the Selwyn Lake upland. Birds such as spruce grouse, willow ptarmigan, gray jay, boreal chickadee, and common raven live here year-round. The surf scoter, mew gull, arctic tern, and least sandpiper nest here but rarely elsewhere in Saskatchewan. Other birds include osprey, sandhill crane, Harris' sparrow, American tree sparrow, gray-cheeked thrush, pine grosbeak, ruby-crowned kinglet, white-crowned sparrow, and blackpoll warbler.

Annual fish production is low at 1 to 2 kg/ha because lake water is cold and nutrient status is low, so that fish grow slowly. Fish include lake trout, arctic grayling, northern pike, lake whitefish, cisco, burbot, and white sucker. The only amphibian of record is the wood frog. Species richness of fish is also low, with 18 species recorded.

HUMAN ACTIVITY. The population of this ecoregion is approximately 600. The major community is Wollaston Lake. The area has no all-weather roads, so transportation is usually by boat in the summer, by snowmobile in the winter, and by plane year-round. Land use activities are limited to trapping, hunting, and recreation. The ecoregion has areas of base metal and gold potential and attracts prospecting activity. None of the ecoregion is contained within parks or other forms of protected areas.

Landscape Areas

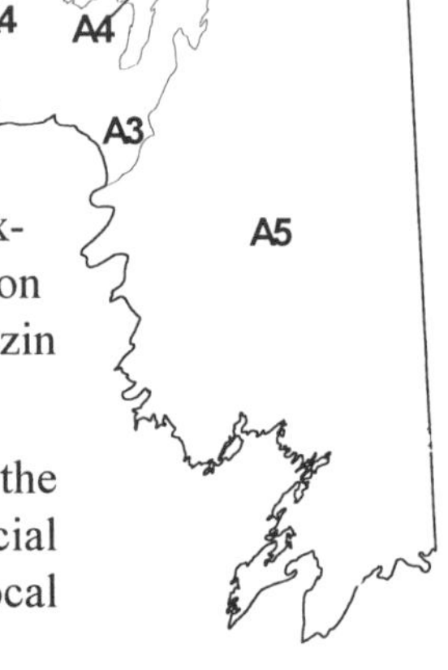

A1. Dunvegan Lake Upland

This is a small area in Saskatchewan but much more extensive in the Northwest Territories. It is an area with broad slopes representing rugged crystalline basement rocks that are largely covered with glacial drift. Elevations range from approximately 420 m at Picae Lake and many smaller lakes that prevail in the area to 500 m on local promontories. The western part of the area drains through the Tazin River to Tazin Lake.

Brunisolic soils formed in a discontinuous blanket of sandy and bouldery glacial till are the dominant soils in the area. Gentle to moderate slopes predominate in this area as the glacial till is sufficiently thick to obscure the underlying bedrock, except for local rises. In local areas, the cover of glacial till is discontinuous and bedrock outcrops dominate a steeply sloping landscape. Eskers and drumlins are prominent local landscape features. Small bogs and fens occur in low-lying depressions and surrounding lakes where gleyed Brunisolic, Gleysolic, and Cryosolic soils prevail.

Due to the deep glacial drift and better soil moisture conditions, the opportunity for fire to start and to spread is reduced. Therefore, this area seems to have suffered less extensive fires than the rest of the Selwyn Lake upland. On the well-drained morainal uplands, lichen woodland is strongly developed, with foam lichens particularly prominent in the reflectant groundcover. Black spruce, jack pine, and white birch dominate the woodland mosaic, while extensive peat plateaus mantle the lowlands.

A2. Eynard Lake Upland

This is a small area in Saskatchewan but much more extensive in the Northwest Territories. It is an area with broad slopes representing rugged basement rocks that are largely covered with glacial drift. Elevations range from approximately 450 m at Sovereign Lake, and many smaller lakes that prevail in the area, to 480 m on local promontories.

The area is dominated by Brunisolic soils formed in a discontinuous blanket of sandy and bouldery glacial till and outwash. In some areas the glacial till is sufficiently thick to mask the underlying bedrock, except for local rises, and moderate slopes prevail. Eskers and drumlins are prominent landscape features, locally. Small bogs and fens occur in low-lying depressions and surrounding lakes where gleyed Brunisolic, Gleysolic, and Cryosolic soils prevail.

Open lichen woodland is the prevalent vegetation on both glacial till and outwash plains. In drumlinized areas, peatlands often comprise 40 to 50% of the landscape cover.

A3. Robins Lake Upland

This is a large area with broad steep slopes representing rugged basement Precambrian rocks with only a discontinuous cover of glacial drift. Elevations range from approximately 450 m at Scott and Premier lakes to over 500 m in local promontories in the northwestern part of the area, and from 400 m at Herbert and Milton lakes to 450 m on local rises in the eastern part of the area. There is drainage to the south from these and many other lakes in the area through the Grease and the Porcupine rivers and many small creeks.

The area is dominated by steep ridges of bedrock. Brunisolic soils form in a thin veneer of sandy and bouldery glacial till that is scattered between bedrock outcrops and on prominent sandy, gravelly eskers. Patterned rock fields formed by frost action, called felsenmere, are a common occurrence where bedrock crops out, as are small bogs and fens in low-lying areas.

While very open lichen woodland and rock lichen is common on the rougher bedrock landscapes, the existence of open lichen woodland on subdued landscapes in this landscape area is indicative of the subarctic climate. The presence of lichen-covered, polygonal peat plateaus and palsas further attests to the harshness of the climate in this area.

A4. Striding River Upland

This area is fragmented into two small parts in Saskatchewan by the border with the Northwest Territories. It is a broadly sloping area dominated by rugged basement rocks that are largely covered with glacial drift. There are numerous large, shallow lakes oriented in a northeast to southwest direction, which reflect the bedrock structure. Elevations range from approximately 450 m in the western part of the area to 400 m in the east. The Striding River drains part of this area into Wignes Lake in the Northwest Territories.

Brunisolic soils formed in a discontinuous blanket of sandy and bouldery glacial till are the dominant soils in the area. In some areas the till is sufficiently thick to obscure the underlying bedrock, except for local rises, and moderate slopes prevail. Eskers and drumlins are prominent landscape features, locally. Felsenmere is commonplace in association with bedrock outcrops. Strandlines of former glacial lakes have been cut into the glacial sediments in uplands at higher elevations. A large, flat bog occurs near Waptya Lake and small bogs and fens occur in numerous low-lying areas and surrounding lakes. Organic soils are present in some of the fens, but most of the fens and bogs are Cryosolics.

The western edge of this landscape area follows the "bog treeline," meaning that the peat plateaus are generally treeless in the Striding River upland. The lowland terrain is extensive, and the treeless polygonal peat plateaus frequently show signs of erosion. The glacial till veneer supports open lichen woodland on well-drained sites. Where the glacial till is quite sandy and bouldery, the lichen woodland stand becomes very open.

A5. Nueltin Lake Plain

This is a very large area in the northeast corner of the province. Elevations of this broadly sloping area range from 420 to 450 m, occasionally 480 m, in areas to the north and south of Phelps Lake and northeast of Wollaston Lake. They recede to approximately 350 m at Hasbala Lake and Zangeza Bay of Reindeer Lake on the Manitoba border. The southern part of the area is part of the Wollaston Lake basin. It drains to Wollaston Lake, which drains northward through the Cochrane River to Hudson Bay as well as through the Fond du Lac River to Lake Athabasca and the Beaufort Sea. The western part, including Hatchet, Phelps, and Hannah lakes also drains to Lake Athabasca. The extreme northeastern part, including Patterson and Misaw lakes, drains northward into the Northwest Territories, and the eastern part, including Charcoal and Hara lakes, drains eastward into Manitoba.

The area is dominated by Brunisolic soils formed in a blanket of sandy and bouldery glacial till and on the many prominent sandy and gravelly eskers that occur in the area. The ground moraine is thicker and more continuous in this area than in many other areas in this ecoregion. In addition, hummocky moraines and drumlins add to the mantle of materials that subdues the underlying bedrock topography. There are numerous bogs and fens in this area, some of them very large. In the southern part, Organic soils are commonly associated with these peatlands, but Cryosolics are associated with peat plateaus on permanently frozen deposits further north. Pools of water on the margins of peat plateaus in the fens, called thermokarst, are further evidence of frozen soils in this area.

Black spruce, somewhat smaller than in forests to the south and west, occupies a variety of habitats from dry esker ridges to wet bogs and stream margins. Individuals of jack pine, white birch, and tamarack may be associated with the black spruce, but pure stands of these other species are uncommon. Open lichen woodland occupies the tops and slopes of eskers, till ridges, old beach ridges, and outcrops covered with shallow soil. On lower, well-drained slopes, feather mosses dominate the forest floor, the black spruce form a more closed canopy, and shrubs like dwarf birch, green alder, and beaked willow are scattered through the understory. Bogs may be treed, but are usually treeless. If treed, the black spruce are closely spaced. Bare silt frost boils are sometimes observed in intermittent drainage channels between sphagnum hummocks. These boils contain rush and sedge species common to an arctic ecosystem. Rocky lake margins also harbour arctic species. Some tundra areas are found on high rocky elevations, or in moist boulder fields; here dwarf birch, sedges, and ericaceous shrubs are common.

A6. Seale River Plain

This is a small area along the Manitoba border, east of Wollaston Lake. Elevations of this broadly sloping area range from 400 to 450 m. They diminish to approximately 350 m at Zangeza Bay of Reindeer Lake on the Manitoba border. The southern part of the area drains southward to Zangeza Bay, and the northern part drains eastward to the Brochet River in Manitoba.

The area is dominated by Brunisolic soils formed in a moderately sloping blanket of sandy and bouldery glacial till. Cryosolic soils occur in lower slope positions in these glacial materials. Sedge bogs are numerous, and many of them contain permafrost.

The sandy blanket of glacial materials on uplands is covered with an open lichen forest, while rock lichens coat exposed bedrock. The numerous permanently frozen bogs are usually treeless and lichen covered.

Tazin Lake Upland Ecoregion

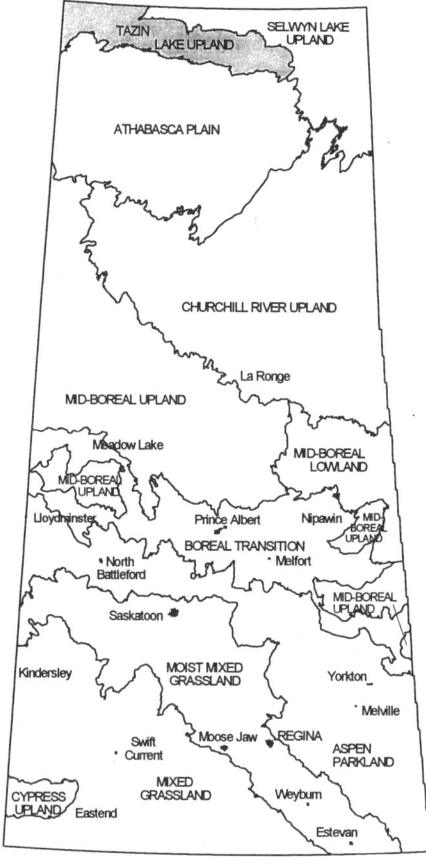

In Saskatchewan, the Tazin Lake Upland Ecoregion stretches northward from Lake Athabasca to the border with the Northwest Territories, but it is part of a larger region that extends to Great Slave Lake. It is one of the smallest ecoregions in Saskatchewan, occupying 1.8 million hectares or 3% of the province.

PHYSIOGRAPHY. Ridged to hummocky crystalline bedrock forms broad, steeply sloping terrain, with local relief of 100 m or more. Most of the Tazin Lake Upland Ecoregion in Saskatchewan drains southward to Lake Athabasca and from there to the Athabasca, Slave, and Mackenzie rivers, but the Tazin Lake area drains northward through the Tazin River to the Taltson River, which empties into Great Slave Lake, and from there through the Slave and Mackenzie rivers to the Beaufort Sea.

GEOLOGY. Major geologic boundaries trend northeast in the crystalline basement rocks of northern Saskatchewan. All of this ecoregion is underlain by a variety of metamorphic rocks collectively referred to as the Rae Province. This province is thought to represent an early continent involved in a Himalayan-style continental collision. In the Tazin Lake Upland Ecoregion it comprises a number of blocks of ancient continental crust, each bounded by faults and younger metamorphosed volcanic and sedimentary rocks.

The ground moraine is very thin and sparse in this ecoregion. Bare bedrock outcrops predominate and a thin veneer of ground moraine covers low areas between outcrops and, occasionally, the highland areas.

CLIMATE. The subarctic climate of the Tazin Lake Upland Ecoregion is characterized by cool summers and very cold winters. The mean annual daily temperature is -3.5°C. The mean July temperature is 16.2°C and

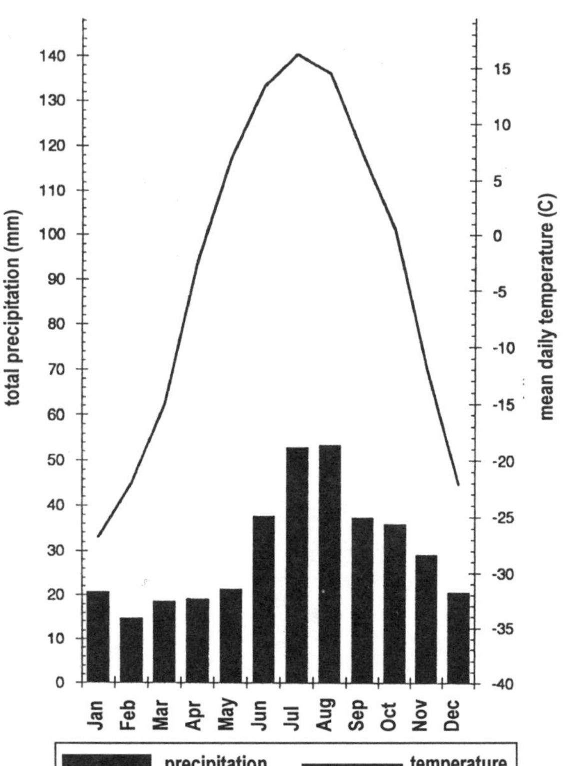

Figure 13. Mean monthly temperature and precipitation for the Tazin Lake upland as represented by the meteorological record from Uranium City.

Shallow rapids are common throughout the ecoregion.

the mean January temperature is -26.8°C. The mean annual precipitation is 362 mm, with 197 mm of rainfall occurring from May to September. The summers are short and cool, with a frost-free period of 105 days and 1,103 degree days with temperatures above 5°C.

A large water body such as Lake Athabasca has a moderating effect on the climate in its vicinity, maintaining a higher than normal evening temperature during its unfrozen period, so that the frost-free period on surrounding lands is extended.

LANDFORMS AND SOILS. Bedrock outcrops dominate the rises and Brunisolic soils are scattered thoughout the intervening intermediate slopes, where they are associated with sandy and frequently stony glacial deposits. Organic soils prevail in fens, with Cryosolics occurring in occasional bogs that are permanently frozen.

GROUNDWATER. Groundwater in the Tazin Lake upland is associated with the discontinuous sandy and bouldery glacial deposits that mantle the bedrock surface. Supply, however, is severely limited by widespread distribution of permafrost.

VEGETATION. The vegetation of the Tazin Lake upland is distinguished from that of the Selwyn Lake upland by the prevalence of closed-crown black spruce-jack pine forests with shady forest floors occurring on both upland and lowland areas. The high boreal climate is less harsh than the subarctic climate in the Selwyn Lake upland; therefore, trees tend to be larger and the area more productive. Black spruce-jack pine forest, rock lichen, lichen woodland, peatlands (peat plateaus and sedge fens), and boreal wetlands are the major plant associations that occur in this ecoregion.

Three-toothed saxifrage found in a rock outcrop.

In the black spruce-jack pine forest, jack pine with lichen ground cover is the prevalent vegetation on warm and dry sites; in the absence of fire, the trend is toward black spruce on the moist and cool sites. White spruce and balsam fir prefer moist sites associated with river valleys or lake shorelines. Stands of trembling aspen or white birch are occasionally present. Where the till veneer is deep enough for adequate rooting, the canopy is underlain by a shrub layer including narrow-leaved and Labrador tea, small bog cranberry, and a mossy ground cover.

A shrub-heath woodland is found on very shallow till veneers and on south-facing esker slopes, where bare ground accounts for up to one-third of the surface. Stunted black spruce, jack pine, and white birch are found scattered among various shrubs. Lichens, mosses, and herbs are not abundant, and purple reed grass is the only significant grass.

This area is prone to fire, which can be expected in a landscape where there is fuel continuity (closed-crown forest) on surface materials that are subject to rapid drying (thin glacial drift over bedrock); however, the rough topography does make local burning difficult in some areas. Jack pine is particularly suited to survival on these sites with coarse drift and in fissures of rock outcrops, due to its low moisture requirements. This, in combination with its early production of serotinous cones, displays its adaptation to fire-driven ecosystems. This ecoregion has an approximate fire cycle of one fire every 100 years.

While medium to tall closed stands of trembling aspen, white birch and balsam poplar are common after a fire, they are a minor component of the forest. White spruce, balsam fir, and black spruce occur in late successional stages.

The peatlands are dominated by sedge fen, composed of sedges, cotton-grasses, horsetails, and bulrushes. The floating mats of aquatic vegetation along the edge of lake shores are wider than those found in the Selwyn Lake upland. Shrubs, with willows, green alder, and dwarf birch predominating, are found around the margins of the fens.

The peat plateaus are wooded, covered with low open stands of black spruce or mixed stands of black spruce and tamarack. Peat, or sphagnum moss, is the main groundcover, interspersed with common and narrow-leaved Labrador tea, bog cranberry, and cloudberry. In areas that are very poorly drained, sedge-dominated fens are associated with tamarack. The permafrost is less extensive than in the Selwyn Lake upland, and no polygonally patterned peat plateaus exist in this area. However, the peatlands do display thermokarst features such as melt-out pools, which are less acidic than the peat plateau itself. The vegetation associated with these includes various sedges and bulrushes, dwarf birch, and tamarack.

Rock lichen is associated with bedrock outcrops that are coated with thin, flat, rock lichens as well as with shrubby filamentous lichens. Along bedrock fractures, where soil is deeper, there is increased diversity of shrubs, lichens, and mosses.

The rock lichen woodland occurs on very shallow till veneers, where droughty conditions are common. A very open stand of stunted jack pine grows in local pockets of drift and in bedrock fissures, while the surrounding bare rock is covered with rock lichens; Cladina and Cladonia lichens cover areas of very shallow drift.

WILDLIFE. Populations of wildlife are low, but there is a larger number of species here than in the Selwyn Lake upland, due to a greater diversity in plant communities. It is estimated that 39 mammal species occur within the ecoregion. Black bear and moose occur at densities of about one of each species

Bald eagle chicks sitting on nest.

Many communities are accessible only by air, by winter roads, or by cargo barges.

per 25 km^2. Barren-ground caribou migrate into the ecoregion, but less frequently and in smaller numbers than in the Selwyn Lake upland. Other mammals include beaver, snowshoe hare, red squirrel, red-backed vole, meadow jumping mouse, and northern bog lemming. Predators include gray wolf, wolverine, marten, lynx, arctic fox, red fox, and ermine.

One hundred and seventeen bird species, which is considered a low level of species richness, have been reported to occur in the Tazin Lake upland. Year-round residents include gray jay, spruce grouse, black-capped chickadee, boreal chickadee, red crossbill, and pine grosbeak. Red-throated loon and semipalmated plover nest in this ecoregion but seldom elsewhere in the province. Birds that breed in this area include surf scoter, arctic tern, mew gull, common redpoll, and greater yellowlegs. Those species that nest in the Tazin Lake upland, but have a wider distribution beyond the taiga shield, include golden eagle, yellow warbler, horned lark, white-winged crossbill, dark-eyed junco, blackpoll warbler, olive-sided flycatcher, and Bohemian waxwing. The willow ptarmigan, rock ptarmigan, and gyrfalcon can be found wintering in the area.

Twenty-one fish species, considered a low level of species richness, are estimated to occur within the Tazin Lake upland. Annual productivity of lake waters is about 1 to 2 kg/ha. Game fish include northern pike, walleye, lake trout, lake whitefish, yellow perch, goldeye, and arctic grayling. Forage fish include cisco, lake chub, emerald shiner, spottail shiner, trout-perch, slimy sculpin, and ninespine stickleback.

Only two amphibians occur in the ecoregion, namely, the northern leopard frog and the wood frog.

HUMAN ACTIVITY. The population of this ecoregion is approximately 600. Major communities include Uranium City and Fond-du-Lac. Land uses include outdoor recreation, wildlife trapping, and hunting and fishing. There is a small hydroelectric facility north of Lake Athabasca near Tazin Lake. There is base metal potential in the area between Lake Athabasca and Tazin Lake and gold exploration and potential development near Goldfields. None of the ecoregion is contained within parks or other forms of protected areas.

Landscape Areas

B1. Uranium City Upland

This is a large area lying to the north of Lake Athabasca, Fond du Lac, and Black Lake. It is an area with broad slopes representing rugged crystalline basement rocks that are sparsely covered with glacial drift. The topography is very rugged, with local relief often approaching 100 m. Elevations range from less than 300 m on the large lakes along the southern margin to approximately 500 m in the northern part of the area. The Oldman, Bulyea, Grease, and Porcupine rivers and numerous other rivers and creeks provide drainage to Lake Athabasca, Fond du Lac, and Black Lake.

The area is dominated by steep bedrock ridges. Brunisolic soils form in a thin veneer of sandy and bouldery glacial till scattered between the bedrock outcrops. Organic and Cryosolic soils occur on numerous small, low-lying and poorly drained areas.

The surface-dry upland terrain is very susceptible to lightning fires. Even-aged forests of jack pine are, therefore, prominent along with the ubiquitous black spruce. White spruce occurs on the margins of some fens and marshes, and some trembling aspen occupy low, sheltered areas.

B2. Territories Upland

In Saskatchewan, this is a small area along the border with the Northwest Territories, but it is much more extensive in the territories. It is an area with broad slopes, representing rugged basement rocks that are largely covered with glacial drift. Elevations range from approximately 420 m at Ena Lake and many smaller lakes that prevail in the area, to 480 m on local promontories. The Abitau River, with headwaters in the Northwest Territories, drains part of this area into Ena Lake.

The area is dominated by Brunisolic soils formed in a discontinuous blanket of sandy and bouldery glacial till. The till is generally sufficiently thick to mask the underlying bedrock, and gentle to moderate slopes predominate. Occasionally, eskers and drumlins interrupt this pattern, but they are not as common as in the Dunvegan area to the north. Organic and Cryosolic soils occur in numerous small, low-lying and poorly drained areas.

Because of sufficient drift and favourable climate, the prominent vegetation is black spruce forest on both uplands and peaty lowlands. Most exposed granitic bedrock is covered by rock lichens, although clumps of Cladina and Cladonia lichens are prominent; jack pine and black spruce grow in bedrock crevices where soil development is sufficiently thick to support plant growth.

Boreal Shield Ecozone

The Boreal Shield Ecozone extends from the Atlantic coast to the Rocky Mountains, separating the warmer boreal plains to the south from the colder taiga shield to the north. It occupies a huge area of northern Saskatchewan, covering 18.7 million hectares, or nearly one-third of the total area of the province. It extends across Saskatchewan from Lake Athabasca on the Alberta border to Flin Flon on the Manitoba border. As the name implies, it represents boreal forest associated with the Canadian Shield in Saskatchewan.

PHYSIOGRAPHY. The Boreal Shield Ecozone comprises two topographically and geologically distinct regions. In the northwest, glacial deposits mantle flat-lying sandstone bedrock and provide most of the local relief. Topography to the south and east is much more typical of the Canadian Shield found in other parts of Canada. Precambrian basement rocks prevail, with extensive areas of rock that form, at first glance, broad, smooth uplands and lowlands. In detail, however, the surface is very uneven and the local relief is often high. The boreal shield straddles the divide between drainage to Hudson Bay and the Beaufort Sea. The area slopes from a general high of 550 m near Cree Lake to 300 m in the southeast around Amisk Lake, and to 275 m in the northwest around Lake Athabasca.

GEOLOGY. This ecozone comprises two highly contrasting geological areas. The Athabasca basin, an area of predominantly sandstone bedrock, occurs in the northwestern part of the ecozone. Precambrian basement rocks occupy the remainder of the area. The sandstones were easily eroded by glaciers; hence, this area has a relatively thick cover of glacial drift. The harder, basement rocks were difficult to erode; consequently, the bedrock is sparsely covered with glacial drift and bedrock outcrops are commonplace.

CLIMATE. The subarctic climate of the Boreal Shield Ecozone is characterized by long, very cold winters and short, cool summers. The winters last about seven months. The summers have periods of daylight close to 18.5 hours per day. The long summer days offset to some degree the shorter growing season and the less intensive solar radiation as compared to other ecozones in the south. Temperatures decrease from southwest to northeast across the ecozone. Total precipitation is variable and low and tends to decrease from south to north. Maximum precipitation occurs from July through September.

LANDFORMS AND SOILS. The ecozone is dominated by a broadly rolling mosaic of uplands and associated wetlands. Precambrian bedrock outcrops interspersed with ridged to hummocky deposits of glacial till, glaciolacustrine, and glaciofluvial deposits are characteristic of its surface materials. Brunisolic soils are associated with the sandy glacial deposits and Luvisols with clayey glaciolacustrine materials. There is virtually no soil development on the numerous bedrock outcrops. Extensive peatlands are found throughout this ecozone. Like the Taiga Shield Ecozone to the north, the landscape of the boreal shield is dotted with numerous small to medium-sized lakes. Peatlands with Organic soils are confined to low-lying depressional areas in the landscape, usually in association with open fens and bogs.

GROUNDWATER. The groundwater conditions in this ecozone closely reflect the contrasting geology that characterizes the area. In the Athabasca basin, both the glacial drift and the underlying sandstone bedrock are highly permeable; hence, the area is likely one large surficial aquifer that extends to considerable depth. In the remaining part of the area, the crystalline basement rocks are only permeable along fractures and faults; hence, they serve as an impermeable barrier at the base of the glacial drift. Consequently, the discontinuous, but usually highly permeable, drift functions as a large but discontinuous surficial aquifer.

VEGETATION. A closed black spruce forest with an understory of feather mosses is the climax vegetation for this region, where soil conditions allow reasonable tree growth. Black spruce dominates the area, forming mixed stands with jack pine on thin soils of uplands and with tamarack on the poorly drained lowlands. Frequent fires have favoured the spread of jack pine, especially on the thin, sandy soils of the Athabasca plain. These fires are likely responsible for the general, scattered occurrence of white birch. White spruce, balsam fir, trembling aspen, and balsam poplar are confined to sites of optimal conditions of soil, drainage, and aspect found in such places as river valleys, around some lakes, and on some south-facing slopes.

Exposed bedrock and sparsely treed bedrock areas are covered with a range of plant communities, dominated by lichens, shrubs, and forbs.

WILDLIFE. Wildlife population and richness varies markedly within this ecozone. They are considerably higher in the Churchill River uplands than in the Athabasca plain, reflecting greater diversity of plant life and consequently more varied habitat for animals and birds.

More than 40 mammal species occur within the ecozone, considered a medium species richness. Moose, black bear, lynx, caribou, gray wolf, beaver, river otter, mink, marten, arctic fox, snowshoe hare, and masked shrew are representative of this group.

Bird diversity is moderately low, with 218 species reported to occur in the ecozone. Representative birds include common raven, gray jay, spruce grouse,

Open pine-lichen woodland reflects the arid and nutrient-poor conditions that prevail in soils developed in sandy glaciofluvial deposits.

The snowshoe hare changes its colour to white in the fall to camouflage with the winter surroundings.

boreal chickadee, white-winged crossbill, red-breasted nuthatch, pileated woodpecker, olive-sided flycatcher, bald eagle, Philadelphia vireo, red-tailed hawk, belted kingfisher, palm warbler, and hermit thrush.

The fish diversity is moderately low in this ecoregion, with 30 species reported. Representative fish include lake whitefish, lake trout, northern pike, and arctic grayling.

The boreal shield has a medium richness of amphibians and reptiles, with five species reported. The Canadian toad and the boreal chorus frog are representative species.

HUMAN ACTIVITY. Approximately 9,000 people live in this zone, or less than 1% of the Saskatchewan population. The economy of the Boreal Shield Ecozone is based on its natural resources. Within the primary labour force, mining (uranium, gold, and other heavy metals) and forestry are the number one employers, followed by fisheries and then agriculture. In the manufacturing sector, the pulp and paper industry employs the largest proportion of workers, although there is less forestry activity in this ecozone than in the boreal plain. Natural landscapes and relatively abundant wildlife and fish support Aboriginal subsistence trapping and hunting, sport hunting and fishing, and commercial harvesting activities, as well as a growing ecotourism industry. Wild rice (a grass, not related to rice) is mechanically harvested in shallows of woodland lakes in this zone. Tourism activities are primarily related to sport fishing, canoeing, wildlife viewing, and ecotourism.

Approximately 3% of the ecozone is contained within a park or protected area, most notably the Lac La Ronge and Clearwater River provincial parks.

Athabasca Plain Ecoregion

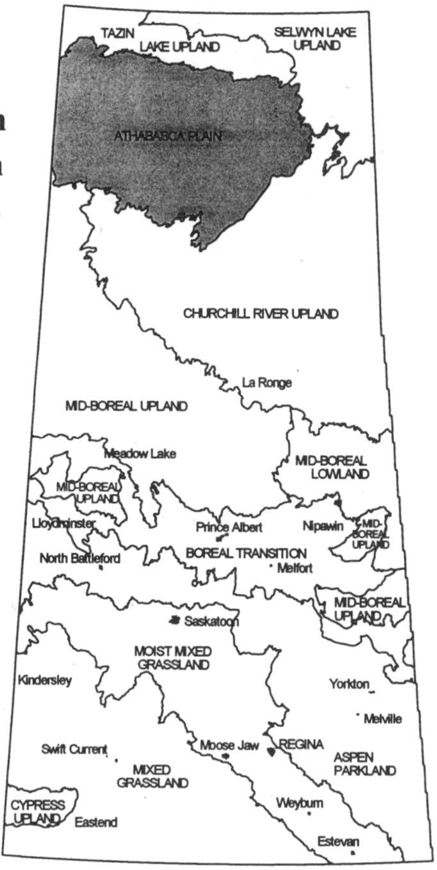

The Athabasca Plain Ecoregion occupies the northwestern part of the boreal shield in the province, extending south from Lake Athabasca to Cree Lake and as far east as Wollaston Lake. Unlike the Churchill River upland, where glacial deposits provide a thin and discontinuous veneer on Precambrian rocks, the glacial deposits in the Athabasca plain provide a relatively thick and continuous cover on flat-lying sandstone bedrock. It is one of the larger ecoregions in the province, occupying 7.4 million hectares or 11% of the province.

PHYSIOGRAPHY. The Athabasca plain is developed on the sedimentary rocks of the Athabasca Group, which are relatively flat-lying with some surface expression of faults and fractures. The bedrock is almost entirely covered by a mantle of glacial drift in the form of ground moraine, outwash plains, and lacustrine plains. The plain slopes gently to the northwest and most of it drains to the Beaufort sea by way of the Athabasca, Slave, and Mackenzie rivers. Elevation of the plain ranges from 485 to 640 m, with local relief of 30 to 60 m due mainly to the occurrence of drumlins, eskers, and meltwater channels. The predominance of sandy glacial deposits contributes to the strongly rolling nature of the terrain.

GEOLOGY. The Athabasca Plain Ecoregion occupies nearly one-third of the surface area of the Saskatchewan portion of the Precambrian Shield. The boundary of this ecoregion corresponds to the erosional edge of the Athabasca basin. The basin is filled by the postmetamorphic Athabasca Group which comprises predominantly sandstones deposited 1.7 to 1.6 billion years ago on the pre-existing crystalline basement rocks. In the central part of the basin, the Athabasca Group is about 1,400 m thick. It is not deformed, with the exception of faulting, local thrust folding, and the Carswell meteorite impact structure. The richest uranium

Smooth shorelines and sandy beaches, such as we see along Lake Athabasca, can be attributed to the sandy nature of the Athabasca Sandstone bedrock which prevails in this ecoregion.

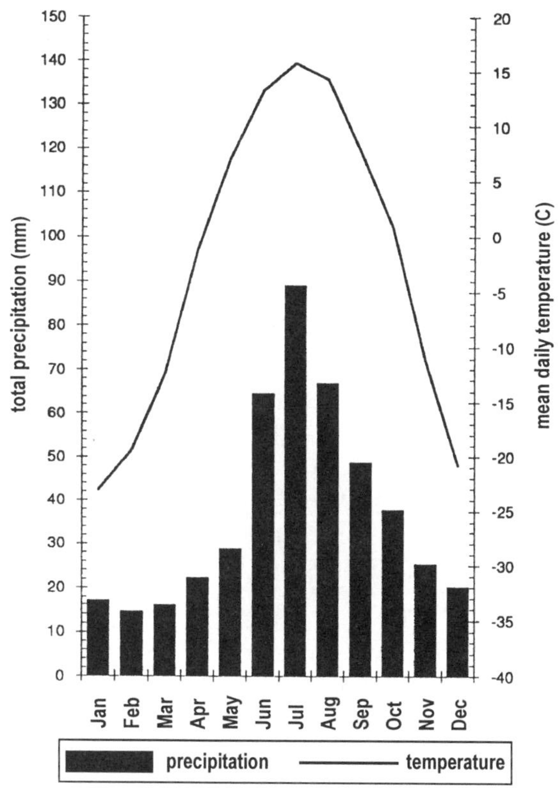

Figure 14. Mean monthly temperature and precipitation for the Athabasca plain as represented by the meteorological record from Cree Lake.

deposits in the world occur at or near the base of the Athabasca basin sandstone sequence, near the erosional unconformity with the underlying crystalline rocks.

In contrast to the areas where crystalline basement rock is exposed, the landscape of the Athabasca basin is dominated by depositional landforms. The soft sandstone of the Athabasca basin was easily eroded by advancing glaciers. The resulting sandy sediment was redeposited as thick ground moraine of sandy till, drumlins, eskers, and other glacial landforms. This terrain has a dendritic drainage pattern. South of Lake Athabasca, the sand has been reworked by wind to form sand dunes over 30 m high.

Ground moraine is generally thicker and more continuous in the Athabasca plain than in the Churchill River upland. Surface forms range from a veneer to a plain, and drumlinoid forms also occur. Lakes and bogs are common but less abundant than in the Churchill River upland. Outwash sands and gravels, eskers, and sand dunes commonly cover the ground moraine. The glacial till averages about 20 m thick, but may be as much as 37 m thick in the western part of the ecoregion. The ground moraine is very sandy and contains numerous quartzite pebbles and cobbles. Relief is due primarily to depositional and erosional processes within the drift, rather than being a reflection of the underlying bedrock structure.

CLIMATE. The subarctic climate of the Athabasca plain is characterized by short summers and cold, very long winters. The mean annual temperature is -2.4°C. The mean July temperature is 15.8°C and the mean January temperature is -23.1°C. The mean annual precipitation is 451 mm, with 288 mm occurring as rain from May to September. The summers are short, with a frost-free period of 97 days, but relatively warm, with 1,106 degree days with temperatures above 5°C.

LANDFORMS AND SOILS. The Athabasca Plain Ecoregion is dominated by a broadly rolling mosaic of uplands and wetlands. The sandstone bedrock is largely obscured by a mantle of sandy glacial deposits, giving a smoother topography than in other parts of the boreal and taiga shield.

Gently sloping glaciofluvial plains and ground moraine are the dominant landscapes throughout much of the area; however, strongly sloping hummocky moraines, prominent drumlins, and sand dunes are striking features locally. The cigar-shaped drumlins are usually hundreds of metres long and tens of metres high, and oriented southwest to northeast. Glacial lakes were once present in the Cree Lake and Lake Athabasca areas.

All sand dunes in the region have a general parabolic shape, reflecting their development in a wet sand environment. Concentrations of active sand dunes occur south of Lake Athabasca and Black Lake. Inactive dunes are widespread but are particularly abundant north and south of the Cree Lake Moraine.

The more common form of inactive dune has a V shape, with the apex pointing to the northwest. These dunes were formed by strong southeasterly winds, which originated from the continental ice sheet. Marked changes in hydrology following the retreat of the glaciers from the area resulted in the stabilization of these dunes, which has persisted to this day. The second form has a U or circular shape with very ragged or zigzag edges. They have been formed mainly by northwesterly winds from the sandy sediments of glacial lake Athabasca. Most of these dunes are anchored by a covering of vegetation, but some are still active.

The soils of the boreal shield are largely Brunisols, but Regosols, Gleysols, Organics, and Cryosols also occur. Brunisols are associated with well to imperfectly drained slopes on the sandy glacial deposits. Regosolic soils prevail in the active and recently stabilized parts of sand dunes. While bogs and fens are not as common as in the Churchill River upland or in the taiga shield, there are numerous small bogs and fens scattered throughout much of the area and several large flat bogs in the western part of the ecoregion. Organic and peaty phases of Gleysolic soils dominate these peatlands. On occasion, permafrost, associated with Cryosolic soils, is present. Soils formed in the moraines and drumlins are often very stony.

GROUNDWATER. The glacial drift and eolian sands that dominate the surficial sediments in this ecoregion are highly permeable and relatively thick and continuous. They are underlain by the Athabasca sandstone, which is more permeable, especially in fractures, than the crystalline basement rocks in other parts of this ecozone, but less permeable than the materials above. As a result, the entire region can be considered to be one large, continuous aquifer. The depth to groundwater is dependent upon local and regional topographical conditions and proximity to the less permeable sandstone. Groundwater can be at considerable depth where the materials are highly permeable and the relief is great, but may be shallow near lakes or where the bedrock is near the surface. Strong groundwater flow exists from regional uplands to local and regional lakes, as well as into rivers and streams.

VEGETATION. Stands of small jack pine with a ground cover of lichens such as reindeer moss are abundant in the Athabasca plain due to the prevalence of dry sandy soils, a harsh climate, and the ensuing frequency of fire. In moister areas such as topographic lows or on fine-textured soils, jack pine-black spruce forests are common. Black spruce and tamarack forests occur in poorly drained, peaty areas. White spruce, balsam poplar, and trembling aspen are rare, but can be found along water courses and lake shores. A small amount of balsam fir occurs along the southern edge of the area. There are six major vegetation groups in the Athabasca Plain Ecoregion: jack pine forests, black spruce forests, black spruce-jack pine forests, mixedwood forests, peatlands (fens and bogs), and boreal wetlands.

Jack pine regeneration after a forest fire.

Where moisture conditions are adequate, jack pine stands with a somewhat open canopy prevail on well-drained sandy glaciofluvial or morainal soils. The ground cover is a carpet of lichens with a wide scattering of various shrubs. On lower slopes, where soil moisture conditions are more favourable, the canopy closes to form a jack pine forest, and the shrub layer becomes more diverse. Tall shrubs like green alder or willow are absent in the upland jack pine forests, being confined to lower, imperfectly drained areas.

Fire is common and creates a mosaic of evenly aged jack pine stands. White birch often appears first after fire, but is of short duration and soon jack pine is more prominent. Jack pine in mature stands attains a height of 8 to 12 m.

An open black spruce forest with lichen carpet occurs on well-drained uplands where soils are less sandy. A closed canopy black spruce forest with feather mosses and lichen, and a scattering of shrubs, occurs in areas that have a more favourable moisture regime such as north-facing slopes, medium to fine-textured deposits, and well to imperfectly drained soils, and on fire-protected islands. In poorly drained areas, where a thin layer of peat often overlies the mineral soil, tamarack, willows, and swamp birch become mixed with black spruce.

The black spruce-jack pine forest represents a transitional moisture gradient between dry conditions found in jack pine and more favourable moisture conditions in black spruce forests. It can be found near lakes and larger streams, just above peatlands, and on slopes of drumlins and eskers. Trembling aspen and white birch may occur and are locally frequent. Green alder is fairly common, and other shrubs are interspersed with an intermittent ground cover of feather mosses and lichens.

Mixedwood forests occur locally within the jack pine forests. They are usually found on finer textured sands and sandy loams, particularly near lake and stream shores. Trembling aspen is found on somewhat higher ground adjacent to the shores. Some trembling aspen-white birch stands occur locally.

Along small, swift-flowing, multichanneled streams, there is a narrow strip of white birch, black spruce, and river alder. They are accompanied by a high grassy groundcover and a mossy, non-sphagnum stream bank interspersed with various low shrubs and herbs.

In low wet areas, peatlands cover the mineral soil, occasionally harbouring pockets of permafrost. Peats are shallow, with a maximum depth of 3 to 4 m. Fens are associated with mineral-rich water along streams and seepages. They are slightly acid and consist largely of aquatic plants and brown mosses, in which sedges, shrubs, and sometimes tamarack grow. Bogs are formed upslope from the fens, where mineral-rich water does not influence the peatland. They are nourished by precipitation and are nutrient poor. This favours the growth of acid-loving sphagnum mosses, various shrubs, herbs, and stunted black spruce (1 to 3 m tall). Bogs burn less frequently than upland areas. The only fireproof sites are saturated fens and rare mineral soil islands within them, as well as moist lakeshore strips.

The most dense and varied wetland vegetation is found along narrow streams and in small, shallow lakes. Plants found here include pondweeds, pond lilies, bulrushes, and sedges. The shrub shorelines are essentially wetlands, flooded in spring and wave-lashed throughout the growing season. As a result, they are intermittently wet, but not waterlogged. The sandy shorelines of large lakes and rivers are fairly clear of vegetation except for occasional pondweeds, bur-reeds, and emergent sedges. This is due to shifting sand, ice scour, wave action, and fluctuating water levels.

Bedrock exposures have a few scattered jack pine growing in various crevices. The rock surfaces are covered with plants of the rock lichen association and ferns.

The open sand dunes, occurring primarily along the south shore of Lake Athabasca, are very sparsely vegetated. Although some shrubs may be present, the vegetation is largely herbaceous. This locale harbours 10 endemic plant species, along with numerous other species considered rare in the province. Dry, open, jack pine forests with scattered open sand patches are characteristic of stabilized dune areas. The ground is covered with lichens, interspersed with sand heather and ericaceous shrubs. Seepage areas support black spruce and white birch with undergrowth of shrubs, herbs, and feather mosses.

Common loon incubating eggs on nest.

WILDLIFE. In contrast to the presence of unique vegetation, the wildlife diversity and populations are low as compared to elsewhere on the boreal shield, and few distinctive species occur. The dry uplands provide poor habitat for most species; however, the riparian areas have diverse, abundant vegetation that attract many mammals and birds. The low diversity of fauna is the result of a harsh environment created by adverse climate, sandy, sometimes shallow soils, and high fire frequency.

It is estimated that 43 mammal species occur within the ecoregion, considered a medium species richness. Moose and black bear populations average about one per 25 km^2. A low population of woodland caribou is also present, and barren-ground caribou are sometimes found wintering here when food is scarce further north. Red-backed vole, meadow vole, and masked shrew are found in damp coniferous forest. The pygmy shrew, arctic shrew, deer mouse, and taiga vole like a dry habitat associated with lichen forest. The meadow jumping mouse is limited to pockets of moist grassy areas. Due to limited hardwoods, beaver populations are limited. Other mammals include little brown bat, porcupine, woodchuck, northern flying squirrel, northern bog lemming, snowshoe hare, and river otter. Predators include gray wolf, least weasel, lynx, wolverine, and marten. If lemming and vole populations are low in the subarctic, the arctic fox follows the caribou migration into the area, dining on carcasses left by wolves. A few species are found only in the western third of the ecoregion, namely coyote, mule deer, and big brown bat.

Bird diversity is low, with 176 species recorded in the ecoregion. Overall bird density is estimated to be 140 individuals per 100 ha, but in dry pine forest uplands, that figure drops to between 12 and 37 individuals per 100 ha. Populations are, therefore, concentrated in riparian areas. Resident birds include common raven; gray jay; hairy, downy, and three-toed woodpeckers; boreal chickadee; white-winged crossbill; red-breasted nuthatch; spruce grouse; and sharp-tailed grouse. Breeding densities of the bald eagle near Key Lake approach the high levels found in the Churchill River upland. Other birds that breed in the ecoregion include red-tailed hawk, belted kingfisher, palm warbler, hermit thrush, yellow warbler, dark-eyed junco, olive-sided flycatcher, and Bohemian waxwing. Waterfowl densities are low because of low habitat productivity. Species in the area include mallard, common merganser, common loon, ring-necked duck, lesser scaup, and bufflehead.

The headframe (centre) and living quarters (foreground) of the Cigar Lake uranium project in the Athabasca Basin.

The invertebrate fauna of rivers and lakes, as well as the fish that feed upon them, are typical of cold northern waters. The fish diversity is low in this ecoregion, with 22 species reported. Large fish include lake whitefish, lake trout, walleye, northern pike, arctic grayling, yellow perch, burbot, white sucker, and longnose sucker. Forage species include trout-perch, cisco, lake chub, spottail shiner, ninespine stickleback, slimy sculpin, and longnose dace. Aquatic fauna are much less abundant than in southern Saskatchewan lakes. In general, sandy bottoms of lakes and streams are not productive; since organisms cannot attach to sediments that are continually being sifted by waves and currents, water bodies in the ecoregion support low fish populations.

The amphibian and reptile diversity is medium, consisting of 5 species. The Canadian toad is the most common, even found wandering across the sand dunes. Wood frogs, northern leopard frogs, and boreal chorus frogs are found in moist areas. The red-sided garter snake also occurs in the ecoregion, eating small frogs.

HUMAN ACTIVITY. The population of this ecoregion is approximately 900, less than 0.1% of the Saskatchewan population. Stony Rapids and Cree Lake are the main communities. Northern Saskatchewan is the world's largest producer of uranium — with 28% of world production and 93% of Canadian production in 1994. Saskatchewan has the highest quality uranium reserves in the world and the majority of uranium mined in Saskatchewan comes from this ecoregion.

Timber resources in the southern section of the ecoregion are used for local sawlog forestry. In addition to logging and mining, trapping, hunting, and fishing are the dominant uses of land in this ecoregion.

Approximately 3% of the ecoregion is within some form of protected area management for conservation purposes, practically all of which is contained within the Athabasca Sand Dunes Provincial Wilderness Park on the south shore of Lake Athabasca.

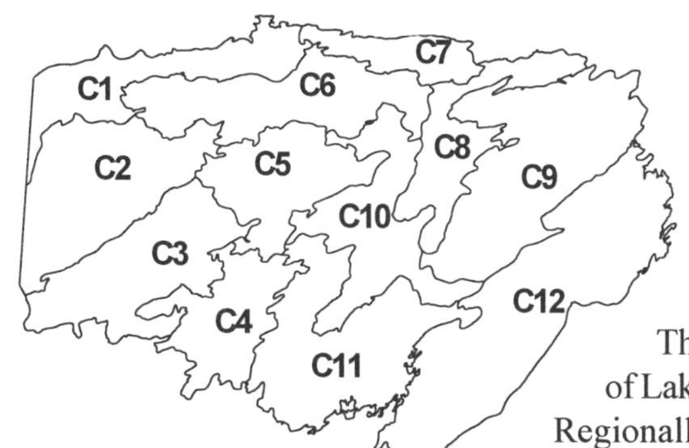

Landscape Areas

C1. Athabasca Dunes

The Athabasca dunes occupy a narrow band along the south shore of Lake Athabasca, extending from Richards Lake to the Alberta border. Regionally, the area is one of low relief as it slopes from highs of 360 m to 209 m at Lake Athabasca. It can be quite rugged, locally, with relief of 40 m in the vicinity of Campbell Lake. The William and MacFarlane rivers were formed as meltwater channels and spillways that carried water northward from the melting glacier to glacial Lake Athabasca. Today they are under-fit streams, carrying small amounts of surface water and an appreciable amount of seepage from the groundwater, to Lake Athabasca. This area contains a diversity of soils, landforms, and vegetation, some of which are unique to Saskatchewan and to Canada. The underlying Athabasca sandstone crops out in only a few places in this area. Depth to bedrock is often 20 m, and is as much as 100 m in the William River area. The surficial materials are very sandy, and as a consequence, the entire area is an aquifer. This has a profound effect on the vegetation and animal life, and the activity of dunes in the area.

Ground moraine, which may be ridged, drumlinoid, hummocky, or planar, occurs in large patches throughout the area. Prominent end moraines, which trend from northwest to southeast, and eskers, which trend from northeast to southwest, also occur in several places, especially in the southern part of the area. Many of the small lakes, such as Campbell Lake and nearby ponds, represent kettles in hummocky moraine. Brunisolic soils predominate on the well-drained slope positions of these sandy deposits, with Gleysols and Organics in the poorly drained lower slopes. Extensive areas of bog cover the glacial sediments in the western part of the area. Palsas in these areas suggest the presence of permafrost.

Not all of the landforms are of glacial origin. The precursor to Lake Athabasca, pro-glacial Lake McConnell, inundated the land surface below 305 m following the retreat of the last glacier. Strandlines, or former beaches of this lake, are found at several locations within the northern part of the area. Shoreline features such as berms, point bars, and spits are also present. Sand dunes are found throughout the area but are most common in the northern part, along the shore of Lake Athabasca. All of these dunes have a parabolic shape, reflecting the moist sands below the surface. The well-stabilized V-shaped dunes in the southern part of the area formed during glacial times on land that was not inundated by glacial Lake McConnell. The easterly oriented active and stabilized U-shaped dunes formed soon after the drainage of glacial Lake McConnell. Evidence suggests that, in some cases, fire has contributed to the initiation of wind erosion and to the expansion of sand sheets.

The combination of dune landform and boreal climates makes the Athabasca dunes a unique and special ecological place in Saskatchewan and in the world. Ten rare plants, Saskatchewan's only endemic species, are scattered through the open dune areas. Seventy additional plant species, designated as rare in Saskatchewan, have been found in the area. Much of this area is contained within the Athabasca Sand Dunes Provincial Wilderness Park on the south shore of Lake Athabasca.

Active dunes are colonized by felt-leaved willow, Tyrrell's willow, field chickweed, Mackenzie hairgrass, and fluccose tansy (all endemic species), as well as sea lime grass, northern bromegrass, narrow reed grass, and proliferous red fescue. The gravel pavements that occur among the dune areas have a sparse scattering of moss campion, inland sea thrift (endemic), northern wormwood, felt-leaved willow, and arctic rock-cress.

Stabilized dunes become a dry, open jack pine woodland with scattered open sand patches. Ground is covered with lichen interspersed with low shrubs and herbs. Seepage areas support black spruce and white birch with undergrowth of low shrubs and herbs.

Large white spruce occur on beach ridges adjacent to Lake Athabasca, one of the few places in the Athabasca plain where conditions favourable for its survival exist (adequate moisture and humidity and low fire risk). Fens, composed of sedges, willows, and sometimes tamarack, occur in low areas adjacent to streams. In other wet, depressional areas, sphagnum mosses, various shrubs, and black spruce comprise the bog community.

C2. Carswell Plain

This is a large area with a gentle northward slope from 450 m in the southeastern part of the area to 300 m at Bartlett Lake near the Alberta border. The Douglas, Carswell, William, and Charbonneau rivers drain some of the numerous lakes and bogs that occur in parts of this area. There is a "window" between Cluff and Carswell lakes where the Athabasca sediments are missing, revealing a circular patch of Precambrian basement rocks. These are encircled by a ring of dolomites, the "dolomite cliffs" of the Carswell Formation. This unusual rock sequence, which is structurally deformed, is thought to be the result of a meteorite impact event.

Most of the south-southeastern part of the area is covered with a smooth blanket of sandy glacial till, upon which numerous eskers and occasional drumlins are superimposed. Brunisolic soils dominate these well-drained slopes. The west-northwestern part has stronger relief in the form of hummocky moraine with moderately steep slopes. Brunisolic soils predominate on the well-drained slope positions in these areas, with Gleysols and Organics, and local Cryosols, in the numerous poorly drained areas. There are extensive areas of Organic soils in the northwestern part of the area.

The area is dominated by jack pine forest on upland sandy areas, with some black spruce forest on peatlands; however, the most unique species associations are found on the "dolomite cliffs." The dolomite outcrops support greater diversity than the acidic rock outcrops found elsewhere on the Shield. Most of the dolomite uplands are covered by jack pine, but with frequent local stands of trembling aspen-jack pine on the ridge crests, and jack pine-black spruce on lower slopes and on Precambrian basement rock found in the centre of the meteorite impact structure. White spruce, white birch, saskatoon, choke cherry, snowberry and buffaloberry are found associated with the dolomite bedrock. The open dolomite cliffs support a unique flora including the rare ferns smooth Woodsia and western smooth cliff-brake.

C3. McTaggart Plain

This is a large area with a gentle northward slope from 540 m in the southern part of the area to 450 m at Hale Lake and the boundary to the Carswell plain. The Richardson and Douglas rivers and Bourassa Creek provide some drainage westward into Alberta. The headwaters of the William and MacFarlane rivers also occur in this area and flow northward to Lake Athabasca, providing drainage for some of the numerous lakes, fens, and bogs that occur in this area.

Most of the area is covered with undulating and hummocky sandy glaciofluvial materials, and eskers are widely distributed throughout the area. Brunisolic soils predominate on the well-drained slope positions, with Gleysols and Organics, and local Cryosols, in the numerous poorly drained areas. Glacial till plains that are strongly gullied occur in the headwaters of the Richardson and Douglas rivers and Bourassa Creek. Brunisolic soils predominate on these well-drained slopes. There is a large area of flat bog north of McTaggart and Dunning lakes. Organic soils dominate these areas but permanently frozen Cryosols also occur.

Open jack pine woodlands dominate on the sandy glaciofluvial materials. A mixture of black spruce and jack pine can be found on the slopes of many eskers. Closed stands of stunted black spruce forest can be found in the boggy lowland areas.

C4. MacFarlane Upland

This area has a gentle northward slope from 570 m in the southern part to 480 m at Brudell and Bernard lakes, at the boundary to the Livingstone plain in the north. External drainage for some of the numerous lakes, fens, and bogs that occur in this area is limited to the MacFarlane and Snare rivers, which flow northward to Lake Athabasca.

Most of the area is covered with a blanket of glacial till. Drumlins and eskers are prominent landscape features. Brunisolic soils predominate on the well-drained slope positions, with Gleysols and Organics, and local Cryosols, in the numerous poorly drained areas. There are numerous relatively small flat bogs scattered throughout the area. Organic soils dominate these areas, but permanently frozen Cryosols also occur.

The area is dominated by an open jack pine woodland with a lichen understory. On the slopes of the drumlins, where moisture conditions are more favourable, black spruce is intermixed with the jack pine. Lower down the slopes, the peaty areas between drumlins are covered by a black spruce forest.

C5. Livingstone Plain

This area has a gentle northward slope from 500 m in the southern part to 420 m at the boundary to the Squirrel Lake plain in the north. External drainage for some of the numerous lakes, fens, and bogs that occur in this area is limited to the MacFarlane River, which flows northward to Lake Athabasca, and its tributary, the Snare River.

Most of the area is covered with a blanket of sandy glacial drift. The eastern part is an undulating glaciofluvial outwash plain with occasional eskers and drumlins of higher relief. Eskers and drumlins are more prominent in the western part of the area. Brunisolic soils predominate on the well-drained slope positions in these landscapes, with Gleysols and Organics, and local Cryosols, in the numerous poorly drained areas. There are numerous relatively small flat bogs scattered throughout the area. Organic soils dominate these areas, but permanently frozen Cryosols also occur.

A mixture of open jack pine and black spruce are associated with the morainal, drumlinized upland areas. On the lowland bog areas, black spruce becomes dominant. On the eastern side of the Livingstone plain, where sandy outwash features are more common, jack pine becomes more prevalent.

C6. Squirrel Lake Plain

This area has a prominent northward slope from 420 m on its boundary with the Livingstone Lake plain to the south to 240 m at Richards, Engler, and Riou lakes in the northern part of the area. The Otherside and Riou rivers drain some of the lakes, fens, and bogs that occur in this area northward to Lake Athabasca.

Most of the southern part of the area comprises undulating glaciofluvial outwash deposits, but eskers and drumlins are prominent landscape features. Glacial till is more common northward, associated with a strong drumlinoid surface form. Brunisolic soils dominate the well-drained slope positions in these landscapes, with Gleysols and Organics, and local Cryosols, in poorly drained areas. There are extensive areas of sand dunes in the vicinity of Richards, Engler, and Riou lakes, in the northeastern part of the area, as well as in the Atchison Lake and Davy Lake areas to the southwest. Brunisolic soils are most common in areas where the dunes are stabilized, but Regosolic soils dominate where the dunes are active or have been recently stabilized. There are often small areas of peatlands with Organic soils in swales between the dune ridges.

Because the surface sediments are dominantly sandy glaciofluvial deposits, open jack pine is the prevalent forest cover. Some black spruce occurs on north-facing esker slopes, and in sandy glacial till areas, associated with jack pine on the drumlin slopes. In addition, a dominantly black spruce canopy occurs in the many boggy areas, and associated with occasional tamarack in fen areas. The sand dune areas are dominantly stabilized with a dry, open jack pine forest with a ground cover of lichens interspersed with Canada blueberry, bearberry, and sand heather. There are scattered open sand patches, where various grasses and herbs are trying to survive and stabilize the sand.

C7. Fond du Lac Lowland

This is a small area extending along the south shore of Fond du Lac from Lake Athabasca to Black Lake. It is a nearly level area, with slopes from 330 m on several regional rises to 250 m at Richards, Engler, and Riou lakes in the southern part of the area and Fond du Lac in the north. These lakes are drained by the Riou River, which joins with the Otherside River before it empties into Lake Athabasca.

The higher, southern part of the area is dominated by a blanket of sandy glacial till with prominent drumlins and local outwash deposits. Sandy glaciolacustrine plains occur at lower elevation, bordering Fond du Lac and Black Lake. Brunisolic soils dominate the well-drained slope positions in these landscapes, with Gleysols and Organics, and local Cryosols, in poorly drained areas. There are extensive areas of peatlands with Organic soils in swales between the drumlins and mantling the glaciolacustrine materials north of Richards and Riou lakes.

Black spruce dominates on the extensive peatlands in the western part of the area. It is frequently intermixed with dwarf birch. This is the only landscape area within the Athabasca plain that has significant mixedwood stands. Black spruce, jack pine, and white birch occur on the upland areas. On the glaciolacustrine sediments near the Fond du Lac River, stands of trembling aspen are common; white spruce and balsam poplar are also present.

C8. Lower Cree River Plain

This is a long and narrow area extending along the lower reaches of the Cree River before it empties into Black Lake. It has a very gentle regional slope from 400 m in the southern part to 300 m at Black Lake. The Cree River and its tributaries, the Pine, Pipestone, Timson, Little Cree, Rapid, and Badwater rivers and Hunter Creek, provide drainage for Thomson, Wapata, Giles, and many smaller lakes, as well as for numerous fens and bogs that are scattered throughout much of the area. The Fond du Lac and Perch rivers provide drainage for the lower, eastern part.

Most of the area is a drumlinoid moraine that is extensively, but not completely, covered with undulating glaciofluvial outwash deposits. Sandy glaciolacustrine plains cover some of the drumlinoid moraine in the Thomson Lake area. Brunisolic soils dominate the well-drained slope positions in these landscapes, with Gleysols and Organics, and local Cryosols, in the numerous, small, poorly drained swales and flats. There are small areas of sand dunes along the south shore of Black Lake, along the Pipestone River near Locker Lake, and northwest of Poitras Lake. Extensive areas of peatlands, with Organic soils, occur in swales between the drumlins and mantling the glaciofluvial materials south of Wapata Lake.

The prevalence of sandy glaciofluvial sediments dictates that open jack pine woodlands will dominate the area. In the occasional dune area, there are dry, very open stands of jack pine with an understory of lichens, Canada blueberry, bearberry, and sand heather. Open sand patches contain pioneering grasses and herbs. Some short black spruce are mingled with the jack pine on the north slopes of eskers. Riparian areas contain black spruce, jack pine, and white birch, as well as alders and willows. The boggy areas are dominated by black spruce, with some tamarack associated with the black spruce on fen margins.

C9. Pasfield Lake Plain

This is a large area in the northeastern part of the Athabasca Plain Ecoregion. It has a gentle regional slope to the north from 480 m south and east of Pasfield Lake to 360 m at the Fond du Lac River. This slope drains most of the area into Black Lake, which drains to the Beaufort Sea. Some of the area, however, drains eastward to Wollaston Lake and Hudson Bay. The Little Cree, Rapid, and Badwater rivers drain much of the southern part of the area into Black Lake through the Cree River. The Fond du Lac River and its tributary, the Hawkrock River, drain much of the northern part of the area. Ward Creek and Waterfound River provide most of the drainage to Wollaston Lake.

Most of the area is a drumlinoid moraine that is extensively, but not completely, covered with undulating glaciofluvial outwash deposits. Prominent eskers occur in the southeastern part, some of them extending more or less continuously for 80 km or more. Brunisolic soils dominate the well-drained slope positions in these landscapes, with Gleysols and Organics, and local Cryosols, in the numerous, small, poorly drained swales and flats. Peatlands with Organic and Cryosolic soils are most extensive in the area between Wigham, Forsyth, and Bell lakes, but wetlands are much less abundant in the southern part of the area. There are extensive areas of sand dunes throughout the southern part of the area and prominent V-shaped dunes in the general Pasfield Lake area. Brunisolic soils are most common in areas where the dunes have been stabilized for a considerable period of time, but Regosolic soils dominate dune areas in the vicinity of Locker and Poitras lakes, where the dunes are either active or more recently stabilized.

The aridity of the area makes fire common, favouring the growth of very open jack pine stands on the extensive very sandy outwash soils. Some open black spruce occurs on north-facing slopes of eskers and drumlins. Bogs often have up to 40% cover by stunted black spruce, intermingled with tamarack near fens. The numerous small dune areas are primarily stabilized by grasses, ericaceous shrubs, lichen, and scattered jack pine.

C10. Pine River Plain

This irregularly shaped area, extending along the upper reaches of the Cree and MacFarlane river watersheds, slopes northward from prominent highs approaching 600 m in the southern part to 500 m on the plains of the Timson, Pipestone, Pine, and Riou rivers and Hunter, Mitchell, and Miller creeks. Drainage is eastward to the Cree River except for a small part that drains north and west through the Otherside River to the MacFarlane River.

Most of the area is a drumlinoid moraine that is covered with undulating glaciofluvial outwash deposits. Prominent eskers, often 5 to 10 km long, occur in the Dautremont Lake area. Sandy glaciolacustrine plains, with prominent wave-cut terraces from a former glacial lake, cover some of the drumlinoid moraine between Dautremont Lake and the Hunter River. Brunisolic soils dominate the well-drained slope positions in these landscapes, with Gleysols and Organics, and local Cryosols, found in the numerous, small, poorly drained swales and flats. There are extensive peatlands in swales between the drumlins and mantling the glaciofluvial and glaciolacustrine materials in the southern part of the area. Sand dunes, occasionally with a prominent V shape, occur in the southern part of the area. Brunisolic soils characterize the stabilized dunes; Regosolic soils dominate those dunes that are presently or were recently active.

Jack pine, with lesser amounts of black spruce, dominates north-facing slopes of eskers and drumlins, as well as some areas of finer-textured glacial till. Black spruce is also the main tree associated with bogs, along with dwarf birch and some tamarack. Trembling aspen and white birch are mixed with the conifers on the small area of glaciolacustrine deposits.

C11. Cree Lake Upland

This area includes Cree Lake and a large area to the north of it. It slopes gently from 600 m on a regional high northwest of Cree Lake to 450 m at Cree Lake. It also slopes from this regional high to 450 m in the northern part of the area. The southwestern part of the area drains from this same regional high through the Karros River to Cree Lake. The northern part also drains from this regional high, but through the Bolding River, Engemann Lake, and Hunter Creek into the Cree River. The eastern part of the area, including Cree Lake, drains northward through the Cree River.

Most of the area is a drumlinoid moraine that is extensively, but not completely, covered with undulating glaciofluvial outwash deposits. Prominent eskers, sometimes more than 10 km long, are scattered throughout the area. Sandy glaciolacustrine plains cover some of the drumlinoid moraine in local areas between Mayson and Engemann lakes, northwest of Weitzel Lake, and north of Cree Lake. Brunisolic soils dominate the well-drained slope positions in these landscapes, with Gleysols and Organics, and local Cryosols, in the numerous, small, poorly drained swales and flats. There are local areas of sand dunes, occasionally with prominent U-shaped dunes, in the southern and northeastern parts of the area. Brunisolic soils are most common in areas where the dunes are stabilized, but Regosolic soils dominate where the dunes are active.

Open jack pine woodland with lichen and Canada blueberry ground cover is prevalent on the dominantly sandy glaciofluvial materials. Fire is common, so the woodlands are often in some stage of regeneration. Some black spruce will be found associated with jack pine on the north-facing slopes of eskers and drumlins, and sometimes on fire-protected islands. A dominantly black spruce forest occurs in boggy areas, associated with occasional tamarack in fens. The sand dune areas are largely stabilized with a dry, very open jack pine and a groundcover of lichens along with Canada blueberry, bearberry, and sand heather. There are scattered open sand patches, where various grasses and herbs are trying to survive. In the transition area between bog and upland, poorly to imperfectly drained soils support black spruce and white birch, Labrador tea, bunchberry, twinflower, and feather mosses.

C12. Wheeler Upland

This is a large area that extends from Cree Lake to Hatchet and Wollaston lakes. It has a moderate northward slope from 600 m in the southern and western parts of the area to 400 m at Hatchet and Wollaston lakes. Drainage in this area is very weakly developed, usually one lake emptying into the next through a small creek.

Most of the area is a drumlinoid moraine that is extensively, but not completely, covered with undulating glaciofluvial outwash deposits. Prominent eskers, some of which are 100 km or more in length, traverse the area from northeast to southwest. Hummocky moraine and hummocky glaciofluvial deposits are also widely scattered throughout the area. Brunisolic soils dominate the well-drained slope positions in these landscapes, with Gleysols and Organics, and local Cryosols, in the numerous, small, poorly drained swales and flats.

Generally, jack pine and black spruce dominate the uplands. Fires are common, and most forests are in some stage of regeneration. Open stands of jack pine are found in older burn areas, sandy outwash areas, on south sides of eskers, on linear ridges of till, and on soils that are shallow to bedrock. Lichen, Canada blueberry, and green alder occur in the understory. North-facing aspects have black spruce as the codominant or subdominant species. Patches of white birch are sometimes present in the well-drained gullies between ridges. Abundant lichen is suspended from jack pine branches within these inter-ridges. Open black spruce stands with a lichen-Canada blueberry understory are more common toward the northeastern part of the landscape area, north of Waterbury Lake. Fewer glaciofluvial deposits are found here. As a result, more favourable soil moisture conditions support a dense black spruce forest, and the extent of jack pine is reduced.

Depending upon intensity of fire and regeneration pattern, bogs may have up to 40% cover of black spruce in unburned sites, and down to none in some burned bogs. Riparian areas of white birch, black spruce, and willow have a denser and taller tree cover. The increased diversity in these areas represents the most productive areas for plant and animal life.

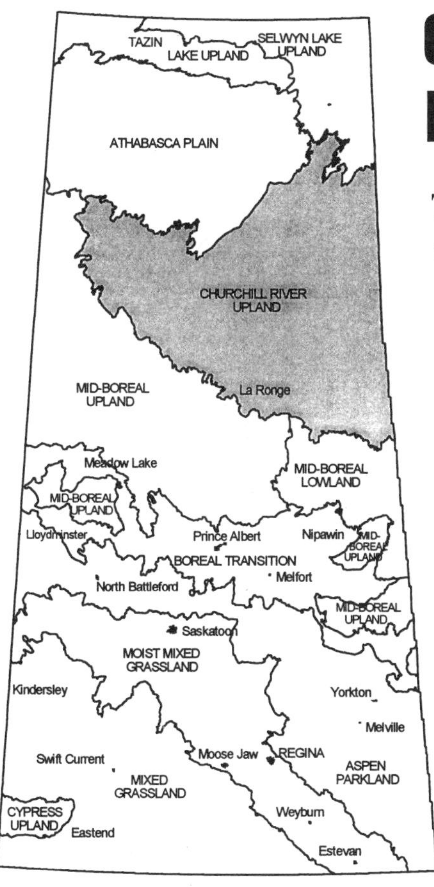

Churchill River Upland Ecoregion

The Churchill River Upland Ecoregion is located along the southern edge of the Precambrian Shield in north-central Saskatchewan. It is a horn-shaped area, with Wollaston and Amisk lakes on the rim and Turnor Lake, in the northwestern part, at the mouth. It is a beautiful area with hundreds of small, clear lakes with broken shorelines connected by rapid streams. Unlike the Athabasca plains, where glacial deposits provide a relatively thick and continuous cover on flat-lying sandstone bedrock, the glacial deposits in the Churchill River upland provide a thin and discontinuous veneer on crystalline Precambrian rocks. It is the largest ecoregion in the province, occupying 11.3 million hectares or 17% of the total area of Saskatchewan.

PHYSIOGRAPHY. The Churchill River upland is developed on crystalline Precambrian basement rocks. The topography of the area is typical of the Precambrian Shield, with extensive areas of rock that form broad, smooth uplands and lowlands. The broader landscape has a monotonous, nearly planar skyline; however, the local topography is extraordinarily uneven and chaotic. Local relief can as much as 90 m but is generally less than 60 m. Lakes, fens, and bogs fill the valleys and depressions between the ridges, hills, and knolls.

Gently rolling hills that slope gradually from 550 m in a central highland around and west of Cree Lake, to 300 m in the southeast around Amisk Lake, and to 275 m in the northwest around Lake Athabasca, reflect the major influence that bedrock has on the landscapes and drainage characteristics of this region.

The hills comprise a complex series of ridges, valleys, and shallow basins that are largely a reflection of folding, faulting, and fracturing of the bedrock. Other ridges and valleys are related to differential erosion of the various rock units. Much of this occurred in the vast period of time prior to glaciation as the former mountains eroded to a peneplain. The glacial ice completed the process by scouring out low-lying areas, especially in zones of more easily eroded rock, thus enhancing the relief. The ice also smoothed and polished the faces and crests of resistant bedrock knobs and hills, while simultaneously plucking rock from the lee sides.

Although some of the bedrock relief has been masked by overburden, particularly in areas of thick drift south of the Athabasca basin in the western part of the area, the bedrock relief is usually discernible through a thin veneer of glacial material.

Present-day drainage of the south and eastern parts of these rolling hills to Hudson Bay via

Figure 15. Mean monthly temperature and precipitation for the Churchill River upland as represented by the meteorological record from Whitesand Dam.

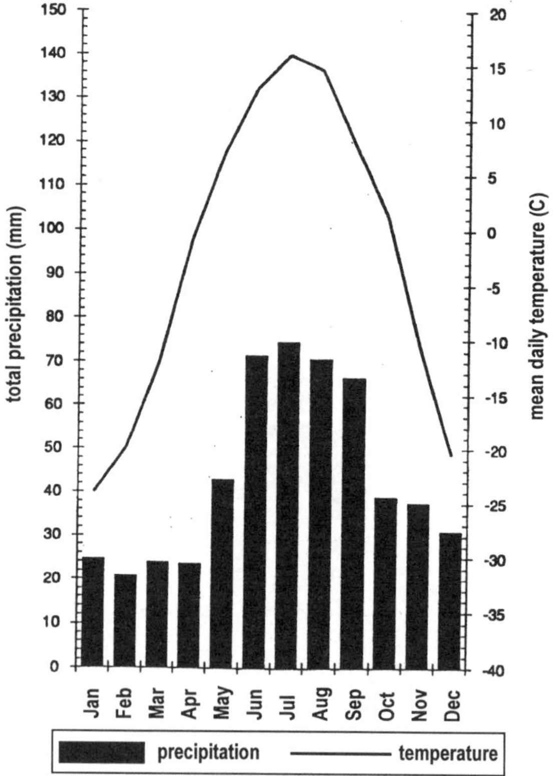

the Churchill and Nelson rivers, and of the northwestern parts to Lake Athabasca and the Beaufort Sea, further demonstrates the control that the bedrock has on the characteristics of this ecoregion.

GEOLOGY. The Churchill River Upland Ecoregion is similar, geologically, to the Taiga Shield Ecozone, described earlier, as both are underlain by crystalline basement rocks of the Precambrian Shield.

CLIMATE. The subarctic climate of the Churchill River upland is characterized by cool and short summers and very cold and long winters. The mean annual temperature is 2.3°C. The mean July temperature is 16°C and the mean January temperature is -24°C. The mean annual precipitation is 528 mm, with 318 mm occurring as rain from May to September. The summers are short, having a frost-free period of approximately 94 days, but relatively warm, with 1,128 degree days with temperatures above 5°C.

LANDFORMS AND SOILS. The Churchill River upland has a thin, patchy cover of ground moraine. The surface expression of these materials closely reflects the topography of the bedrock. Generally these deposits are less than 3 m thick and, in the southeastern part of the ecoregion, are usually covered by silts and clays of Glacial Lake Agassiz, which covered the eastern part of the Churchill River upland. The associated silt and clay deposits range from less than 1 m thick on topographic rises to as much as 5 m in depressions in the bedrock surface. The Reindeer Lake basin also was partially occupied by a glacial lake. Lacustrine sands, silts, and some clays, generally less than 3 m in thickness, are concentrated in low-lying areas and are generally covered by bog.

Heavy frost coating white spruce boughs.

The Cree Lake moraine, not much more than a series of low mounds in the eastern part of the region, becomes a continuous ridge about 10 m high in some locales and as much as 35 m as it is traced to Black Birch Lake in the western part of the ecoregion. It is an imposing topographic feature which likely represents a major still-stand of ice in northern Saskatchewan during glacial times.

Brunisolic soils are associated with sandy and bouldery glacial tills as well as sandy and gravelly glaciofluvial deposits. Luvisols are the dominant soil on silty and clayey glaciolacustrine deposits. Organic and peaty phases of Gleysolic soils dominate numerous small bogs and fens that prevail in the ecoregion. On occasion, permafrost and associated Cryosolic soils occur in peatland areas. There is virtually no soil development on the numerous outcrops of crystalline basement rocks.

GROUNDWATER. The crystalline basement rocks that dominate the bedrock in this ecoregion are generally massive and dense. Permeability is usually determined by fractures and faults, which are not necessarily interconnected. There are no known wells drilled in this kind of rock in Saskatchewan, and any wells in materials such as this are likely to provide very limited water supply. The shallow depth of the glacial drift minimizes the opportunity for inter-till aquifers; however, the sandy nature of the glacial drift provides for extensive surficial aquifers. Bogs are likely to have permafrost, diminishing the opportunity for shallow groundwater.

VEGETATION. Black spruce dominates the region, with significant stands of jack pine on dry sand plains. A mosaic of forest types in various stages of succession is common because the rate of recovery of a burned area is dictated by timing and severity of fire, as well as by the supply of recolonizing material in adjacent unburned vegetation. As a result, there are six vegetation associations in the Churchill River upland: black spruce forest, jack pine forest, white spruce forest, mixedwood forest, peatlands (treed and open bogs, and fens), and wetlands. There are very few areas of unvegetated rock outcrops.

An old-growth black spruce forest, with a closed canopy of black spruce, occurs where glacial sediments are relatively thick, the soils are moderately well drained, and there is no evidence of recent fire. Shrubs and other tree species occur only where windfall has created breaks in the canopy. The ground is covered by a dense carpet of feather mosses. Scattered Labrador tea and bog cranberry and various herbs occur on well-drained southern aspects. Lichens and green alder occur in canopy breaks, where there is more sunlight.

A closed black spruce forest mixed with occasional jack pine and white birch can be found on ridges and clay plains. Beaked willow occurs throughout as tall, dense, shrubby trees, while green alder forms the short shrub layer. The ground vegetation consists of mosses, small shrubs, and herbs.

Male catkins on a white spruce tree.

An open jack pine forest develops on the ridges of exposed bedrock. The jack pine persist in shallow crevices and depressions, and rarely become taller than 8 m. White birch, pin cherry, and willow are widely scattered among the pine. A dense lichen carpet covers the rock, while in crevices and shallow hollows, a number of small shrubs, ferns, and small sedges are abundant.

On sandy areas, like outwash plains and eskers, a closed jack pine forest with a uniform understory is found. The ground vegetation is a dense carpet of lichens, mixed with mosses, low shrubs, and herbs.

A white spruce forest occurs

sporadically, usually on south-facing slopes along lake shores where soil moisture and drainage conditions are favourable, and on rich alluvial soils of river valleys. On south-facing slopes, several old trees of trembling aspen and balsam poplar are scattered among widely spaced white spruce, while black spruce and white birch occur less commonly. The understory is composed of low shrubs, mosses, and lichens. On alluvial plains white spruce, balsam poplar, trembling aspen, and white birch form a closed canopy. There is a very conspicuous shrub layer. Ground vegetation includes feather mosses and various herbs.

A dense mixedwood forest is associated with large streams and rivers, and loamy to clayey glaciolacustrine deposits. These forests contain roughly equal amounts of deciduous and coniferous trees, including trembling aspen, white birch, balsam poplar, white spruce, jack pine, and black spruce. The understory is dense, including various tall and low shrubs, as well as young aspen and spruce. Bunchberry and dewberry are common forbs as well. Oak fern may be present.

Peatlands vary from treed bogs (covered with a stunted black spruce stand and having an understory of ericaceous shrubs and feather mosses) to open bogs. Shrubs such as beaked willow and dwarf birch form a discontinuous layer under the canopy of black spruce, and tamarack may occur with black spruce in wetter locations. Low shrubs are common, while sphagnum and other feather mosses dominate the surface cover. Trees are more stunted in the northern part of the ecoregion. South of the Churchill River, white birch occurs occasionally with black spruce. Since this ecoregion lies near the southern limit of the discontinuous permafrost zone, permafrost tends to be widespread only in the drier bogs.

There is little aquatic vegetation in the characteristic deep, steep-sided lakes. Extensive offshore marshes distinguish lakes of the Churchill River from others in the area. These marshes form where sediments are deposited in shallow water in protected bays and small backwater eddies. The vegetation mats in these marshes comprise several pondweeds, pond lilies, sedges, and rushes. Near shore, a thick mat of decayed organic matter is found on the lake bottom, supporting such species as water calla, marshmarigold, and buck-bean. Offshore vegetation mats also occur in shallow basins of smaller lakes, especially in deltaic offshore deposits of clay and silt washed out of the glacial drift along shore. On small, irregular lakes away from the Churchill River, flooded forest is prominent along the shores. This is often due to rising water levels controlled by beaver dams, which are very common at the heads of tiny outlet streams. On protected shorelines, glacial deposits extend under a cloak of willows to the water's edge. On exposed reaches, the bedrock is washed clean of the glacial sediments.

Bedrock outcrops are characterized by thinly scattered black spruce or jack pine growing in rock crevices. These have a sparse understory of lichens and club mosses, interspersed with ground juniper, other shrubs and herbs, and various ferns. Shady locations typically have fewer species.

WILDLIFE. Wildlife population and richness is higher in the Churchill River upland than elsewhere on the Shield. Higher diversity of plant life due to better climatic and soil conditions creates more varied habitat for animals and birds. Of significance, the Churchill River system contains the second highest concentration of nesting bald eagles in North America — only in Alaska do higher concentrations exist.

Mammal richness is rated medium, with an estimated 41 different species occurring in the ecoregion. Moose and black bear are common here. Woodland caribou are not common, but are more plentiful here than in any other ecoregion. Barren-ground caribou may winter occasionally between Cree and Wollaston lakes. Other mammals include masked shrew, snowshoe hare, beaver, muskrat, river otter, porcupine, northern flying squirrel, least chipmunk, woodchuck, and deer mouse. Predators include gray wolf, red fox, mink, marten, least weasel, lynx, and striped skunk.

Bird diversity is medium, with 204 species reported to occur in the ecoregion. Of particular note is the high concentration of nesting bald eagles observed along the Black Bear Island Lake to Otter Rapids section of the Churchill River, as well as a lesser number of ospreys. Resident birds include: great horned owl, common raven, gray jay, spruce grouse, ruffed grouse, black-capped chickadee, red-breasted nuthatch, hairy and downy woodpeckers, and great gray owl. Birds that migrate into the area to breed include the Philadelphia vireo, red-tailed hawk, hermit thrush, and fox sparrow. Numerous waterfowl species breed in the many water bodies, including red-breasted merganser, common goldeneye, common loon, mallard, and bufflehead.

Thirty species of fish are reported to occur in the ecoregion, which is considered a medium species richness. Lake sturgeon are found in the Churchill River system below Island Falls Dam. Both lake trout and lake whitefish live in the many cool deep lakes where they can descend to cooler water in summer. Other game fish include northern pike, walleye, and yellow perch. Arctic grayling are found in the fast-flowing streams in the northern part of the ecoregion. Goldeye prefer the quiet, turbid water of large rivers, small lakes, ponds, and muddy shallows of large lakes. Longnose sucker, white sucker, and burbot also occur extensively in considerable numbers. Forage fish species include cisco, which are a primary food source for lake trout, lake chub, trout-perch, ninespine stickleback, slimy sculpin, and spoonhead sculpin. Emerald and spottail shiners are very important, being eaten by all species of fish; the emerald shiner is also important food for fish-eating birds because of its surface swimming habits.

The occurrence of shorthead redhorse and sauger in the Otter Rapids to Island Falls section of the Churchill River is unusual for the province. The former is mainly restricted to the Saskatchewan and Qu'Appelle rivers, and the latter has been collected only in the Saskatchewan River and its tributaries. The presence of the fathead minnow (which is rare or absent from lakes in the Shield, yet abundant in the rest of the province) throughout the Churchill system, suggests that the fish fauna resembles that of the south more than that of the Shield, presumably due to the influence of relatively warm river flow.

Lone timber wolf on the forest edge.

Amphibians and reptiles are represented by five species: Canadian toad, wood frog, boreal chorus frog, northern leopard frog, and red-sided garter snake.

HUMAN ACTIVITY. The population of the Churchill River Upland Ecoregion is approximately 8,500, less than 1% of the Saskatchewan population. Major communities include La Ronge and Creighton. Trapping, hunting, fishing, and tourism are the dominant land uses in this ecoregion.

This ecoregion also contains the largest areas of base metal potential in the province. Gold and uranium are in a mining development phase. A pulpwood and dimension lumber industry operates to a limited extent in the southern part of the ecoregion.

Approximately 4% of the ecoregion is managed as a protected area for conservation purposes, most of which is contained within Lac La Ronge Provincial Park.

Sport fishing is a popular recreational activity in the ecoregion.

Landscape Areas

D1. Black Birch Plain

This area extends eastward from Preston and Lloyd lakes to the south shore of Cree Lake. The northwestern part of the area is drained by the Clearwater River and has a very gentle southward slope from 570 m in local uplands to 480 m at Careen Lake. The lower central part has a drainage divide from which the Brustad River drains the northern part into Cree Lake and the Gwillim River drains the remainder southward to the Mudjatik River. The eastern part is much higher in elevation, sometimes exceeding 600 m, and is drained by the Mudjatik River.

The bedrock surface has only a thin veneer of sandy glacial till, glaciofluvial, and glaciolacustrine deposits; hence, the surface is very irregular and hummocky in nature. Outcrops of Precambrian rocks dominate the landscape in a large block south of Cree Lake and in several smaller blocks further west. Gently sloping, sandy glaciolacustrine deposits occur north of Black Birch Lake and in the Lloyd Lake areas. Brunisolic soils dominate the well-drained positions in these landscapes, with Gleysols and Organics, and local Cryosols, in the numerous, small, poorly drained swales and flats. Large areas of peatlands occur only in the upper reaches of the Virgin and Brustad rivers. Scattered, and occasionally V-shaped, sand dunes occur in the western part of the area. Brunisolic soils are most common in areas where dunes are stabilized, but Regosolic soils dominate where they are active.

Open jack pine stands with lichen and Canada blueberry ground cover are prevalent on the sandy surface materials. Black spruce is mixed with jack pine on dry esker and drumlin slopes and in the sandy glacial till areas. A dominantly black spruce forest occurs in the many boggy areas and is associated with occasional tamarack in fens. The transition area between bog and upland supports black spruce and white birch, Labrador tea, bunchberry, twinflower, and feather mosses. The sand dune areas are most often stabilized with a dry, open jack pine woodland with a ground cover of lichens interspersed with Canada blueberry, bearberry, harebell, and sand heather. There are scattered open sand patches, where various grasses and herbs attempt to stabilize the sand.

D2. Frobisher Plain

This area extends from north of the Clearwater River in the northwest to Little Flatstone Lake in the southeast. The Cree Lake moraine, an ice-frontal feature that is important in the deglaciation of northern Saskatchewan, extends along the northern margin of this area. The area has a gentle regional slope from 540 m in the northwest and in a local upland south of Black Birch Lake to 420 m along the southern border of the Shield. The Descharme and Clearwater rivers drain the northwestern part of the area into the Athabasca River in Alberta. A series of southward-flowing creeks drains the central part to Wasekamio, Turnor, Frobisher, and a number of smaller lakes at the southern margin of the Shield. These lakes, in turn, drain in a southeasterly direction, emptying into the Mudjatik River before it enters the Churchill River in the southeastern part of the area. The Mudjatik River also drains the eastern part of the area into the Churchill River. The lower Mudjatik River represents a former glacial meltwater channel that carried meltwater from the ice during the formation of the Cree Lake moraine.

A thin veneer of glacial till and glaciofluvial deposits covers the bedrock surface throughout most of the area. The close proximity of the underlying bedrock, however, imparts a very irregular, hummocky nature to the surface. Sandy glaciolacustrine deposits occur in the Little Flatstone Lake area, representing the northern reaches of glacial Lake Agassiz. Crystalline Precambrian rocks on rugged slopes dominate the landscape in a large block east of Wasekamio and Turnor lakes and in a smaller block further west. Brunisolic soils dominate the glacial deposits in well-drained slope positions in these landscapes, with Gleysols and Organics, and local Cryosols, in the numerous, small, poorly drained swales and flats. There are extensive areas of peatlands with Organic soils mantling the glacial materials, especially in the Clearwater River, Frobisher Lake, and Heddery Lake areas. Sand dunes, occasionally V-shaped, are widely scattered throughout the northwestern part of the area. Brunisolic soils are most common in areas where the dunes are stabilized, but Regosolic soils dominate where the dunes are active.

The area is characterized by extensive stands of jack pine on the sand plains and glacial till ridges that are shallow to bedrock. Black spruce becomes dominant where the glacial till deposits are thicker. The poorly drained bogs are forested with black spruce and tamarack. Fens are also common. Where drainage and soil conditions are favourable, such as on alluvial areas near the Churchill River and on south-facing lake shores, stands of white spruce, trembling aspen, and balsam poplar occur. Balsam fir and white birch are present, but are not abundant. The sand dune areas are dominantly stabilized with a dry, open jack pine forest with a ground cover of lichens interspersed with Canada blueberry, bearberry, harebell, and sand heather. There are scattered open sand patches, where various grasses and herbs attempt to stabilize the sand.

D3. Pinehouse Plain

This area lies between the Haultain River on the east side and the Mudjatik River on the west, and from Haultain Lake in the north to Pinehouse Lake, on the southern margin of the

Shield, in the south. Except for areas of local relief in excess of 100 m in the northern part, this area has a gentle regional slope from highs of approximately 600 m in the north to 400 m in the south. Some of these isolated highlands drain westward into the Mudjatik River through Girard and Porter creeks, while others drain eastward to the Haultain River through several unnamed creeks. The lower Haultain River represents a former glacial meltwater channel that carried meltwater from the ice during the formation of the Cree Lake moraine.

A thin, discontinuous veneer of glacial till covers the bedrock surface in lower topographic positions throughout most of the area, but Precambrian basement rocks crop out on numerous rises and dominate in a large area that extends from Blackstone Lake to Dipper Lake. The close proximity of the underlying bedrock imparts a very irregular, hummocky nature to the surface. Sandy glaciofluvial outwash deposits, usually on gentle slopes but occasionally interrupted by eskerine ridges, occur east of Porter Lake and in the Knee Lake vicinity. Brunisolic soils dominate the glacial deposits in well-drained slope positions in all of these landscapes, with Gleysolics and Organics, and local Cryosolics, in the numerous, small, poorly drained swales and flats. Extensive areas of peatlands are limited in this area and are generally associated with low relief in the bedrock surface, such as occurs north of Porter and Dipper lakes.

Extensive stands of jack pine occupy the sand plains and low ridges, while black spruce occurs on the thin glacial till upland soils. Bogs are treed with black spruce, and tamarack is associated with fen margins. South of the Churchill River, trembling aspen, white birch, and green alder are common on glacial till. The associated shrubs include Canada blueberry, prickly rose, low bush-cranberry, and pin cherry. The ground cover includes two-leaved Solomon's seal, bunchberry, fireweed, Indian rice grass, mosses, and lichens. The moist to wet alluvial terrain, found along the Churchill and Haultain rivers and other major streams, is dominated by white birch and black spruce, and stands of white spruce occur occasionally.

D4. Foster Upland

This large, predominantly bedrock area forms a wide arc that extends from Reindeer Lake to Lac La Ronge. The area has a gentle slope from a regional high of approximately 600 m in the Upper Foster Lake area to less than 400 m at Reindeer Lake and Lac La Ronge. The Haultain, Norbert, Belanger, and Foster rivers all drain this upland southward to the Churchill River. The Wathaman River provides for most of the drainage northward to Reindeer Lake. The Belanger and Foster rivers represent former glacial meltwater channels that carried meltwater from the ice during the formation of the Cree Lake moraine.

The area is dominated by outcrops of Precambrian basement rocks, with only a thin, discontinuous veneer of sandy glacial till covering this bedrock surface in lower topographic positions. Many granite cliffs, sometimes rising as high as 20 m above the lake, surround Black Bear Island Lake.

Hummocky moraines and glaciofluvial outwash deposits, which are also sandy, provide thicker cover on the bedrock in local areas. The close proximity of the underlying bedrock in these areas imparts a very irregular, hummocky nature to the surface. Prominent sandy and gravelly eskerine ridges occur throughout the northern part of the area. The southern part was inundated by glacial Lake Agassiz with the resultant deposition of glaciolacustrine clays. In well-drained slope positions, Brunisolic soils dominate on the sandy and gravelly glacial deposits and Gray Luvisols on clay deposits. Gleysols and Organics, and local Cryosols, dominate in the numerous, small, poorly drained swales and flats. Extensive areas of peatlands are limited in this area and are generally associated with low relief in the bedrock surface.

In the southern portion of the area, a productive mixedwood forest occurs wherever glacial deposits are relatively deep. About two-thirds of the forest consists of mixed stands of white spruce and trembling aspen, with lesser amounts of other conifers. Poorly drained sites are dominated by black spruce, which is also prominent on the thin-soiled ridges. Jack pine is abundant only on local sandy areas. North of Paul and McTavish lakes, coniferous forest becomes dominant. Black spruce forms open stands on the thin-soiled uplands, and closed stands on deeper soils or in moist areas. On the extensive rock outcrops, jack pine accompanies the spruce and dominates on recently burned areas. The scattered white birch stands are the result of fire. Open sedge fens and sparsely treed bogs are common.

The greatest nesting densities of bald eagles in Saskatchewan are found on the Churchill River between Pinehouse Lake and Otter Rapids. Most nests are within 200 m of water and are commonly situated in mixedwood stands. Golden eagle nests are also found in significant numbers between Black Bear Island Lake and Otter Rapids.

D5. Highrock Lake Plain

This area is largely covered by sediments originating from the Athabasca sandstone to the north, but is underlain by Precambrian basement rocks. The area has a very gentle northeasterly slope from a regional high of approximately 570 m in the Highrock Lake area to less than 420 m at Geike River. The Geike River provides for most of the drainage northward to Wollaston Lake. This area is essentially a drumlinoid moraine that is extensively, but not completely, covered with undulating glaciofluvial outwash deposits. Prominent eskers, some of which are 50 km long, are also common in this area. Sandy glaciolacustrine plains cover some of the drumlinoid moraine and outwash in local areas such as around Costigan Lake. Brunisolic soils dominate the well-drained slope positions in these landscapes, with Gleysols and Organics, and local Cryosols, in the numerous, small, poorly drained swales and flats.

Generally, jack pine dominates the uplands because the glacial till deposits are very sandy. Fires are common, and most forests are in some stage of regeneration. An open jack pine forest is found on sandy outwash areas, south sides of eskers, linear ridges of till, and on soils that are shallow to bedrock. Lichen, Canada blueberry, and green alder occur in the understory. North-facing aspects have black spruce as the codominant or subdominant species. A mixture of jack pine and black spruce also occurs on the margins of bogs. Black spruce is more common in the area south of Costigan Lake. Sedges, willows, dwarf birch, and tamarack are associated with fens. Riparian areas are more diverse and dense, comprising white birch, black spruce, and willow, making them better wildlife habitat than upland areas.

D6. Wollaston Lake Plain

This area is largely covered by sediments originating from the Athabasca sandstone to the north, but it is underlain by crystalline Precambrian bedrock. The area has a very gentle northeasterly slope from a regional high of approximately 450 m in the southern part of the area to less than 400 m at Wollaston and Reindeer lakes. The Geike River and a number of smaller rivers provide for most of the drainage northward to Wollaston and Reindeer lakes.

This area is essentially a hummocky moraine with occasional drumlins and prominent eskers, some of which are 50 km long. Although the hummocky surface is largely a reflection of the underlying bedrock, rarely does the bedrock crop out. Brunisolic soils dominate the well-drained slope positions in these landscapes, with Gleysols and Organics, and local Cryosols, in the numerous, small, poorly drained swales and flats.

Black spruce dominates in this landscape area. It exists as an open canopy with a lichen ground cover where glacial till is shallow to bedrock; this is quite common between Reindeer and Wollaston lakes. As the glacial till becomes thicker toward the south, a more closed canopy with feather mosses and lichen ground cover becomes common. Open stands of jack pine occur locally on the sandy and gravelly glaciofluvial deposits and on rocky areas where soils are very thin. Scattered, stunted black spruce and occasional tamarack grow on the abundant bogs associated with low-lying areas.

D7. Reindeer Lake Plain

This is a very small area in Saskatchewan, but it is part of a larger area in Manitoba. It is largely covered by sediments originating from the Athabasca sandstone to the north, but is underlain by crystalline Precambrian bedrock. The area in Saskatchewan lies at approximately 380 m. Most of it drains eastward to the Nelson River in Manitoba.

This area is essentially a hummocky moraine with occasional drumlins and prominent eskers. Although the hummocky surface is largely a reflection of the underlying bedrock, the bedrock is rarely exposed. Brunisolic soils dominate the well-drained slope positions in these landscapes, with Gleysols and Organics, and local Cryosols, in the numerous, small, poorly drained swales and flats.

The area is dominated by open black spruce stands on the shallow, sandy glacial till, which become more dense in the lower areas where peat deposits are very thin. Jack pine occurs on the rocky areas where soils are very thin. Scattered, stunted black spruce and occasional tamarack are associated with low boggy areas.

D8. Macoun Lake Plain

This area lies to the west of the south end of Reindeer Lake. It is largely covered by glacial sediments, but is underlain by crystalline Precambrian bedrock. The area has a very gentle northeasterly slope from a regional high of approximately 450 m in the Macoun Lake area to less than 400 m at Reindeer Lake.

This area is essentially a hummocky moraine with prominent eskers. Although the hummocky surface is largely a reflection of the underlying bedrock, rarely does the bedrock crop out. Brunisolic soils dominate the well-drained slope positions in these landscapes, with Gleysols and Organics, and local Cryosols, in the numerous, small, poorly drained swales and flats. Sandy glaciolacustrine plains cover some of the morainal deposits in local areas such as around May, Oliver, Nokomis, and Perry lakes.

Black spruce is dominant on the thin glacial till veneer, varying from an open canopy on the thin veneer to a closed canopy where the glacial till is thicker. Jack pine occurs where the soils are very thin or on sandy and gravelly glaciofluvial materials. The glaciolacustrine areas support a mixedwood forest composed of trembling aspen, white spruce, balsam fir, and white birch, as well as black spruce and jack pine. Black spruce and tamarack are associated with the peatlands.

D9. Sisipuk Plain

This large, predominantly bedrock area extends from Deep Bay on Reindeer Lake to Lac

La Ronge and Wapawekka Lake. The area has a very gentle slope from regional topographical highs of approximately 500 m in the McLennan Lake area north of the Churchill River to less than 400 m at Reindeer Lake and Lac La Ronge and to less than 350 m along the Manitoba border. The Reindeer and Pagota rivers drain this upland southward to the Churchill River. The area south of the Churchill River largely drains into Lac La Ronge and Wapawekka Lake.

The area is dominated by outcrops of ice-scoured crystalline Precambrian rocks. A thin, discontinuous veneer of sandy glacial till covers this bedrock surface in lower topographic positions in the northern part of the area. Hummocky moraines and glaciofluvial outwash, both of which are sandy, provide thicker cover on the bedrock in local areas. The close proximity of the underlying bedrock in these areas imparts a very irregular, hummocky nature to the surface. A large part of the area was inundated by glacial Lake Agassiz with the resultant deposition of glaciolacustrine clays. In well-drained slope positions, Brunisolic soils dominate on the sandy and gravelly glacial till and glaciofluvial deposits, and Gray Luvisols on glaciolacustrine clay deposits. Gleysols and Organics, and local Cryosols, dominate in the numerous, small, poorly drained swales and flats. Extensive areas of peatlands are limited in this area and are generally associated with low relief in the bedrock surface.

A mixture of coniferous forest and mixedwood forest is characteristic of the Sisipuk Plain. Pure stands of black spruce or jack pine are not as extensive as elsewhere in the Shield. The wide distribution of clayey glaciolacustrine materials supports trembling aspen, white birch, balsam poplar, jack pine, white spruce, and black spruce. Small trembling aspen stands occur on well-drained, south-facing slopes along rivers. On sandy glacial till areas, closed forests of black spruce and/or jack pine occur, depending on the depth of the glacial deposits. Jack pine are found on very thin soils associated with bedrock outcrops. White birch, willow, and green alder are scattered throughout the area. Black spruce and tamarack are associated with the low-lying bogs and fens.

D10. Flin Flon Plain

This predominantly bedrock area represents the southern limits of the Precambrian Shield in eastern Saskatchewan. It slopes gently southward from regional topographical highs of approximately 400 m in the vicinity of Pelican and Mirond lakes to regional lows of 330 m at Deschambault and Amisk lakes. The Sturgeon-weir River drains these lower lakes into the Saskatchewan River.

The area is dominated by outcrops of ice-scoured crystalline Precambrian rocks. A thin, discontinuous veneer of sandy glacial till covers the bedrock surface locally, but a veneer of glaciolacustrine silts and clays is more extensive. The close proximity of the underlying bedrock imparts a very irregular, hummocky nature to the surface. In well-drained slope positions, Brunisolic soils dominate on the sandy and gravelly glacial deposits, and Gray Luvisols on clay deposits. Gleysols and Organics dominate in the numerous, small, poorly drained swales and flats. Extensive areas of peatlands are limited in this area and are generally associated with low relief in the bedrock surface.

A mixedwood forest is characteristic of the Flin Flon plain. Black spruce is the most common tree, but it does not dominate the landscape to the same extent that it does in the rest of the boreal shield. White spruce is a significant component of the forest, as is trembling aspen. Jack pine stands are extensive where sandy glaciofluvial materials are present. Some balsam fir is associated with the white spruce. Poorly drained peaty areas are forested with black spruce and tamarack. The water in the Sturgeon-weir River is warmer and more productive than rivers farther north. As a result, waterfowl, especially the American white pelican, are numerous along its length.

D11. Reed Lake Plain

This is a very small area in Saskatchewan but is part of a larger area in Manitoba. The area in Saskatchewan lies at approximately 330 m and drains eastward to the Nelson River.

This area includes hummocky morainal deposits with a discontinuous veneer of glacial lake clays. The deposits are shallow, and the bedrock crops out frequently. Brunisolic soils dominate the well-drained glacial tills, with Gray Luvisols prevailing on the imperfectly drained clays. Gleysols and Organics occur in the numerous, small, poorly drained swales and flats. There is a large flat bog in the Saskatchewan portion of the area.

Since the northern half of the area in Saskatchewan is predominantly a bog, stunted black spruce and tamarack dominate the landscape area. The uplands in the south are characterized by a mixedwood forest of black spruce, trembling aspen, white spruce, and white birch, with jack pine on thinly soiled rocky areas.

Boreal Plain Ecozone

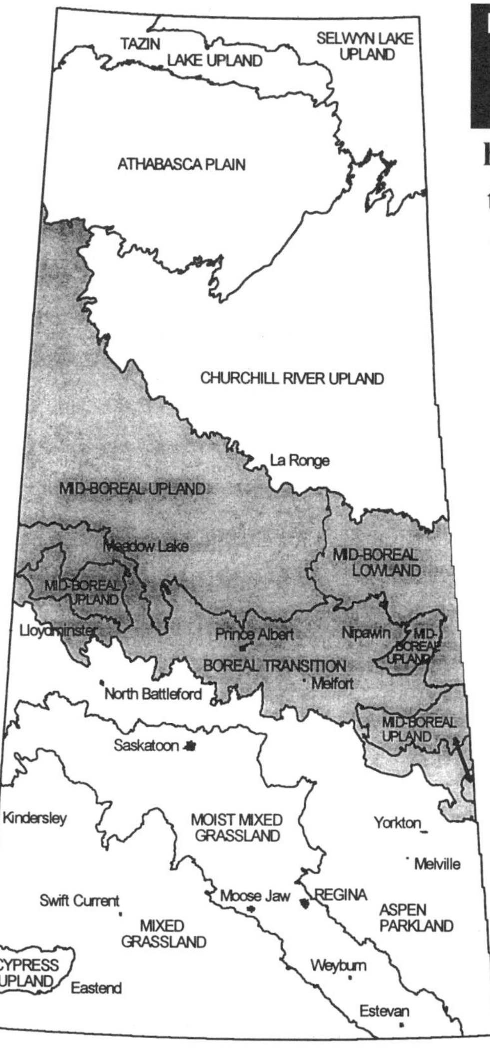

The Boreal Plain Ecozone extends across Canada from Newfoundland to the Rocky Mountains. In Saskatchewan it covers more than 17 million hectares, or about 27% of the area of the province. As the name implies, the bulk of the region is characterized by northern boreal forest, although about 25% of the ecozone along its southern boundary in Saskatchewan is used for agricultural production.

PHYSIOGRAPHY. The boreal plain in Saskatchewan extends in a band from the Precambrian Shield south to the aspen parkland, which is the northern boundary of the Prairie Ecozone. It is essentially a level to gently rolling plain with numerous subdued uplands dispersed throughout most of its extent. Elevations are lowest in the northeastern part of the area. The Manitoba Escarpment and then the northern extension of the Missouri Coteau represent successive increases in elevation from approximately 500 m in the east to 600 m in the west, with some uplands reaching nearly 900 m.

GEOLOGY. The Boreal Plain Ecozone lies south of the Precambrian Shield where the crystalline basement rocks exposed on the Shield are covered by younger sedimentary rocks. The Boreal Plain Ecozone is host to resources of peat, sand and gravel, and natural gas.

Ordovician and Silurian carbonate (limestone and dolomite) bedrock, deposited 500 to 400 million years ago, is exposed just south of the Precambrian Shield margin; otherwise, bedrock outcrops are restricted mainly to stream valleys. Glacial sediments are 100 to 250 m thick throughout most of the Boreal Plain Ecozone. The glacial deposits are markedly less sandy in character than those of the Boreal Shield Ecozone. The surface of the Boreal Plain Ecozone is generally flat to hummocky, dominated by ground moraine deposited beneath the continental glacier. The moraine deposits are characterized by an abundance of lakes, but the northeast-southwest elongation of lakes seen in the crystalline portion of the Precambrian Shield is not evident in the boreal plain.

Although glacial deposits represent the surficial sediment throughout nearly all of the boreal plain, and in places they are hundreds of metres thick, the topography of the ecozone closely mirrors the bedrock surface. The higher plains and uplands in the southwestern part of the ecozone are associated with thick deposits of Upper Cretaceous shales that form the bedrock surface. These shales become thinner and eventually disappear to the north and east, with older, Lower Cretaceous sands forming the bedrock surface. In the extreme eastern part of the ecozone, the Lower Cretaceous sand disappears, exposing still older Paleozoic bedrock.

Mixedwood forests are common on the well-drained escarpment of the Wapawekka Hills.

Glacial deposits strongly influence the nature of the local landscape throughout the ecozone. Till plains and hummocky moraines, often with an abundance of glacial kettles, are a dominant feature of the Mostoos, Waskesiu, Wapawekka, and other uplands. Nearly level glacio-lacustrine plains are also common, as are glaciofluvial areas that are often modified by wind into dunes. Valleys and rivers cross this plain, flowing through the Beaver, Saskatchewan, and Assiniboine river systems to the Churchill and Nelson rivers and into Hudson Bay.

CLIMATE. The climate of the Boreal Plain Ecozone is humid continental at lower elevations in the southern part, becoming more typical of a subarctic climate at higher elevations in the southern part and throughout the northern part. It is characterized by long, cold to very cold, and snowy winters and short, warm, and moist summers. Temperatures generally decrease from south to north and from east to west within the ecozone in response to increasing latitude and decreasing altitude, respectively. Total precipitation is variable and low and tends to decrease from south to north. Maximum precipitation occurs from July through September.

LANDFORMS AND SOILS. Landforms and soils in the Boreal Plain Ecozone contrast sharply with those to the north. Glacial deposits are much thicker, and topography is usually totally related to these deposits. Only in the eastern part of the ecozone, where Paleozoic dolomites form the bedrock surface, are there extensive bedrock outcrops. Except for a band on the margin of the Canadian Shield where the soils are sandy, they usually contain more clay-sized materials and have a much more diverse mineralogy.

The soils in the boreal plain are largely Luvisols, Brunisols, and Organics. As a general rule, Luvisolic soils occur on loamy- and clayey-textured sediments, while sandy deposits are characterized by Brunisolic soils. Organic soils or those developed from organic peaty materials are confined to low-lying depressional areas where water accumulates due to runoff and where internal drainage is restricted. Extensive peatlands are found throughout the northern parts of the ecozone, particularly in the Mid-Boreal Lowland Ecoregion. Permanently frozen soils, or Cryosols, are found occasionally throughout the Mid-Boreal Upland Ecoregion. These soils typically develop in undecomposed sphagnum peat deposits under a dense coniferous tree cover. Chernozemic soils, which are commonly associated with grassland environments, are found along the southern boundary of the ecozone in the Boreal Transition Ecoregion.

GROUNDWATER. Groundwater conditions in the boreal plain vary markedly from the adjoining Churchill River upland to the north, but are quite similar to those in the Prairie Ecozone to the south. The basal aquitard of Precambrian basement rocks is covered by a major aquifer developed in Lower Cretaceous sandstone. This aquifer is confined by Upper Cretaceous shales in the numerous regional uplands that prevail in the area, and may be confined by glacial deposits in regional lowlands. Where the glacial deposits are thin or highly permeable, there is a continuous aquifer from the surface to the Lower Cretaceous aquifer. The Lower Cretaceous aquifer in the boreal plain is not as highly mineralized as it is in the Prairie Ecozone; hence, it is a valuable source of water for domestic and industrial use.

VEGETATION. The climate of the boreal plain is warmer and, consequently, species richness and productivity are higher than in ecozones to the north. Generally, the ecozone is characterized by a closed-crown mixedwood and coniferous forest. The deciduous component is represented mainly by trembling aspen, white birch, and balsam poplar, which become most numerous in the Boreal Transition Ecoregion along the southern boundary adjoining the prairie grasslands. White and black spruce, jack pine, and tamarack are the main coniferous species, with black spruce and tamarack increasing in dominance along the northerly sections of the ecozone. A mixedwood forest of white spruce and aspen occupy well-drained sites, and jack pine occurs on sand ridges and terraces. Lowlands are extensive, supporting willow-sedge fens and marshes. There is more fen peatland than in the Shield to the north, where bog peatland occurs more often due to lower nutrient status of water flowing over Shield bedrock. Extensive floating mats of aquatic plants are characteristic along lake shores.

An assortment of less common hardwoods such as American elm, green ash, and Manitoba maple occur locally under warmer climatic conditions that are associated with regional lowlands. Peatlands supporting open stands of black spruce and tamarack occur extensively in regional lowlands and in more northerly local depressions.

WILDLIFE. There is a gradual increase in wildlife productivity and diversity from north to south in this ecozone, reflecting progressively warmer climates and greater diversity of vegetation from the boreal shield to the Prairie Ecozone.

More than 50 mammal species occur within the ecozone, considered a high species richness. Moose, black bear, white-tailed deer, elk, muskrat, gray wolf, beaver, red squirrel, and least chipmunk are representive of this group.

Black bear are common in this ecozone.

Species richness of birds is high, with approximately 300 species reported to occur in the ecozone. Representative birds include common raven, great gray owl, gray and blue jay, ruffed grouse, boreal chickadee, common loon, mallard, Canada goose, several species of hawks, and many species of warblers.

The fish diversity is high throughout most of this ecozone, with nearly 40 species reported. Representative fish include northern pike, walleye, yellow perch, lake whitefish, lake trout, white sucker, burbot, goldeye, and fathead minnow.

The boreal plain has a medium richness

of amphibians and reptiles, with six species reported. The Canadian toad, the boreal chorus frog, and the red-sided garter snake are representative species.

HUMAN ACTIVITY. Approximately 151,000 people live in this zone, or 15% of the Saskatchewan population. The principal uses of this ecozone include forestry, agriculture, mining, oil and gas exploration and production, hunting and trapping, outdoor recreation, and tourism. The largest employment sectors are service industries and public administration.

Rapids provide entertainment to white-water canoers.

About 72% of the ecozone is forested and 16% is cultivated. Roughly half of the zone is actually productive commercial forest land. The rate of forest harvesting — especially of the previously little-used trembling aspen stands — has increased greatly in recent years. Forestry operations focus on harvesting large volumes of wood fibre for pulp and paper. There are large pulp mills at Prince Albert and Meadow Lake.

Some of Saskatchewan's most productive agricultural lands occur in the southern part of this ecozone, where climate and soils are suited to the production of a variety of cereal, oilseed, pulse, and hay crops. Livestock production is also common in this area.

Water resources are abundant in the Boreal Plain Ecozone. The local residential impact on water quality is low compared with that of more populated areas. However, variations in the soils, land cover, and land uses in the ecozone make water quantity and quality highly variable.

The Boreal Plain Ecozone has very little mining development, although there are two peat mines and several quarrying activities for silica and gravel in the zone. This ecozone has hydroelectric dams at Squaw Rapids and Nipawin. Most of the oil and gas activity in this ecozone is located in the Lloydminster area. Approximately 6% of the province's oil reserves and less than 1% of its gas reserves are located in this ecozone. Numerous smaller industrial operations service the lumber, pulp and paper, oil and gas, or agricultural industries (grain, seed, fertilizer).

The mid-boreal upland is the heart of the timber industry.

Most of the commercial fishing in the province occurs within the Boreal Plain Ecozone. Over 65% of the 200 lakes fished annually in Saskatchewan are contained within this zone. More than 40% of all provincial sport angling occurs within this zone. The boreal plain is the most significant ecozone for trapping in the province with nearly 70% of the pelts harvested in Saskatchewan coming from this zone. This ecozone is also the most significant in the province for outfitting services, containing approximately 55% of all Saskatchewan's outfitters.

Approximately 8% of this ecozone is managed within parks and protected areas, principally national and provincial parks and Wildlife Habitat Protection Act lands. These include Prince Albert National Park and Duck Mountain, Greenwater Lake, Narrow Hills, and Meadow Lake provincial parks.

Mid-Boreal Upland Ecoregion

The Mid-Boreal Upland Ecoregion includes rolling uplands and undulating plains in the north, as well as prominent rolling uplands in the south. It is a large area, occupying over 10 million hectares or 16% of the province. It includes a major block that extends westward from the east central part of the ecozone, as well as several outliers in the south and eastern part of the ecozone. It is characterized by a mosaic of forests, open and treed fens, bogs, and water. A combination of cold climate, sandy soils, and hilly topography has limited agricultural development to less than 10% of the area.

PHYSIOGRAPHY. The Mid-Boreal Upland Ecoregion comprises a series of rolling uplands surrounded by gently undulating plains. The uplands, proper, are usually highest in their central portions, sloping in all directions to the plains below. These plains, in turn, tend to slope downward from the south and west to the east and north, in accordance with the slope of the bedrock surface. Most of the region has a cover of glacial drift that is sufficiently thick to obscure the underlying bedrock topography.

The uplands are dominated by hummocky morainal landscapes. They generally protrude 50 to 200 m above the adjacent plain, with the Pasquia and Mostoos hills reaching elevations of 900 m and more. Although the break from the plains to the uplands is usually gradual and unspectacular, prominent escarpments are striking features, locally. The surrounding plains are dominated by level to undulating glaciofluvial and glaciolacustrine deposits with an abundance of wetlands and organic soils.

The valleys of the Assiniboine and Beaver rivers, which are part of the Nelson River drainage basin, add to the beauty of the region. There are also a number of prominent lakes in the region: Candle, Wapawekka, Waskesiu, Montreal, Dore, Crean, La Plonge, Canoe, Primrose, Churchill, Peter Pond, and Methy, to name but a few.

The fall colours of the trembling aspen, as seen here on the well-drained uplands, are in sharp contrast to the black spruce and tamarack on the poorly drained lowlands.

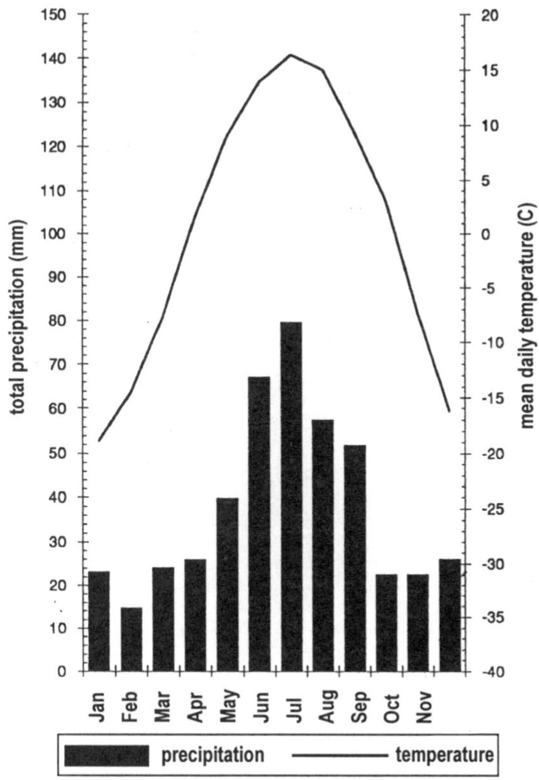

Figure 16. Mean monthly temperature and precipitation for the mid-boreal upland as represented by the meteorological record from Waskesiu Lake.

GEOLOGY. The bedrock underlying the southern part of the Mid-Boreal Upland Ecoregion is mudstone and shale of the Upper Cretaceous Riding Mountain Formation, while the portion bordering the Precambrian Shield is sandstone and siltstone of the Manville and Lower Colorado group of Lower Cretaceous age. The bedrock surface has a general slope from 480 m in the south to 360 m in the north. This surface is covered with 100 m or more of glacial deposits throughout most of the area.

Hummocky moraines are most common at higher elevations on the various uplands, with ground moraine and glaciofluvial deposits more common in the intervening plains. The glacial deposits in the northern part of the area are more sandy than to the south, reflecting the influence of Precambrian and underlying sandy bedrock on the composition of these materials.

CLIMATE. The subarctic climate of the mid-boreal upland is cooler and drier than the Mid-Boreal Lowland and the Boreal Transition ecoregions, but warmer and wetter than the boreal shield to the north. The mean annual daily temperature is 0.3°C. The mean July temperature is 16.3°C and the mean January temperature is -18.9°C. The mean annual precipitation is 452 mm, with 291 mm of rainfall occurring from May to September. The summers are short and cool, having a frost-free period of 91 days and a total of 1,256 degree days above 5°C.

LANDFORMS AND SOILS. Gray Luvisolic and Eutric Brunisolic soils prevail on the well to imperfectly drained slopes of hummocky and ground moraines. Brunisols prevail on sandy glaciofluvial, glacial till, and eolian deposits, except for recently stabilized sand dunes where Regosolic soils dominate. Gleysols and Organic soils dominate the lower slope positions in morainal areas as well as extensive nearly level areas that are common in the area.

GROUNDWATER. Groundwater occurs in glacial drift as well as in the bedrock. A major bedrock aquifer occurs extensively throughout the northern part of the ecoregion, within the sandy and silty beds of the Lower Cretaceous Mannville Formation. There is a major buried valley aquifer, the Hatfield Valley aquifer, in the western part of this ecoregion. It is part of a major valley that entered the province near Cold Lake on the Alberta border and extended to the Manitoba border east of Regina. Inter-till aquifers are thought to be widely distributed throughout the ecoregion, but they are poorly defined. They are most common in the older and deeper Floral Formation, but may also occur within the Battleford Formation. Surface aquifers are common in association with the sandy materials, especially in the northern part of the area.

Bedrock, glacial, and surficial aquifers influence the ecology of the area. The sandy surficial deposits that prevail in the northern part of the ecoregion provide a water source for lakes such as Peter Pond, Churchill, Dore, and Candle. These lakes have a low salt content that reflects concentrations in the glacial deposits. The surface aquifers also provide a ready water supply for vegetation, and the low salt content of the water influences the composition of the plant communities.

White spruce intermingled with trembling aspen.

VEGETATION. The characteristic forest of well-drained uplands in this ecoregion is a mixture of coniferous and deciduous trees, with varying proportions of medium to tall, closed stands of trembling aspen, jack pine, black spruce, white spruce, and balsam poplar, listed in order of dominance. White birch and balsam fir are present, but not abundant. Deciduous stands have a diverse understory of shrubs and herbs; coniferous stands tend to promote a predominantly feather moss understory.

Eight major vegetation groups are recognized in the mid-boreal upland: aspen forest, jack pine forest, white spruce forest, mixedwood forest, black spruce-jack pine forest, black spruce forest, peatlands, and boreal wetlands.

Aspen forests dominate on medium to fine textured soils. On typical well-drained sites, a dense hazelnut shrub layer is present, under which grows twinflower, bunchberry, bishop's-cap, wild sarsaparilla, cream-colored vetchling, two-leaved Solomon's-seal, and starflower. Dewberry, fireweed, American wild strawberry, ground cedar, and tall lungwort are locally abundant. On drier well-drained sites, beaked hazelnut, hairy wild rye grass, and wild sarsaparilla are common. Green alder and some willow species are also common, especially in open areas. Other small shrubs include prickly rose and high bush-cranberry. Mosses are relatively unimportant on the forest floor. Of interest are several species common to the eastern part but rare elsewhere in the province, including bush honeysuckle, red elderberry, and mountain maple. The forest matures at 65 to 70 years of age, and as the aspen rots, it leaves behind a sparse aspen-white spruce forest.

Jack pine forests occupy the relatively well-drained sandy or gravelly plains and low ridges. On very rapidly drained sites, open stands of jack pine exhibit a stunted twisted form with wide-spreading, lightly foliaged branches and a stocky stem. The forest floor is densely carpeted with Cladonia lichens, along with some Canada blueberry, bearberry, and bog cranberry. There is a sparse scattering of two-leaved Solomon's-seal, blue grasses, and early blue violet.

On well-drained soils or in local depressions, some aspen, white birch, white spruce, black spruce, or balsam fir may be present under the closed jack pine canopy. The crown of the jack pine is reduced to the upper fifth of the tree, and the trunk is slender and relatively straight, with little taper. Green alder is a common tall shrub in openings. Other characteristic smaller shrubs include prickly rose and twinflower, with some saskatoon, bristly black currant, and Labrador tea present. The forest floor is often surprisingly bare of herbs, with an abundant feather moss and lichen cover. The scattered herbs most characteristic are bunchberry, starflower, ground cedar, rattlesnake plantain, two-leaved Solomon's-seal, horsetail, early blue violet, and wild sarsaparilla.

White spruce forest commonly occurs on well-drained, hummocky glacial till uplands. The best stands occur on moderately well to imperfectly drained sites, such as on alluvial materials along streams. Very good stands occur on Dark Gray Chernozemic soils on relatively level, water-modified glacial till or lacustrine materials. Leaf litter and feather and other mosses form the ground cover. On the most moist sites, the feather moss is very dominant, associated with vine-leaved coltsfoot. On well-drained sites, a variety of shrubs are characteristic, such as bog cranberry, twinflower, Labrador tea, high bush-cranberry, prickly rose, skunk currant, wild red currant, and dwarf birch. Common herbs are wild sarsaparilla, bishop's-cap, horsetail, stiff club-moss, bunchberry, dewberry, northern bedstraw, and palm-leaved coltsfoot. On fairly flat, poorly drained areas encircling lowlands, short, narrow-diameter, white spruce is found, having an understory of horsetails, sedges, and reed grasses.

Mixedwood forests occur under well and imperfectly drained conditions where white spruce is mixed with trembling aspen and balsam poplar.

Black spruce forest occurs extensively in the wetter, more poorly drained forest areas, but it also occurs extensively on moderately well-drained sites. On the moderately well-drained sites, it occurs in a very high stand density, causing trees to be tall and thin without much taper. Complete feather moss ground cover and an absence of shrubs is characteristic, due to low light levels. Only small amounts of bunchberry, bog cranberry, common horsetail, bishop's-cap, northern comandra, blueberry, twinflower, and Labrador tea can be found on these sites. On imperfectly drained sites, balsam poplar and tamarack are minor components; at an earlier stage in succession, tamarack was likely codominant. A dry phase of black spruce forest can also occur, where feather mosses are replaced by lichens as the ground cover.

On the wettest sites, peat is commonly characterized by sphagnum mosses. The stand is more open, causing the trees to become limby. Tamarack is a common associate of black spruce under these conditions. Common shrubs are leather-leaf, pale laurel, dwarf birch, and Labrador tea. Common herbs include cloudberry, round-leaved sundew, three-leaved Solomon's-seal, horsetail, small bog-cranberry, and wintergreens.

Bull elk in velvet.

Black spruce-jack pine forests, often mixed with trembling aspen, dominate the northern part of the ecoregion. They occur mainly on imperfectly drained morainal uplands, but also occur on wet to arid glaciofluvial plains and on horizontal or raised bogs characterized by forest and sphagnum peat.

Peatlands are common throughout this ecoregion. They include open and treed fens and treed bogs. They range in occurrence from level, plateau-like areas on the top of regional uplands, to nearly level to flat areas between these regional uplands.

WILDLIFE. Moose and black bear are common in the northern part of the ecoregion; woodland caribou are less common. There is greater diversity southward to include white-tailed deer, mule deer, and elk. Other mammals include muskrat, gray wolf, beaver, meadow vole, northern flying squirrel, and least chipmunk.

Bird diversity is low in the northern part but increases southward. Ruffed grouse are common, and birds such as chimney swift and whip-poor-will range in the eastern part of the area. Other birds include great gray owl, blue jay, sharp-shinned hawk, broad-winged hawk, yellow-bellied sapsucker, common goldeneye, sandhill crane, many species of warblers, solitary vireo, western tanager, rose-breasted grosbeak, and ruby-throated hummingbird.

A peat processing and baling plant near Carrot River.

Northern pike, walleye, and lake whitefish are the most common fish in the northern part of the ecoregion; yellow perch and scattered populations of lake trout are more common further south. Other fish include white sucker, burbot, goldeye, and fathead minnow.

A moderately diverse population of amphibians and reptiles occurs in this ecoregion, including red-sided garter snake, Canadian toad, and the boreal chorus frog.

HUMAN ACTIVITY. The population of this ecoregion is approximately 22,000, or 2% of the Saskatchewan population. Major communities include La Loche, Buffalo Narrows, Île-à-la-Crosse, and Waskesiu. Pulpwood and local saw-log forestry, water-oriented recreation, hunting, and trapping are the main land use activities. Agricultural activities are significant in the southern part of the ecoregion, mainly crop production, livestock management, and beekeeping. This ecoregion also has large areas of major peat resource potential. Projects involving bulk sampling of diamonds have occurred in the Fort à la Corne kimberlite field and its northwest extension in the Candle-Whiteswan lakes area. About 1% of the total land area in this ecoregion is under cultivation. Approximately 9% of the ecoregion is within some form of park or protected area. Saskatchewan's largest national park, Prince Albert, is located in this ecoregion, along with Clearwater River, Narrow Hills, Wildcat Hills, Greenwater Lake, and Duck Mountain provincial parks.

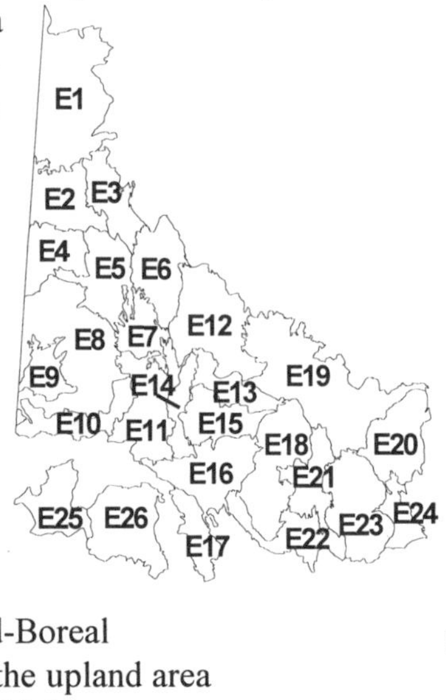

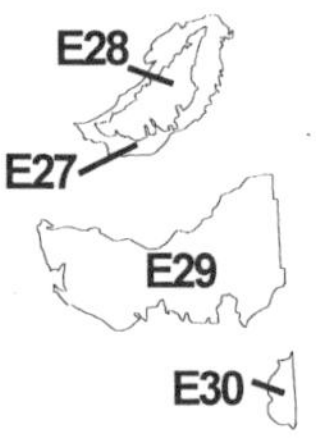

Landscape Areas

E1. Firebag Hills

The Firebag Hills area is located in the northernmost part of the Mid-Boreal Upland Ecoregion and includes the Clearwater River Valley and the upland area along the Alberta border that extends northward to the Canadian Shield.

The landscape throughout the northern part of the area is a predominantly gently to strongly rolling morainic plain, with elevations ranging from 480 m to over 580 m. The prominent, deeply-incised Clearwater River Valley, which in places is up to 250 m deep, is located in the south. The entire area drains to the west via the Clearwater River and its tributaries.

The surficial deposits, which are derived in part from the underlying Lower Cretaceous sandstone bedrock, are mostly sandy glacial tills and glaciofluvial deposits. Organic deposits overlie the sandy tills in local depressional areas.

In the northern part, the upland soils are predominantly Dystric Brunisols developed on the sandy glacial till deposits. In the valley itself the soils have developed largely on sandy loams and sands presumably derived from erosion and slumping of the sandy till and outwash deposits. Since the slopes are excessively drained and there are numerous eroding slopes and intermittent water courses, many of the soils are Regosols. Weakly developed Dystric Brunisols are found on some of the more stable slope positions.

The vegetation in the northern part of the area is predominantly short scrubby jack pine with a lichen understory, a reflection of the extremely sandy soils and the frequency of fire. Black spruce and tamarack occupy the poorly drained peatland areas. Along the Clearwater River valley itself, the vegetation is much more diverse, reflecting the varying surficial deposits and drainage conditions within the valley. Along the valley walls the vegetation is characterized by trembling aspen, often mixed with jack pine and white spruce. The poorly drained areas in the bottom of the valley are characterized by sedges, grasses, willows, and local stands of tamarack and black spruce.

E2. Garson Lake Plain

The Garson Lake plain extends northwestward from Peter Pond Lake to La Loche and west to the Alberta border. The area is relatively level with elevations ranging from about 425 to 450 m. Local drainage for the most part is southeast into Peter Pond Lake via the La Loche and Kimowin rivers.

The relatively low-lying, gently rolling landscape is characterized by a mosaic of peatlands and intermittent upland areas. The peatlands are relatively shallow and are often densely treed, with black spruce and tamarack being the dominant species. The uplands are a mix of sandy glacial till and glaciofluvial deposits, as well as loamy glacial till sediments. The sandy areas are often poorly drained and support dense stands of black spruce. The soils are dominantly Brunisolic and peaty Gleysolics. The more hummocky landscapes are generally comprised of loamy glacial till deposits. Gray Luvisolic soils supporting trembling aspen, often mixed with pine, are characteristic of these landscapes.

E3. Palmbere Plain

The Palmbere plain occurs along the Shield north of Churchill Lake. The area slopes gradually from about 500 m east of McLean Lake, east and south toward the Shield. Local drainage is into Wasekamio, Turnor, Frobisher, and Churchill lakes, which occur on the Shield at an elevation of about 425 m.

The landscape is, for the most part, a gently to strongly rolling glacial till plain. Outwash sands and gravels occur sporadically throughout the area, along with organic or peaty materials which overlie the till in many of the level and depressional areas. The depressional areas tend to be elongated in a northwest-southeast direction, a reflection of the underlying bedrock and the direction of glacial ice movement. The glacial till itself is extremely sandy, being derived largely from the underlying Cretaceous sandstone as well as from material moved into the area from the Shield by glacial erosion. There are no loamy-textured soils here, unlike the Garson Lake plain to the west.

Typical vegetation in the upland areas consists of open stands of jack pine, occasionally mixed with black spruce and a lichen or feather moss understory, reflecting the droughty nature of the sandy Brunisolic soils that are characteristic of these upland areas. Dense stands of black spruce, with an understory of Labrador tea, sphagnum, and feather mosses, are typical of the depressional area, although treeless sedge fens are also found.

E4. Christina Plain

The Christina plain occurs between Peter Pond Lake and the Alberta border. The plain is reasonably level, ranging in elevation from 600 m in the Grizzly Bear Hills west of Peter Pond Lake to about 500 m along the Kimowin River. With the exception of a small area along the Alberta border, which drains west into the Athabasca River, the area drains into Peter Pond Lake via the Kimowin and Dillon rivers.

The landscape ranges from strongly rolling in the Grizzly Bear Hills, to level and gently undulating along the Alberta border, where large tracts of shallow peatlands are common. Peatlands occupy about 15% of the landscape. Otherwise the surficial deposits consist mainly of loamy textured glacial till with lesser amounts of sandy glaciofluvial deposits. Gray Luvisolic soils are typically associated with the loamy till deposits, whereas Dystric Brunisols are found on the sandy materials.

The vegetation is predominantly coniferous forest, with black spruce and, to a lesser extent, jack pine being the dominant trees. The dense but short black spruce stands are commonly associated with the shallow organic deposits along the Alberta border. Coniferous stands along with stands of trembling aspen and mixed stands of trembling aspen and white spruce or jack pine are common elsewhere.

E5. Dillon Plain

The Dillon plain is a relatively level to gently undulating area that slopes gently northward from an elevation of about 500 m at the base of the Mostoos upland to about 400 m at Peter Pond Lake. Surface drainage is via the Dillon, Nipin, and McCusker rivers, which originate to the southwest in the Mostoos upland.

The surficial deposits comprise largely loamy textured glacial till, which is overlain in places by sandy glaciofluvial sediments. Gray Luvisolic soils are found on the loamy textured sediments, whereas Dystric Brunisols are characteristic on the sandy materials. About 40% of the landscape is peatland.

The vegetation is largely a mixedwood forest of trembling aspen, white spruce, and jack pine. Local stands of jack pine are found in some of the sandy sites, and some black spruce stands are found on the peatlands. Most of the peatlands, however, are treeless or sparsely treed fens.

E6. Île-à-la-Crosse Plain

The Île-à-la-Crosse plain is a relatively level to gently rolling area between Lac Île-à-la-Crosse and Churchill Lake. Elevations only range from about 425 to 450 m. Surface drainage is either directly into Lac Île-à-la-Crosse, or into Churchill Lake and then southward into Lac Île-à-la-Crosse via the MacBeth channel.

Typical of landscapes adjacent to the Shield, this area exhibits a ridged and swale pattern oriented in a northwest-southeast direction, reflecting the underlying bedrock surface and the direction of glacial ice movement. The ridges comprise, for the most part, sandy glacial till sediments and Brunisolic soils. Dense stands of jack pine, sometimes mixed with black spruce, are common on the ridges. The intervening depressions or swales are largely treeless fens, although scattered tamarack and black spruce occur in some areas.

Along either side of the MacBeth channel, Luvisolic soils, developed on loamy glacial materials, are dominant. The landscape here does not exhibit the ridge and swale pattern found elsewhere. Moreover, better soil conditions favor the growth of trembling aspen and white spruce, which are rarely found on the sandy Brunisolic soils. In the vicinity of Lac Île-à-la-Crosse, forest cover is mostly trembling aspen with some white spruce toward northern portions of the lake. The water in the lake, unlike other parts of the Churchill River system, contains floating algae and pollen, increasingly so in the latter part of summer.

E7. Canoe Lake Lowland

The Canoe Lake lowland is a level, low-lying area extending north from Canoe Lake to Kazan Lake. This area has a very gentle regional slope from 470 m on the western side to 440 m on its eastern margin. Canoe Creek enters the area from the west, and flows into Canoe Lake. The Canoe River flows eastward from Canoe Lake and is joined by the Apps River before reaching Lac Île-à-la-Crosse.

Over 95% of the area is organic terrain. The remainder comprises islands of sandy glaciofluvial sediments scattered throughout the peatlands, along with loamy textured sediments found along the shore of Canoe Lake itself. The bulk of the peatland is of fen origin, although there are significant areas of bog.

Scattered tamarack and black spruce, along with sedges and swamp birch, are characteristic of the fens, whereas in the bogs, black spruce, as usual, gains prominence. Discontinuous permafrost occurs near Canoe Lake. Scrubby jack pine are found on the islands of mineral soil, while trembling aspen with a few white spruce can be found along the shores of Canoe Lake.

E8. Mostoos Upland

The Mostoos upland is a major, bedrock-controlled upland located along the Alberta border near Primrose Lake. Elevations range from about 525 m along the upper escarpment to over 750 m in the Mostoos Hills themselves. Surface drainage is, for the most part, to the north and east, either into Peter Pond Lake via the MacCusker and Nipin rivers, or locally into Canoe Lake and eventually into Île-à-la-Crosse and the Churchill River system. A small area at the upper elevations drains locally into Primrose Lake and south via the Martineau River into Cold Lake and the Waterhen River system.

The landscape is mainly a hummocky moraine, although along the moderately sloping north-facing slopes, the terrain is often dissected by numerous drainage channels. The surficial deposits are mainly weakly calcareous, loamy textured glacial till deposits, although in many areas the till is overlain by sandy and gravelly glaciofluvial sediments. Gray Luvisolic and Dystric Brunisolic soils are dominant on the loamy and sandy materials, respectively. The poorly drained depressional areas account for about 30% of the area and, as usual, are characterized by organic or peat materials. Most of the organic landforms are fens, although permafrost in bogs has been reported near Cold Lake.

Coniferous stands of jack pine, occasionally mixed with black spruce, are dominant on the well-drained sites, while mixed stands of trembling aspen and jack pine or white spruce, along with pure stands of trembling aspen and white spruce, also occur. The bulk of the peatlands are characterized by sedges and scattered tamarack and black spruce.

E9. Primrose Plain

The Primrose plain is a level, low-lying tract of organic terrain surrounding Primrose Lake. The elevation is about 600 m, and surface drainage is into Primrose Lake.

The surficial glacial materials are loamy textured glacial till and clayey glaciolacustrine sediments. The glaciolacustrine deposits were derived from erosion of the surrounding uplands during deglaciation. These sediments are generally less than 2 m thick, and along with the glacial tills are, for the most part, overlain by organic deposits. Most of the peatlands are of fen origin.

The vegetation, typical of fens, is characterized by sedges, swamp birch, and a scattering of tamarack and black spruce. Dense black spruce stands occur on the few isolated bogs in the area. Permafrost has been reported in bogs near Primrose Lake. The well and imperfectly drained mineral soils, which occupy about 20% of the area, are characterized by jack pine and black spruce.

E10. Mostoos Escarpment

The Mostoos escarpment, as the name implies, comprises the prominent steep south- and east-facing slopes of the Mostoos Hills. Elevations range from 525 m at the base of the escarpment to over 750 m. Surface drainage is either south into the Waterhen River or east into Keeley Lake.

The landscape is characterized by a moderately to steeply sloping, eroded escarpment dissected by numerous deep-set, well-defined valleys. Many of these large valleys have relatively small streams, called "misfit streams," indicating the valleys were former glacial meltwater channels. The oblique alignment of the valleys relative to the slope is also indicative of their glacial origin. The surficial deposits are largely glacial till with some shallow glaciofluvial sands and gravels. This landscape, in contrast to the surrounding terrain, is almost devoid of wetlands.

The forests are mostly of trembling aspen, reflecting the south-facing exposure, although in the valleys themselves, the aspen is often mixed with white spruce or jack pine.

E11. Waterhen Plain

The Waterhen plain lies east of the Mostoos escarpment, sloping gradually northward from an elevation of 525 m southeast of Waterhen Lake to about 430 m at Canoe Lake. Surface drainage is either to the east and north via the Waterhen and Beaver rivers, or north into Canoe Lake via the Keeley River.

The landscape of the Waterhen plain is extremely variable due in part to the nature and origin of the stratified surface sediments which overlie the glacial till in most areas. The bulk of the stratified sediments was derived initially from erosion of the valleys in the Mostoos escarpment. These sediments were carried eastward and deposited in confined basins or channels on the ice surface in the adjacent lowland. Later the sediments were redeposited when the ice melted. This type of deposition almost predictably yields a chaotic distribution of sediments and landscape features. Evidence of this type of deposition can be found east of Waterhen Lake, where hummocky, steeply sloping, water-lain sediments are found at elevations considerably above the surrounding terrain. In the northern part of the plain, between Keeley and Canoe lakes and along the base of the escarpment, the glacial tills are overlain by a shallow layer (50 cm) of sandy stratified sediments. Along the west side of the Beaver River, hummocky, steeply sloping, sandy, stratified sediments are also found at elevations significantly above that of the surrounding terrain. Organic terrain accounts for about 15% of the area and, as usual, is confined to the low-lying depressional areas of the landscape.

Reflecting the influence of the underlying sediments, the vegetation is diverse, varying from stands of pure trembling aspen and mixed stands of trembling aspen and white spruce on the loamy glaciolacustrine deposits in the south, to mixedwoods along the base of the escarpment, to sparse stands of jack pine associated with the sands south of Keeley Lake and along the Beaver River.

E12. La Plonge Plain

The La Plonge plain extends north from Lac La Plonge to the Shield and is bounded on the west by Lac Île-à-la-Crosse and on the east by Pinehouse Lake. The highest elevation, at about 550 m, occurs near the geographic centre of the plain, from which the landscape slopes away in all directions. Surface drainage ultimately ends up into the Churchill River system, which follows the northern boundary of the La Plonge plain, although in the western part of the area, most of the streams first empty into the Beaver River or Lac Île-à-la-Crosse. In the eastern part, most streams empty directly into Pinehouse Lake at an elevation of about 400 m.

The landscape in the La Plonge plain exhibits a distinctive ridge and swale pattern similar to that of the Île-à-la-Crosse plain and other landscape areas neighbouring the Shield. The ridges are oriented in a northwest-southeast direction, which reflects the nature of the underlying bedrock and the direction of glacial ice movement. The surficial deposits consist of sandy glacial till derived largely from the Cretaceous sandstone bedrock. In the depressional areas or swales, the glacial till sediments are overlain by organic deposits mostly of fen origin.

As expected on these dry sandy deposits, the vegetation is dominated by jack pine with an understory of either lichen or feather moss, depending upon the stand density. In the poorly drained depressional areas, the vegetation comprises mainly sedges and swamp birch, along with scattered tamarack and black spruce.

E13. Mahigan Lake Plain

The Mahigan Lake plain extends south from Lac La Plonge to Dore Lake and then eastward past the north shore of Smoothstone Lake. The plain itself slopes eastward from an elevation of 550 m along the north shore of Dore Lake to 425 m northeast of the Swan Lakes. Apart from a few streams that empty directly into Lac La Plonge and Dore Lake, surface drainage is via the Smoothstone River, which flows northeastward through the area and eventually empties into Pinehouse Lake.

The Mahigan Lake plain comprises two distinct landscapes. In the western part, between Lac La Plonge and Dore Lake, the terrain is largely a gently to moderately sloping hummocky moraine. Gray Luvisolic soils, developed in loamy textured glacial till, are dominant, although in some cases, the till is overlain with sandy deposits that are less than 1 m thick. The vegetation consists mainly of mixed stands of trembling aspen and white spruce. The undrained depressions are dominated by organic deposits. Most of the organic landforms are bowl bogs, which are characterized by dense stands of black spruce.

The eastern part of the plain is dominated by large tracts of organic terrain. Most are of fen origin, although densely treed black spruce bogs are also found. Scattered throughout the fen landscape are islands of sandy glaviofluvial sediments occasionally mixed with or underlain by loamy glacial till. These sandy mineral soils support mainly jack pine, although occasionally the pine is mixed with black spruce, particularly along the margins of the upland where soil drainage is slightly restricted. A prominent esker extends from the eastern boundary of the area northwest, past the Swan Lakes and then north past Budd Lake. Some parts of the esker have yet to become stabilized by vegetation and are continually being eroded by the wind.

E14. Dore Lake Lowland

The Dore Lake lowland extends northward from Sled Lake, past the west side of Dore Lake, to Lac La Plonge. Elevations range from 425 to 525 m. Surface drainage is northward via the Beaver River, although some streams drain locally into Dore and Sled lakes.

The relatively level landscape is dominated by expanses of both bogs and fens in roughly equal proportion. The bogs, being slightly drier, support dense stands of black spruce, while the fens are dominated by sedges along with sparse stands of tamarack and, to a lesser extent, black spruce. Isolated upland areas of loamy glacial till and glaciolacustrine sediments, often overlain or mixed with sandy glaciofluvial materials, also occur throughout the lowland. The loamy tills and clayey lacustrine sediments support medium to tall stands of trembling aspen and white spruce. Jack pine is generally the dominant component of stands found on the sandy materials. Black spruce is often associated with the jack pine along the transition area between the well-drained uplands and poorly drained organic soil areas.

E15. Smoothstone Plain

The Smoothstone plain comprises the area extending from Sled and Dore lakes eastward past Smoothstone Lake. Elevations range from 460 m at Dore Lake to over 600 m south of Smoothstone Lake. The western part of the area is drained via the Beaver River, while waters from the eastern part empty into the Smoothstone River.

The eastern part of the region is a reasonably uniform, gently undulating glacial till plain characterized by Gray Luvisolic soils and supporting productive stands of trembling aspen and white spruce. Steeply sloping moraines occur near the shore of Smoothstone Lake, and prominent glacial flutings oriented in a northwest-southeast direction are common east of Philion Lake. The depressional areas, as usual, contain organic soils.

West of Smoothstone Lake, however, the landscapes become highly variable, ranging from steeply sloping hummocky moraines with high local relief along the south shores of both Dore and Beaupré lakes, to almost level, clayey glaciolacustrine plains southeast of Mirasty Lake. Several large peatlands of both bog and fen origin can also be found in the vicinity of Sled and Beaupré lakes. Sandy glaciofluvial sediments, including a prominent esker, can be found between Beaupré and Dore lakes. Apart from the organic soils, which are either treeless or support tamarack and black spruce, and the isolated sandy areas, which support jack pine, medium to tall stands of trembling aspen and white spruce are dominant vegetation types.

E16. Clarke Lake Plain

The Clarke Lake plain is an extensive area of low relief extending west from the base of the Waskesiu upland to the Beaver River. Elevations range from 500 to 575 m. The eastern part of the area drains locally into the Clarke Lakes and then north into Smoothstone Lake; the western part drains north via the Cowan and Beaver rivers, or directly into Sled Lake.

The Clarke Lake plain is characterized by two major landscapes. About 60% of the area is a gently undulating glacial till plain, although shallow clayey glaciolacustrine sediments are commonly found overlying the till on the lower slopes. Productive stands of trembling aspen and white spruce, along with scattered stands of pure trembling aspen, are the most common types of vegetation on these landscapes. The remaining 40% of the area is peatland, with large tracts being found in the vicinity of the Clarke Lakes. Most of the peatlands are fens, which are often either treeless or support sparse stands of tamarack and black spruce. Numerous bogs supporting moderate to dense stands of black spruce also occur in the area.

E17. Leoville Hills

The Leoville hills is a rugged upland area of moderate to high local relief, extending from Green Lake south almost to Highway 3 east of Spiritwood. Elevations range from 525 m near the south end of Green Lake to over 670 m in the southern part of the region. Apart from the extreme northern part of the upland, which drains into Green Lake, the area drains eastward into the Big River, which empties into Cowan Lake and eventually into the Beaver River.

The Leoville hills are largely a hummocky glacial till plain. Rugged, steeply sloping landscapes are common, particularly in the southern part of the plain, and along Tea Creek, which empties into Green Lake. The surficial deposits are mainly loamy textured glacial till, although significant areas of sandy glaciofluvial sediments are also found. In some cases the sandy materials overlie the till on the lower slopes. Organic soils are confined to small undrained depressions or along stream channels.

Pure and mixed stands of trembling aspen and white spruce dominate on the well-drained, loamy glacial till, while balsam poplar occurs on imperfectly drained soils. Mixed stands of trembling aspen, white spruce, and jack pine occur to a lesser extent. Balsam fir and white birch are present, but not abundant. Black spruce and tamarack are the dominant tree species on the poorly drained peatlands.

E18. Waskesiu Upland

The Waskesiu upland includes the upper elevations of Prince Albert National Park as well as the upland area north of the park known as the Thunder Hills. Elevations range from 550 m at the base of the upland to over 750 m. The system of external drainage consists mainly of streams that originate in the upland and, controlled by its relief, drain downslope to the adjacent lowlands. The upland in the southern part drains to the south via the Sturgeon and Spruce rivers, which empty into the North Saskatchewan River near Prince Albert. The remainder of the upland drains eastward into Montreal Lake and then northward into the Churchill River system via the Montreal River.

Like most major uplands in the province, the landscape is primarily a hummocky glacial till plain. At the upper elevations the landscapes are gently undulating to moderately rolling, although those in the northern part are generally rougher and have steeper slopes than those in the south. Surficial sediments are comprised mainly of loamy textured glacial till, although clayey glaciolacustrine sediments, derived from erosion of the surrounding uplands during deglaciation, occur sporadically in the southern regions. In most instances, the knolls and upper slopes are comprised of glacial till, with the clayey stratified sediments overlying the till on the lower slopes. Glaciolacustrine sediments are rare in the northern part of the upland, but shallow sandy materials are commonly found overlying the till on the lower slopes. As usual in these types of landscapes, the depressional areas are filled with organic materials. Steeply sloping escarpments dissected by numerous large, deep-set valleys occur in the southern part of the upland. Many have relatively small streams, called "misfit streams," indicating the valleys were likely former glacial meltwater channels. Areas of sandy and gravelly sediment are often found at the base of the escarpment. The steeply sloping escarpments, in contrast to the upper plateau-like tops of the uplands, are almost devoid of wetlands except along the small creeks themselves.

Mixed stands of trembling aspen and white spruce are dominant on the well-drained sites in the southern part of the upland. In the northern part of Prince Albert National Park and to the south in the Thunder Hills, coniferous stands of jack pine and black spruce are by far the most prevalent. Black spruce and tamarack are, as expected, the dominant tree species on the poorly drained peatlands.

E19. La Ronge Lowland

The La Ronge lowland lies between the northern escarpments of the Waskesiu and Wapawekka uplands and the Canadian Shield. In general, the area slopes gently northward from an elevation of about 535 m at the base of the Wapawekka hills to 400 m along the south boundary of the Shield. Surface drainage is provided by the Smoothstone, Montreal, Bow, and Nipekamew rivers and their tributaries. Many of these streams originate in the Waskesiu and Wapawekka uplands, flow north through the La Ronge Lowland itself, and empty into Lac La Ronge and Pinehouse Lake.

The relatively level landscape is considered to be an ice-scoured plain developed from glacial-modified lower Cretaceous sand and Precambrian erratics. Topography ranges from gently undulating to moderately rolling. In the southern part, between the Thunder and Wapawekka hills, the surficial deposits are a mix of sandy loam glacial till and sandy glaciofluvial deposits. Some of the area of glaciofluvial origin appears to have been reworked by wind, giving the local topography a dune-like appearance. Near the Shield, between Lac La Ronge and Pinehouse Lake, the materials are dominantly of sandy glacial till origin similar to those in the La Plonge and Île-à-la-Crosse plains, which also border the Shield. Poorly drained bogs and fens account for over 40% of the area. Large tracts are found in the vicinity of Emmeline Lake.

As expected on these dry sandy-textured soils, the upland vegetation is dominated by jack pine with an understory of lichens or feather mosses. The intervening, poorly drained areas are forested with tamarack and black spruce. Long stretches of sluggish, marshy streams connect scattered lakes as they wind through a relatively flat topography compared to the Shield. Trembling aspen and white spruce are of much less importance here than in the uplands to the south.

E20. Wapawekka Upland

The Wapawekka upland extends from Wapawekka Lake south to East Trout Lake and east to Big Sandy Lake, and comprises what is known locally as the Wapawekka and Cub hills. It represents the northern extent of the Manitoba escarpment. Elevations range from 400 m to over 800 m, with the strongly dissected escarpments rising in places as much as 240 m in less than 5 km. Apart from the extreme southwest corner, which is drained by the Nipekamew River northward into the Churchill system, the upland drains locally into Deschambault and Wapawekka lakes, which are part of the Saskatchewan River system.

The upland itself is a gently undulating to hilly morainic plain, with strongly dissected north- and east-facing escarpments. Surficial deposits consist mainly of loam and clay loam textured glacial till, and to a lesser extent, of sandy glaciofluvial and organic deposits. Along the western boundary, fluvial sands are commonly found overlying the loamy glacial till on the lower slopes.

On the plateau-like top of the upland, the landscapes exhibit a ridged or fluted pattern oriented in a northwest-southeast direction, marking the direction of glacial ice movement. The intervening swales contain organic deposits. The glacial tills are reddish coloured and are extremely impermeable, resulting in an abundance of imperfectly and poorly drained soils.

The vegetation is dominated by coniferous stands of black and white spruce. There are large blocks of upland black spruce near Little Bear Lake. The fluted moraine on the hilltop supports a black spruce forest on the ridges, while a fen-like, very wet bog inhabits the swales. Black spruce also occurs together with jack pine throughout much of the upland. Mixedwood stands are confined mainly to the steeply sloping escarpment areas. Peatlands, which occupy about a quarter of the area, support mostly black spruce and, to a lesser extent, tamarack. A rare orchid called the northern twayblade has been found here, along with several other species recorded in fewer than 10 provincial locations.

E21. Montreal Lake Plain

The Montreal Lake plain parallels the eastern and western sides of Montreal Lake between the Waskesiu upland to the west and the Whiteswan upland to the east. Elevations range from about 480 m to 520 m. Local drainage is into Montreal Lake and thus to the Churchill River.

The western part of this relatively low-lying area is an undulating to gently rolling till plain, which slopes eastward toward Montreal Lake. Loamy textured glacial tills, which are occasionally overlain with shallow (less than 1 m) sandy glaciofluvial deposits, local areas of sandy and gravelly outwash, and organic deposits, are the major surficial deposits. The area east of the lake is a mix of organic deposits and shallow sandy deposits overlying till. Prominent ridges oriented in a north-south direction are common. Nearly one-half of the Montreal Lake plain is organic terrain, with extensive areas found east of Montreal Lake.

The Montreal Lake plain is characterized by a diversity of forest types including pure and mixed stands of trembling aspen and white spruce, particularly along the western boundary of the area. Pure stands of jack pine are, as usual, found on the sandy outwash deposits, although areas of jack pine, occasionally mixed with black spruce, are also found on the well-drained glacial till landforms. Black spruce and tamarack are dominant on the peatlands.

E22. Emma Lake Upland

The Emma Lake upland extends in an arc south of the Waskesiu upland and then east almost to Candle Lake. In general the terrain slopes to the south from an elevation of about 600 m at the base of the Waskesiu and Whiteswan uplands to about 525 m along its southern boundary. Drainage is to the North Saskatchewan River mainly via the Sturgeon, Spruce, and Whitefox rivers.

The landscape, for the most part, is a hummocky glacial till plain characterized by a series of knolls, intermediate slopes, and undrained depressions. Near the south-facing escarpment of the Waskesiu Hills, however, there are numerous sandy and gravelly outwash areas.

These sandy and gravelly sediments were likely derived from the eroded valleys of the adjacent Waskesiu hills escarpment and were subsequently deposited in the flood plains of the Spruce River and other streams. Glaciolacustrine silts and clays also occur there occasionally.

Along the southwest corner of Prince Albert National Park, the landscapes consist of a level to gently sloping glacial till plain, which is considered to be the result of glacial erosion. The northwest-southeast orientation and the elongated shape of many of the lakes and depressional features in this region mark the direction of glacial ice movement.

Loamy textured Gray Luvisolic soils supporting medium to tall stands of trembling aspen are characteristic of most of the upland. In the southern part of the upland, the sandy glacoiofluvial sediments are characterized by Dark Gray Chernozemic soils, which support mainly trembling aspen, although some small areas of isolated fescue grasslands are found. These areas represent the northernmost extension of grassland plant communities and Chernozemic soils in this part of Saskatchewan. Organic soils supporting sparse stands of tamarack and black spruce account for about 15% of the total area.

E23. Whiteswan Upland

The Whiteswan upland extends south and west from the Wapawekka upland. Elevations are slightly lower than in the Wapawekka upland, ranging from about 450 to 670 m. Like most major uplands, external drainage consists mainly of streams that originate in the upland and, controlled by its relief, drain downslope to the adjacent lowlands. Apart from the northwest part of the upland, which drains north via the Bow River and eventually into the Churchill River system, the upland is drained by the Torch and White Gull rivers south and east into the Saskatchewan River system.

The landscape consists mainly of a roughly undulating to strongly rolling morainic plain, although in the northern part the glacial till is often overlain by 15 to 60 cm of sandy sediments of glaciofluvial origin. Large tracts of organic deposits along with some sandy glaciofluvial sands occur at the lower elevations east of Candle Lake.

At the upper elevations north of Candle Lake, the forests comprise mainly mixed and pure stands of trembling aspen and white spruce, along with significant areas of jack pine, which is sometimes mixed with black spruce. The organic terrain is characterized mainly by black spruce, although scattered tamarack are commonly found in the fen areas.

E24. White Gull Plain

The White Gull plain is a low-lying area that slopes gently southward from an elevation of 450 m at the base of the Whiteswan upland to about 400 m at its southern boundary. Surface drainage is via the Torch River and the White Gull and Falling Horse creeks, all of which flow south and east into the Saskatchewan River.

The landscape is mainly a level to gently undulating outwash plain comprising sandy and gravelly glaciofluvial sediments derived from the erosion of the uplands to the north and west. The prominent exception is the Narrow Hills in the extreme northern part. The hills themselves, which are only a few kilometres wide and several kilometres in length, are composed of a series of ascending ridges oriented in a northwest-southeast direction and are probably part of an esker complex. Some steeply sloping dunes are also found in this region. Organic deposits are scattered throughout the plain, and account for about 20% of the area.

As expected on these coarse-textured sediments, Brunisolic soils supporting moderate to dense stands of jack pine are dominant. Isolated mixedwood stands occur along the eastern edge of the area. Black spruce and tamarack are confined to the poorly drained organic soils.

E25. Bronson Upland

The Bronson upland is located near the Alberta border and forms the divide between the Churchill River drainage system to the north and the Saskatchewan River system to the south. From the height of land north of Bronson and Peck lakes, at an elevation of about 640 m, surface waters flow both to the south into the North Saskatchewan River via the Monnery and Englishman rivers and Pipestone Creek, and to the north into the Beaver River via Makwa River and Vermilion Creek. Elevations at the base of the upland are about 525 m.

The bulk of the Bronson upland is a moderately sloping, hummocky glacial till plain, although significant areas of gravelly, glaciofluvial deposits occur in the vicinity of Bronson, Peck, and Worthington lakes. Rugged, steeply sloping landscapes are found south of Makwa Lake. Organic deposits are confined to the low-lying, undrained, depressional areas in the landscape and are not extensive.

The forests in the Bronson upland consist mainly of trembling aspen, as opposed to dominantly coniferous and mixedwood stands found to the east in the Thickwood upland. Well-drained glacial till is covered with a dense, continuous canopy of trembling aspen. When left undisturbed, white spruce will form nearly pure stands. Open aspen-white spruce stands occur on dry sandy soils, and the dry sites on heavier soils are covered by aspen of poor height growth. Jack pine is present and may cover large areas following fires. White spruce, together with tamarack or balsam poplar, occur on some wet sites.

E26. Thickwood Upland

The Thickwood upland extends south from Meadow Lake to just past Turtle and Helene lakes. Like the Bronson upland to the west, this upland forms the divide between the Churchill and Saskatchewan river systems. This height of land occurs at an elevation of about 730 to 760 m a few kilometres to the north of Turtle and Helene lakes. South of the divide, most waters flow south into the North Saskatchewan via the Turtlelake River. The bulk of the upland drains north into Meadow Lake and then into the Beaver River, which is part of the Churchill River system.

The Thickwood upland is largely an undulating glacial till plain, although some ridged landforms can be found northeast of Turtle Lake. The ridges are oriented in a northeast-southwest direction, and mark the direction of glacier movement. Surficial deposits are almost exclusively loam to clay loam textured glacial till. Organic deposits, as usual, overlie the till in the low-lying depressional areas and account for up to 20% of the area. Large tracts occur northeast of Turtle Lake. Most of the better drained soils are Gray Luvisols, but because of the relatively level landscapes and compact nature of the till itself, many exhibit evidence of restricted drainage.

The Thickwood upland is considered to have a slightly cooler and more moist climate than the adjacent Bronson upland, in part due to its slightly higher elevation. This, coupled with its slightly finer-textured soils and more subdued topography, favours the growth of coniferous and mixedwood as compared to trembling aspen forests. The latter are largely confined to lower elevations along the margins of the upland. This is similar to other major uplands in this ecoregion such as the Mostoos and Waskesiu uplands. The northern half of the area represents the southern limit of black spruce, and the southern boundary represents the southern extent of jack pine.

In the northern half of the area, jack pine grows on dry sands and on sandy to loamy soils; aspen occurs on most loamy sites. White spruce is an occasional component of the stands on well to imperfectly drained sites. Peat occurs frequently in depressions under open sedge and tamarack vegetation, or under sphagnum moss and black spruce cover.

In the southern half, areas of adequate soil moisture are covered with a dense, continuous canopy of trembling aspen. When left undisturbed, white spruce will form nearly pure stands. Open aspen-white spruce stands occur on dry sandy soils, and the dry sites on heavier soils are covered by aspen of poor height growth. Jack pine is present and may cover large areas following fires. White spruce, together with tamarack or balsam poplar, occur on some wet sites. Peat may accumulate in poorly drained areas under a sedge or willow cover.

E27. Pasquia Escarpment

Over a distance of less than 10 km, the Pasquia escarpment slopes steeply from the edge of the Pasquia plateau at an elevation of over 600 m, to the base of the hills at an elevation of less than 300 m. The entire Pasquia Hills upland, which is a thinly glaciated plateau overlying an Upper Cretaceous shale bedrock core, forms part of the Manitoba escarpment, or First Prairie Steppe. As described in the Pasquia Plateau landscape area, fine-textured, shale-modified glacial till was deposited on the top of the bedrock. Although the drift is thick at the top of the escarpment, it is thin and discontinuous on the mid to lower parts, resulting in shale outcrops. Gray Luvisols have developed on the glacial till deposits, while Dark Gray Chernozemic soils have developed on the highly calcareous, shallow, clayey glaciolacustrine deposits, which occupy a small section of the southwestern part of the area.

Included in this landscape area are the Pasquia beaches, a narrow belt of shoreline deposits left by former Lake Agassiz. It consists of a series of parallel, sandy and gravelly beach ridges descending from the base of the main escarpment at 390 m to an elevation of around 275 m on the north and 335 m on the east. A mix of colluvial sands, clays, and shales have intermixed with the beach deposits and, depending upon the texture and relative slope position, are characterized by Regosolic, Brunisolic, and weakly developed Chernozemic soils. Organic terrain, accounting for about 15% of the entire Pasquia escarpment, is common between the ridges. External drainage here is poor except where the streams and rivers descending from the hills cut through the beach ridges.

The dominant landscape is a moderate to steeply sloping, dissected morainal escarpment, with gently undulating terrain, both glaciolacustrine and colluvial, sloping away from the base. The steep dissected landscape allows for extensive external drainage on the escarpment. Considerable water is carried by the many streams and rivers during spring thaw or after heavy rains. The northern escarpment drains into the Carrot River via rivers such as the Papikwan, Cracking, Waskwei, Man, Pasquia, and Jordan, on its route to the Saskatchewan River. The Fir, Greenbush, and Prairie rivers drain the southern escarpment into Lake Winnipegosis via the Red Deer River, while the Overflowing River drains directly into this lake. The entire drainage system for the Pasquia escarpment eventually terminates in Hudson Bay.

The tree species include a mixture of trembling aspen, balsam poplar, white birch (most common on the northeast part of the escarpment), white spruce, and balsam fir, while high and low bush-cranberry, beaked hazelnut, willow, green alder, mountain maple, and wild red raspberry often occur as the understory. In the beaches area, vegetation ranges from a mixture of jack pine, trembling aspen, and white spruce on the ridges, to a luxuriant growth of balsam poplar, white spruce, and white birch on the better drained colluvial soils, to black spruce and tamarack on the poorly drained colluvial and organic deposits.

E28. Pasquia Plateau

The Pasquia plateau forms the top of the Pasquia Hills upland. Successive ice advances and retreats removed materials from lowland areas and deposited a thick mantle of drift (up to 300 m thick) on the Upper Cretaceous shale bedrock. Ice eventually advanced over the top of the upland, leaving pronounced northwest-southeast flutings in the central area. Organic deposits account for approximately 50% of the plateau, occurring mainly in the southwest half of the area. Gray Luvisol soils have formed in the heavy-textured, shale-modified glacial till in the northeast portion of the plateau. The glacial till in the central area does not have the shale modification and, as a result, is coarser textured. Throughout the Pasquia plateau, the surface on the glacial till is very stony.

The land rises from elevations of 550 m to over 825 m and contains much internal relief. The landscape is composed of gently sloping organic terrain and moderately to strongly sloping hummocky morainal areas. A drainage divide runs from the southwest to the northeast of the plateau, and extensive external drainage occurs on both sides of this divide. North of the divide, water flows into the Carrot River by way of the Man, Cracking, Waskwei, Pasquia, and Papikwan rivers, eventually flowing into the Saskatchewan River. South of the divide, rivers such as the Fir and Greenbush join the Red Deer River on its way to Lake Winnipegosis, while the Overflowing River drains directly into this lake. All the water from the Pasquia plateau eventually enters the Nelson River system on its way to Hudson Bay.

The well-drained uplands are covered with a mixture of trembling aspen, balsam poplar, white birch, white spruce, and balsam fir, while low and high bush-cranberry, beaked hazelnut, willow, green alder, mountain maple, and wild red raspberry often occur as the understory. Jack pine occurs with black spruce on the plateau-like tops of the higher hills. The poorly drained peatlands are dominantly moss peat supporting stunted stands of black spruce and tamarack of varying densities depending on the thickness of the organic deposit.

E29. Porcupine Hills

The Porcupine Hills area, located in the east-central part of the province, is an island of the Mid-Boreal Upland Ecoregion within the Boreal Transition Ecoregion. It is part of the Manitoba escarpment, and includes the physiographic upland features known as the Greenwater, High Tor, and Piwei hills, as well as Porcupine Mountain and Porcupine escarpment. The Porcupine Hills are underlain by Upper Cretaceous shale bedrock. Glacial drift ranges from 30 to 135 m in depth, although erosion has exposed the shale in some locations, especially along the Swan River Valley. Surficial deposits are largely loam to clay loam, strongly calcareous glacial till; however, clayey glaciolacustrine materials occur on the west side of the Porcupine Hills upland, almost exclusively within the High Tor Hills. Organic deposits, which make up about 10% of the area, overlie the glacial till in low-lying depressional areas. Almost all of the soils in the area are Gray Luvisols, but some Dark Gray Chernozemics occur toward the outer fringes.

The landscape is predominantly a strongly to moderately sloping knob and kettle glacial till plain, with some gently rolling lacustrine plains and many dissected escarpments. Elevations generally exceed 600 m and rise to approximately 760 m on Porcupine Mountain. Because of the knob and kettle landscape, external drainage is limited. The northern part of the area drains northward via the Red Deer River and such tributaries as Etomami, Piwei, and Pepaw rivers, eventually reaching Lake Winnipegosis. The southern part is drained southeast by the Assiniboine, Lilian, Swan, and Woody rivers into Lake Winnipeg and Lake Winnipegosis. All water in this area ultimately drains into Hudson Bay.

The upland forest consists mainly of trembling aspen and white spruce. Swamp birch, black spruce, tamarack, and Labrador tea are associated with the more common bog peatlands, while sedges, cattails, and willows are associated with the fens. Large blocks of black spruce are found on the upper rims of the Hills due to fire and cooler, moister local climate. Approximately 15% of the area is cultivated.

E30. Duck Mountain

Duck Mountain is an island of the Mid-Boreal Upland Ecoregion that occurs along the Manitoba border. This upland area is considered to be part of the Manitoba escarpment and is an Upper Cretaceous shale bedrock high that has been covered with over 200 m of glacial drift. The soils are predominantly a mixture of strongly calcareous, loam to clay loam glacial till and shallow, clay loam glaciolacustrine materials overlying glacial till. Local areas of clayey glaciolacustrine materials, as well as sandy and gravelly materials, occur throughout the area. Organic deposits occur occasionally. Gray Luvisolic soils occur across most of the area; however, along the margins of Duck Mountain, Dark Gray Chernozemics are more common.

The irregular relief is marked by low hills with long, moderate to steep slopes and many deep, wet depressions. Some localized areas of gently to moderately undulating terrain also occur. Elevations rise to over 820 m at the highest point in Manitoba, while the highest elevation reached in Saskatchewan is 685 m. Surface runoff is rapid to excessive, but much water is retained locally in potholes. The entire area drains externally into lakes Winnipeg and Winnipegosis. The Saskatchewan part of Duck Mountain is drained by the Assiniboine and Swan rivers and their tributaries, while the rest of the upland area is drained by rivers such as Pine, Garland, and Drifting.

Duck Mountain is covered with a mixedwood vegetation. The dominant tree is trembling aspen, accompanied by varying proportions of white spruce, balsam poplar, white birch, black spruce, and tamarack. Large white birch can be found along the escarpment of Boggy Creek. There is typically a dense understory of green alder, beaked hazelnut, red-osier dogwood, willows, and mountain maple. Mountain ash is a rare component of the understory. There are numerous wetlands, some of which are peaty. Approximately 15% of the Duck Mountain area in Saskatchewan is cultivated.

Mid-Boreal Lowland Ecoregion

The Mid-Boreal Lowland Ecoregion, as the name implies, represents the nearly level, low-lying part of the Boreal Plain Ecozone. It is situated near the Manitoba border, below the Manitoba escarpment. It is the smallest of the three ecoregions in the Boreal Plain Ecozone, occupying only 2 million hectares or 3% of the province. This lowland area is dominated by fens and other peatlands, with lesser amounts of woodlands, rock, and open water. Less than 10% of this area is used for agricultural purposes.

PHYSIOGRAPHY. The Mid-Boreal Lowland Ecoregion slopes in accordance with the bedrock surface from 450 m at the base of the Wapawekka, Pasquia, and Porcupine hills, to less than 300 m in the central and eastern parts of the area. Glacial deposits mantle the underlying bedrock adjacent to the uplands in the western part of the area but limestone bedrock frequently outcrops further east. Peat and open water also are common in the central and eastern part of the area. Levees border the numerous rivers and creeks, particularly the Sipanok channel, and the Saskatchewan and Red Deer rivers that enter from the uplands to the west and traverse the area. There are also a number of prominent lakes in the region, including Suggi, Namew, Cumberland, and Windy.

GEOLOGY. The bedrock underlying the Mid-Boreal Lowland Ecoregion comprises interbedded sands, silts, and clays of Lower Cretaceous age in the borderlands to the uplands. Limestone and dolomite of Ordovician and Silurian age occur extensively in the north and eastern parts. The bedrock surface slopes

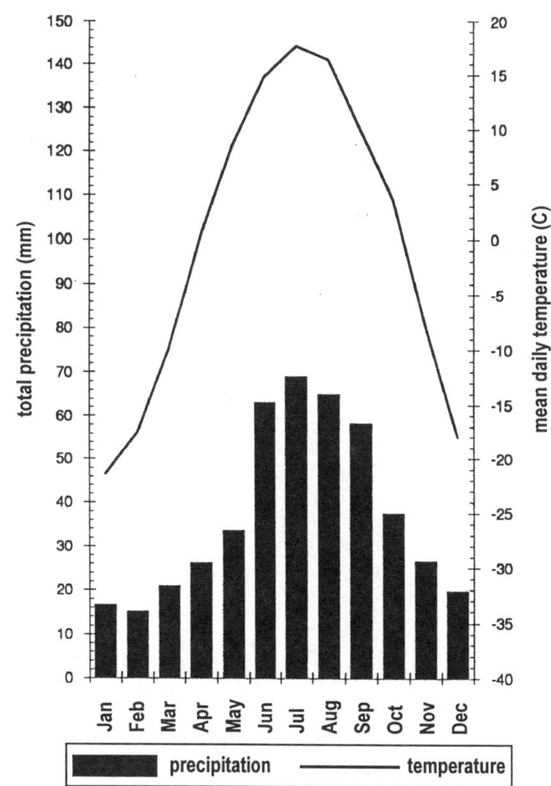

Figure 17. Mean monthly temperature and precipitation for the mid-boreal lowland as represented by the meteorological record from The Pas.

from 300 m on the margin of the uplands to 260 m in the central portion of the area.

Expanses of fen peatland are typical of the Mid-Boreal Lowland Ecoregion.

CLIMATE. The climate of the Mid-Boreal Lowland Ecoregion is transitional between the subarctic climate to the north and humid continental climate to the south. It is generally warmer and wetter than the mid-boreal upland to the west and the boreal shield to the north, but cooler than the more southerly Boreal Transition Ecoregion. The mean annual daily temperature is -0.3°C. The mean July temperature is 17.7°C and the mean January temperature is -21.4°C. The mean annual precipitation is 452 mm, with 282 mm of rainfall occurring from May to September. The summers are short and cool, having a frost-free period of 114 days and a total of 1,395 degree days above 5°C.

LANDFORMS AND SOILS. Dark Gray Chernozemic, Gray Luvisolic, and Eutric Brunisolic soils prevail on the higher elevations adjacent to the uplands, with Organic soils dominating the lower elevations. Regosolic and Gleysolic soils prevail on river levees. The Dark Gray Chernozemic soils are dark-coloured soils that are relatively high in organic matter and are usually calcareous at or near the surface. They are usually associated with imperfectly drained conditions and nearly level landscapes. The Gray Luvisolic soils are named for the prominent gray layer that lies below a thin leaf mat. This gray layer, which is usually depleted in organic matter and clay, is underlain by a layer that is enriched in clay. Gray Luvisolic soils are generally associated with well-drained conditions in areas of higher relief. The Brunisolic soils also have a gray layer beneath the leaf mat that is usually depleted in organic matter and clay, but unlike the Gray Luvisolic soils, this is underlain by a brownish-red layer that is not enriched in clay. The Organic soils are associated with flat bogs and patterned and horizontal fens.

GROUNDWATER. Groundwater in the Mid-Boreal Lowland Ecoregion occurs in association with the drift that covers the bedrock as well as within the bedrock. The Cumberland aquifer occurs within the limestone and dolomite bedrock that prevails throughout most of this ecoregion, and the Mannville aquifer occurs in Lower Cretaceous sands along the southern fringe of the area. Small inter-till and sandy surficial aquifers are also likely to occur along the southern margin where the glacial drift is thicker.

Bedrock, glacial, and surficial aquifers influence the ecology of the area. The sandy surficial deposits that prevail in the western and northern part of the ecoregion provide a water source for lakes such as Big Sandy. The low salt content of these lakes is a reflection of the low salt concentrations in the glacial deposits throughout much of the area. These surface aquifers provide a ready water supply for the vegetation in surrounding areas where the low salt content of these aquifers influences the composition of the plant communities.

VEGETATION. The Mid-Boreal Lowland Ecoregion has the most diverse flora of any ecoregion in the province. The climate favours frost-hardy evergreen species; black spruce would dominate the vegetation on all sites if all disruptive forces were eliminated. The greatest proportion of the mid-boreal lowland is composed of cold, wet peatlands, where peat averages 2 m deep but ranges up to 4 m deep. On saturated sites, black spruce is the only tree of consequence, although tamarack may occur as a pioneer species when light levels are high. On slightly higher ground, marginally merchantable black spruce grows with a willow understory. Given adequate time, white spruce will invade into black spruce on imperfectly drained sites, but competition from black spruce keeps it from becoming a dominant component. On very wet sites, fen vegetation of sedges, willows, and tamarack will dominate. Dolomite outcrops are associated with open jack pine forest. Shallow, highly calcareous till over limestone bedrock supports jack pine, but grades to black spruce if left undisturbed. The high lime content occurring in such areas hinders the growth of trees to some degree.

The levees, which are built up by the periodic deposition of river sediments, rise abruptly from the river channel and then slope gently into a back-swamp area of marshes, fens, and poorly drained meadows. Most of the levees are well drained and represent the most productive forest lands in the province. Large white spruce, balsam poplar, and trembling aspen are found there, sometimes in mixture with balsam fir and white birch, along with an assortment of less common hardwoods such as American elm, green ash, and Manitoba maple. Hardwoods will persist in the mix until spruce forms a closed canopy; they can reproduce under their own canopy, but not under a dense spruce canopy. The rich alluvium supports a luxuriant understory that includes ferns and horsetail. On slightly higher land and back from the floodplain, ridges of sand and gravel, which are beach remnants of postglacial lakes, carry pine and spruce forests with a heath-shrub undergrowth.

There are five major vegetation groups in the ecoregion: peatlands, black spruce forest, mixedwood forest, jack pine forest, and boreal wetlands.

Black spruce forest occurs extensively in the wetter, more poorly drained forest areas, but it also occurs extensively on moderately well-drained sites. On the latter, it occurs in a very high stand density, causing trees to be tall and thin without much taper. Complete feather moss ground cover and an absence of shrubs is characteristic, due to low light levels. Only small amounts of bunchberry, bog cranberry, common horsetail, bishop's-cap, northern comandra, Canada blueberry, twinflower, and Labrador tea can be found on these sites. On imperfectly drained sites, balsam poplar and tamarack are minor components; at an earlier stage in succession, tamarack was likely codominant. A dry phase of black spruce forest can also occur, in which feather mosses are replaced by lichens as the ground cover.

Juniper at the forest edge.

Jack pine forests occupy the relatively well-drained sandy or gravelly plains and low ridges. On very rapidly drained sites, open stands of jack pine exhibit a stunted, twisted form with wide-spreading, lightly foliaged branches and a stocky stem. The forest floor is densely carpeted with Cladonia lichens, along with some Canada blueberry, bearberry, and bog cranberry. There is a sparse scattering of two-leaved Solomon's-seal, blue grasses, and early blue violet.

On well-drained soils or in local depressions, some trembling aspen, white birch, white spruce, black spruce, or balsam fir may be present under the closed jack pine canopy. The crown of the jack pine is reduced to the upper fifth of the tree, and the trunk is slender and relatively straight with little taper. Green alder is a common tall shrub in openings. Other characteristic smaller shrubs include prickly rose and twinflower, with some saskatoon, bristly black currant, and Labrador tea present. The forest floor is often surprisingly bare of herbs, with an abundant feather moss and lichen cover. The scattered herbs most characteristic are bunchberry, starflower, ground cedar, rattlesnake plantain, two-leaved Solomon's-seal, horsetail, early blue violet, and wild sarsaparilla.

Northern pike is one of the most predominant fish species in the ecoregion.

Mixedwood forests occur under well and imperfectly drained conditions, where white spruce is mixed with trembling aspen and balsam poplar.

Peatlands are common throughout this ecoregion, especially in the Saskatchewan River delta. They include open and treed fens and treed bogs.

WILDLIFE. The wildlife populations of this ecoregion are relatively high, reflecting a more favourable climate and greater diversity of vegetation than occurs in most parts of the boreal forest and taiga regions in the province. Although the diversity of mammals is relatively low, populations of some species, such as moose, are the highest in the province. Black bear, white-tailed deer, and elk are inhabitants of this ecoregion. Other mammals include beaver, muskrat, woodland caribou, red squirrel, and porcupine.

Camping is a popular tourist activity in the Mid-Boreal Lowland Ecoregion.

This is an important area for waterfowl habitat. Bird diversity is moderately high. There are large numbers of barred owls, and the black-throated blue warbler, which is rarely seen in other parts of the province, breeds in this ecoregion. Other birds include common loon, wood duck, Nashville warbler, blue-winged teal, American coot, Franklin's gull, mallard, and Canada goose; rare species include the barred owl and whip-poor-will.

Northern pike, walleye, and lake whitefish are the most common fish in this ecoregion, but lake sturgeon are also present in the Cumberland House area. Other species include yellow perch, lake trout, goldeye, and mooneye.

Five species of reptiles and amphibians occur in this ecoregion, including the red-sided garter snake, Canadian toad, and wood frog.

HUMAN ACTIVITY. The population of this ecoregion is approximately 5,000 or less than 1% of the Saskatchewan population. The major community is Cumberland House. This ecoregion has large areas of major peat resource potential. Tourism activities include camping, snowmobiling, hunting and sport fishing, ecotourism, hiking, wildlife viewing, cross-country skiing, and canoeing. About 1% of the total land area in this ecoregion is under cultivation. Approximately 1% of the ecoregion is within some form of park or protected area, principally *Wildlife Habitat Protection Act* lands. Forestry is the most important land use. Fishing, trapping, seasonal hunting, and some ranching are other resource uses. Agricultural activities occur locally on the margins of the Porcupine and Pasquia hills uplands.

F1
F2
F3
F4

Landscape Areas

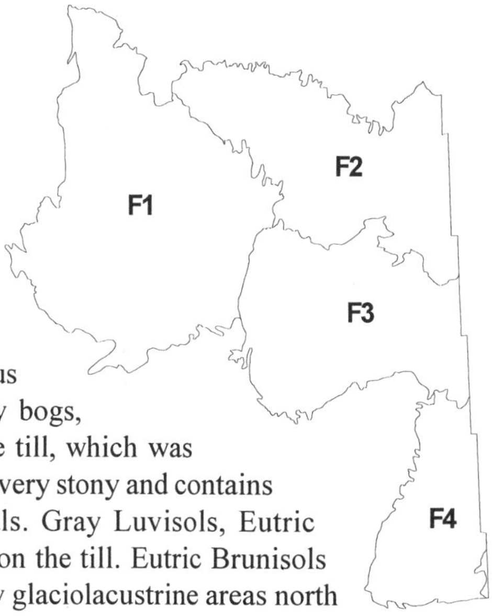

F1. Mossy River Plain

The Mossy River plain lies at the western edge of the Mid-Boreal Lowland. It consists of a mixture of eroded glacial till and sandy glaciolacustrine materials underlain by Cretaceous bedrock. Organic deposits, comprising mainly bogs, occupy approximately 70% of the surface. The till, which was eroded by the waters of former Lake Agassiz, is very stony and contains an abundance of sandy and gravelly materials. Gray Luvisols, Eutric Brunisols and Regosolic soils have developed on the till. Eutric Brunisols and Regosolic soils have developed in the sandy glaciolacustrine areas north and east of Big Sandy Lake.

The landscape is flat to gently undulating, and slopes eastward from 442 m at its western edge to 280 m at the Saskatchewan delta. The striking features of the area are the former beaches. The highest strandline, at an elevation of 442 m, is clearly visible along the Wapawekka upland. This marks the western limit of the Mossy River plain. Other strand lines and beaches run more or less transverse to the slope and strongly impede the surface drainage, thereby promoting the development of organic soils. They also provide reasonably continuous thoroughfares for wildlife. The area drains eastward to the Saskatchewan River via the Missipuskiow, Torch, Mossy, and Scarth rivers, and McDougal Creek. The Bear and Ballantyne rivers empty into Deschambault Lake, which is also part of the Saskatchewan River drainage system.

The dominant vegetation on much of the mineral soils is a mixture of black spruce and jack pine. Jack pine dominates the tree layer on the rapidly drained sandy soils, with Canada blueberry, bog cranberry, bearberry, and reindeer moss composing the understory. White spruce and trembling aspen are less prevalent than in other mixedwood areas, although both species are well represented where drainage conditions are favourable, often growing on the well-drained Gray Luvisolic soils. Bogs support stunted black spruce with lesser amounts of tamarack. Common shrubs are willows, swamp birch, Labrador tea, leather-leaf, and bog cranberry, and the ground cover is dominated by sphagnum moss. The fens are composed primarily of sedges, sometimes with a sparse cover of tamarack, swamp birch, or willows.

F2. Namew Lake Upland

The Namew Lake upland is located in the northeastern part of the mid-boreal lowland along the Manitoba border, extending north to the Canadian Shield. Outcrops of the Paleozoic dolomite and dolomitic limestone bedrock occur over approximately 20% of the land area. The dominant surficial deposit is a shallow, sandy loam, strongly to extremely calcareous glacial till, in which Eutric Brunisols have developed. A significant portion of the area is covered by a deposit of weakly to moderately calcareous, clayey glaciolacustrine materials, (deposited in glacial Lake Agassiz) in which Gray Luvisols are the predominant soil. About one-third of the area is a mixture of bogs and fens. The landscape is nearly level to gently undulating, sloping eastward from about 365 m near Deschambault Lake to approximately 275 m at the Manitoba border. The area drains into the Saskatchewan River via the Grassberry River and its tributaries.

The prevailing vegetation on the flat, poorly-drained peatlands consists of patches of black spruce and tamarack, with intervening meadows of sedges and swamp birch. Good stands of white spruce, trembling aspen, and balsam poplar, sometimes in mixture with balsam fir and white birch, occur on the better drained soils. Shallow, extremely calcareous soils often have stands of scrubby trembling aspen. The south shore of Amisk Lake lies ouside the Shield and is lined in places by spectacular dolomite cliffs. A few palsas and peat plateaus, with permafrost, and collapsed palsas occur on fibric organic materials.

Jack pine is common on sand and on bare dolomite outcrops. Trembling aspen and white spruce are dominant on clayey lacustrine deposits, with low bush-cranberry, dewberry, wild sarsaparilla, bunchberry, and prickly rose as characteristic understory.

F3. Saskatchewan Delta

The Saskatchewan delta is a flood plain of the Saskatchewan River and its tributaries which has been subjected periodically to deposition of alluvial materials carried by waters flowing from the Saskatchewan River through the Sipanok and Dragline channels. The delta itself is a gently sloping, poorly drained, alluvial and lacustrine plain often overlain by organic materials. It is underlain by Paleozoic dolomite and dolomitic limestone, which crops out occasionally.

Regosolic soils, which occupy 20% of the area, are found on the fine-textured, stratified, recent levee deposits along rivers and streams. The remainder of the area is characterized mainly by peaty Gleysolic soils. Those near Cumberland House are formed on shallow, clayey, strongly calcareous alluvial materials underlain by glacial till.

The landscape is predominantly level, with elevations that vary from about 280 m at Kennedy Creek in the west to about 265 m at the Manitoba border, a descent of about 15 m in 80 km. Surface drainage is via the Saskatchewan, Carrot, Birch, and Saskeram rivers and their many tributaries.

The bulk of the area is covered by organic deposits, the majority of which are fens, due to the high nutrient status of the water moving through the area. They are frequently saturated with water at or near the surface, and are largely treeless, with a surface cover of cattails, rushes, reeds, sedges, and scattered willows. Some salinity is found in the fens north of the Carrot River, around Goose Lake.

F4. Overflowing River Lowland

The Overflowing River lowland is located along the Manitoba border in the southern part of the Mid-Boreal Lowland Ecoregion. This flat-lying glacial till plain has many subdued beach features and large tracts of organic deposits which cover almost 75% of the landscape; the northern part is almost completely overlain by organic materials. The remainder of the lowland comprises Dark Gray Chernozemic soils formed in a mixture of sandy glaciofluvial materials and clay loam, highly calcareous, water-modified glacial till derived from Paleozoic limestone. Upper Cretaceous shale bedrock underlies the glacial drift at a depth of 3 to 30 m.

The entire lowland is nearly level, gently sloping to the northeast from a western high of 335 to 275 m in the northeast at the Manitoba border. External drainage is to the east into Lake Winnipegosis via the Overflowing, Red Deer, and Armit rivers and to the northeast into Carrot River via the Pasquia River and Niska Creek.

The best stands of forest occur on the better drained mineral soils along the banks of streams, rivers, and drainage ways. They include white spruce, trembling aspen, balsam poplar, American elm, green ash, and Manitoba maple. Willows occur on the more poorly drained mineral soils. Beach ridges and imperfectly drained morainic uplands commonly support jack pine, black spruce, tamarack, and, occasionally, trembling aspen. The dominant vegetation of the bog areas is stunted stands of black spruce and tamarack with an undergrowth of sphagnum moss and Labrador tea. Fen areas support sedges, willows, common cattails, and swamp birch. About 5% of the area is under cultivation.

Boreal Transition Ecoregion

The Boreal Transition Ecoregion represents a transitional area between boreal forest to the north and grasslands to the south. It is a large area of undulating to gently sloping plains, occupying approximately 5.3 million hectares or 8% of the province in a belt extending across central Saskatchewan from the Alberta to the Manitoba border. In several instances, uplands of the Mid-Boreal Upland Ecoregion interrupt this belt. Unlike the other regions in this ecozone, agriculture is a major land use in the Boreal Transition Ecoregion, with nearly 50% of the lands under cultivation.

PHYSIOGRAPHY. The Boreal Transition Ecoregion comprises a series of nearly level to gently sloping glacial till, glaciolacustrine, and glaciofluvial plains interrupted by hummocky morainal uplands. Elevations of the plains drop from 485 m in the Meadow Lake area to 350 m at the break to the Manitoba escarpment near the town of Hudson Bay. Uplands can attain elevations of nearly 800 m. While this topography mirrors the slope of the bedrock surface, most of the region has a cover of glacial drift that is sufficiently thick to obscure the underlying bedrock.

The valleys of the Beaver, North and South Saskatchewan, Saskatchewan, Carrot, Red Deer, and Assiniboine rivers add to the beauty of the region. These river valleys form part of the Nelson River drainage basin. There are few lakes in this ecoregion, especially in comparison to the mid-boreal upland.

GEOLOGY. The bedrock underlying the Boreal Transition Ecoregion is silt and clay shales of late Cretaceous age. The bedrock surface has a general slope from 540 m in the south to 360 m in the north. This surface is covered with 100 m or more of glacial deposits throughout most of the area. Hummocky moraines are most common at higher elevations on these uplands, with glaciolacustrine,

Remnant grasslands found on the arid, south-facing slopes of the Sturgeon River represent the northern extension of grasslands in this ecoregion.

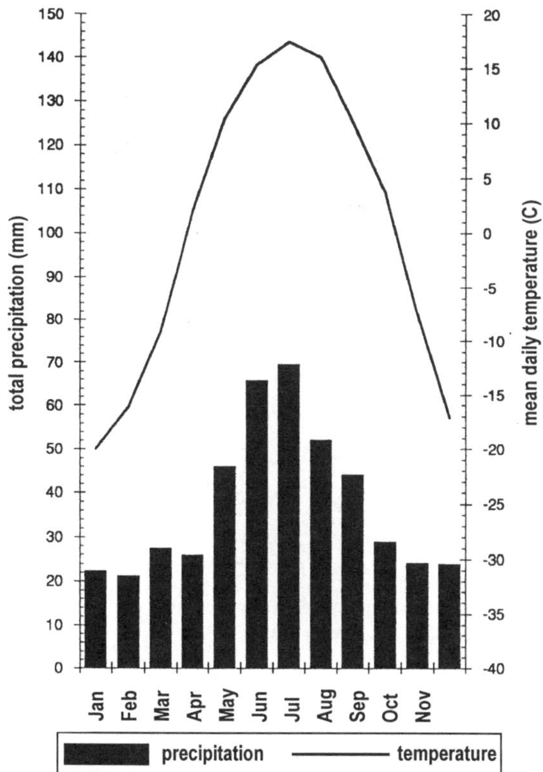

Figure 18. Mean monthly temperature and precipitation for the boreal transition as represented by the meteorological record from Lost River.

glaciofluvial, and glacial till deposits more common on the intervening plains. The glacial tills contain more clay than those to the north, reflecting a stronger influence of the silts and clays that form the bedrock surface in this area.

CLIMATE. The climate of the Boreal Transition Ecoregion is more typical of humid continental climates at lower elevations in the southern part but more like subarctic climates at higher elevations, and in the northern part of the area. As such, it is warmer and drier than the mid-boreal lowland and the mid-boreal upland, but cooler than the more southerly Aspen Parkland Ecoregion. The mean annual daily temperature is 0.4°C. The mean July temperature is 17.4°C and the mean January temperature is -20.0°C. The mean annual precipitation is 452 mm, with 272 mm of rainfall occurring from May to September. The summers are short and cool, having a frost-free period of 94 days and a total of 1,453 degree days above 5°C.

LANDFORMS AND SOILS. The Boreal Transition Ecoregion includes a diverse group of soils, reflecting the transitional ecoclimatic conditions described earlier. Black and Dark Gray Chernozemic soils prevail in areas bordering the aspen parkland where, historically, grasslands have dominated the vegetation, whereas Dark Gray Luvisolic soils occur where forest vegetation has prevailed. Gray Luvisolic soils occur locally on uplands where grasslands were never significant. Regosolic soils occur in sandy brush and shrublands, while Eutric Brunisolic soils occur in well-drained sandy areas under more heavily wooded vegetation. Gleysolic soils occupy imperfectly to poorly drained soils associated with grasslands, and Organic soils are associated with poorly drained portions of forested areas.

GROUNDWATER. Groundwater in the Boreal Transition Ecoregion is associated with the drift that covers the bedrock as well as with the bedrock. There are no major bedrock aquifers in this ecoregion, since much of the bedrock surface is covered with aquitards composed of Cretaceous shale. There is a major buried valley aquifer, the Hatfield Valley aquifer, in this ecoregion. It is part of a major valley that entered the province near Cold Lake on the Alberta border and extended to the Manitoba border east of Regina. Blanket aquifers are important sources of groundwater in the Pathlow area near Melfort. Inter-till aquifers are widely distributed throughout the ecoregion. They are most common in the older and deeper Floral Formation but may also occur within the Battleford Formation. Surficial aquifers are most common along the North and South Saskatchewan rivers southwest of Prince Albert and along the Saskatchewan River west of Nipawin.

Bedrock, glacial, and surficial aquifers influence the ecology of the area. Lakes such as Brightsand derive a considerable amount of their source from aquifer discharge. The quality of the water in these lakes is largely dependent upon the source of the groundwater; higher salt concentrations are associated with discharge from bedrock aquifers and low salt concentrations from near-surface glacial aquifers or from surface aquifers.

Aquifers also impact on the water supply to vegetation. The prevalence of trembling aspen in sandy areas is often a reflection of a surface aquifer in these sediments. Saline soils and salt-tolerant vegetation is often associated with surface concentrations of salts derived from glacial and bedrock aquifers.

VEGETATION. The Boreal Transition Ecoregion is dominantly a deciduous boreal forest characterized by a mix of forest and farmland. It marks the southern limit of closed boreal forest and the northern advance of arable agriculture. Although the native tree species are the same as in the mid-boreal upland, stand composition, development, and tree growth are different. Compared to similar stands on Luvisolic soils in the mid-boreal upland, trembling aspen-white spruce stands have a higher aspen component on Chernozemic soils, and growth for both species is more rapid.

The bulk of the ecoregion was occupied at one time by grassland vegetation, as suggested by the presence of Chernozemic soils, most of which are now cultivated. In the absence of regular fires, the forest has encroached on remaining small isolated patches of grassland, in which the dominants include needlegrasses, wheatgrasses, and plains rough fescue.

Characteristic vegetation of hilly upland areas is a closed cover of tall trembling aspen with a dense understory of herbs and tall shrubs. Balsam poplar is a significant component growing mainly on imperfectly drained soils. Although the understory plants parallel those in the mid-boreal upland, grasses are more common, and northern wheatgrass and hairy wild rye are prominent.

Pure, even-aged jack pine stands characterize fire-prone, dry, nutrient-deficient sandy and gravelly soils. They are occasionally found on dry ridges of loamy till, in association with stunted shrubby aspen.

Before dropping its needles in the fall, the tamarack turns a golden colour.

Black spruce is rarely found on uplands, being confined, along with tamarack, to wet places such as peatlands, which are less common here than elsewhere on the boreal plain; peat thickness usually exceeds 2 m. Tamarack attains its best growth in this ecoregion. Secondary bog flora is the same as that found further north. Occasionally, white spruce is associated with the tamarack.

White spruce is found on all soil materials from peat and sand to clayey lacustrine and loamy till. It prefers north-facing slopes of river valleys, allowing it to penetrate deeply into the aspen parkland. In the absence of other competing conifers, it is able to occupy unusual habitats. Patchy white spruce can be found struggling on rapidly drained areas that seem more appropriate to jack pine. It likely became established during very favourable weather conditions and continues to survive due to lack of competition. This represents an invasion of aspen parkland due to reduced incidence of fire. Openings in the thin white spruce canopy are occupied by struggling aspen, shrubs, and grass. The understory is composed primarily of bluegrass and wheatgrasses, with bearberry as the main low shrub. Saskatoon is scattered throughout. Plants typical of the prairie are also found here, such as plains rough fescue, June grass, early blue violet, and Richardson's needle grass.

There are seven major vegetation groups in this ecoregion: agricultural land, aspen forest, mixedwood forest, jack pine forest, grasslands, peatlands, and boreal wetlands.

Aspen forests prevail under natural conditions, where they are dominated by trembling aspen, but include balsam poplar and occasional white spruce. They dominate rapidly to well-drained slopes and escarpments of major uplands, as well as moderately well to imperfectly drained landscapes at the base of these uplands. Understory plants parallel those of the mid-boreal upland, including broad-leaved herbs such as bunchberry, twinflower, wild sarsaparilla, bishop's-cap, and dewberry.

Mixedwood forests occur on well-drained soils, where white spruce is mixed with trembling aspen and balsam poplar.

Jack pine forests occur throughout the ecoregion, usually associated with rapidly drained, nutrient-poor sandy glacial till, glaciofluvial, and eolian deposits, although they are limited by fire, disease, and weed infestations. Mature stands of jack pine may have an understory of either Canada blueberry or lichens.

Grasslands occur in the drier locations within the Boreal Transition Ecoregion, often mixed with shrubs and trembling aspen. Grasslands dominated by needlegrasses survive in dry habitats and, as a result, are less susceptible to invasion by forest species. Dominant species are porcupine grass, June grass, and dryland sedges. Common shrubs and herbs include snowberry, prickly rose, saskatoon, prairie sage, pasture sage, plains wormwood, and bastard toadflax. Fescue grasslands, which are important elk habitat, are dominated by plains rough fescue. Other typical species include northern bedstraw, yarrow, veiny meadow rue, wild vetch, cream-coloured vetchling, prickly rose, snowberry, and saskatoon. Although forb and shrub species outnumber the grasses, grass cover is typically double that of broad-leaved plants. The proportion of grasses in the cover decreases with increasing moisture. The moister sites are most susceptible to forest invasion, since their existence depends upon fire. In the absence of fire, they will commonly succeed to either an aspen, aspen-pine, or pine forest.

A glint of yellow betrays the presence of a yellow warbler.

Boreal wetlands are not as common in this ecoregion as in other ecoregions of the boreal plains. Both open and treed fens and treed bogs are present. They range in occurrence from plateau-like areas on the top of regional uplands, to nearly level to flat areas between the regional uplands.

WILDLIFE. There is greater diversity of wildlife in the Boreal Transition Ecoregion than in the aspen parkland to the south, but it is not as great as in other parts of the Boreal Plain Ecozone.

Species richness of mammals and birds is high. Mammals include white-tailed deer, moose, elk, black bear, beaver, northern short-tailed shrew, red squirrel, raccoon, and coyote. Birds include boreal chickadee, gray jay, black-and-white warbler, common loon, and red-necked grebe.

The diversity of fish species is high in this ecoregion, with northern pike, walleye, yellow perch, lake whitefish, lake trout, white sucker, burbot, and fathead minnow representative of this diversity.

A moderately rich population of amphibians and reptiles occurs in this ecoregion. It includes red-sided garter snake, tiger salamander, Canadian toad, and the wood frog.

HUMAN ACTIVITY. The population of this ecoregion is approximately 124,000, or 12% of the Saskatchewan population. Major communities include Meadow Lake, Prince Albert, Nipawin, and Melfort. Land uses include forestry, agriculture, hunting, fishing, and recreation. Located within this ecoregion are a panelboard mill, pulp and paper mills at Meadow Lake and Prince Albert, and three saw mills.

The Boreal Transition Ecoregion marks the northern limit of arable agriculture.

The climate in the Boreal Transition Ecoregion is warmer than in the other ecoregions in the Boreal Plain Ecozone and, consequently, it accounts for 95% of the total land under crop production in the ecozone. About 50% of the ecoregion is farmland, producing spring wheat and other cereals, oilseeds, and hay. Forage production for seed and dehydration is also a popular activity in this ecozone. Crop diversity has resulted in long rotations being practiced, with the virtual exclusion of summerfallow.

Approximately 9% of the ecoregion is within some form of park or protected area, the majority of which are *Wildlife Habitat Protection Act* lands.

Landscape Areas

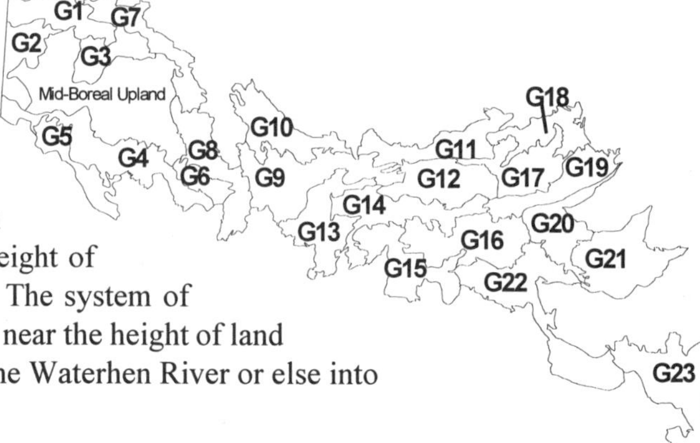

G1. Beaver River Plain

The Beaver River plain encompasses the area between the Beaver and Waterhen river systems extending east from the Alberta border to Golden Ridge. Elevations range from about 560 m at the height of land to about 525 m along the Beaver River itself. The system of surface drainage consists of streams which originate near the height of land and, controlled by the slope, either flow north into the Waterhen River or else into the Beaver River.

The landscape is largely a gently sloping, hummocky moraine. Surficial deposits are mainly loamy textured glacial till, although some sandy glaciofluvial deposits occur along the Beaver and Waterhen rivers. Isolated areas of silty glaciolacustrine sediments are found north of Goodsoil. Extensive areas of organic deposits occur near the Alberta border. Gray Luvisolic soils are characteristically associated with the glacial till sediments, although Dark Gray Luvisols and minor amounts of Dark Gray Chernozemic soils also occur.

About 80% of the area is native forest, with most of the upland areas consisting of trembling aspen and, to a lesser extent, jack pine, which is most often found on the sandy soils. Black spruce and tamarack dominate the organic soil areas. About 35% of the roughly 35,000 ha of cultivated land is sown annually to cereals, with a roughly equal amount planted to perennial forage. Oilseeds represent about 15% of the cultivated land.

G2. Frog Lake Upland

The Frog Lake upland occurs along the Alberta border south of the Beaver River Valley. The bulk of the upland occurs above the 600 m contour and, in places, rises above 670 m. The north slope of the upland descends to an elevation of about 525 m along the Beaver River. The bulk of the area drains northward into the Beaver River; the remainder drains south into the North Saskatchewan River via the Pipestone Creek.

The landscape is dominantly a gently rolling moraine, with moderately and, in places, steeply sloping topography, particularly along the Alberta border north of Onion Lake. Surficial deposits are mainly loamy glacial till with significant areas of sandy or gravelly glaciofluvial deposits. Organic deposits are found in the depressional areas but are not extensive. Gray Luvisolic soils are characteristic of most upland areas, although minor occurrences of Dark Gray Luvisols and Dark Gray Chernozemic soils have been found on the relatively coarse textured sediments at the lower elevations. The vegetation is largely an aspen forest, similar to that further east in the Bronson upland.

G3. Meadow Lake Plain

The Meadow Lake plain extends along the base of the Thickwood Hills escarpment northeast from Makwa Lake through to Meadow Lake. The area slopes in a northeast direction from an elevation of 575 m at the base of the hills to less than 480 m north of Meadow Lake. Apart from local drainage into Meadow Lake, the area is drained mainly by the Makwa River and Morin Creek, which empties into the Meadow River.

The Meadow Lake plain is a level to gently undulating plain that appears to have been eroded during glaciation. Evidence of glacial erosion includes the level landscapes, glacial flutings oriented in a northeast-southwest direction, and the stony nature of the till. In the northeastern part of the plain, near Meadow Lake, the glacial till is overlain by 1 m or more of silty and clayey glaciolacustrine deposits. These deposits support mainly Black and Dark Gray Chernozemic soils and, to a lesser extent, Black Solonetzic soils. In the southern part of the Meadow Lake plain, the surficial deposits consist largely of glacial till, although isolated silty or clayey lacustrine deposits are found occasionally on the lower slopes. Shallow, sandy glaciofluvial deposits are also found to overlie the till in some areas. Dark Gray Chernozemic soils are dominant in this region.

The bulk of the Meadow Lake plain is cultivated, with about 65% used for annual crops (mainly cereals and oilseeds). Perennial forages account for about 20% of the arable land. On average, about 10% of the cultivated land is left in fallow each year. The non-arable land is mainly wetlands, or land which is too stony to cultivate, most of which supports aspen forests.

G4. Onion Lake Plain

The Onion Lake plain extends from the Alberta border eastward along the southern boundary of the Thickwood Hills. Elevations range from almost 800 m south of Meeting Lake to about 550 m along the North Saskatchewan River near the Aberta border. Surface drainage, for the most part, is provided by streams which originate in the Thickwood Hills to the north, flow south through the Onion Lake plain, and empty into the North Saskatchewan River.

With the exception of the steeply sloping glaciofluvial landscapes near the Alberta border, the Onion Lake plain is mainly a gently undulating to moderately rolling glacial till plain. Silty glaciolacustrine sediments are found near Turtleford, but occupy less than 5% of the area. Sporadic occurrences of sandy glaciofluvial sediments also occur there. Dark Gray Chernozemic soils are dominant in most landscapes, while Black Chernozemic soils characterize the sandy glaciofluvial deposits near Turtleford. Luvisolic soils are associated with some of the loamy glacial till deposits along the northern boundary.

Slightly more than half of the area is cropland, with cereals being the main crop. A significant area is planted annually to oilseeds. About 10% of the arable land is in perennial forages, and an equal amount is fallowed. Uncultivated areas are mainly aspen-white spruce forest. The southern boundary of the Onion Lake plain is approximately the southern limit of white spruce. Areas of adequate soil moisture are covered with a dense, continuous canopy of trembling aspen; if left undisturbed, white spruce will invade and form nearly pure stands. Open trembling aspen-white spruce stands occur on dry sandy soils, and the dry sites on heavier soils are covered by trembling aspen of poor height growth. Jack pine is also present and may cover large areas following fires. White spruce, together with tamarack or balsam poplar, occur on some wet sites. Peat may accumulate in poorly drained areas under a sedge or willow cover.

G5. Turtle River Plain

The Turtle River plain lies between the North Saskatchewan River and the Onion Lake plain. Elevations range from over 640 m near Paradise Hill to about 500 m at the river.

The Turtle River plain is mainly an undulating glaciofluvial plain with moderately sloping topography. Glacial till landscapes occur throughout the area and form a prominent upland south of Paradise Hill. Black Chernozemic soils developed on the sandy and sandy loam textured glaciofluvial sediments are dominant, while most of the loamy glacial till is characterized by weak Black Solonetzic soils. The upland south of Paradise Hill is characterized mainly by loamy Dark Gray Chernozemic soils.

The bulk of the Turtle River plain is cropland, with cereals being the dominant crop, accounting for about half of the arable land. About 20% is planted to oilseeds and 15% to forages. Fallow accounts for about 10% to 15% of the cultivated land. Grasslands dominate the natural vegetation of this area, with aspen bluffs of several acres in size, but the extent of woodlands increases toward the north. Grasses grow mainly where moisture is deficient in heavier soils, such as on hills and south slopes. Trees occur in slight depressions or on the northern side of hills where they are not exposed to direct sunshine. Tree species are mainly trembling aspen, with some balsam poplar in moist areas. The height of trees seldom exceeds 15 m. Open aspen stands grow on dry sandy sites and also show poor height growth. Wet sites in depressions are occupied by sedges and by some willows, or by salt-tolerant plants. Scattered white spruce and white birch may occur on favourable sites, such as on gully slopes near rivers.

G6. Meeting Lake Upland

The Meeting Lake upland is part of the Thickwood Hills southwest of Spiritwood. The upland slopes to the northeast from an elevation of about 775 m along its southwestern boundary to 600 m at the base of the Upland near Spiritwood. The bulk of the upland drains northward into Witchekan Lake, which in turns drains north into the Churchill River system. The remainder of the area along its southern and eastern boundaries forms part of the Saskatchewan River drainage system.

The upland itself is largely a hummocky glacial till plain characterized by Gray Luvisolic soils and moderately to steeply sloping togography. Organic soils occupy the undrained depressions.

Only about one-quarter of the land is cultivated, due to the relatively cool climate and stony, infertile soils. The remainder of the area is mostly trembling aspen forest.

G7. St. Cyr Plain

The St. Cyr plain extends in a narrow band southeastward from Greig Lake in the Meadow Lake Provincial Park, along the east-facing slopes of the Thickwood Hills to Chitek Lake. In general, the terrain slopes northward with elevations averaging about 500 to 600 m. With the exception of the northernmost areas, which are drained by the Waterhen River, the plain drains into Meadow Lake and then north into the Beaver River.

The landscape is dominantly a hummocky glaciofluvial plain, with moderately rolling topography. The sandy sediments occurring in this area were likely derived from erosion of the neighboring Mostoos and Thickwood hills. Relatively level landscapes, characterized by silty glaciolacustrine sediments, occur in the vicinity of Dorintosh. The prominent steeply sloping St. Cyr Hills, which occur along the eastern edge of the plain east of Meadow Lake, also comprise varved lacustrine materials. The presence of the water-lain sediment, at an elevation considerably above the surrounding terrain, suggests that the sediments were first laid down in channels or basins in the glacial ice and later redeposited when the ice melted.

Trembling aspen occasionally mixed with pine and white spruce, along with a few pure stands of jack pine, are characteristic of the St. Cyr plain. Because of the sandy soils and, in places, steeply sloping topography, only about 7% of the land is cultivated, mostly on the silty lacustrine soils near Dorintosh.

G8. Witchekan Plain

The Witchekan plain extends from Chitek Lake south along the base of the Thickwood Hills escarpment. Elevations range from over 700 m in the southern part of the plain to about 600 m near Witchekan Lake. The northern part of the plain drains locally into Witchekan Lake and then north via the Big River into the Churchill River system. The remainder of the area drains south and east into the North Saskatchewan River.

In the southern part of the plain, hummocky glacial till landscapes with moderately sloping topography are dominant. The soils are mainly Dark Gray Chernozems with Gray Luvisols found at the upper elevations. Around Witchekan Lake itself, the glacial till landscapes are relatively level, and glaciolacustrine deposits occupy a significant area. Glaciofluvial sands are prevalent between Witchekan Lake and the escarpment to the southwest. Dark Gray Chernozemic soils are dominant, although Gray Luvisols are commonly found at the higher elevations north of the lake.

G9. Shellbrook Plain

The Shellbrook plain lies north of the North Saskatchewan River and east of the Witchekan plain. The terrain, which is at an elevation of about 450 to 500 m, is relatively level but slopes gradually toward the North Saskatchewan River. It is drained by a number of streams which originate in the uplands to the north and flow through the Shellbrook plain on their way to the North Saskatchewan River.

The area is a gently undulating to moderately rolling plain. Along its southern boundary the landscape is characterized mainly by sandy loam fluvial-lacustrine deposits and Dark Gray Chernozemic soils. Extremely sandy stratified deposits, often reworked by wind, also occur, and exhibit typical dune topography characterized by short steep slopes and circular undrained depressions. The soils found on these sandy materials are mainly Brunisols and, to a lesser extent, Regosols and Dark Gray Chernozems.

In the northern part, the surficial deposits are mainly loamy glacial till and glaciolacustrine sediments, although a large tract of sandy eolian sediments occurs south of Canwood. Dark Gray Chernozems are associated with the finer textured deposits, while Brunisolic soils are dominant on the sandy eolian sediments.

Roughly 60% of the area is cultivated, with cereals and oilseeds being the main crops. Forages account for about 15% of the cultivated area. The native areas are mostly pine forest associated with the extremely sandy eolian deposits. Isolated wetlands supporting black spruce and tamarack also occur.

G10. Sturgeon River Plain

The Sturgeon River plain is a moderately rolling glacial till plain forming an arc around the southwestern corner of the Waskesiu Hills. While the overall landscape exhibits a hummocky pattern characterized by numerous undrained depressions or potholes, many of the small lakes and wetlands are elongated in a northwest-southeast direction. This feature, coupled with the fact that the prominent Sturgeon River Valley — which is a former glacial meltwater channel — is oriented in a similar direction, is evidence of the direction of glacier movement.

Elevations range from about 525 m at the base of the Waskesiu Hills and in the northern part of the area, to about 450 m along its southern boundary. Along the northern boundary, water flows northward into either Cowan Lake or Delaronde Lake and from there into the Churchill River system. The remainder of the area drains southward into the Saskatchewan River system, although with the exception of Sturgeon River Valley, external drainage is not well developed and groundwater tables are often high.

In the southern part of the area, Dark Gray Chernozemic soils developed on loamy textured glacial till are dominant. Many of these soils are calcareous at the surface or show evidence of restricted drainage due to a high water table. The low-lying depressional areas are characterized by organic soils, many of which contain marl deposits. Isolated areas of virgin Black Chernozemic soils can be found on the steep south-facing slopes of the Sturgeon

River Valley, as well as on some very sandy deposits along the southwestern boundary of Prince Albert National Park. Gray Luvisolic soils, developed on loamy glacial till which is occasionally overlain with sandy stratified sediments, are dominant in the northwestern part of the area.

Slightly less than half of the Sturgeon River plain is cultivated, with cereals and oilseeds accounting for about 70% of the seeded area. The remaining area is largely trembling aspen forest or wetlands.

G11. Whitefox Plain

The Whitefox plain slopes gently southeastward from an elevation of 500 m at the base of the White Swan upland to an elevation of about 400 m west of Nipawin. Surface drainage is provided by the Whitefox, Torch, and Missipuskiow rivers, all of which empty into the Saskatchewan River east of Tobin Lake.

The terrain is a relatively level glacial till plain which, in places, has been eroded and subsequently overlain by stratified waterlain sediments. Most of the stratified sediments are loamy in texture, except in the Smeaton area where they are mostly sandy and gravelly. Where the eroded till occurs at or near the surface, the soils are often stony. Dark Gray Chernozemic soils are dominant, except in the northeast where Gray Luvisols are commonly found.

About 65% of the area is cultivated, with the usual mix of cereals and oilseeds being dominant. The remainder, uncultivated, occurs mainly north of Smeaton and in the northeast corner and comprises jack pine, trembling aspen, and mixedwood forest.

G12. La Corne Plain

The bulk of the La Corne plain occurs along the Saskatchewan River east of the forks. The landscape is mainly an undulating fluvial-lacustrine plain, with gently sloping topography. However, where the deposits are extremely sandy, they have often been reworked by wind into dunes, giving the landscape a hummocky appearance with short steep slopes and, at times, high local relief. Finer textured deposits occur on rolling topography along the north side of the river near the eastern border.

The coarse, sandy deposits are characterized largely by Brunisolic soils. Gray Luvisolic soils are common on the finer textured sands and silty deposits. Dark Gray Chernozemic and Organic soils each occupy about 10% of the area.

G13. Nisbet Plain

The Nisbet plain extends southwest from Prince Albert along the North Saskatchewan River, east past Duck Lake and then south along the South Saskatchewan River as far as Rosthern. The landscape is primarily a level, sandy glaciofluvial plain, although in places the sediments have been reworked by the wind into dunes. The majority of soils are Eutric Brunisols and Regosols, which are associated with the extremely sandy sediments. Black Chernozemic soils are associated with slightly finer textured materials. Fens occupy about 5% of the area.

The elevation averages about 490 m to 500 m, with local highs above 520 m. The South Saskatchewan River is entrenched to 435 m. Given the high permeability of the soils, there is little surface runoff and limited external drainage.

The extremely sandy areas are dominated by relatively open stands of jack pine with an understory of lichens and ericaceous shrubs. Open stands of scrubby trembling aspen, occasionally mixed with jack pine and the isolated white spruce, are characteristic of most of the area. Cultivated land, which occurs mostly along the southern boundary of the area on the Chernozemic soils, accounts for about one-third of the area.

G14. Prince Albert Plain

The Prince Albert plain is a hummocky glaciolacustrine plain that lies south of Prince Albert and extends east from the third meridian to north of Melfort. In general the area slopes to the north and east with elevations ranging from a high of 520 m on top of Red Deer Hill to about 410 m at the eastern edge of the Plain. Surface drainage, particularly in the rougher landscapes, ends up in local sloughs and small lakes. External surface drainage is into the Carrot River or the North and South Saskatchewan rivers via Red Deer, McFarlane, and Peonan creeks.

Most landscapes in the region exhibit a hummocky pattern with moderately steep slopes. Strongly sloping landscapes are common between the Saskatchewan rivers, while toward the eastern part of the plain, gently undulating landscapes prevail. Black Chernozemic and, to a lesser extent, Dark Gray Chernozemic soils dominate the area. Some of the soils south of the South Saskatchewan River have an abnormally thick topsoil layer and are referred to as Thick Black soils. These soils are the most productive agricultural soils in the province, and the area as a whole is one of the more productive.

Approximately 80% of the area is under cultivation, with the bulk of the land seeded to cereals and oilseeds. Only about 10% is planted to forages.

G15. Tiger Hills Upland

The Tiger Hills upland lies along the southern edge of the Boreal Transition Ecoregion in the vicinity of Basin, Jumping, and Lenore lakes. The landscape is fundamentally a moderately sloping, hummocky glacial till plain, although the till is often overlain by a shallow (less than 1 m) veneer of silty glaciolacustrine materials. At the upper elevations the lacustrine veneer is found only on the mid and lower slopes. An area of dominantly sandy materials occurs south of Struthers Lake. Because of the dominantly hummocky nature of the landscape, surface runoff ends up largely in sloughs and small lakes. External drainage is via the Carrot River and Melfort Creek.

Elevations range from 530 to 600 m, which is on average 100 m higher than that of the neighbouring Prince Albert and Melfort plains to the north. The relatively high elevation and resulting cool temperatures promote the formation of Gray and Dark Gray Luvisolic soils. Dark Gray Chernozemic soils are found mainly at the lower elevations at the base of the upland.

About 70% of the area is cultivated, with cereals being the main crop. Oilseeds account for about 20% of the cultivated land annually, while forages occupy only about 5%. The remnant areas of native vegetation are mainly trembling aspen with an undergrowth of pin cherry, choke cherry, saskatoon, and prairie rose.

G16. Melfort Plain

The Melfort plain is a level glaciolacustrine plain located near the centre of the Boreal

Transition Ecoregion. Black and Thick Black Chernozemic soils developed on silty and clayey lacustrine sediments dominate the area, but Dark Gray Chernozemic and some Gray Luvisolic soils occur in the northeast. The glacial drift, overlying Upper Cretaceous shales, averages less than 90 m and on the eastern side of the Melfort plain, the drift is commonly less than 60 m.

The very gently undulating landscape is dissected by the many tributaries of the Carrot River. Elevations average around 450 m, sloping from the southwest at 460 m to the northeast at 410 m. Some local areas exceed 485 m in elevation.

Over 90% of the area is cultivated, with cereals (50%), oilseeds (25%) and forages (10%) being the major crops in 1991. According to long-term yield records, this area is the most productive agricultural region in the province.

G17. Nipawin Plain

The Nipawin plain is located toward the northern edge of the Boreal Transition Ecoregion and is a mixture of sandy loam to clayey lacustrine materials deposited in former Lake Agassiz. Dark Gray Chernozemic soils have formed on the clays south of Tobin Lake, while Black Chernozemics are dominant on the silts and clays south of Aylsham. The remainder of the area is characterized by Dark Gray Chernozemic soils. Many soils show evidence of imperfect drainage, although construction of roads and ditches subsequent to original land cultivation has improved drainage. The glacial drift, overlying Upper Cretaceous shales, is commonly less than 60 m thick.

The landscape is very gently to gently undulating, sloping eastward from 395 m northwest of Nipawin to 315 m at Tobin Lake. Most drainage is into the Saskatchewan River directly or via the Petaigan and Whitefox rivers. There is limited drainage southward into the Carrot River.

About 80% of the area is cultivated, with cereals and oilseeds being the dominant crops. On native sites, trembling aspen, along with the occasional white spruce, are common on well-drained soils, while balsam poplar occupy moist lowland areas. Interspersed among the forest in the original vegetation was some prairie and patches of meadow, but most have disappeared under the plow.

G18. Tobin Lake Lowland

The Tobin Lake lowland is located to the north and east of Tobin Lake. North of the lake is a silty and sandy fluvial lacustrine plain with some eolian sand deposits. Dark Gray Chernozemic soils occur on these materials, except for the very sandy sites where Eutric Brunisols and Regosols are most likely. Many of the soils are imperfectly drained. To the east of Tobin Lake, organic soils along with Gray Luvisols, Eutric Brunisols, and Regosols have formed on beach ridges and eroded glacial till. Upper Cretaceous shale bedrock underlies the glacial drift, which averages less than 90 m thick, and is commonly less than 60 m.

The landscape is very gently to gently undulating, sloping to the east from an elevation of 390 m at the western edge to an elevation of 280 m where it adjoins the Saskatchewan delta. External drainage is east via the Torch and Saskatchewan rivers. To the east of Tobin Lake, surface drainage is restricted by beach ridges.

The better drained beach ridges and eroded till deposits commonly support jack pine, black spruce, tamarack, and occasionally trembling aspen. Due to the stoniness of the till and, in some cases, excessive wetness, none of these species attain a large size. Jack pine is the most vigorous. Organic soils support sphagnum moss, willows, swamp birch, Labrador tea, leather-leaf, and bog cranberry, along with stunted black spruce and occasional tamarack.

About 40% of the Tobin Lake lowland is cultivated, with cereals, oilseeds, and forages being the most important crops.

G19. Red Earth Plain

The Red Earth plain is a clayey glaciolacustrine plain underlain by Upper Cretaceous shales. The depth of the glacial drift is commonly less than 60 m and is particularly thin near the base of the Pasquia escarpment, where lacustrine materials lie directly on shales. The soils are dominantly Dark Gray Chernozemics, with a few Gray Luvisols in well-drained areas and organic deposits in poorly drained areas.

The relatively uniform landscape is very gently undulating, sloping to the northeast from 390 m in the south at the base of the Pasquia escarpment to 275 m in the vicinity of Red Earth and Pakwaw Lake. There is extensive external drainage to the northeast by the Carrot River and its tributaries, the Papikwan, Jordan, and Cracking rivers.

About 80% of the area is cultivated, with cereals and oilseeds being the main crops. About 20% of the cultivated area is planted to forage. The native vegetation is dominantly deciduous forest, although pockets of grassland likely existed before cultivation. The imperfectly drained clays south of the Red Earth settlement support a luxuriant growth of trembling aspen, balsam poplar, and white birch; in older stands, white spruce is also present.

G20. Mistatim Upland

The Mistatim upland is located directly southwest of the Porcupine Hills. It is dominated by Gray Luvisols formed in glacial till, most of which is overlain by shallow, clayey glaciolacustrine materials. In the southern part, highly calcareous, clayey, water-modified glacial till derived mainly from Paleozoic limestone is more common. Along its northern edge, significant Gray Solonetzic soils occur in the shallow clayey glaciolacustrine deposits. A large organic deposit occurs southwest of Mistatim.

Most of the landscape is very gently to gently undulating, with numerous dissections. Near the Porcupine Hills, the glacial till tends to have a moderately sloping hummocky surface with numerous potholes. Elevations reach 610 m along the edge of the Porcupine Hills, descending to 410 m in the north and 470 m in the south. External drainage is south into the Red Deer River and north into the Carrot River via the numerous dissections and streams in the area.

Approximately 35% of the Mistatim upland is cultivated, with the remaining area dominated by mixedwood forest. Trembling aspen and balsam poplar are the main components. Black spruce and tamarack occur in the bogs.

G21. Hudson Bay Plain

The Hudson Bay plain lies between the Porcupine and Pasquia hills. The area itself is underlain at a depth of between 3 m and 30 m by Upper Cretaceous shale bedrock which is exposed along the Etomami, Pepaw, and Red Deer rivers near Hudson Bay. The dominant surface deposit is a clay loam to clay-textured, highly calcareous, water-modified glacial till that has been derived in part from Paleozoic limestone, as evidenced by its pink colouration. Soils formed in the till are dominantly Dark Gray Chernozemics, but some Gray Luvisols occur in the northwest. Dark Gray Chernozemic soils have also formed in the shallow, clayey glaciolacustrine deposits that are found interspersed with the till, and in a local area of sandy glaciofluvial materials found on the western side of the area. Organic deposits account for about 10% of the total area.

The entire landscape is gently undulating, descending gradually from an elevation of 490 m on the western side to an elevation of about 365 m near Hudson Bay. The area drains eastward into Lake Winnipegosis via the Red Deer River and its tributaries.

The Hudson Bay plain is on the northern edge of a transitional area between the mixedwood forest and the aspen parkland. The vegetation is dominantly trembling aspen with an undergrowth of willow, red-osier dogwood, saskatoon, pin cherry, and choke cherry. Balsam poplar is found on imperfectly drained soils. Small pockets of grassland, and mixedwood forest consisting of mainly trembling aspen and white spruce, occur in local areas. Black spruce, occasional tamarack, mosses, swamp birch, and Labrador tea are associated with bogs, while cattails, bulrushes, sedges, and willows are associated with fens. About 35% of the area is under cultivation.

G22. Barrier River Upland

The Barrier River upland is located along the southern edge of the Boreal Transition Ecoregion to the east of the Porcupine Hills, stretching west almost as far as Pleasantdale. It is a gently to roughly undulating glacial till plain interspersed with local sandy and silty glaciolacustrine plains. The region surrounding Bjorkdale is dominated by Gray Luvisolic and Dark Gray Chernozemic soils developed in shallow, sandy to sandy loam glaciolacustrine materials underlain by glacial till. Thick Black Chernozemic soils formed in glacial till are common in the vicinity of Pipestone Creek. The remainder of the area is dominated by Gray Luvisolic and Dark Gray Chernozemic soils formed on loamy glacial till, interspersed with local sandy and silty materials.

Elevations range from 610 m south of Nut Mountain to 470 m near Bjork Lake. The bulk of the area drains externally into the Barrier and Red Deer rivers via such streams as Pipestone and Duck creeks. In the extreme north, drainage is into the Carrot River, and a local area in the southeast drains into the Assiniboine River.

G23. Swan River Plain

The Swan River plain occupies the area between the Duck and Porcupine uplands, and extends southward around Duck Mountain and along the Assiniboine River. Surface deposits in the central part of the plain are glaciolacustrine sands, silts, and clays and in the peripheral area are thin lacustrine sediments over glacial till. Gravels and sands tend to occur in association with the rivers. Thick Black Chernozemic soils dominate the area, with a high proportion of Dark Gray Chernozemics and some Gray Luvisols. Drift thickness ranges from 15 m to 60 m. Upper Cretaceous shales are exposed in the Swan and Assiniboine river valleys and on Thunder Hill. The outcrops appear as grayish or brownish clay almost or entirely devoid of vegetation. These shales slake in water and when moist expand to form a highly plastic clay. On drying, the clay shrinks to form a honeycomb-like surface pattern. These shales are generally low in carbonates but contain the mineral gypsum. Ironstone concretions are distributed irregularly or in layers in the shale and are often found scattered on the surface of outcrops. Solonetzic soils can be found in association with these shales.

Topography is gently undulating to moderately sloping hummocky, and dissections are common. The landscape slopes southward from an elevation of 550 m at the base of the Porcupine Hills, and inward toward the valleys of the Swan and Assiniboine rivers, decreasing to 450 m on the flood plain of the Assiniboine. External drainage is to lakes Winnipeg and Winnipegosis via the Assiniboine and Swan rivers and their many tributaries.

About two-thirds of the area was cultivated in 1991, with cereals being the major crop. Oilseeds accounted for about 20% of the cultivated land, while 10% was seeded to forages. Native grassland vegetation comprises June grass, plains rough fescue, slender and northern wheatgrasses, marsh reed grass, and shrubs such as prairie rose and wolf-willow. Deciduous forest occurs in moist locations and comprises trembling aspen, balsam poplar, willow, red-osier dogwood, saskatoon, pin cherry, and choke cherry. Bur oak can be found growing on southern exposures in the southern Assiniboine Valley. In the more northern parts of the Swan River plain, mixed stands of trembling aspen and white spruce are common. On Thunder Hill, bur oak, green ash, and Manitoba maple are present. Bur oak also occurs in isolated, warm, south-facing pockets of the Assiniboine River Valley north of Lake of the Prairies.

Prairie Ecozone

Grasslands occupy a vast area in North America, from the Rocky Mountains on the west to the deciduous forests on the east, and from the boreal forests in the north to the Gulf of Mexico. In Canada, mixed-grass and fescue prairie dominate these grasslands. The aspen parkland — a narrow band of grassland with scattered occurrences of aspen groves — separates these grasslands from the forests. The grasslands surround a small, geologically unique upland that has a lodgepole pine vegetation similar to that found in montane regions to the west. Thus grassland, aspen parkland, and montane forest regions constitute the Prairie Ecozone in Canada. This ecozone covers the southern one-third of Saskatchewan, approximately 24 million hectares, extending from the boundary with the United States to the Boreal Plain Ecozone.

PHYSIOGRAPHY. The Prairie Ecozone is essentially a level to gently rolling plain with numerous subdued uplands dispersed throughout most of its extent. Small but prominent uplands rise above this plain in its southern part. Elevations in the Prairie Ecozone are lowest in the northeastern part of the area. The Missouri Coteau and then the Wood Mountain and Cypress Hills plateaus represent successive increases in elevation from approximately 1,000 m in the northeast to 1,100 m in the southwest.

GEOLOGY. Glacial deposits represent the surficial sediment throughout the Prairie Ecozone, and they may be hundreds of metres thick. These deposits are generally thinner in the Prairie Ecozone than in the Boreal Plain Ecozone, and parts of the Cypress Hills and Wood Mountains were not glaciated. As a consequence, the regional topography of today closely mirrors the shape of the bedrock surface that existed prior to glaciation. Also, the composition of the glacial deposits is strongly influenced by the nature of this underlying bedrock.

Late Cretaceous and Tertiary age rocks cover older Phanerozoic rocks throughout the Prairie Ecozone. The Tertiary rocks formed mainly in river and lake environments, whereas the Cretaceous rocks are of marine origin.

The youngest rocks of Tertiary age contain appreciable amounts of gravels and quartzites, which have resisted millions of years of geological erosion. This has maintained the surface in the Cypress Hills far above the surrounding lands, where the softer and older sands and clays have been largely or entirely removed. Geologists believe that a thickness of about 1 km of Tertiary rocks has been eroded from Saskatchewan's landscape and that before erosion, the extent of the Tertiary deposits may have been much greater than presently known. Even the underlying and still older Cretaceous shales have undergone extensive erosion, carving the slope and drainage to the northeast that prevails to this day.

Glacial deposits, however, have a profound influence on the nature of the local landscape throughout the ecozone. Till plains and hummocky moraines, often with an abundance of glacial kettles, are a dominant feature of the area. Nearly level glaciolacustrine areas are also common, as are glaciofluvial areas that are often modified by wind to form dunes. Valleys and rivers cross this plain, flowing through the Beaver, North and South Saskatchewan, Red Deer, Assiniboine, Qu'Appelle and Souris rivers to the Churchill and Nelson rivers and into Hudson Bay, and through the Frenchman River to the Missouri River and the Gulf of Mexico.

Fertile black soils develop under parkland environment.

A dominant regional feature is the Missouri Coteau, a major northeast-facing bedrock escarpment. Many large ice-pushed ridge complexes are located along this escarpment. The Dirt Hills, south and southwest of Regina, are among the largest and best developed ice-pushed ridges in the world. The soft shale and mudstone bedrock was thrust upward by the force of the advancing glacier so that, in places, bedrock overlies younger glacial deposits.

Postglacial events have also impacted on Saskatchewan's landscape. Underfit streams, with their characteristic floodplains, are active in channels that originated as meltwater channels from the ice or spillways from glacial lakes. Lakes such as those in the Qu'Appelle Valley have formed between alluvial fans that blocked the glacial valley where present-day creeks enter it. Sand dunes have been active since glaciation.

CLIMATE. The climate in the Prairie Ecozone ranges from semiarid to humid continental, with long and cold winters, short and very warm summers, and cyclonic storms. Temperatures are highest at lower elevations in the south, progressively decreasing with increasing altitude and latitude. Precipitation is generally low, but it increases slightly from south to north and more markedly from west to east. This precipitation trend, when combined with temperature gradients described above, has created a series of climatic zones from cool semiarid in the southwest to moderately cold subhumid in the northeast. Climatic zonation also occurs in response to altitude, as moderately cold semiarid to subhumid conditions prevail on uplands in what is otherwise the driest part of the ecozone.

LANDFORMS AND SOILS. Most landforms in the Prairie Ecozone are of glacial origin. Nearly level ground moraine (till plains), glaciolacustrine and glaciofluvial plains are major contributors to the "flat prairie" landscape, although glacial kettles break this monotony in some areas. Gently rolling to hilly hummocky and ridged moraines and sand dunes add to the diversity of the landscape. Valleys and coulees, sometimes with enclosed lakes, are often the most striking landscape features.

Soils strongly reflect climate and natural vegetation and the associated landform. Soils formed in glacial till, the sediment that constitutes ground moraine and hummocky moraine, are usually loam textured, while those formed in glaciolacustrine deposits have higher proportions of silt and clay, and those formed in glaciofluvial deposits have more sand and gravel.

Chernozemic soils are synonymous with a grassland vegetation, so the entire Prairie Ecozone is dominated by them. Brown Chernozemic soils are associated with mixed grasses in the sub- to semiarid region; Dark Brown Chernozemic soils with a more productive mixed-grass vegetation in the semiarid region; and Black Chernozemic soils with a fescue prairie-aspen grove parkland vegetation in the subhumid region. Dark Gray Chernozemic soils occur in areas transitional to the boreal forest.

Solonetzic soils occur in all of the soil climatic zones in association with parent materials containing a high content of sodium salts. Regosolic soils prevail on recent deposits such as alluvial flood plains and sand dunes. Gleysolic soils prevail in wetland areas.

GROUNDWATER. In the Prairie Ecozone, the basal aquitard of Precambrian and Paleozoic rocks is overlain by bedrock aquifers. These aquifers in turn are confined by an upper aquitard of Cretaceous shale. The Judith River and Ravenscrag aquifers are the most important of these bedrock aquifers in this ecozone. The Hatfield and Tyner valley and several other buried valleys lie on the bedrock surface and provide valuable sources of groundwater for the ecozone. Aquifers also occur within the glacial sediments, most notably within and at the surface of the Floral Formation. Surficial aquifers, representing sandy and gravelly glacial deposits, are scattered throughout the ecozone.

VEGETATION. The Prairie Ecozone is a grassland region. A mixed-grass community dominates the southwestern, warmer, and more arid part of the ecozone, represented by the Mixed Grassland Ecoregion. A late summer moisture deficit, caused by low precipitation and high evapotranspiration, and periods of extensive droughts typify the climate of this area. The resulting mixed-grass vegetation includes what are often referred to as "short grasses" (blue grama grass and sedge) and "mid to tall grasses" (wheatgrasses, June grass, needle-and-thread, and porcupine grass), along with pasture sage and moss phlox.

Grassland vegetation has adapted to the semiarid climate of the Mixed Grassland Ecoregion in the Prairie Ecozone.

Northward and eastward from the mixed grassland, moisture deficits are less severe and droughts are less prolonged. "Mid-grasses" dominate these areas, along with an increase in the extent of shrublands, aspen grove woodlands, and wetlands. This is the Moist Mixed Grassland Ecoregion.

A belt, representing a transition from the grasslands to the south and the boreal forest to the north, extends diagonally from southeast to northwest across the southern part of the province. Summers are cooler in this region, winters are longer and colder, and snow cover is more continuous than in the regions to the south and west. Summer evaporation and precipitation rates in this area are almost equal, which minimizes the potential severity of the late summer moisture deficits. Here, a mosaic of trembling aspen surrounds numerous wetlands. These form groves in a sea of plains rough fescue grasslands. This is the Aspen Parkland Ecoregion.

The smooth climatic and vegetation zonation that extends from southwest to northeast across the southern part of the province is interrupted by a prominent upland. High elevations result in a climate that is cooler and more moist than the surrounding dry grasslands. Vestiges of a montane forest, dominated by lodgepole pine, that once extended all the way to the Rocky Mountains remain to this day. This is the Cypress upland.

Many small wetland areas, or sloughs, occur throughout the Prairie Ecozone. In the more humid parts, these sloughs tend to be more permanent, the water is relatively fresh, and they are ringed by willows and trembling aspen; in drier parts of the ecozone, however, the sloughs are less permanent and more saline, and the transition from the wetland to the grassland is a sharp one. Most freshwater wetlands are characterized by emergent vegetation such as sedges, bulrushes, cattails, and reed grasses on their margins. In the open water, submerged growth of pondweeds, yellow watercrowfoot, and greater bladderwort may be present. Saline wetlands do not have a marginal ring of willows, but rather have shorelines heavily encrusted with white salts and usually bare of vegetation except for a few salt-tolerant plants like red samphire. Salt-tolerant grasses, such as seaside arrow-grass and alkali grass, grow at the margin of the salt crusts.

WILDLIFE. Historically, the prominent species on the prairie was the bison. The pronghorn antelope, though an animal of the open plains, ranged well into the parkland. Elk grazed on the grassland around the edges of aspen groves. The wolf was the main predator of the ungulates. Settlement and widespread cultivation of the grasslands has caused some species to come near the brink of extinction (as in the case of bison) or to currently occupy a small portion of their former range.

An abundance of assorted mice and voles inhabit the matted vegetation in unburned or ungrazed grassland. The thirteen-lined ground squirrel also prefers longer grasses. Richardson's ground squirrel forms extensive colonies on knolls, gravel ridges, and overgrazed areas. The northern pocket gopher spends most of its life underground, feeding on succulent roots in pastures and haylands; its mounds of soil become an annoyance during haying. Coyote, red fox, and the re-introduced swift fox feed chiefly on rodents, birds, and insects. The badger feeds predominantly on ground squirrels, which it captures by digging. The snowshoe hare inhabits aspen groves during the day, emerging to feed at night, while the white-tailed jack rabbit frequents pastures, cultivated fields, and open, arid prairie, seldom penetrating wooded areas except as

Bison were once a dominant species of the prairie.

shelter from blizzards. The striped skunk reaches its highest densities in agricultural areas, and the woodchuck has also prospered as a result of agricultural and forestry practices.

Characteristic grassland birds include western meadowlark, horned lark, upland sandpiper, and chestnut-collared longspur. The vesper sparrow, clay-colored sparrow, chipping sparrow, and sharp-tailed grouse are more abundant on prairie adjacent to woodland. The brown-headed cowbird followed the bison herds and fed on insects associated with them; its migratory nature led it to lay eggs in other birds' nests rather than build its own. The ferruginous hawk and Swainson's hawk will nest on the ground in open arid prairie, while the red-tailed hawk is common to parts of the prairie that supply trees for nesting. In the winter, large flocks of snow bunting and common redpoll frequent grasslands, fields, and road edges, feeding on seeds of forbs and grasses exposed above the snow.

The prairie has more fish species than the boreal plain, this being the result of additional warm water species being found in the Qu'Appelle, Assiniboine, and Souris river systems.

Reptile species are most numerous in the prairie, preferring the warmth of a dry arid region. Fourteen species of reptiles occur here, 11 of which occur in the mixed grassland. An additional three species of amphibians occur in the prairie as compared to the boreal plain.

HUMAN ACTIVITY. More than 80% of the economic activity of the province is generated in this ecozone, with agriculture as the dominant land use. Called the breadbasket of Canada, much of Canada's and Saskatchewan's cropland and rangeland and pasture are located in the Prairie Ecozone. The other major activities contributing to the economy are mining (coal, potash, mineral, and aggregates) and oil and gas production. Despite the dominance of agricultural activities on the landscape, the majority of the population is found in urban communities. The 1991 population of this ecozone was approximately 827,000 or 84% of the total population of Saskatchewan. Ten of Saskatchewan's 12 cities are located in this zone, and 81% of the population lives in urban centres. Also, this ecozone has a higher proportion of its labour force in secondary industries than the national average, reflecting the importance of its major urban centres in serving national and international markets.

Trembling aspen are associated with the wet depressional areas that frequent the northern part of the Prairie Ecozone.

Agriculture has diversified considerably in recent years in the Prairie Ecozone, from traditional grain crops to more oilseed crops, such as canola, flax, and sunflowers. Producers have increasingly adopted more sustainable farming practices, including conservation tillage and reduced summerfallow, reducing the risk of water and wind erosion. The Prairie Ecozone has also been experiencing a trend towards increased livestock production.

Agriculture, and to a lesser degree urbanization, have transformed more than 80% of the native prairie landscape. Most of the rough fescue grassland has been ploughed, and much of the remainder has been significantly modified by livestock grazing and haying. Almost all of the tall-grass prairie is gone. Less than 20% of the once abundant mid-grass prairie remains in its native state, about one-quarter of the mixed-grass prairie and aspen parkland. Approximately 40% of the original 2 million hectares of wetlands have been converted to agricultural use. All landscape areas within this ecozone have been cultivated or grazed for at least 20% of their area, and many show 100% cultivation or grazing levels.

Over the past 100 years, the Prairie Ecozone has undergone development by natural resource industries, largely agriculture and forestry, but also oil and gas extraction and refining, hydroelectric power generation, fisheries, and mining. Although these industries have fostered a thriving economy and high standard of living, they have also greatly modified the original ecosystems, diminishing wildlife and plant populations.

The Prairie Ecozone has vast amounts of a wide range of non-renewable resources, including oil, natural gas, potash, coal, sodium sulphate, and clay products. There are currently 14,000 active oil wells and 7,000 active gas wells in the Prairie Ecozone.

Forested lands are scattered, occurring in gullies, ravines, and areas of higher elevation. Generally the use of such forests has been for recreation or as a source of fuel wood. There is relatively limited commercial fishing activity in this zone. Commercial aquaculture, gill netting and harvesting of brine shrimp, minnows, and leeches occur on selected prairie lakes. There are several private trout hatcheries. The Prairie Ecozone is a popular destination for anglers, providing almost half of all recreational fishing in the province. Twenty-two percent of the provincial trapping harvest occurs from this ecozone. Over half of the provincial total of hunting of big game and more than 80% of the hunting for bird species occurs in the Prairie Ecozone.

Just under 9% of this ecozone is in some form of park or protected area. Canada's only national park dedicated to the protection of grasslands, Grasslands National Park, occurs in this zone. Saskatchewan's Watchable Wildlife Society has identified 90 "eco-sites" in the province that represent areas with a high degree of natural significance for ecotourism. The Prairie Ecozone contains 55 of those sites.

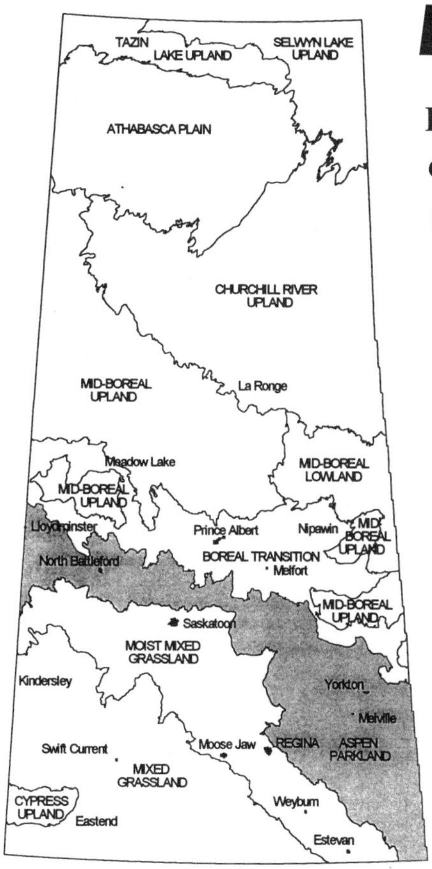

Aspen Parkland Ecoregion

In its native state, the Aspen Parkland Ecoregion is characterized by a mosaic of aspen groves and fescue grasslands. It represents a zone of transition between the open grasslands of the south and the continuous forests of the north. It forms a belt of 8 million hectares (13% of the province) that extends in an arc from the Manitoba border in the extreme southeast corner of the province to the Alberta border near Lloydminster. This ecoregion is named after its unique pattern of native vegetation, where aspen groves occur on the moister sites, such as north-facing slopes and depressions, while grasslands occur on the drier hilltops and south-facing slopes. The pattern changes across the region, with gradual expansion of grassland toward the southern edge and more continuous aspen cover toward the north or on north-facing regional slopes and at higher elevations. This unique vegetation pattern has formed in response to climate, geology, and fire. However, this ecoregion has been drastically altered by agricultural use, as 80% of the ecoregion is cropland.

PHYSIOGRAPHY. The Aspen Parkland Ecoregion comprises a broad plain that is interrupted by deep, scenic valleys and subdued, hilly uplands. The primary slope of the plain is downward to the north and east, in accordance with the slope of the bedrock surface. Most of the region has a cover of glacial drift that is sufficiently thick to obscure the underlying bedrock topography; hence, striking bedrock landscapes (such as occur in the Mixed Grassland and Cypress Upland ecoregions) are lacking. Secondary slopes from the uplands to drainage systems such as the North Saskatchewan and Qu'Appelle rivers occasionally break the general northward slope of the plain.

Elevations of the plain, where level to undulating glaciofluvial and glaciolacustrine deposits prevail, range mostly from 500 to 600 m, occasionally rising above 700 m and dropping below 425 m. Uplands, dominated by hummocky morainal landscapes, generally protrude 50 to 200 m above the adjacent plain, with the Touchwood Hills and Moose Mountains reaching elevations of 800 m and more. Although the break from the plains to the uplands is usually gradual and unspectacular, prominent escarpments such as the Eagle Hills are locally striking features.

The valleys of the Souris, Qu'Appelle, Assiniboine, South and North Saskatchewan, and Battle rivers, often entrenched 100 m or more into the plain, are major contributors to the beauty of the region. These river valleys form part of the Nelson River drainage basin, but in spite of their prominence they often drain only the area in close proximity to the valleys. There are also a number of prominent lakes in the region: Manitou, Jackfish, Basin, Lenore, Quill, Little Quill,

Good Spirit, Kenosee and the Qu'Appelle Lakes, to name but a few.

The beautiful Qu'Appelle Valley with its underfit stream was once a major spillway that drained Glacial Lake Regina.

GEOLOGY. The bedrock underlying the Aspen Parkland Ecoregion is almost entirely marine sedimentary rocks of the Riding Mountain Formation (Pierre Shale) and Lea Park Formation of the Upper Colorado Group in the western part of the ecoregion. These sediments typically consist of gray-green silty clays and shales with local deposits of bentonite. Localized occurrences of younger, fluvial or alluvial deposits include: Paleocene siltstones capping the Frenchman, Whitemud, and Eastend formation clays, siltstones, and sandstones; Tertiary chert gravels; and gray muddy sands, silts and clays with thin coal seams and bentonites of the Judith River Formation. In the subsurface, older sedimentary rocks of marine origin host deposits of potash and other salts, and petroleum.

CLIMATE. The Aspen Parkland Ecoregion has a humid continental climate. It is cooler and wetter, and, consequently, less arid than the grassland ecoregions to the south and west, but warmer and slightly drier than in the boreal ecoregions to the north and east. Within the Aspen Parkland, temperature and precipitation are lower in the northwest than in the southeast. Temperatures are also lower at high elevations than on nearby plains.

The mean annual daily temperature is 1.4°C. The mean July temperature is 18.0°C and the mean January temperature is -18.9°C. The mean annual precipitation is 420 mm, with 262 mm of rainfall occurring from May to September. The summers are short and warm, having a frost-free period of 106 days and a total of 1,584 degree days above 5°C.

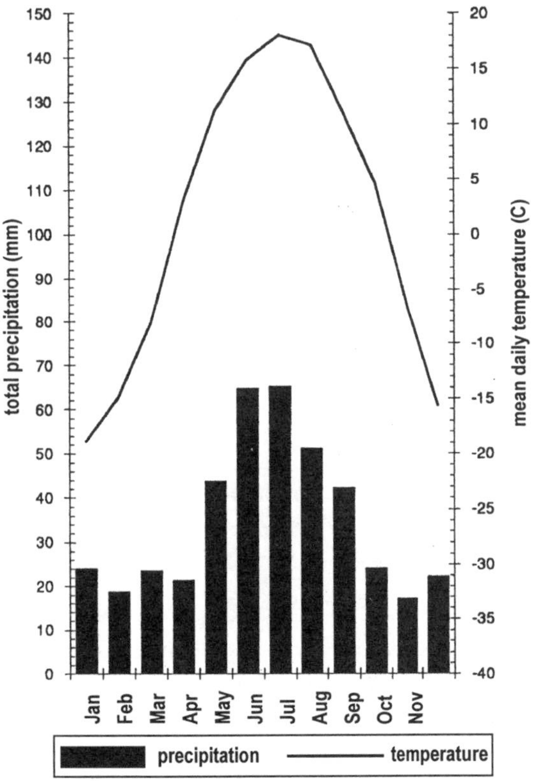

Figure 19. Mean monthly temperature and precipitation for the aspen parkland as represented by the meteorological record from Pilger.

LANDFORMS AND SOILS. Black Chernozemic soils prevail throughout this ecoregion in response to the large additions of organic matter in these fescue grasslands and slower rates of decomposition in this cooler part of the Prairie Ecozone. As their name implies, these soils have a dark-coloured surface layer that is high in organic matter. Typically, this layer is separated from a grayish-brown layer, which represents the soil parent material, by a reddish-brown layer that is free of carbonates of calcium and magnesium.

Soils tend to be thin and lower in organic matter on upper slopes, becoming progressively thicker and higher in organic matter on mid and lower slopes in response to an increased supply of soil moisture and plant growth. Dark Brown soils occur on prominent south-facing local and regional slopes where more arid conditions result in reduced growth. Dark Gray Chernozemic and Dark Gray and Gray Luvisolic soils occur at higher elevation and on prominent north-facing slopes, where grassland vegetation has been displaced by trembling aspen.

GROUNDWATER. Groundwater in the Aspen Parkland Ecoregion is associated with the drift that covers the bedrock as well as with the bedrock. Bedrock aquifers are limited in this ecoregion. The sandy and silty beds of the Judith River Formation extend into part of the ecoregion in the west, and the Bredenbury and Estevan aquifers occur in the southeast; however, much of the bedrock surface is covered with aquitards comprising Cretaceous shale. There are several major buried valley aquifers within the ecoregion. The Battleford Valley aquifer is an extensive system in the western part of the ecoregion. The Hatfield Valley aquifer in this ecoregion is part of a major valley that once extended from Cold Lake on the Alberta border to the Manitoba border east of Regina. The Estevan Valley aquifer also extends into this ecoregion. Blanket aquifers are also important sources of groundwater in the Meacham and the Wynyard-Melville aquifers that extend south and east from Saskatoon. Inter-till aquifers are widely distributed throughout the ecoregion. They are most common in the older and deeper Floral Formation but may also occur within the Battleford Formation. The Dalmeny aquifer, north of Saskatoon, is one that has been well defined. Surficial aquifers are most common along the North Saskatchewan River west of North Battleford, with only small, isolated occurrences in the eastern part of the ecoregion.

Both the bedrock and glacial aquifers have a marked influence on the ecology of the area. For example, Manitou Lake, the Quill Lakes, Redberry Lake, and the Qu'Appelle Lakes derive a considerable amount of their source from aquifer discharge. The quality of the water in these lakes is largely dependent upon the source of the groundwater; higher salt concentrations are associated with discharge from bedock aquifers and low salt concentrations from near-surface glacial aquifers or from surface aquifers.

The black choke cherry is common to edges of wooded areas and coulees of the ecoregion.

Aquifers also impact on the water supply to vegetation. The prevalence of trembling aspen in sandy areas is often a reflection of a surface aquifer in these sediments. Saline soils and salt-tolerant vegetation are often associated with surface concentrations of salts derived from glacial and bedrock aquifers.

VEGETATION. The mosaic pattern of the aspen parkland vegetation is best expressed in hummocky landscapes where the frequent changes of slope produce a regular alternation between woodlands in the lower areas and grasslands on the upper slopes. Many of these landscapes are focussed on glacial kettles, or "sloughs," with associated wetland vegetation. Flat areas, especially with clay soils, are usually devoid of wetlands and woodlands, while sandy areas may have a nearly continuous woodland cover. In pre-settlement times, fires prevented the trembling aspen from encroaching on the grasslands. However, since settlement, the incidence of fire has been reduced and the aspen has advanced upslope from the sloughs.

Most woodlands are represented by open stands of trembling aspen with an understory of shrubs (western snowberry, prairie rose, beaked hazelnut, and saskatoon), herbs (wild sarsaparilla, showy and smooth asters, wild peavine, and western Canada violet), and grasses (fowl and Kentucky bluegrass; water, awned, beaked, and woolly sedges; and white-grained mountain and Canadian ricegrass).

Stands in the drier, southern part of the ecoregion tend to have a shrub layer of western snowberry, prairie rose, and saskatoon, and a diverse mixture of herbs, whereas in the moister, northern parts, or at high elevations, beaked hazelnut becomes the dominant shrub and wild sarsaparilla the dominant herb. Aspen stands on sandy soils are characterized by prostrate shrubs (creeping juniper and bearberry). Meadow-sweet and poison ivy appear in the shrub layer, along with western snowberry, prairie rose, and choke cherry, while hay sedge is often an important herb.

Balsam poplar is associated with aspen throughout the region, becoming most prominent in the lowest, wettest parts of stands. Green ash, Manitoba maple, American elm, and cottonwood are more restricted in distribution and are found in riparian woods along major streams. Even more limited is bur oak, which is found on the slopes of the eastern part of the Qu'Appelle Valley.

Shrublands frequently appear in depressions or on the margins of aspen stands. The main shrub species are: western snowberry, Wood's rose, wolf-willow, saskatoon, choke cherry, and hawthorn. Lesser vegetation is often sparse under shrub stands, but may include species of either woodland or grassland.

The Aspen Parkland Ecoregion is the home of the fescue prairie grassland, dominated by plains rough fescue. Other major graminoids include sedges, western porcupine grass, June grass, awned wheat grass, and slender wheat grass. Broad-leaved herbs include low goldenrod, field chickweed, yarrow, prairie crocus, white prairie aster, and small-leaved pussy-toes.

Most of the fescue prairie that has not been cultivated is used for livestock grazing. Rough fescue has been eliminated from many pastures by overgrazing, leaving a mixed-prairie community of spear grasses, blue grama, and pasture sage that has been typically invaded by Kentucky bluegrass. In the eastern part of the ecoregion, rough fescue is less common. Many areas are dominated by western porcupine grass, wheatgrasses, and Kentucky bluegrass. Sandy soils also reduce the dominance of rough fescue, in favor of spear grasses, sand grass, sedges, and shrubs such as creeping juniper and choke cherry. Sand dunes introduce some distinctive species such as sand dropseed, Indian rice grass, and skeletonweed.

The frequent depressions throughout the ecoregion have distinctive wetland vegetation zones with increasing soil wetness: wet meadows (marsh reed grass, northern reed grass, Kentucky bluegrass, fowl bluegrass, Baltic rush, and willows), shallow marsh (reed canary grass, spangletop, awned sedge, beaked sedge, creeping spike-rush, and water smartweed), deep marsh (bulrushes, cat-tail, and giant reed grass), and open water (pondweeds).

Increasing salinity in wetlands shifts the vegetation to salt-tolerant species such as saltgrass, Nuttall's alkali grass, red samphire, sea blite, and alkali bulrush.

Red fox cubs.

WILDLIFE. The Aspen Parkland Ecoregion, with its grasslands, wooded groves, and numerous wetlands, supports more species of birds than the simpler grassland ecoregions to the south, but fewer than in the boreal transition to the north.

Fifty-five mammal species occur in this ecoregion. Mule deer and elk were common before settlement, but now are largely replaced by white-tailed deer, which is now the characteristic large mammal of this ecoregion. The cover provided by the aspen stands with their dense shrub understory, combined with the high nutritional value of agricultural crops common in the region, provide excellent habitat for these deer. Moose and pronghorn also occur in the area.

Snowshoe hare is a dominant mammal of the aspen groves, but the white-tailed jack rabbit and eastern cottontail also frequent the area. Chief predators are the coyote and red fox. Red-backed vole, Franklin's ground squirrel, and the striped skunk are common on the aspen edges. Other squirrels include the red squirrel, eastern gray squirrel, fox squirrel, Richardson's ground squirrel, thirteen-lined ground squirrel, least chipmunk, and woodchuck.

Although beaver are more characteristic of the boreal plain, they inhabit streams and large waterbodies if an aspen or willow food supply is convenient. The muskrat is the dominant mammal of sloughs and marshes. It consumes roots and bulbs of aquatic plants, helping to keep sloughs more open. Other rodents include: voles, mice, northern pocket gopher, and porcupine. There are 6 shrews, 6 bats, 13 carnivores, including 6 members of the weasel family (striped skunk, short-tailed weasel, prairie long-tailed weasel, least weasel, mink, and badger), 3 felines (bobcat, lynx, and cougar), raccoon, and black bear.

In this ecoregion, 320 bird species have been recorded, among a wide variety of habitat choices. The most abundant birds living in open, non-treed habitats are savannah sparrow, horned lark, and western meadowlark, while those that depend on shrub and forest habitats are clay-colored sparrow, American crow, house wren, vesper sparrow, yellow warbler, American robin, least flycatcher, American goldfinch, mourning dove, Brewer's blackbird, warbling vireo, black-billed magpie, and tree swallow. Abundant songbirds associated with wetlands are red-winged blackbird, yellow-headed blackbird, and song sparrow. The most common waterbirds are mallard, lesser scaup, sora rail, American coot, blue-winged teal, black tern, northern shoveler, and green-winged teal. Ducks are common here, where numerous potholes are major components of the "duck factory of North America," an area which is centred on Saskatchewan parklands and extends into Alberta, Manitoba, and North Dakota.

Species such as the house sparrow and barn swallow are abundant but are not tied to specific habitats. While not as abundant as the smaller songbirds, two predatory birds – the red-tailed hawk and the great horned owl – are commonly observed in this ecoregion.

Some eastern areas have birds that are unusual to this ecoregion or even to the province; the great crested flycatcher, black-billed cuckoo, eastern wood-pewee, and indigo bunting are among the more common ones.

Most of the birds that breed in the aspen parkland are migratory. Species that are normally year-round residents include the black-capped chickadee, black-billed magpie, downy woodpecker, hairy woodpecker, ruffed grouse, sharp-tailed grouse, blue jay, and great horned owl, as well as the introduced rock dove (pigeon) and house sparrow. Other species migrate into the aspen parkland from the north and winter there.

Fish diversity is high, with 47 species. The most common game fish are walleye, northern pike, yellow perch, and burbot. Several trout species have been introduced. The goldeye and sauger occur in the larger river systems. Some species of fish not found elsewhere in the province occur in the southeastern part of the ecoregion, including brown bullhead, channel catfish, chestnut lamprey, and rock bass.

Reptiles and amphibians are represented by 11 species, a relatively high number for the province. The largely vegetarian western painted turtle is an inhabitant of sluggish backwater and oxbows in the eastern parkland, while the large predacious snapping turtle is less abundant. The western plains garter snake is widespread in occurrence, but the red-sided garter snake is limited to major river valleys. The smooth green snake and the redbelly snake live in the southeastern part of the region. Tiger salamanders sometimes use northern pocket gopher mounds as moist daytime refuges. Large numbers of frogs can be heard calling in the evening. Wood frogs and boreal chorus frogs can be found in small temporary sloughs, while the increasingly rare leopard frog requires more permanent water to allow the large tadpoles time for full development. The Canadian toad is also common throughout the ecoregion.

HUMAN ACTIVITY. The population of the Aspen Parkland Ecoregion is approximately 195,000, or 20% of the Saskatchewan population. Four of Saskatchewan's 12 cities occur in the ecoregion, namely Lloydminster, North Battleford, Yorkton, and Melville.

The aspen parkland, with its favorable climate and highly productive soils, is suited to the production of a wide variety of field crops. Thus agriculture is the major land use throughout the ecoregion, with many areas being almost entirely farmland. In some areas nearly all farmland is cropland, used for the production of annual crops such as cereals and oilseeds or planted to a perennial forage crop. Longer rotations than in the adjacent moist mixed grassland means there is less summerfallow practiced. The sloughs also tend to be wetter, often resulting in remnant aspen groves dispersed throughout the cultivated fields. Such areas sometimes provide habitat for waterfowl and other wildlife.

In many parts of the ecoregion, the cultivated fields contain small patches of wet, stony, or hilly land that are not cultivated and that may provide habitat, albeit often poor, for some forms of wildlife. In other parts, there are large tracts of land that are wet, sandy, saline, stony, or hilly and are therefore not suited for cultivation. They are often intended for pasturing livestock, but also provide the majority of available habitat for birds, deer, coyote, fox, hare, squirrels, and many other animals.

This mechanic is adjusting the teeth of a continuous mining machine. He is about 1,000 m below the surface, in a Saskatchewan potash mine.

The urban centres in this region as well as a large number of towns and villages impact on land use within their boundaries as well as in surrounding neighbourhoods, with residential development and light industries being the most important. This ecoregion is also home to major heavy industry, in particular, the heavy oil upgrader at Lloydminster, potash refineries at Lanigan, Esterhazy, and Rocanville, and potassium sulphate development at Quill Lake.

Dams and reservoirs are present on all of the major drainage basins in the Prairie Ecozone. They are used primarily to store water for use during drought and to alleviate flooding during peak flows. The Aspen Parkland Ecoregion contains three dams (Moosomin, Alameda, and Shellmouth).

Hunting for big game, recreational hiking, camping, and fishing for northern pike, walleye, and perch are all accessible activities enjoyed in the aspen parkland. Ten provincial parks, including Good Spirit Lake, Moose Mountain, Echo Valley and the Battlefords, occur in this region. Approximately 5% of the ecoregion is within some form of park or protected area.

Landscape Areas

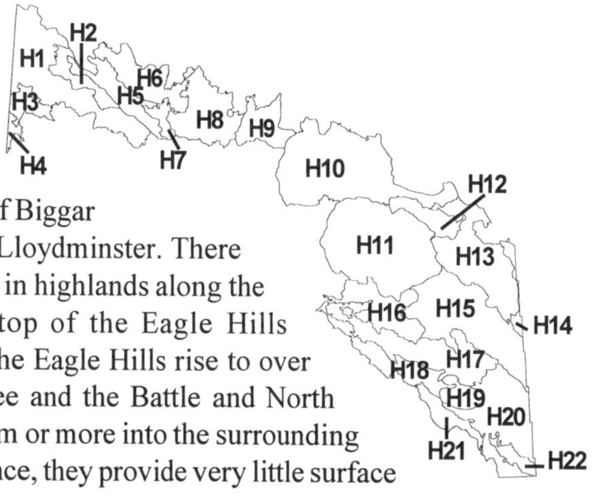

H1. Lloydminster Plain

H1 H2 H3 H4 H5 H6 H7 H8 H9 H10 H11 H12 H13 H14 H15 H16 H17 H18 H19 H20 H21 H22

The Lloydminster plain is a nearly level plain that extends westward from north of Biggar to the Alberta border, in the vicinity of Lloydminster. There is a general northward slope from 650 m in highlands along the southern boundary to 600 m at the top of the Eagle Hills escarpment. Morainal uplands such as the Eagle Hills rise to over 700 m. Valleys of the Big Gully Coulee and the Battle and North Saskatchewan rivers are entrenched 100 m or more into the surrounding plain. However, in spite of their prominence, they provide very little surface drainage to the surrounding plain.

Native vegetation most commonly occurs along river valleys or on steeply sloping hummocky moraines. The valleys of the North Saskatchewan and Battle rivers and Big Gully Coulee have fescue prairie and aspen forest along their slopes. The North Saskatchewan, at the north edge of the area, even has scattered white spruce (outliers of the boreal forest) on north-facing slopes. Aspen parkland with fescue prairie is also well expressed in hummocky moraines in the Neilburg-Freemont area and in the Eagle Hills. Continuous aspen forest occurs at the higher elevations of the Eagle Hills. This area supports a small population of moose, one of the few in the aspen parkland.

The dominantly Black loamy soils have developed mainly in level to undulating silty glaciolacustrine deposits formed where the Battle River emptied into Glacial Lake Saskatchewan, which extended a long distance to the east. Black loamy soils also formed in hummocky morainal deposits on adjacent uplands. Dark Gray and Gray Luvisolic soils are common on the more heavily treed north-facing slopes of the Eagle Hills. Shallow Regosolic soils occur on the eroded valleys of the Battle and North Saskatchewan rivers and Big Coulee.

Most of the Lloydminster plain is cropland. Cereals are the major crop, with large amounts of oilseeds. Less than 20% of the cropland area is summerfallow. The majority of the rangeland and pasture is associated with the very steep, hummocky morainal and gullied landscapes along and within Big Gully Coulee and the North Saskatchewan River valley and the Eagle Hills.

H2. Lower Battle River Plain

The Lower Battle River plain is a hummocky sand plain that occurs between North Battleford and Maidstone. This area is dominated by glaciofluvial plains at approximately 550 m, but it includes the Eagle Hills escarpment, which presents a drop of 75 to 100 m from the adjacent Lloydminster plain, and Maskwa Hill, which rises over 100 m above the glaciofluvial plain. The Battle River bisects this area, being entrenched 50 m in the upper reaches but much less than this at its confluence with the North Saskatchewan River.

The sandy soils in this area have resulted in a high percentage of uncultivated land, in which there is an extensive cover of trembling aspen. There are also eolian areas that have sand dune grassland, and riparian vegetation and wetlands are associated with the Battle River. Some large areas of native vegetation on sand are included in PFRA community pastures (Battle River-Cutknife, Paynton). Northern parts of the area, near the North Saskatchewan River, have some white spruce, as well as peatlands with black spruce and tamarack, features which are outliers of the boreal forest to the north. The mouth of Big Gully Creek is considered a particularly interesting area for diversity of vegetation and wildlife.

The weakly developed Regosolic soils have developed in sandy glaciofluvial deposits formed where the Battle River emptied into Glacial Lake Saskatchewan, which extended a long distance to the east. These sands were subsequently altered by wind erosion in prehistoric times to form the low-relief dunes that prevail today.

Most of this area is rangeland and pasture, occupied by the Lucky Man and Poundmaker Indian reserves and two large PFRA community pastures. There are only small amounts of cropland. Cereals are the major crop, with small amounts of oilseeds and forages. Summerfallow occupies less than 20% of the cropland area.

H3. Ribstone Plain

The Ribstone plain is a small area that includes Manitou Lake and the sand hills to the south of it. General elevations are 600 m, but some of the hills reach 700 m.

This sandy area has a high proportion of uncultivated land, much of which is in native vegetation. Most of this is included in 13 large grazing co-operatives. As in other sandy areas, the cover of low aspen woodland is very extensive. However the rougher dunes have more open grassland, and there are limited areas of active dunes with their distinctive species. Also, a significant part of the naturally wooded area has been cleared to produce grasslands similar to those that occur naturally. Seepage through the sand has created a wide array of wetlands, ranging from freshwater to saline, and including some peatlands similar to those found in the boreal forest far to the north. This area may support the largest population of mule deer within the aspen parkland, although in recent years mule deer have been increasing in other parts of the region.

The weakly developed Regosolic soils have developed in sandy glaciofluvial deposits formed where the Sounding Channel emptied into Glacial Lake Unity. These sands were subsequently altered by wind erosion in prehistoric times to form the hummocky relief that prevails today.

Most of this area is rangeland and pasture, occupied by 13 grazing co-operatives. There is a very small amount of cropland. Cereals are the major crop, with small amounts of oilseeds and forage crops. Approximately 20% of the cropland is summerfallow.

H4. Provost Plain

The Provost plain is a very small area of glaciofluvial and glaciolacustrine deposits located along the Alberta border near Macklin. Elevations in the area range from 650 to 700 m.

Nearly all of this area is suitable for cropland; hence, there is very little native vegetation remaining.

Dark Brown loam and sandy loam soils reflect the more arid climate and associated vegetation of this portion of the aspen parkland. These soils have developed primarily in level to undulating glaciolacustrine and glaciofluvial deposits formed where Sounding Creek emptied into Glacial Lake Unity.

Nearly all of this area is cropland. Cereals are the major crop, with small amounts of oilseeds. Less than 30% of the cropland area is summerfallow.

H5. Maymont Plain

The Maymont plain is a nearly level plain that extends from Radisson to Jackfish Lake. The area slopes gently southward from 580 m at the base of the Whitewood Hills to a nearby basin at 550 m. It then rises again to 580 m before falling to 490 m near the North Saskatchewan River. The North Saskatchewan River is entrenched 30 m or more into the surrounding plain, but it provides drainage for a band up to 10 km in width along the river. The remainder of this area drains into several large lakes.

Most of the native vegetation in this area has been cultivated. The slopes of the North Saskatchewan River valley provide the main area of aspen parkland that remains, but scattered patches remain in hummocky morainal areas and along coulees.

The dominantly Black loamy soils have developed in shallow silty glaciolacustrine deposits formed in Glacial Lake Saskatchewan. These deposits cover the underlying glacial till at lower elevations but do not cover the higher areas where Black loamy soils formed in hummocky and ridged morainal deposits prevail. Shallow Regosolic soils occur on the eroded valleys of the North Saskatchewan River.

Nearly all of the Maymont Plain is cropland. Cereals are the major crop, with large amounts of oilseeds and small amounts of peas and beans. Less than 20% of the cropland is summerfallow. The Battlefords Provincial Park is located in this area.

H6. Whitewood Hills

The Whitewood Hills is a hilly upland northeast of North Battleford that represents the south-facing flank of the much larger Thickwood Hills area. Elevations exceed 730 m in isolated highs, dropping to 580 m at the margin of the plains to the south. Surface drainage is limited to local sloughs and lakes within the area and to the plain below.

Cultivation is fairly extensive in this area but the steeply sloping hummocky landscape has resulted in significant areas being left in native vegetation. Classic aspen parkland with fescue prairie can be seen in the area north and east of Jackfish Lake, with the Hatherleigh provincial pasture being a notable area for natural vegetation composition. The hills north and west of Blaine Lake also have a high proportion of native aspen parkland, some of which is protected in Wildlife Development Fund land. All of this area is within the more moist part of the aspen parkland, being both close to the northern edge of the ecoregion and relatively high in elevation, and aspen stands with beaked hazelnut understory are extensive in uncleared areas. There are regionally important breeding habitat for the endangered piping plover in this area, with the shoreline of Redberry Lake offering a good opportunity to view this species.

The dominantly Black loamy soils have developed primarily in glacial till deposits associated with steep to very steep hummocky morainal landscapes. The southern part of the area has loamy and sandy Black soils formed in sandy and silty glaciolacustrine and sandy and gravelly glaciofluvial deposits associated with moderately to steeply sloping hummocky landscapes. These latter deposits are believed to have formed in a glacial lake that rested on the glacier prior to its retreat from the area.

Most of the Whitewood Hills is cropland. Cereals are the major crop, with large amounts of oilseeds and small amounts of forages. Approximately 20% of the cropland area is summerfallow. There are small areas of rangeland and pasture scattered throughout the area, usually in association with steeply sloping landscapes or sandy soils. The Hatherleigh provincial pasture occupies some of this land.

H7. Hafford Plain

The Hafford plain is a nearly level plain lying between Radisson and Hafford. Elevations on this plain drop from 600 m in the north to 520 m in the south. Surface drainage is limited to local sloughs and lakes.

Sandy soils have resulted in large amounts of this area being uncultivated. Native grassland and aspen woodland on sand can be seen in the Hafford and Fielding provincial pastures, and in the area around Borden.

Black soils developed in sandy glaciofluvial and silty glaciolacustrine deposits formed in Glacial Lake Saskatchewan are the most common soils in this area. They are associated with gently undulating and moderately sloping hummocky landscapes. Regosolic sands occur on glaciofluvial deposits that were subsequently altered by wind erosion in prehistoric times to form the low-relief dunes that prevail today.

Most of the Hafford plain is cropland. Cereals are the major crop, with small amounts of oilseeds and forages. More than 20% of the cropland area is summerfallow. The rangeland and pasture area is also extensive, usually associated with extremely sandy or saline areas.

H8. Waldheim Plain

The Waldheim plain is a nearly level plain that extends from Borden, west of the North Saskatchewan River, to Alvena, east of the South Saskatchewan River. Elevations throughout most of the plain are approximately 520 m, rising to 550 m at the Whitewood Hills, to the west, and the Minichinas Hills, to the east. The North Saskatchewan River is entrenched 30 m or more into the surrounding plain, but the South Saskatchewan River is not as deeply entrenched. The North Saskatchewan River provides drainage for a band along the river that is less than 10 km wide through Radouga, Turtle, and some smaller creeks; however, except for Fish Creek, there is virtually no surface drainage to the South Saskatchewan River. The remainder of the area drains into numerous sloughs and lakes. In particular, Kohleschmidt, Friesen, and Rosthern creeks drain to Duck Lake.

Most of the native vegetation in this level glaciolacustrine area has been cultivated. However, there is native aspen parkland on stony, eroded till plains in the area west of the North Saskatchewan River, between the Borden and Petrofka bridges. The valleys of the North and South Saskatchewan rivers create narrow belts of slope grasslands, wooded coulees, and riparian woods.

The Black loamy and sandy soils that dominate this area have developed in shallow sandy and silty glaciolacustrine deposits, formed in sediments of former Glacial Lake Saskatchewan. These deposits provide cover for the underlying glacial till at lower elevations but do not cover the till at higher elevations or along the North and South Saskatchewan rivers, where they have been eroded off, leaving a lag of boulders, sands, and gravels. Shallow Regosolic soils occur on the eroded valleys of the North and South Saskatchewan rivers.

Nearly all of the Waldheim plain is cropland. Cereals are the major crop, with small amounts of oilseeds and forages. Less than 20% of the cropland area is summerfallow.

H9. Cudworth Plain

The Cudworth plain comprises a series of undulating plains in the central part, flanked by hilly uplands on the west and east sides of the area. Elevations in upland areas in the south reach 610 m, with prominent uplands such as Manatinaw and the Tiger Hills in the north reaching 580 m. The intervening plains fall from 580 m in the south to 490 m in the north. With the exception of McKay Creek and the upper reaches of the Carrot River, which drain out of the area to the northeast, most of the surface drainage is limited to local flow to Buffer, Boucher, Wakaw, and several smaller lakes and sloughs in the area.

Most of the native vegetation in this area has been cultivated, particularly on the level lacustrine plains. However, in the hummocky moraine of the Minichinas Hills, west of Wakaw, there is extensive aspen parkland vegetation, although much of it is interspersed with cultivated fields.

The Black loamy soils that are dominant in this area have developed in silty glaciolacustrine deposits associated with gently undulating to rolling topography, with numerous glacial kettles, in the central plains region. The glaciolacustrine deposits were lain down in Glacial Lake Saskatchewan as the glacier retreated northward from the area. The upland areas are also Black loamy soils, but moderately to steeply sloping hummocky moraines with numerous glacial kettles are the most common landscapes.

Nearly all of the Cudworth plain is cropland. Cereals are the major crop, with small amounts of oilseeds. Less than 20% of the cropland is summerfallow.

H10. Quill Lake Plain

The Quill Lake plain is a large, nearly level area that extends eastward from Humboldt almost to Canora. Elevations reach 600 m at the margins of the Porcupine and Touchwood hills, but essentially lie between 520 and 550 m throughout most of the area. There is considerable drainage from the Porcupine and Touchwood hills into the Quill Lakes, but there is no surface drainage out of this area.

Most of the native vegetation in this area has been cultivated. The only significant area of aspen parkland with fescue prairie is Wolverine PFRA community pasture, near Plunkett. A large part of this landscape area has been rated as nationally important for migratory birds. It includes several large, shallow lakes that are used by large populations of ducks as breeding, moulting, and staging areas. It is also important as a breeding and staging area for geese, and some lakes are regionally important for colonial waterbirds (double-crested cormorant, great blue heron, black-crowned night-heron). The Quill Lakes support one of the world's larger breeding populations of the endangered piping plover. These lakes and Lenore Lake are also nationally important as staging areas for other shorebirds.

The thick Black loamy soils reflect the more humid climate and associated vegetation that prevailed in the area. These soils have formed in glacial till deposits in association with gently sloping till plains and moderately sloping hummocky moraines.

Most of the Quill Lake Plain is cropland. Cereals are the major crop, with small amounts of oilseeds. Less than 20% of the cropland is summerfallow. There are small areas of rangeland and pasture scattered throughout the area, usually in association with sandy soils. The PFRA community pasture near Plunkett occupies some of this land.

H11. Touchwood Hills Upland

The Touchwood Hills is a large upland area that extends southward from Wynyard and Foam Lake to near Balcarres. Elevations range from 600 m at the base of the hills to 730 m in the Touchwood and Little Touchwood hills. There is considerable drainage from the north flank of the hills through Birch and Duckhunting creeks to the Quill Lakes and through Beaver and Becket creeks to Foam Lake. The eastern flanks drain to the Whitesand River through Lawne, Cussed, and Willow Brook creeks. There also is drainage to the Qu'Appelle River through Kaposvar, Pearl, Pheasant, Jumping Deer, and Loon creeks.

About 30% of this area is uncultivated, usually represented as significant areas of aspen parkland on hummocky terrain. The largest areas of native vegetation are in the vicinity of Punnichy (much of this on Indian reserves), and further east around Parkerview. Much of the latter area is in the Ituna-Bon Accord and Garry PFRA community pastures, the Insinger provincial pasture, and Wildlife Development Fund land. Much of the native vegetation in all of these areas consists of nearly continuous aspen forest on Gray Luvisol soils.

The Black loamy soils reflect the climate and vegetation that prevailed throughout much of the area. These soils have developed mostly in glacial till deposits associated with moderately sloping hummocky morainal landscapes; however, the Little Touchwood Hills area has Black loamy and sandy soils formed in sandy and silty glaciolacustrine deposits associated with moderately to steeply sloping hummocky landscapes. These latter deposits are believed to have formed in a glacial lake that rested on the glacier prior to its retreat from the area.

Most of the Touchwood Hills is cropland. Cereals are the major crop, with small amounts of oilseeds. There is a very small area of forages and over 20% of the cropland is summerfallow. There are extensive areas of rangeland and pasture scattered throughout the area, usually in association with steeply sloping or heavily treed landscapes. Several PFRA community pastures, a provincial pasture, and several Indian reserves near Punnichy represent some of these areas.

H12. Whitesand Plain

The Whitesand plain, situated between Foam Lake and Canora, slopes gently to the southeast, from elevations of 550 m near Fishing Lake to 490 m near Good Spirit Lake. There is considerable drainage from the Porcupine Hills, to the north, into Fishing Lake and through Spirit Creek into Good Spirit Lake. Similarly, there is drainage from the Touchwood Hills to the south, into the Whitesand River, which drains much of the Whitesand plain into the Assiniboine River.

Because of the predominance of sandy soils in this area, only about half of the area is cultivated. Significant areas of aspen parkland occur, for example in the Foam Lake PFRA community pasture. A small area of sand dunes with woodland and grassland can be seen at Good Spirit Lake Provincial Park.

The dominantly Black sandy loam soils have developed in sandy and gravelly glaciofluvial deposits formed when glacial meltwater poured over the area. Landscapes are most commonly gently undulating in nature.

There is an almost equal amount of rangeland-pasture and cropland in this area. Cereals are the major crop, with small amounts of oilseeds and forage crops. More than 20% of the cropland is summerfallow. There are extensive areas of rangeland and pasture scattered throughout the area, usually in association with extremely sandy or saline soils. Small PFRA community pastures are located on some of these areas, as is Good Spirit Provincial Park.

H13. Yorkton Plain

The Yorkton plain is a large, nearly level area extending from Canora to Spy Hill. It slopes gently from 520 m in the south to 490 m in the north. Yorkton, Wallace, and Crooked Hill creeks drain to the Assiniboine River through the Whitesand River; Kamsack, Stony, and Cutarm creeks drain directly to the Assiniboine.

Most of this area has been cultivated, and the remaining aspen parkland is interspersed with farmland. The thick Black loamy soils reflect the humid climate and associated vegetation of the area.

Soils formed in glacial till deposits associated with nearly level till plains with numerous kettles are most common, but soils formed in silty glaciolacustrine deposits in association with gently undulating landscapes are also common. These glaciolacustrine deposits were lain down in Glacial Lake Saltcoats. Cutarm Creek was formed as a meltwater channel that drained this lake.

Most of the land in the Yorkton Plain is cropland. Cereals are the major crop, with small amounts of oilseeds and forage crops. Less than 20% of the cropland is summerfallow. Pastureland is dispersed throughout the area.

H14. St. Lazarre Plain

The St. Lazarre plain is a very small area in Saskatchewan, situated near the Assiniboine River valley on the Manitoba border. Elevations are approximately 520 m throughout this area. There is considerable surface drainage to the Assiniboine River.

This landscape is largely uncultivated. Some of this is associated with valleys. Along the Assiniboine River, the valley slopes are covered with trembling aspen, with some grassland on south-facing slopes, and with occasional bur oak. The Qu'Appelle, at the south end of the landscape area, has abundant bur oak on south-facing slopes, along with aspen stands and grassland. Spy Hill PFRA community pasture, just north of the Qu'Appelle Valley, consists of sandy plains with extensive native grassland.

Black soils developed in sandy and gravelly glaciofluvial and eroded glacial till deposits, formed by glacial meltwater in the early stages of development of the Assiniboine River, are the most common soils in this area. They are associated with gently undulating till plains and gullied glaciofluvial landscapes.

Most of the St. Lazarre plain is rangeland and pasture, occupied at least in part by a PFRA community pasture. Cereals are the major crop, with small amounts of oilseeds. There is a large amount of cropland that is planted to forages and more than 20% of the cropland is summerfallow.

H15. Melville Plain

The Melville plain is a nearly level area that lies on both sides of the Qu'Appelle River valley in the eastern part of the region. Except for the Pheasant Hills in the western part of the area and the Broadview-Whitewood area south of the Qu'Appelle Valley, where elevations exceed 600 m, most of the plain slopes from 550 m in the north to 520 m at the edge of the Qu'Appelle Valley. Surface drainage of the area north of the Valley is provided through Kaposvar, Pearl, and Pheasant creeks to the Qu'Appelle River.

Most of this area consists of farmland with only small areas of aspen parkland vegetation. The largest areas of native vegetation are associated with the Qu'Appelle Valley. This contains extensive slope forests of trembling aspen and green ash, grassland on south-facing slopes, and a rich variety of wetlands and riparian vegetation, along with hayfields and cultivated land, in the valley bottom. The eastern part of the valley, within this landscape area, is the main area of bur oak in Saskatchewan, which appears most abundantly on south-facing slopes. This is an outlier of the "aspen-oak parkland" of southern Manitoba. This portion of the valley is also interesting for its inclusion of other eastern forest species, as well as pockets of grassland typical of the "tall grass prairie" which occurs in Manitoba and the midwestern states of the United States.

The riparian and valley-slope forests along the Qu'Appelle Valley provide unusual animal habitats. Wood duck, an uncommon species in Saskatchewan, can be found along the river in this area. The eastern-most portion of the valley has eastern wood-pewee as well as lazuli and indigo bunting as uncommon summer birds. In general, the valley, with its diversity of habitats, has a large variety of bird species relative to comparable areas in the surrounding uplands. The Qu'Appelle River and drainages entering it also have painted and snapping turtles. Other eastern animal species found in the Qu'Appelle Valley include eastern gray squirrel, redbelly snake, and smooth green snake. The Qu'Appelle system also has fish that are uncommon in Saskatchewan, including rock bass, brown bullhead, and channel catfish, as well as the chestnut lamprey.

The Black loamy soils that prevail in this area have formed in glacial till deposits associated with moderately sloping hummocky moraine.

Most of the land in the Melville plain is cropland. Cereals are the major crop, with small amounts of oilseeds and forages. More than 20% of the cropland is summerfallow. Pastureland is generally dispersed, but there is some concentration in sandy soil areas along the Qu'Appelle River valley and within several Indian reserves. Crooked Lake Provincial Park is located in this area.

H16. Indian Head Plain

The Indian Head plain is a clay plain lying on either side of the Qu'Appelle River valley in the eastern part of the region. Elevations fall from 600 m at the Pheasant Hills and Moose Mountain upland to 570 m at the edge of the Qu'Appelle Valley. Pheasant, Jumping Deer, Redfox, Adair, and Summerberry creeks, which all flow to the Qu'Appelle Valley, provide a considerable amount of external drainage for this area.

Most of this level plain has been cultivated. As with the Melville plain, the main area of native vegetation is the Qu'Appelle Valley and the numerous coulees leading into it. This portion of the valley is further west than that in the Melville plain, and there is a lower proportion of wooded cover and no bur oak. However, the valley still creates a diverse landscape of slope forests of trembling aspen and green ash, grasslands on south-facing slopes, riparian woods of Manitoba maple and balsam poplar, and wetlands. Many of the animal species with eastern affinities that occur in the Melville plain also occur in this landscape area, although with reduced abundance in many instances.

Black clayey soils formed in glaciolacustrine clays associated with level to gently undulating landscapes are most common, but appreciable areas of Black loamy soils formed in glacial till deposits associated with gently undulating till plains and moderately sloping hummocky moraines with numerous kettles are also present. The clay deposits were lain down as part of Glacial Lake Indian Head. This lake, formed by meltwater from the ice that collected in a basin created by the high ground to the south and the glacier to the north, drained through the Pipestone Spillway to Lake Souris, in Manitoba. The Qu'Appelle Valley formed later, as a spillway for Glacial Lake Regina.

Most of the land in the Indian Head plain is cropland, with cereals the major crop. More than 30% of the cropland is summerfallow. Pastureland is generally dispersed, but there is some concentration in sandy soil areas along the Qu'Appelle River valley and in several Indian reserves within the area. Echo Valley Provincial Park is located in this area.

H17. Kipling Plain

The Kipling plain represents the north flank of the Moose Mountain upland. It extends eastward from the Qu'Appelle River valley, north of Regina, almost to the Manitoba border. Elevations rise from 600 m on the lower plains to the north to over 670 m throughout much of the area and to 700 m in isolated areas. There is a considerable amount of surface drainage to the Qu'Appelle River through Echo, Indian Head, Redfox, Adair, and Elcapo creeks, to the east through Montgomery and Pipestone creeks, and to the south through Moose Mountain Creek.

This morainal plain is mostly cultivated, with aspen parkland interspersed with farmland over much of it. The Pipestone Creek valley provides more continuous native vegetation, with slope forest, grassland, and wetlands. Upland aspen parkland is represented in Strawberry Lake provincial pasture. Black loamy soils formed in glacial till deposits associated with moderately sloping hummocky moraines with numerous kettles are most common in this area.

Most of the land in the Kipling plain is cropland, with cereals the major crop. More than 30% of the cropland is summerfallow. Pastureland is generally dispersed, but there is some concentration in several sandy soil areas and in several Indian reserves within the area.

H18. Moose Mountain Upland

The Moose Mountain upland represents the south-facing, drier part of the larger upland region. It parallels the Kipling plain as it extends eastward from the Qu'Appelle Valley, north of Regina, to Moose Mountain. Elevations rise from 600 m on the lower plains to the south to over 670 m throughout much of the area and to 730 m near Moose Mountain. There is a limited amount of surface drainage — to the east through Montgomery Creek to Pipestone Creek, and to the south through Wascana and Moose Mountain creeks.

Most of the native vegetation in this area has been cultivated. What remains is limited to areas of hummocky morainal landscapes, where it is interspersed with farmland.

Dark Brown soils reflect the more arid climate and associated vegetation of the area. Dark Brown loamy soils formed in glacial till deposits associated with moderately sloping hummocky moraines with numerous kettles are most common.

Nearly all of the land in the Moose Mountain upland is cropland. Cereals are the major crop, and more than 30% of the cropland area is summerfallow.

H19. Moose Mountain

Moose Mountain represents the uppermost part of the larger Moose Mountain upland. Elevations rise from 730 m at the margin with the surrounding plains to 800 m in isolated highs. Surface drainage in this area is limited to the numerous small lakes and sloughs within the area.

This landscape area has more uncultivated land than any in the Aspen Parkland Ecoregion. The core of the area is a prominent upland which is covered with continuous forest. The forest is dominated by trembling aspen, but balsam poplar also appears in moist sites. Green ash and, to a much lesser extent, Manitoba maple appear as a shade-tolerant understory beneath the aspen, especially in the eastern part of the area. Trees reach heights similar to those in the boreal ecoregions. In reality, this area belongs with the Boreal Transition Ecoregion, but it is included in the Aspen Parkland Ecoregion to avoid fragmentation of regions. The hummocky landscape of Moose Mountain also creates a high density of lakes and wetlands, ranging from deep marsh to shallow marsh to wet meadow. Around the periphery of the wooded core, mixed and fescue grasslands appear, especially on the prominent south-facing slope that bounds the area.

Moose Mountain has a distinctive bird community compared to the surrounding parklands. This may be the only place in Saskatchewan where the yellow-throated vireo occurs regularly. While yellow warbler and common yellowthroat are the only warbler species found regularly throughout most of the ecoregion, in this landscape area, ovenbird and American redstart are common, and the northern waterthrush, and black-and-white, mourning, and chestnut-sided warblers can be found. This area also has populations of elk and moose, usually found only in the boreal ecoregions.

Black and Dark Gray soils reflect a more humid climate and associated vegetation than in the surrounding area. Black loamy soils formed in glacial till deposits associated with steeply sloping hummocky moraines with numerous kettles are most common, but appreciable areas of Dark Gray loamy soils, formed in similar deposits and with the same associated landscapes, are also present.

Nearly all of the land in Moose Mountain is either rangeland and pasture, in association with Indian reserves, or Moose Mountain Provincial Park.

H20. Gainsborough Plain

The Gainsborough plain is a nearly level area that extends eastward from Moose Mountain to the Manitoba border and southward to the border with the United States. The area slopes from 730 m against Moose Mountain to 480 m at the Manitoba and United States borders. Surface drainage from this area is extensive. Smith, Morrison, and Cowper creeks drain the western part to Moose Mountain Creek. Auburnton, Lightning, and Gainsborough creeks drain to the Antler River before it leaves the province to join the Souris River in the United States. Graham, Jackson, Stony, and Pipestone creeks all flow into Manitoba before joining the Souris River.

Most of the native vegetation in this area has been cultivated. What remains is limited to areas of hummocky morainal landscapes, where it is interspersed with farmland.

Black soils reflect the climate and associated vegetation of the area. Black loamy soils formed in glacial till deposits associated with gently undulating till plains with numerous kettles are most common.

Most of the land in the Gainsborough plain is cropland. Cereals are the major crop, with only small amounts of oilseeds and forage crops. Less than 20% of the cropland is summerfallow. Pastureland is generally dispersed throughout the area.

H21. Moose Mountain Creek Plain

The Moose Mountain Creek plain is a small area along Moose Mountain Creek, extending from north of Stoughton to Oxbow. The area slopes from 640 m in the upper reaches of Moose Mountain Creek to 580 m at its confluence with the Souris River.

Native aspen parkland vegetation occurs in association with sandy soils such as in the Tecumseh PFRA community pasture.

Dark Brown and Black soils reflect the more arid climate and associated vegetation of the area. Dark Brown sandy loam soils formed in sandy glacial till deposits associated with moderately sloping hummocky landscapes are most common, but Dark Brown sands on nearly level glaciofluvial and Black sandy loams formed in moderately sloping hummocky morainal landscapes also occur.

There is an almost equal amount of rangeland-pasture and cropland in this area. Cereals are the major crop, with small amounts of forage crops. Approximately 30% of the cropland is summerfallow. There are extensive areas of rangeland and pasture scattered throughout the area, usually in association with extremely sandy or saline soils. A small PFRA community pasture is located on some of these areas.

H22. Oak Lake Plain

The Oak Lake plain is a small area along the Antler River, in the extreme southeast part of the region. It is part of a much larger area in Manitoba. It slopes from 580 m in the north to less than 490 m where the Antler River enters Manitoba in the south. Auburnton and Lightning creeks and the Antler River provide a considerable amount of surface drainage to this area.

Most of this landscape area consists of farmland interspersed with small areas of aspen parkland. The lower Antler River area supports a number of eastern forest and prairie species which are rare in Saskatchewan.

Black soils reflect the relatively arid climate and associated vegetation of the area. Black sandy loam soils formed in sandy, nearly level glaciofluvial deposits are most common.

Most of the land in the Oak Lake plain is cropland. Cereals are the major crop, with small amounts of forages. Approximately 20% of the cropland is summerfallow. Pastureland is generally dispersed throughout the area.

Moist Mixed Grassland Ecoregion

The mixed prairie is a vast region that extends from Saskatchewan to the high plains of Texas. It is characterized by mid-grasses (wheatgrasses and speargrasses) and short-grasses (blue grama grass), all growing in mixed stands. The Moist Mixed Grassland Ecoregion represents the northernmost extension of these open grasslands. It occupies 6.8 million hectares or 11% of the province. Wheatgrasses and speargrasses are the dominant grasses, and aspen commonly occur in association with local wetlands. The ecoregion closely correlates with a semiarid climate and Dark Brown soils. Agriculture has drastically modified the natural landscape in this ecoregion, with approximately 80% of the ecoregion under cultivation.

PHYSIOGRAPHY. The Moist Mixed Grassland Ecoregion comprises a broad plain that is interrupted by deep, scenic valleys and subdued, hilly uplands. The primary slope of the plain is downward to the north and east, in accordance with the slope of the bedrock surface. Most of the region has a cover of glacial drift that is sufficiently thick to obscure the underlying bedrock topography; hence, striking bedrock landscapes such as occur in the Mixed Grassland and Cypress Hills Upland ecoregions are uncommon. Secondary slopes from the uplands to drainage systems such as the South Saskatchewan, Qu'Appelle, and Souris rivers occasionally break the general northeastward slope of the plain.

Level to gently undulating glaciolacustrine and glacial till plains that seem almost endless typify this ecoregion, but hummocky morainal uplands, sand dunes, and local "badlands" provide some diversity. The plains generally lie between 500 and 600 m. The uplands protrude 50 to 200 m above the adjacent plain, with the Neutral and Bear hills reaching elevations of 700 m and more. Although the break from the plains to the uplands is usually gradual and unspectacular, prominent escarpments such as the Missouri Coteau are striking features.

The valleys of the Souris, Qu'Appelle, and South Saskatchewan rivers,

Cereal crops dominate the landscape of the Moist Mixed Grassland Ecoregion.

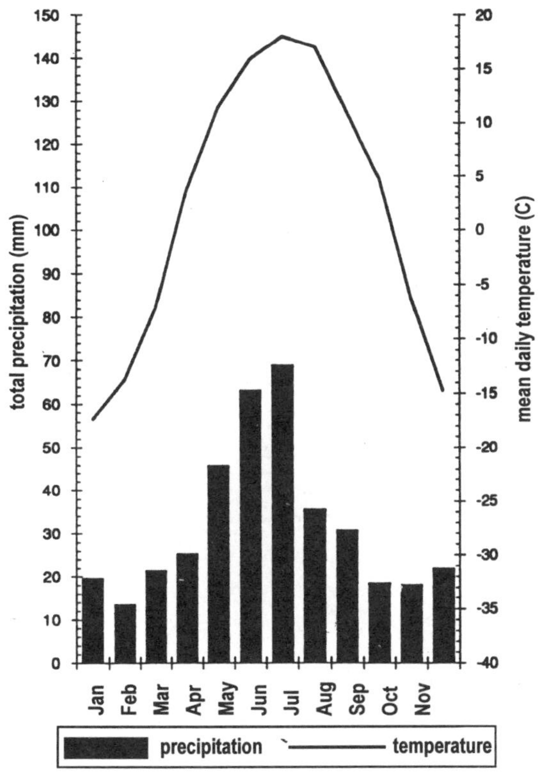

Figure 20. Mean monthly temperature and precipitation for the Moist Mixed Grassland Ecoregion as represented by the meteorological record from Harris.

sometimes entrenched 100 m or more into the plain, are major contributors to the beauty of the region. These river valleys form part of the Nelson River drainage basin. There are also a number of lakes that add diversity and beauty: Muddy, Tramping, Diefenbaker, Goose, Last Mountain, Little Manitou, and Buffalo Pound, to name but a few.

GEOLOGY. The bedrock underlying most of the ecoregion is marine sedimentary rocks of the Bearpaw Formation. These rocks typically consist of gray-green silty mudstones and shales with localized deposits of bentonite. In the southeastern part of the ecoregion, near the United States border, the Upper Cretaceous Frenchman, Whitemud, and Eastend formations are overlain by the coal-bearing Ravenscrag Formation. In the subsurface, older sedimentary rocks host important deposits of potash and salt, numerous oil fields, and a few gas fields of considerable economic importance to the province.

CLIMATE. The Moist Mixed Grassland Ecoregion has a subhumid continental climate. It is cooler and wetter, and consequently less arid, than the Mixed Grassland Ecoregion to the south and west of it but warmer and slightly drier than in the Aspen Parkland Ecoregion to the north and east. Within the moist mixed grassland, temperature and precipitation are lower in the northwest than in the southeast. Temperatures are also lower at high elevations than on nearby plains. The mean annual daily temperature is 2.4°C. The mean July temperature is 18.4°C and the mean January temperature is -16.7°C. The mean annual precipitation is 383 mm, with 240 mm of rainfall occurring from May to September. The summers are short and warm, having a frost-free period of 110 days and a total of 1,663 degree days above 5°C.

LANDFORMS AND SOILS. Dark Brown Chernozemic soils prevail throughout this ecoregion in response to the relatively large additions of organic matter in these mixed grasslands and slower rates of decomposition in this cooler part of the mixed-grass prairie. As their name implies, these Dark Brown soils have a dark-coloured surface layer that is higher in organic matter than those in the Brown soil zone, but lower than in the Black zone. Typically, this layer is separated from a grayish-brown layer, which represents the soil parent material, by a reddish-brown layer that is free of carbonates of calcium and magnesium.

Soils tend to be thin and lower in organic matter on upper slopes, becoming progressively thicker and higher in organic matter on mid and lower slopes, in response to an increased supply of soil moisture and plant growth. Brown soils occur on prominent south-facing local and regional slopes where more arid conditions result in reduced growth. Black soils occur on prominent north-facing slopes and in lower-slope positions on steeply sloping topography, where fescues and other grasses that typify the aspen parkland prevail.

GROUNDWATER. Groundwater in the ecoregion is associated with the drift that covers the bedrock as well as with the bedrock. Bedrock aquifers within the sandy and silty beds of the Judith River Formation prevail throughout all except the southeastern part of the ecoregion, where the aquifers in the Ravenscrag Formation prevail. The Tyner Valley, Swift Current Valley, and Estevan Valley aquifers represent major buried valley aquifers of the Empress Formation that have been incised into the bedrock surface. Glacial aquifers are widely distributed throughout the ecoregion. Inter-till aquifers are most common in the older and deeper Floral Formation. The City of Regina obtains some of its water supply from such systems. Surficial aquifers are common in the sandy glacial lake deltas that blanket the present surface between the North and South Saskatchewan rivers from Borden to Saskatoon, along the South Saskatchewan River from Elbow to Saskatoon, along the Qu'Appelle River east of Elbow, and along Thunder Creek west of Moose Jaw.

Both the bedrock and glacial aquifers have a marked influence on the ecology of the area. Lakes such as Tramping, Last Mountain, Little Manitou, Goose, and Buffalo Pound derive a considerable amount of their source from aquifer discharge. The quality of the water in the lake is largely dependent upon the source of the groundwater; higher salt concentrations are associated with discharge from bedrock aquifers and low salt concentrations from near-surface glacial aquifers or from surface aquifers.

Aquifers also impact on water supply to vegetation. The prevalence of aspen in sandy areas such as the Moose Woods and Harris Sand Hills, south of Saskatoon, is often a reflection of a surface aquifer in these sediments. Saline soils and salt-tolerant vegetation is often associated with surface concentrations of salts derived from glacial and bedrock aquifers.

VEGETATION. The regular alternation between woodland, shrubland, and grassland that characterized the Aspen Parkland Ecoregion still prevails in the Moist Mixed Grassland Ecoregion. However, the woodland is restricted to tiny rings around sloughs. Northern wheatgrass and western porcupine grass dominate on loamy soils, while sandy areas have a unique community of grasses, shrubs, and trees. In presettlement times, fires prevented aspen from encroaching on the grasslands; however, since settlement, the incidence of fire has been reduced and the aspen has advanced southward across the region as well as upslope from the sloughs.

The prickly rose is a common native rose that grows in shrubby patches throughout the prairies.

The Moist Mixed Grassland Ecoregion is the home of the mid-grasses (wheatgrasses and speargrasses). These mid-grasses are often sandwiched between blue grama grass on drier upper slope positions of morainic landscapes and rough fescue and Hooker's oat grass in the better protected lower slope positions. Sedges and June grass are also important components of the moist mixed grassland communities, with June grass being particularly abundant in areas of lacustrine clay soils.

Shrublands frequently appear in depressions, on margins of aspen stands, or in association with sandy soils. The most abundant species among the forbs and shrubs, everywhere, is pasture sage. Mats of club-moss commonly cover parts of the soil surface beneath the two-layered, mixed-grass canopy. Lichens also occasionally occur in this lowest layer. Dwarf individuals of hoary sage brush and prairie rose often are present within the herbaceous cover and patches of western snowberry occur in protected habitats. Valleys and coulees contain patches of brush, including willow, wolf-willow, saskatoon, western snowberry, and choke cherry.

Plant communities in sandy areas, where rainfall rapidly infiltrates the soil and soil water is readily accessible to plants, vary significantly from those on finer textured soils. Grasses unique to sandy areas include sand grass, Canada wild rye, Indian rice grass, and sand dropseed. Grasses such as little bluestem and western porcupine grass, which are common on loamy soils throughout the Aspen Parkland Ecoregion and the northern extremities of the Moist Mixed Grassland Ecoregion, also prevail in these sandy areas. Many species of forbs that are typical of the sandy environment are rare or absent in other habitats. These include hairy golden aster, prairie sunflower, and skeletonweed. Shrubs such as wolf-willow, creeping juniper, choke cherry, saskatoon, and prairie rose thrive in sandy soils.

Wetlands in the moist mixed grassland have a similar assemblage of grasses, sedges, and rushes to that described for the Aspen Parkland Ecoregion. Increasing salinity in wetlands shifts vegetation in these areas to salt-tolerant species such as salt-grass, Nuttall's alkali grass, red samphire, sea blite, and alkali bulrush. Areas with accumulations of soluble salts are represented by desert saltgrass and Nuttall's alkali grass. Where salinity is too high for these species, annual halophytes, especially red samphire and sea blite, contribute some cover.

Most woodlands in the Moist Mixed Grassland Ecoregion are represented by stands of trembling aspen with an understory of shrubs (western snowberry and prairie rose), herbs (western Canada violet, smooth and showy aster, and small bedstraw) and grasses (bluegrass and sedges). Aspen stands on sandy soils are characterized by prostrate shrubs (creeping juniper and bearberry). Hay sedge is often an important herb.

The grassland in areas grazed by domestic livestock generally has a greater component of short-grasses and other "increaser species." Where grazing has been sufficiently intensive to affect the mid-grasses severely, short-grasses such as blue grama and sedge prevail.

Short-eared owl resting on a fence post.

WILDLIFE. The Moist Mixed Grassland Ecoregion, with its grasslands, wooded groves, and numerous wetlands, supports more species of birds than the simpler Mixed Grassland Ecoregion to the south but fewer than in the aspen parkland to the north.

Fifty-one species of mammals have been reported in the grassland zone of southern Saskatchewan. The following mammals prevail in this ecoregion: big brown bat, porcupine, white-tailed jack rabbit, prairie vole, meadow vole, northern grasshopper mouse, olive-backed pocket mouse, white-footed mouse, deer mouse, masked shrew, thirteen-lined ground squirrel, eastern cottontail, northern pocket gopher, meadow jumping mouse, Richardson's ground squirrel, and sagebrush vole. Among the larger mammals that range the area are coyote, striped skunk, least weasel, red fox, mule and white-tailed deer, and pronghorn. Bison once roamed over this ecoregion.

The former Matador Ranch, and more recently one of the grassland biome sites of the International Biological Program, provided a relatively large expanse of open grassland for the study of fauna. One hundred and ninety-eight species of birds (six of which are introduced) were observed within a 1500 km^2 area surrounding the Matador. Of these, 92 are summer residents (breeding in the area) and 10 species are permanent residents. An additional 16 species are summer residents or visitors which do not breed in the district; 7 are winter residents. The remaining 73 species are spring and autumn transients. Only 15 species breed in the normal upland. These include three raptors (short-eared owl, northern harrier, and burrowing owl), three shore-birds (upland sandpiper, marbled godwit, and long-billed curlew), sharp-tailed grouse, and the following passerines: Baird's sparrow, Sprague's pipit, chestnut-collared longspur, horned lark, savannah sparrow, vesper sparrow, McCown's longspur, and western meadowlark.

Fish diversity is somewhat lower than in the Aspen Parkland Ecoregion, with 41 species. The most common game fish are walleye, northern pike, yellow perch, and burbot. Several trout species have been introduced. The goldeye, sauger, and lake sturgeon occur in the South Saskatchewan River.

Five snakes, six frogs and toads, one turtle, and one salamander range into the ecoregion. Of these, the tiger salamander, great plains toad, painted turtle, plains garter snake, boreal chorus frog, wood frog, and northern leopard frog are the most common species.

HUMAN ACTIVITY. The population of this ecoregion is approximately 546,000, 55% of the Saskatchewan population. Major communities include Regina, Saskatoon, Moose Jaw, Weyburn, Estevan, Unity, Biggar, Davidson, Watrous, and Rosetown.

Agriculture is the major land use throughout the ecoregion, with many areas being almost entirely farmland. Approximately 80% of this ecoregion is cultivated; in some areas nearly all farmland is cropland. Spring wheat and other cereal grains are produced by employing a wheat or other grain-fallow rotation. Oilseed crops are also becoming increasingly important. Minor irrigation of these crops occurs near Lake Diefenbaker. In many parts of the ecoregion, the cultivated fields contain small patches of wet, stony or hilly land that are not cultivated and that may provide habitat, albeit often poor, for some forms of wildlife. In other parts, there are large tracts of land that is not suited for cultivation, with the intended use being pasture for livestock. These areas, especially when in as close as possible to the native state, represent better wildlife habitat.

The moist mixed grassland, with its semiarid climate, is not as well suited to the production of a wide variety of

Giant draglines are used to remove overburden and expose the coal seams in Saskatchewan coal mines.

field crops as is the aspen parkland, but it is better suited than the more arid Mixed Grassland Ecoregion. Longer rotations than in the adjacent mixed grassland means there is less summerfallow practiced. The sloughs also tend to be wetter, occasionally resulting in remnant aspen groves dispersed throughout the cultivated fields. Such areas sometimes provide habitat for waterfowl and other wildlife. Areas that are wet, sandy, saline, stony or hilly are generally not cultivated. They often are used for pasturing livestock, but also provide the majority of available habitat for birds, deer, coyote, fox, hare, squirrels, and many other animals.

The Moist Mixed Grassland Ecoregion is also home to major heavy industry. Mining activity includes oil, gas, potash, salt and coal. Substantial production of crude oil occurs in the Weyburn-Estevan areas. Potash is produced from 10 mines in the province, most of which are in this ecoregion. Coal is produced from five open pit mines along the southern boundary of Saskatchewan within this and the Mixed Grassland Ecoregion. There is sodium sulphate solution mine development at Unity. Dams and reservoirs are present on all of the major drainage basins in the Prairie Ecozone. They are used primarily to store water for use during drought and to alleviate flooding during peak flows. Four major dams (the Gardiner, Rafferty, Weyburn, and Boundary Reservoir) are located in the Moist Mixed Grassland Ecoregion.

Waterfowl hunting is common, and recreation is important around several large reservoirs. Six provincial parks occur in this region, including Danielson, Buffalo Pound, and Douglas parks. Approximately 5% of the ecoregion is within some form of park or protected area. Of special note is the Last Mountain Lake National Wildlife Area noted for sandhill crane, duck, geese, and other concentrations of birds.

Landscape Areas

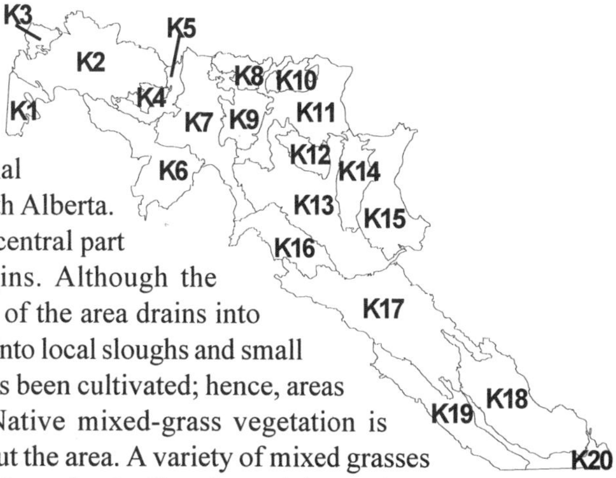

K1. Neutral Hills

The Neutral Hills is a hilly morainal upland located against the border with Alberta. Elevations range from 800 m in the central part of the area to 720 m at the margins. Although the escarpment along the northern edge of the area drains into Cactus Lake, most of the area drains into local sloughs and small lakes. Most of this landscape area has been cultivated; hence, areas of native vegetation are limited. Native mixed-grass vegetation is interspersed with cropland throughout the area. A variety of mixed grasses and various shrubs are common on the uplands. Sloughs and depressions are dominated by sedges, surrounded by willows and aspen. More continuous cover can be found in the steep, hummocky morainal landscapes in the northern part of the area, especially in the Hearts Hill PFRA community pasture.

Dark Brown loamy soils prevail on glacial till deposits associated with steep and very steep hummocky morainal landscapes as well as on local areas of gently undulating glaciolacustrine landscapes.

Most of the Neutral Hills is rangeland or pasture in association with hilly topography. Cropland is associated with the more gently sloping areas, with cereals the major crop.

More than 40% of the cropland area is summerfallow. There are extensive areas of rangeland and pasture scattered throughout the area, usually in association with extremely steep slopes, stones, and numerous sloughs. The Hearts Hill and Antelope Park PFRA community pastures are located on some of these areas.

K2. Tramping Lake Plain

A large basin with prominent lakes and occasional low hills, the Tramping Lake plain extends from near Macklin at the Alberta border almost to Biggar. Elevations drop from more than 700 m on the margin of the basin to 610 m at Tramping Lake. Although the Tramping Lake and Shepards sloughs played important roles in carrying meltwater into glacial lakes to the south of the area, today these channels drain only small areas in their immediate vicinity. There also is a limited amount of drainage to Grill, Muddy, Ear, Fire, Cactus, and several other lakes.

Native mixed-grass vegetation is limited to steep hummocky morainal landscapes — where it is generally interspersed with croplands — and to sandy soils, gullies, and valley sides. A variety of mixed grasses and various shrubs are common on the uplands. Sloughs and depressions usually comprise sedges surrounded by willows and aspen. More continuous cover can be found in the general area of Muddy Lake.

Dark Brown loamy soils prevail on very gently to gently undulating glaciolacustrine landscapes as well as on moderately sloping hummocky morainal and glaciolacustrine landscapes. Sometimes these landscapes have a network of gullies that drain to lakes or streams.

The loamy glaciolacustrine deposits formed in Glacial Lake Unity provide a thin, continuous cover on the glacial till on nearly level landscapes, but only cover the swales in areas where prominent intersecting till ridges prevail. In level areas, the glacial till is underlain by an eroded, gravelly, and stony surface of an earlier till unit. In hummocky morainal areas, the till thickens to as much as 10 m. Many lakes in the area, such as Muddy, End, and Fire lakes were formed by ice plucking the materials beneath it and creating a depression. Local hills to the south of the depression represent the subsequent deposition of these materials.

Nearly all of the area is cropland. Cereals are the major crop, with small amounts of oilseeds. More than 30% of the cropland area is summerfallow. Rangeland and pasture are limited to small areas of steep hummocky morainal landscapes, such as occur between Ear and Grill lakes, or sandy soils near Unity.

K3. Senlac Hills

The Senlac Hills is a hilly, morainal upland formed when the glacier plucked materials from its base, creating the large depression in the Artland-Winter area, and subsequently deposited these materials nearby, to form a range of hills. Elevations reach 715 m in the centre of the area, dropping to 685 m at the margin. Surface drainage is limited to flow to local sloughs or small lakes.

Native mixed-grass vegetation is limited to steep hummocky morainal landscapes or sandy soils in the northeastern part of the area, where it is interspersed with cropland. A variety of mixed grasses and shrubs are most common on uplands. Sloughs and depressions usually comprise sedges surrounded by willows and aspen.

Dark Brown loamy and sandy soils occur on steep to very steep glaciolacustrine and hummocky morainal landscapes that dominate this area.

Most of the area is cropland. Cereals are the major crop, with small amounts of oilseeds. Approximately 25% of the cropland area is summerfallow. Most of the rangeland and pasture is associated with the very steep, hummocky morainal landscapes in the northeastern part of the area.

K4. Biggar Plain

The Biggar plain is a sandy basin west of Biggar. Elevations drop gently from 670 m on the margins to below 650 m at Richmond and Castlewood lakes. Surface drainage is minimal in this sandy area.

Native vegetation is limited to sandy or saline soils, where it is interspersed with cropland. A variety of sand grasses and shrubs are most common on the uplands. Depressional areas are often saline, with alkali grass, greasewood, gumweed, and red samphire the characteristic vegetation.

Dark Brown sandy loam soils have formed on gently sloping hummocky glaciofluvial landscapes that dominate the area.

Most of the area is cropland. Cereals are the major crop, with small amounts of forages. More than 35% of the cropland area is summerfallow. Rangeland and pasture is limited to the very sandy or saline areas dispersed throughout the area.

K5. Bear Hills

The Bear Hills is a crescent-shaped hilly morainal upland that represents a rise from the Second to the Third Prairie Steppe. There is a distinct drop in elevation from over 700 m in the heart of the hills to 600 m in the southern and eastern parts of the area, but only a slight drop to the west. There is some surface drainage to Eagle Creek and Vanscoy Lake, at the base of the hills.

Native vegetation occurs interspersed with cropland throughout much of the area. More continuous cover occurs in the northern part of the area, primarily in association with steep hummocky morainal landscapes. A variety of mixed grasses and shrubs are most common on the uplands. Sloughs and depressions comprise sedges, usually surrounded by willows and trembling aspen, but alkali grass, gumweed, greasewood, and red samphire are more common on saline flats.

Dark Brown loamy and sandy loam soils formed on steep to very steep hummocky morainal and glaciofluvial landscapes dominate the northern part of the area. The southern part is dominated by Dark Brown loamy soils formed on gently sloping hummocky glaciolacustrine landscapes. The glaciofluvial and glaciolacustrine deposits, in association with hummocky moraine at relatively high elevation, indicate deposits in lake and river environments that were present on top of the glacier as the ice retreated from the uplands to the west.

Most of the area is cropland, with cereals the major crop, and more than 35% of the cropland area is summerfallow. Rangeland and pasture is limited to the more steeply sloping and stony areas in the northern part of the area.

K6. Rosetown Plain

The Rosetown plain is a large, nearly level glacial lake plain that extends from the base of the Coteau Hills near Dinsmore to the Bad and Bear hills near Rosetown and then northwestward to Tramping Lake. There is a gentle slope from 600 m at the base of the Coteau Hills to 560 m at MacDonald Creek, followed by a gentle rise to 610 m at Rosetown and a further rise to 680 to 700 m in the northwestern part of the area. Eagle Creek provides a conduit for surface drainage from a considerable portion of the northwestern part of the area but the majority of the area drains into local sloughs and the Whitebear Channel.

Remnant native vegetation is associated with the steep valley sides of Eagle Creek and the sandy soils along the Whitebear channel, where a variety of mixed grasses and shrubs are most common. Except for Eagle Creek and the Whitebear channel, which are incised into this plain, the area is a relatively level glaciolacustrine plain with Dark Brown clayey soils.

Nearly all of the area is cropland. Cereals are the major crop, with small amounts of peas, beans, and other crops. Nearly 40% of the cropland area is summerfallow.

K7. Goose Lake Plain

The Goose Lake plain is a nearly level glacial lake plain that extends from the elbow of the South Saskatchewan River to the North Saskatchewan River west of Borden. This area slopes gently to the north and east from 580 m at the base of the Bear Hills to 520 m along its eastern margin with the Moose Wood Sand Hills and at the North Saskatchewan River. There is limited surface drainage into Eagle Creek and Goose Lake.

Native vegetation is common on sandy soils scattered throughout the area, especially in the PFRA community pasture near Elbow, and along the valleys of Eagle and MacDonald creeks and the South Saskatchewan River. A variety of grasses occur in the poorly stabilized sandy areas, and juniper and other shrubs in the more stable areas. Aspen is common where the water table is near the surface. The vegetation on the river valleys is most commonly shrubs, with trembling aspen on north-facing slopes.

The Goose Lake plain comprises a sequence of silty and sandy glaciolacustrine deposits, formed as the levels in Glacial Lake Saskatchewan dropped in response to the northward retreat of the glacier from this area. The sandy soils have been subsequently modified to dune topography from wind activity. Sandy Regosolic soils prevail on these deposits. Dark Brown loamy soils occur on very gently undulating glaciolacustrine landscapes.

Most of the area is cropland. Cereals are the major crop, with small amounts of oilseeds and forages. Approximately 30% of the cropland area is summerfallow. Rangeland and pasture are limited to areas of sand dunes and include a PFRA community pasture.

K8. Saskatoon Plain

The Saskatoon plain is a level glacial lake and eroded glacial till plain west and north of Saskatoon, with elevations from 500 to 520 m. Limited surface drainage is eastward to the South Saskatchewan River.

Native mixed-grass vegetation is limited to the more sandy soils — where it is interspersed with cropland — and the valley of the South Saskatchewan River. In the sandy areas, a variety of grasses and shrubs are the most characteristic species on the uplands. Depressional areas are often saline, with various salt-tolerant grasses such as alkali grass and red samphire being present. Aspen is also common in nonsaline areas with a relatively high water table. The vegetation on the river valley is most commonly shrubs and aspen.

The area comprises a very gently undulating glaciolacustrine landscape with Dark Brown loamy soils in the southern part. These deposits thin toward the north, providing a discontinuous cover on an eroded, stony, and gravelly glacial till surface. At the northern margin of the area, this eroded till plain has a considerable amount of gravels associated with it. These are covered with a very thin, sandy deposit. Dark Brown sandy soils dominate this part of the area.

The stony and gravelly soils in the Saskatoon plain are used as pasture; however, most of the area has soils that are suited to crop production. Cereals are the most common crop, with small amounts of oilseeds and forages. Approximately 25% of the cropland area is summerfallow.

K9. Moose Wood Sand Hills

The Moose Wood Sand Hills is an area of sand dunes straddling the South Saskatchewan River south of Saskatoon. The area lies at approximately 530 m, except for the alluvial plains along the river, which lie at 490 m. Beaver Creek provides a small amount of surface drainage for this area.

There is an abundance of native vegetation in this area, especially in the three large PFRA community pastures that occupy much of the sandy soils in the area. The poorly stabilized areas are characterized by grasses, with shrubs such as juniper more prevalent in stable areas. Aspen is common in areas where the water table is near the surface. There are also native shrubs, grasses, and aspen on the valley sides, and cottonwood, green ash, and Manitoba maple along the alluvial flats of the South Saskatchewan River.

The dunes in the Moose Wood Sand Hills are moderately to steeply sloping, with associated sandy Regosolic soils. The level alluvial plains in the vicinity of Pike and Moon lakes are loamy-textured Regosols, whereas those in the French Flats are Solonetzic and Regosolic clays. Dark Brown sandy loam soils on very gently undulating glaciofluvial landscapes are present in the northern part of the area.

Most of this area is pasture and rangeland in association with the sand dunes, a considerable portion of which is contained within three PFRA community pastures. Pike Lake Provincial Park is also located in this area. Cropland, which is only 40% of the total area, is limited to sandy loam soils in the northern part of the area and alluvial flats along the river. Cereals are the major crop, with large amounts of forages. Approximately 25% of the cropland area is summerfallow.

K10. Minichinas Upland

The Minichinas upland is a hilly morainal upland east of Saskatoon. Elevations range from 530 m at the base of the hills on the west side to above 600 m at the highest point. There is a limited amount of drainage, locally, to Patience and Blucher lakes.

Native vegetation occurs interspersed with cropland throughout much of the area. More continuous cover occurs in the eastern part of the area primarily in association with steep hummocky morainal landscapes. A variety of mixed grasses and shrubs are most common on the uplands. Sloughs and depressions comprise sedges, usually surrounded by willows and trembling aspen, but saltgrass, alkali grass, and red samphire are more common in saline areas.

Moderately to steeply sloping hummocky morainal landscapes, with numerous glacial kettles, are most common in this area. There are lesser amounts of moderately sloping glaciolacustrine landscapes. Dark Brown loamy soils formed in glacial till are associated with the hummocky moraines, and clay loams and clays are associated with the glaciolacustrine landscapes.

Most of the area is cropland. Cereals are the most common crop, with small amounts of oilseeds. More than 30% of the cropland area is summerfallow. Rangeland and pasture are limited to the more steeply sloping landscapes in the northern part of the area. The St. Denis National Wildlife Area is located in this area.

K11. Elstow Plain

The Elstow plain is a glacial lake plain that slopes from approximately 550 m at the base of the Minichinas and Allan hills to 520 m in the southern part of the area and 490 m at the South Saskatchewan River near Saskatoon. Surface drainage is limited to Blucher and Blackstrap lakes and large sloughs.

Native vegetation occurs interspersed with cropland throughout much of the area. More continuous cover occurs in the northeastern part of the area, primarily in association with steep hummocky morainal landscapes. A variety of mixed grasses and shrubs are most common on the uplands. Sloughs and depressions comprise sedges, usually surrounded by willows and trembling aspen, but saltgrass, alkali grass, and red samphire are more common in saline areas.

Hummocky and kettled glaciolacustrine landscapes are most common in the eastern part of the area, indicating the presence of a former glacial lake resting on glacial ice. The channel of the present Lewis Creek served as a spillway for this glacial lake. In the remainder of the area, the landscapes are very gently undulating glaciolacustrine plains. Dark Brown loamy soils prevail on the various landscapes. Clay soils occur, locally, east of Saskatoon, and Solonetzic Dark Brown soils occur west of Hanley.

Most of the area is cropland. Cereals are the major crop, with small amounts of oilseeds. Nearly 30% of the cropland area is summerfallow. Pastureland prevails in stony and steeply sloping hummocky moraines, especially in the northeastern part of the area, and on sandy soils south of Bradwell.

K12. Allan Hills

The Allan Hills is a hilly morainal upland southeast of Saskatoon. Elevations range from 550 m at the base of the hills on the north and east side to 670 m at the highest points in the hills. There is a limited amount of surface drainage to Blackstrap Coulee, Arm River, and Lewis Creek.

Native vegetation occurs interspersed with cropland throughout much of the area. More continuous cover occurs in association with steep hummocky morainal landscapes. A variety of mixed grasses and shrubs are most common on the uplands. Sloughs and depressions comprise sedges, usually surrounded by willows and trembling aspen but saltgrass, alkali grass, and red samphire are more common in saline areas.

Moderately to strongly sloping hummocky morainal landscapes are most common in this area, with lesser amounts of moderately sloping glaciolacustrine landscapes. Dark Brown loamy soils formed in glacial till are associated with the hummocky moraines, and clay loams and clays are associated with the glaciolacustrine landscapes.

Most of the area is cropland. Cereals are the major crop and nearly 40% of the cropland area is summerfallow. Pasture and rangeland occur on the more steeply sloping, sometimes stony, soils which are scattered throughout the area.

K13. Arm River Plain

The Arm River plain is a very large, relatively level area that extends southward from Dundurn to Lumsden and eastward, almost from Outlook to Imperial. The area slopes gently from 620 m on the southeast flank of the Allan Hills to 530 m at the Last Mountain Lake Plain, and from 610 m in the gentle upland near Hawarden to 580 m in the area to the east and south of it. There is a limited amount of surface drainage through Iskwao Creek and the Arm River channel to the Qu'Appelle Valley.

Native mixed-grass vegetation is limited to hummocky morainal landscapes, where it is generally interspersed with croplands. More continuous cover occurs in areas of sandy soils north of Davidson, especially in the PFRA community pasture; in areas of Solonetzic soils west of Davidson (once again in a PFRA community pasture); and in gullies and valley sides associated with Iskwao Creek, Arm River channel, Qu'Appelle Valley, and Little Manitou Lake. A variety of mixed grasses and various shrubs are common on the uplands. Sloughs and depressions usually comprise sedges, surrounded by willows and trembling aspen, but saltgrass, alkali grass, and red samphire are more common in saline and Solonetzic soil areas. The vegetation on the river valleys is most commonly mixed grasses and shrubs, with aspen on north-facing slopes.

Moderately sloping hummocky moraine with numerous kettles is the most common landscape of the area. Dark Brown loamy soils formed in glacial till are associated with these landscapes. A local area of Solonetzic Dark Brown soils occurs west of Davidson.

Nearly all of the area is cropland. Cereals are the major crop, with a very small amount of irrigated crops. Nearly 40% of the cropland area is summerfallow. A small amount of pasture is associated with Solonetzic, sandy, and stony soils, with PFRA community pastures near Davidson occupying considerable amounts of this kind of land.

K14. Last Mountain Lake Plain

The Last Mountain Lake plain is a nearly level plain that slopes gently westward from 530 m at the Strasbourg and Arm River plains to 500 m at Last Mountain Lake. Limited surface drainage is to Last Mountain Lake through Lanigan and Saline creeks in the north and several small creeks to the south. Extensive areas of native vegetation are associated with the sandy, often wet and saline soils at the north end of Last Mountain Lake, and especially in the Last Mountain Lake Cooperative Wildlife Area and several PFRA community pastures that occupy much of this area. Grasses and shrubs prevail on upland sites with salt grass, sedges, and rushes in saline and wet areas.

The very gently undulating glaciolacustrine landscapes that are common in this area were formed by a small glacial lake, Glacial Lake Last Mountain, that created the prominent valley to the south as water from the glacial lake spilled into the Qu'Appelle Valley. Dark Brown loamy soils are associated with these glaciolacustrine deposits, as well as with glacial till deposits in the southern part of the area. Sandy glaciofluvial deposits with wet saline Gleysolic and Regosolic soils are common in the northern part of the area.

Although soil texture and topography is generally favourable for cultivated crops, there are large areas of saline and wet soils that limit the cropland area in much of the Last Mountain Lake plain. Cereals are the major crop, with small amounts of oilseeds and forages.

Approximately 25% of the cropland area is summerfallow. Pasture and rangeland occurs primarily to the north of Last Mountain Lake, where the Last Mountain Lake Cooperative Wildlife Area and several PFRA community pastures occupy much of the area.

K15. Strasbourg Plain

Except for Last Mountain, a small but prominent upland rising 100 m above the surrounding plain in the southern part of the area, the Strasbourg plain is a nearly level area extending from north of Nokomis to the Qu'Appelle Valley. The area slopes to the west and south from 560 to 580 m at the base of the Touchwood Hills, to 530 m at Last Mountain plain and 550 m at the Qu'Appelle Valley. There are a number of small creeks that drain the northern part of the area into Kutawagon Lake. There is also considerable drainage to Last Mountain Lake through Saline Creek. West and East Loon creeks drain some of the southern part to the Qu'Appelle Valley and several small creeks provide drainage to Last Mountain Lake.

Native mixed-grass vegetation is limited to hummocky morainal areas, where it is interspersed with cropland. Extensive areas of saltgrass, alkali grass, sedges, and rushes occur in association with wet and saline areas in the northern part of the area, especially in several PFRA community pastures. Aspen is more prevalent on the slopes of Last Mountain. Sloughs and depressions comprise sedges, usually surrounded by willows and aspen. When saline, saltgrass, alkali grass, and red samphire are more common.

This is essentially a large, moderately sloping hummocky morainal area with frequent glacial kettles. Dark Brown soils on loamy glacial till deposits prevail throughout, except on Last Mountain where the higher elevation and cooler climate has resulted in the formation of Black loamy soils on the glacial till deposits. Wet and saline Gleysolic and Regosolic soils are common in the Kutawagon Lake area.

Although soil texture and topography are generally favourable for cultivated crops in most of the Strasbourg plain, areas of saline and wet soils limit the cropland area. Cereals are the major crop, with small amounts of oilseeds. More than 30% of the cropland area is summerfallow. Rangeland and pasture is most common in the northern part of the area where two PFRA community pastures are located. Rowan's Ravine Provincial Park is located in this area.

K16. Eyebrow Plain

The Eyebrow plain includes the small, gentle morainal upland near Eyebrow and the slightly lower area straddling the Qu'Appelle Valley from Marquis to Riverhurst. There is a gentle slope from 610 m in the Eyebrow-Keeler area and at the edge of the Arm River plain, to 580 m at the Qu'Appelle Valley. Iskwao Creek drains some of the area north of the valley and numerous small creeks drain the area immediately south of the Qu'Appelle Valley.

Native mixed-grass vegetation is limited to local areas of stony or sandy hummocky moraines, where it is interspersed with cropland, and to patches of sandy soils and in association with the Qu'Appelle and South Saskatchewan river valleys. A variety of mixed grasses and shrubs are the most characteristic species in uplands within the morainal areas, whereas sloughs and depressions comprise sedge, usually surrounded by willows and aspen. A more continuous cover can be found in sandy areas north of the Qu'Appelle Valley, especially in the PFRA community pasture. In these areas, sandgrasses are most common in the poorly stabilized areas, and shrubs such as juniper on the more stable areas. Trembling aspen is also common in areas with a relatively high water table. The vegetation on the river valleys is most commonly shrubs and grasses.

Dark Brown loamy soils developed in glacial till associated with moderately sloping hummocky moraines and gently undulating till plains prevail in the Eyebrow Hills. Nearer the valley, very gently sloping glaciolacustrine and glaciofluvial landscapes prevail. Dark

Brown loams and sandy loams are most common on these landscapes, except south of the elbow of the South Saskatchewan River where Brown loamy soils occur, and north of the elbow where Regosolic soils occur in association with sand dunes.

Nearly all of the area is cropland. Cereals are the major crop, with small amounts of forages. Nearly 40% of the cropland area is summerfallow. Most of the sand dunes are pasture, with the PFRA community pasture occupying a considerable portion of this area. Douglas Provincial Park also occurs in this area.

K17. Regina Plain

The Regina plain is a large, level glacial lake plain that extends from the base of the Missouri Coteau south and west of Moose Jaw to the Moose Mountain upland east of Regina and north to the Qu'Appelle Valley. This area represents a former glacial lake, Glacial Lake Regina, which was drained by the Qu'Appelle Valley as the glacier receded from the area. The Qu'Appelle Valley is incised more than 100 m into the surrounding plain, creating considerable drainage of the land to the south through Moose Jaw River and High Hill, Wascana, Cottonwood, Boggy, and Flying creeks.

Remnant native vegetation occurs on the sides of coulees such as Cottonwood coulee and Moose Jaw Creek, where a variety of mixed grasses and shrubs are the most characteristic species in open areas. North-facing slopes are dominated by cottonwoods.

The area has a level to very gently undulating glaciolacustrine landscape. Dark Brown clay soils are associated with these landscapes. Sandy glaciofluvial deposits along Thunder Creek west of Moose Jaw were formed where glacial meltwater from the west entered Glacial Lake Regina. Brown sandy soils are most common on these deposits, although parts of this area are duned with associated Regosolic soils.

Nearly all of the area is cropland, with cereals the major crop. More than 30% of the cropland area is summerfallow.

K18. Griffin Plain

The Griffin plain is a large, nearly level till plain that extends from Weyburn, east to Oxbow. Elevations drop gradually from 640 m at the edge of the Moose Mountain upland to 590 m in the southern part of the area. Surface drainage is limited to the northwestern part of the area, with flow to the Souris River.

Native mixed-grass vegetation is limited to soils with strong Solonetzic development, especially in the PFRA community pasture, where salt-tolerant grasses, pincushion cactus, gumweed, and greasewood represent the characteristic vegetation.

Most of the area is an undulating till plain with a dominance of loamy Dark Brown Solonetzic soils formed in glacial till. A band on the south side of the area has a moderately sloping hummocky morainal landscape. Dark Brown loams formed in glacial till are the most common soils in this area.

Nearly all of this area is cropland, but strong development of Solonetzic soils, with associated salinity, limits the cropland area somewhat. Cereals are the major crop and nearly 40% of the cropland area is summerfallow. A PFRA community pasture occupies some of the pastureland in the area.

K19. Trossachs Plain

The Trossachs plain is a level glacial till plain that extends along the base of the Missouri Coteau from Avonlea to Estevan. Elevations are highest in the northwest where the plain slopes from 670 m at the Coteau to 580 m at Yellow Grass marsh. Further east, elevations reach to only 600 m at the base of the coteau, dropping to 580 m on the plain. The gradient provided by this slope has resulted in extensive prehistoric erosion in the upper reaches of this plain. Drainage from this more northerly area leads to the Moose Jaw River. Further south, the erosion is not as severe, although a considerable amount of drainage to the Souris River has developed through Roughbark, Jewel, Gibson, and Long creeks.

Extensive areas of native mixed-grass vegetation occur in association with soils strong in Solonetzic development and with coulees, especially in the numerous PFRA community pastures. In the Solonetzic areas, salt-tolerant grasses, pincushion cactus, gumweed, and greasewood are most characteristic.

The landscape of this area is nearly level to undulating, with prominent gullying into the underlying bedrock in the northern part. Loamy Dark Brown Solonetzic soils formed in glacial till deposits are most common on this plain.

Nearly all of this area is cropland, but strong development of Solonetzic soils, with associated salinity, and gullies limit the cropland area somewhat. Cereals are the major crop and nearly 40% of the cropland area is summerfallow. Most of the pastureland in this area is represented by a number of PFRA community pastures.

K20. Souris River Plain

The Souris River plain is an eroded till plain along the part of the Souris River between Weyburn and the United States border. Elevations on this plain drop from 580 m on the valley sides to 520 m in the valley bottom. Surface drainage is extensive, with flows into the Souris River and the Rafferty Reservoir.

Extensive areas of native mixed-grass vegetation occur in association with the sandy and stony sides of the Souris River Valley, and especially in the many PFRA community pastures.

This undulating till plain was severely eroded by glacial meltwater that flowed southeastward along the ice margin, creating the early stages of the Souris River. Stones, sands, and gravels are common landscape features. Although loam-textured Dark Brown soils formed in glacial till are most common, there also are extensive areas of sandy Dark Brown Solonetzic and Black loamy soils formed in glacial till.

Most of the area is cropland. Cereals are the major crop, with small amounts of forages. Approximately 30% of the cropland area is summerfallow. Extensive areas of stony, sandy, and gravelly soils in the Souris River plain are used as rangeland and pasture. Several PFRA community pastures are situated on such soils. The coal field near Bienfait is situated in this area.

Mixed Grassland Ecoregion

The mixed-grass prairie is a vast region that extends from Saskatchewan to the Gulf of Mexico. In its natural state it is characterized by mid-grasses (wheatgrasses and speargrasses) and short-grasses (blue grama grass) growing in mixed stands. The Mixed Grassland Ecoregion typifies much of the northern part of these open grasslands. It occupies 8.6 million hectares or 13% of the province. Wheatgrasses and speargrasses are the dominant grasses, but blue grama grass is an important component. It closely correlates with a semiarid climate and Brown soils. Unlike the Moist Mixed Grassland Ecoregion, aspen rarely occur in association with local wetlands. Agriculture has not modified the natural landscape of this ecoregion to the extent that it has in the aspen parkland and the moist mixed grassland; only 50% of the ecoregion has been cultivated.

PHYSIOGRAPHY. The Mixed Grassland Ecoregion comprises a broad plain that is interrupted by deep, scenic valleys and hilly uplands. The primary slope of the plain is downward to the north and east, in accordance with the slope of the bedrock surface. Most of the region has a cover of glacial drift that is sufficiently thick to obscure the underlying bedrock topography; however, it is not uncommon to experience the unique beauty of striking bedrock landscapes associated with the Wood Mountain, Cypress Bench, Frenchman River, and other valleys. Secondary slopes that extend from the uplands to drainage systems such as the South Saskatchewan, Frenchman, and Big Muddy valleys occasionally break the general northward slope of the plain.

Landscapes in the Mixed Grassland Ecoregion are the most diverse of those in the Prairie Ecozone. Level to gently undulating glaciofluvial, glacio-lacustrine, and glacial till plains are frequently interrupted by hummocky

Prairie grasslands have provided some of the most productive agricultural soils in the country.

morainal uplands, sand dunes, benchlands, and numerous creeks and valleys. The plains in the northern and eastern part of the ecoregion generally lie between 700 and 750 m, while those bordering on the north flank of the Cypress Hills extend to more than 800 m. The plateaus and plains to the south of the Cypress Hills upland reach 1,000 m. Morainal uplands occasionally reach elevations from 50 to 100 m above the adjacent plains, but sometimes they are no higher than these plains.

The valleys of the Frenchman, Big Muddy, and South Saskatchewan rivers and Swift Current Creek, sometimes entrenched 100 m or more into the plain, are major contributors to the beauty of the region. The South Saskatchewan River and Swift Current Creek form part of the Saskatchewan-Nelson River drainage basin, but the Frenchman and Big Muddy contribute to the Missouri River drainage system. Lakes such as Diefenbaker, Clearwater, Old Wives, Fife, Willowbunch, Big Muddy, Crane, and Chaplin add to the diversity and beauty of the region.

GEOLOGY. The bedrock underlying the Moist Mixed Grassland Ecoregion is primarily marine sedimentary rocks of the Bearpaw Formation. These sediments typically consist of gray-green silty clays and shales with localized deposits of bentonite. Near the United States border, the coal-bearing Ravenscrag Formation of Tertiary age overlies Upper Cretaceous Frenchman, Whitemud, and Eastend formation clays, siltstones, and sandstones. Older Cretaceous rocks (Judith River Formation and Upper Colorado group) are exposed in some river valleys. Oil, gas, and sodium sulphate are produced from subsurface marine sedimentary rocks that lie beneath this ecoregion.

CLIMATE. The Mixed Grassland Ecoregion has a semiarid climate. It is warmer and slightly drier than in the Moist Mixed Grassland and the Cypress Upland ecoregions. Within the mixed grassland, temperatures are higher on the plains of lower elevation to the north and east than on the higher plains and plateaus in the southern part of the region, but there is little variability in precipitation throughout the region. The mean annual daily temperature is 4.0°C. The mean July temperature is 18.9°C and the mean January temperature is -12.6°C. The mean annual precipitation is 352 mm, with 219 mm of rainfall occurring from May to September. The summers are relatively short but warm, having a frost-free period of 112 days and a total of 1,797 degree days above 5°C.

LANDFORMS AND SOILS. Brown Chernozemic soils prevail throughout this ecoregion in response to the relatively small additions of organic matter in these mixed grasslands and rapid rates of decomposition in this warmer part of the mixed-grass prairie. As their name implies, these Brown soils have a brown-coloured surface layer that is lower in organic matter than those in the Dark Brown soil zone. Typically, this layer is separated from a grayish-brown layer, which represents the soil parent material, by

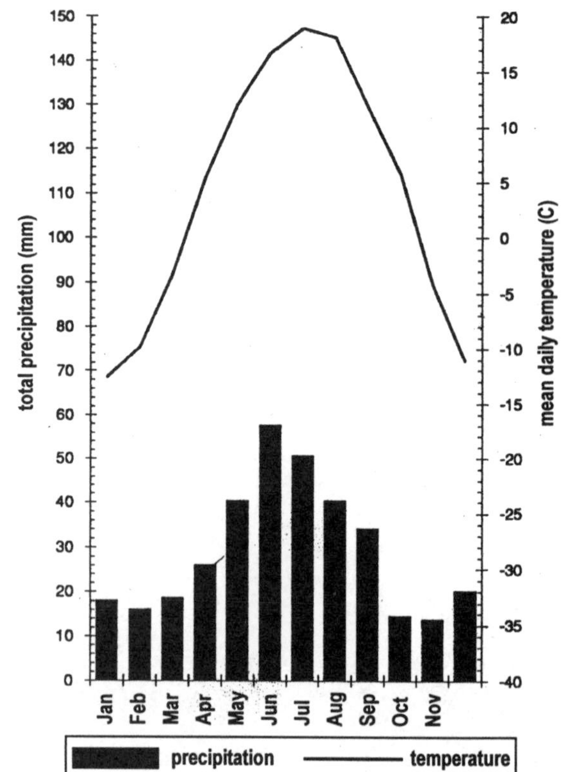

Figure 21. Mean monthly temperature and precipitation for the Mixed Grassland Ecoregion as represented by the meteorological record from Leader.

a reddish-brown layer that is free of carbonates of calcium and magnesium.

Soils tend to be thin and lower in organic matter on upper slopes, becoming progressively thicker and higher in organic matter on mid and lower slopes in response to an increased supply of soil moisture and plant growth. Dark Brown soils occur on prominent north-facing slopes and in lower slope positions on steeply sloping topography, where wheatgrasses, speargrasses, and other grasses that typify the moist mixed grassland prevail.

GROUNDWATER. Groundwater in the Mixed Grassland Ecoregion is associated with the drift that covers the bedrock as well as within the bedrock. Bedrock aquifers are common throughout the ecoregion within the sandy and silty beds of the Judith River, Bearpaw, and Eastend to Ravenscrag formations. The Tyner Valley and Swift Current Valley aquifers represent buried valley aquifers of the Empress Formation that have been incised into the bedrock surface.

Glacial inter-till aquifers are widely distributed throughout the ecoregion. They are most common in the older and deeper Floral Formation but may also occur within or at the surface of the Battleford Formation.

Surficial aquifers occur in association with sandy and gravelly surficial deposits such as the Great Sand Hills, Elbow Sand Hills, and in the vicinity of Maple Creek and Swift Current.

Both the bedrock and glacial aquifers have a marked influence on the ecology of the area. Lakes such as Old Wives and Chaplin derive a considerable amount of their source through discharge from deep aquifers — hence the higher salt concentration — whereas lakes such as Crane and Bigstick have fresher water reflecting a near-surface aquifer.

Aquifers also impact on water supply to vegetation. The prevalence of aspen in sandy areas such as the Elbow and Great Sand Hills is often a reflection of a surface aquifer in these sediments. Saline and Solonetzic soils and salt-tolerant vegetation are often associated with surface concentrations of salts derived from glacial and bedrock aquifers.

Snowberry can be found in dense clumps in coulees and low spots in the open prairie.

VEGETATION. The regular alternation between woodland, shrubland, and grassland that characterized the aspen parkland and the moist mixed grassland is absent in this ecoregion. Wheatgrasses, speargrasses, and blue grama grass dominate on loamy soils, while sandy areas have a unique community of grasses and shrubs.

The natural vegetation of the Mixed Grassland Ecoregion is a mixture of mid-grasses (wheatgrasses and speargrasses) and short-grasses. The mid-grasses dominate on level to gently undulating landscapes, but blue grama grass prevails on drier upper slope positions of morainic landscapes. Sedges and June grass are also important components of the mixed grassland communities, with June grass being particularly abundant in areas of lacustrine clay soils.

Shrublands frequently appear in depressions or in association with sandy soils. The most abundant species among the forbs and shrubs, everywhere, is pasture sage.

Mats of club-moss commonly cover parts of the soil surface beneath the two-layered, mixed-grass canopy. Lichens also occasionally occur in this lowest layer. Sage and roses often are present within the herbaceous cover, and patches of snowberry occur in protected habitats. Valleys and coulees contain patches of brush, including willow, wolf-willow, saskatoon, snowberry, and choke cherry.

The kangaroo rat is well adapted to life in arid grasslands.

Plant communities in sandy areas in the mixed grassland are very similar to those described for the Moist Mixed Grassland Ecoregion.

Various communities of wetlands occur, the dominant grasses, sedges, and rushes of which are shared with wetlands of other grassland and forest regions (see Aspen Parkland Ecoregion).

The grassland in areas grazed by domestic livestock generally has a greater component of short-grasses and other "increaser species." Where grazing has been sufficiently intensive to affect the mid-grasses severely, short-grasses such as blue grama and sedge prevail.

WILDLIFE. The birds, mammals, amphibians and reptiles that occur in the Mixed Grassland Ecoregion are essentially the same as those described for the Moist Mixed Grassland Ecoregion.

Fish diversity is somewhat lower than in the moist mixed grassland but higher than in the Cypress Upland Ecoregion, with 36 species occurring. The most common game fish are walleye, northern pike, yellow perch, and burbot, but they do not extend into the extreme southwest portion of the ecoregion. Several trout species have been introduced, with the brown trout being particularly common in the southwest part of the ecoregion. The goldeye, sauger, and lake sturgeon occur in the South Saskatchewan River.

HUMAN ACTIVITY. The population of this ecoregion is approximately 84,000, just over 8% of the population of the province. Major communities include Swift Current, Leader, Kindersley, Maple Creek, Assiniboia, Shaunavon, and Gravelbourg.

Approximately 62% of this region is used for agricultural purposes, of which about half is pasture or rangeland and the remainder is cropland. Much of Saskatchewan's cattle production occurs in this region. The production of

A pumpjack pumps crude oil from reservoir rocks deep beneath the surface.

spring wheat and other cereal grains uses a grain-fallow rotation. Flaxseed and durum wheat are also grown. Much of Saskatchewan's irrigation occurs in this ecoregion.

The Mixed Grassland Ecoregion, with its semiarid climate, is not as well suited to the production of a wide variety of field crops as is the Moist Mixed Grassland Ecoregion. Shorter rotations than in the adjacent moist mixed grassland means there is less summerfallow practiced. The sloughs also tend to be drier and, consequently, aspen groves are absent in this area. Areas that are wet, sandy, saline, stony, or hilly are generally not cultivated. They often are used for pasturing livestock, but also provide the majority of available habitat for birds, deer, coyote, fox, hare, squirrels, and many other animals.

Irrigation is the largest water use in this region as well as the entire ecozone. Dams and reservoirs are present on all of the major drainage basins in the Prairie Ecozone. They are used primarily to store water for use during drought and to alleviate flooding during peak flows. The Duncairn and Altawan Reservoir dams occur in the Mixed Grassland Ecoregion.

The Mixed Grassland Ecoregion is also home to major heavy industry, in particular, the coal mining at Coronach and sodium sulphate development at Chaplin, Ingebrite, Palo, and Ormiston. Saskatchewan is the second largest oil-producing province in Canada, with substantial crude oil production from the Kindersley-Kerrobert and Swift Current areas in this ecoregion. There is significant heavy oil potential in the Kindersley area. Saskatchewan is the third largest natural gas producing province in Canada. The main natural gas producing areas and reserves are along the western boundary of Saskatchewan, in the Beacon Hill, Kindersley, and Hatton areas.

As part of the North American waterfowl migratory flyway and with its diverse wildlife habitat, the region provides opportunities for hunting and recreation. Sport fishing and ecotourism are also important recreational activities. Four provincial parks, including Saskatchewan Landing and Wood Mountain Post, occur in this region. Approximately 14% of the ecoregion is within some form of park or protected area. A large part of that percentage is made up of PFRA and provincial community pastures and lands designated under the *Wildlife Habitat Protection Act*. Grasslands National Park, the only national park in Canada devoted to the protection of grassland species, occurs in this region.

Landscape Areas

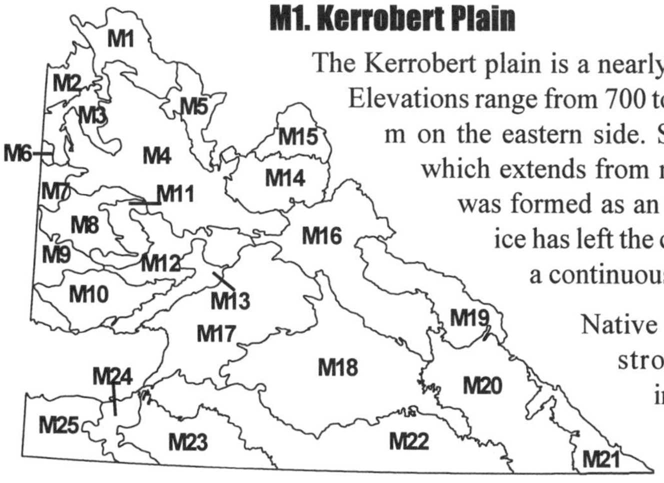

M1. Kerrobert Plain

The Kerrobert plain is a nearly level area that extends southward from Kerrobert. Elevations range from 700 to 725 m on the western margin, sloping gently to 670 m on the eastern side. Street and Teo lakes lie in the Verendrye channel, which extends from near Luseland to south of Kindersley. This channel was formed as an ice-walled channel in glacial times. Melting of the ice has left the channel with poorly defined valley sides and without a continuous stream.

Native prairie vegetation is limited to areas of sandy or strongly developed Solonetzic soils, where it is interspersed in the cropland area, and to the Verendrye channel. A variety of grasses prevail in upland areas with shrubs limited to more moist depressional areas and to coulees. Salt-tolerant grasses, pincushion cactus, greasewood, and gumweed are characteristic of Solonetzic areas. More continuous grassland cover occurs in the several PFRA community pastures in the area.

A nearly level morainal landscape with Solonetzic Brown soils dominates this area. Brown soils on glaciofluvial sands occur north of Kerrobert and Brown soils on glaciolacustrine clays occur in the southeastern part of the area.

Nearly all of the area is cropland; however, Solonetzic and sandy soils limit the extent of cropland somewhat. Cereals are the major crop. More than 40% of the cropland area is summerfallow. Much of the remaining land is rangeland and pasture, with several PFRA community pastures occupying a considerable portion of it.

M2. Sibbald Plain

The Sibbald plain is a nearly level clay plain surrounding a series of small hummocky morainal uplands. It occurs along the Alberta border near Alsask. Elevations on the clay plains range from 700 to 725 m, with the morainal uplands extending to 740 m. Surface drainage is confined to flow into Dewar Lake and small, local sloughs.

Native prairie vegetation is limited to areas of hummocky moraines and sandy soils, where it is interspersed in the cropland area. A variety of grasses prevail in upland areas with shrubs limited to more moist depressional areas and to coulees. More continuous grassland cover occurs in the PFRA community pastures within the area.

Brown clay-textured soils occur on the gently to moderately undulating glaciolacustrine plains and Brown loams on the moderately to strongly sloping hummocky morainal landscapes.

Nearly all of the area is cropland. Cereals are the major crop, with small amounts of a wide variety of other crops being grown. Nearly 40% of the cropland area is summerfallow. There is a PFRA community pasture on some of the strongly sloping lands.

M3. Oyen Upland

The Oyen upland is a hilly area that occurs along the Alberta border west of Eatonia. There is some surface drainage from the hills to nearby lakes and sloughs, particularly into Cabri Lake in the Eston plain. Elevations exceed 760 m in the centre of the uplands, dropping to 720 m in lower areas.

Native prairie vegetation is limited to areas of hummocky moraines and Solonetzic soils, where it is interspersed in the cropland area, and to several PFRA community pastures. A variety of grasses prevail in upland areas, with shrubs limited to more moist depressional areas and to coulees.

The area is dominated by Brown loamy soils developed in glacial till. These soils are usually associated with steeply to very steeply sloping hummocky moraines, but rather extensive areas of Solonetzic Brown soils occur on moderately undulating morainal deposits.

Most of the Oyen upland is cropland, with cereals the major crop. More than 40% of the cropland area is summerfallow. Hilly lands near Flaxcombe are primarily rangeland and pasture, some of which are within PFRA community pastures.

M4. Eston Plain

The Eston plain is a nearly level clay plain that extends from north of Kindersley southward to the Cabri-Leader area. Elevations range from 725 m along the Oyen upland to 600 m in the southeast. Surface drainage is provided by Verendrye Creek and Netherhill coulee which flow into the Verendrye channel, and local flow into Snipe Lake and the South Saskatchewan River. Also, White Bear coulee and Gillanders and Smith creeks drain the southeastern part of the area into the White Bear channel. The Verendrye channel, an ice-walled meltwater channel that originated near Luseland, ends in an area of rolling silt hills south of Cutbank Lake. The South Saskatchewan River is incised 40 to 50 m into this plain.

Native vegetation is limited to local areas of sandy soils and hummocky topography — where it is intermixed with areas of cropland — and to the valley sides of the South Saskatchewan River. In sandy areas, the poorly stabilized dunes are characterized by grasses, with creeping juniper and other shrubs on the more stable areas. Trembling aspen are present where the water table is near the surface. The vegetation on the river valleys is most commonly shrubs. A variety of grasses are common in upland areas within hummocky landscapes, with shrubs limited to more moist depressional areas.

Very gently and gently undulating glaciolacustine plains with Brown clay soils prevail throughout most of the area. There is a prominent ridged morainal area northwest of Cabri and several areas of sand dunes along the South Saskatchewan River.

Most of the Eston plain is cropland; however, the extensive area of gullied and sandy land along the South Saskatchewan River limits the cropland area somewhat. Cereals are the major crop and nearly 40% of the cropland area is summerfallow. Isolated areas of pasture and rangeland are associated with hilly morainal and sandy areas.

M5. Bad Hills

The Bad hills are part of the Missouri Coteau, which represents the rise from the Second Prairie Steppe to the east and the Third Prairie Steppe to the west. General elevations in this hilly area range from 685 to 730 m, dropping to 600 m at the edge of the Rosetown and Eston plains in the southeastern part of the area. There is a limited amount of surface drainage to the South Saskatchewan River in the southern part of the area, and to Eagle Creek in the north, as well as to Bad Lake.

Native mixed-grass prairie is interspersed with cropland throughout the area. A more continuous grassland cover can be found in association with steep hummocky moraines and especially in some of the PFRA community pastures in the area. A variety of grasses are common on the uplands, with shrubs limited to more moist depressional areas and to coulees.

The landscape is primarily a moderately to very steeply sloping hummocky moraine with Brown loamy soils. Moderately to strongly sloping glaciolacustrine areas with Brown clayey soils are also present.

Most of the Bad Hills is cropland; however, steep slopes limit the cropland area somewhat. Cereals are the major crop and more than 40% of the cropland area is summerfallow. Several PFRA community pastures represent a considerable amount of the pasture and rangeland.

M6. Acadia Valley Plain

The Acadia Valley plain is a small, nearly level area along the Alberta border, north of Empress. Elevations range from 725 m in the surrounding Oyen uplands to 700 m adjacent to Empress Creek on the Oyen plain. The area drains through Empress Creek to the South Saskatchewan River.

Native mixed-grass prairie is limited to hummocky morainal areas, where it is intermixed with areas of cropland. A variety of grasses are common on the uplands, with shrubs limited to more moist depressional areas and to coulees.

In Saskatchewan, the area comprises moderately sloping hummocky moraine, with a smaller area of very gently undulating glaciolacustrine plains. Brown loamy soils formed in glacial till prevail on the morainal landscapes and Brown clayey soils in the glaciolacustrine area.

Most of the Acadia Valley plain in Saskatchewan is rangeland or pasture, as steep slopes severely limit the extent of cropland. Cereals are the major crop, with small amounts of peas, beans, and a variety of other crops. Less than 30% of the cropland area is summerfallow.

M7. Bindloss Plain

The Bindloss plain is a sandy area located immediately south of the South Saskatchewan River, along the border with Alberta. Elevations range from 730 m in the south to 685 m at the South Saskatchewan River. Surface drainage is limited to gullying along the river valley.

Extensive areas of native mixed-grass prairie occur in association with this area of sandy soils. These grasslands are intermixed with areas of croplands, but dominate the valley sides of the South Saskatchewan River. In sandy areas, the poorly stabilized dunes are characterized by grasses, with creeping juniper and other shrubs in the more stable areas. Trembling aspen are present where the water table is near the surface. The vegetation on the river valleys is most commonly shrubs and grasses.

Moderately to steeply sloping sand dunes dominate the area, with lesser amounts of very gently undulating glaciofluvial plains. Regosolic sands are associated with the sand dunes and Brown sandy loams with the glaciofluvial plains.

Most of the Bindloss plain is rangeland and pasture, as the extremely sandy nature of the soils severely limits the cropland area. Cereals, including small amounts of fall rye, are the major crop. More than 40% of the cropland area is summerfallow.

M8. Hazlet Plain

The Hazlet plain is a silty glacial lake plain that separates the clay soils of the Eston plain and the sands in the Great Sand Hills. Elevations rise from 685 m in the clay plain to 720 m throughout the northern part of the silty plain. The southern part of the silty plain is considerably higher than in the north, with elevations approaching 780 m. Surface drainage throughout the area is limited to flow to local small lakes and sloughs.

Native mixed-grass prairie is limited to hummocky glaciolacustrine landscapes, where it is interspersed with the cropland area. A variety of grasses are common on the uplands, with shrubs limited to more moist depressional areas.

The landscape in the northern part of the area is a very gently undulating glaciolacustrine plain. In the south it is a moderately sloping hummocky glaciolacustrine plain with numerous glacial kettles. Brown loam soils prevail on both types of landscapes.

Most of the Hazlet plain is cropland; however, appreciable areas of steeper slopes and associated glacial kettles are pasture. Cereals are the major crop and more than 40% of the cropland area is summerfallow.

M9. Schuler Plain

The Schuler plain is a hummocky morainal area extending along the Alberta border from

Burstall to the north-facing slopes of the Cypress Hills upland. The area rises from 760 m at the margin with the Hazlet plain to 820 m in the Wilde Hills. It falls to 760 m at the Maple Creek plain before rising again to 850 m on the flank of the Cypress slopes. Surface drainage of the Wilde Hills is limited to flows to several small lakes in the central part of the area and to Many Islands and Bitter lakes to the south. The southern block has some drainage to the Walsh flats through Abbott Creek and to Maple Creek through McCoy Creek.

Native mixed-grass prairie is limited to steeply sloping hummocky morainal landscapes, where it is interspersed with areas of cropland, and along coulees. A variety of grasses are common on the uplands, with shrubs limited to more moist depressional areas.

Landscapes in the area are moderately to steeply sloping hummocky moraine. Glacial kettles are common, especially in steeply sloping areas. The associated soils are Brown loams formed in glacial till.

Most of the Schuler plain is cropland; however, appreciable areas of steeper slopes and associated glacial kettles are used as rangeland or pasture. Cereals are the major crop and more than 40% of the cropland area is summerfallow. Pasture is associated with steeply sloping hummocky moraines in the Wilde Hills and gullied morainal lands immediately north of the Cypress Hills upland.

M10. Maple Creek Plain

The Maple Creek plain is a sandy area to the north of the Cypress Hills upland. Elevations range from 770 to 800 m along the southern margin, dropping to 720 to 740 m at Bitter, Bigstick, and Crane lakes. Although Maple and Piapot creeks flow through the area, very little of this sandy area drains into them.

Extensive areas of native mixed-grass prairie occur in association with the sandy soils that prevail in this area. In such areas, the poorly stabilized areas are characterized by grasses, with creeping juniper and other shrubs on the more stable areas. Trembling aspen is common in areas where the water table is near the surface.

Landscapes in the southern part of the area are hummocky glaciofluvial with moderate slopes. They are very gently undulating glaciofluvial in the central part and gently sloping sand dunes in the northern part. Brown sandy loam soils are most common on the glaciofluvial landscapes and sandy Regosolic soils prevail in the sand dune areas.

Most of the Maple Creek plain is rangeland or pasture, as sandy soils severely limit the cropland area. Several PFRA community pastures occupy some of this sandy land. Cereals, including relatively large amounts of fall rye are the major field crop. There are also large amounts of forages. Summerfallow occupies only 25% of the cropland area.

M11. Great Sand Hills

The Great Sand Hills occur midway between the South Saskatchewan River and the Cypress Hills, northwest of Swift Current. The hills rise from 700 m on the western margin to 750 m on isolated highs. There is no surface drainage in this sandy area.

Extensive areas of native mixed-grass prairie occur in association with the sandy soils that prevail in this area. In such areas, the poorly stabilized areas are characterized by grasses, with creeping juniper and other shrubs on the more stable areas. Trembling aspen is common in areas where the water table is near the surface.

The most common landscapes are very steeply sloping sand dunes. The slopes are more gentle in the southern part. The associated soils are Regosolic sands.

Nearly all of the Great Sand Hills is rangeland and pasture, as the extremely sandy and hilly soils severely limit the cropland area. Cereals, including relatively large amounts of fall rye, are the major crop. There also are large amounts of forages. More than 40% of the cropland area is summerfallow.

M12. Antelope Creek Plain

The Antelope Creek plain is a nearly level silty glacial lake plain on the east side of the Great Sand Hills. Elevations range from 720 to 730 m. Surface drainage is limited to a few small local lakes.

Native mixed-grass prairie is limited to the more steeply sloping hummocky morainal and glaciolacustrine landscapes, where it is interspersed with cropland, and along coulees. A variety of grasses are common on the uplands, with shrubs limited to more moist depressional areas.

Landscapes in this area are primarily hummocky glaciolacustrine plains with moderate slopes and numerous glacial kettles. There also are several hummocky moraines in the area, some with moderate slopes and others more steeply sloping. Glacial kettles are common features in many of these morainal areas. Brown loam soils are associated with the glaciolacustrine and glacial till deposits.

Most of the Antelope Creek plain is cropland; however, appreciable areas of steeper slopes and associated glacial kettles are used as rangeland or pasture. Cereals are the major crop and more than 40% of the cropland area is summerfallow.

M13. Gull Lake Plain

The Gull Lake plain is a mixed sandy and silty area lying on the north flank of the Cypress Hills and Swift Current plateaus, southwest of Swift Current. Elevations drop from 760 to 820 m at the base of the plateau. There is a limited amount of surface drainage into Bridge Creek, as it flows through the area from the escarpment of Swift Current plateau to Antelope Lake.

Extensive areas of native mixed-grass prairie occur in association with the sandy soils that prevail in this area and especially in the PFRA community pasture. In such areas, the poorly stabilized dunes are characterized by grasses, with creeping juniper and other shrubs on the more stable areas. Trembling aspen is common in areas where the water table is near the surface.

The southern part of the area is primarily a hummocky glaciolacustrine plain. There are steep slopes and numerous kettles in some parts, whereas other parts are more gently sloping with occasional gullies. Hummocky moraines with steep slopes and numerous gullies also occur in the southern part of the area. Brown loamy soils are associated with all of these landscapes. The northern part of the area is more sandy. In places, the landscape is a hummocky glaciofluvial plain with moderate slopes, while in others it is a steeply sloping sand dune. Brown sandy loam soils are associated with the glaciofluvial plains and Regosolic sands with the sand dunes.

Most of the Gull Lake plain is cropland; however, appreciable areas of sandy soils that are used as rangeland or pasture severely limit the cropland area. Cereals, including small amounts of fall rye, are the major crop. There also is a small amount of forages. More than

40% of the cropland area is summerfallow. A PFRA community pasture represents some of the rangeland and pasture in the area.

M14. Beechy Hills

The Beechy Hills is the name given to an area around Beechy that is hilly in some parts and an undulating plain in other parts. The hills in the western part of the area are an extension of the Coteau Hills to the north. Here, elevations reach 760 m. The undulating plain around Luck Lake is considerably lower, with elevations of 600 m at Luck Lake and 580 m at the South Saskatchewan River. Most surface drainage is limited to local flow into Luck Lake.

Native mixed-grass prairie is limited to steeply sloping hummocky morainal landscapes, where it is interspersed with cropland, and along coulees. A more continous cover occurs in the PFRA community pasture. A variety of grasses are common on the uplands, with shrubs limited to more moist depressional areas.

The landscape of the hilly area is that of a steeply to very steeply sloping hummocky moraine with numerous glacial kettles as well as prominent curvilinear ridges. The associated soils are Brown loams formed in glacial till. Sandy glaciofluvial plains with Brown soils occur locally. In the area to the east, landscapes include very gently to gently undulating glaciolacustrine plains and moderately sloping hummocky moraines. Brown clay soils are most common in the glaciolacustrine areas, and Brown loams formed in glacial till are common in the morainal areas.

Most of the Beechy Hills area is cropland; however, appreciable areas of hilly land or sandy soils are used as rangeland or pasture. Cereals are the major crop, with small amounts of peas, beans, and a variety of other crops. More than 40% of the cropland area is summerfallow. A PFRA community pasture includes some of the rangeland and pasture that occurs in the area.

M15. Coteau Hills

The Coteau Hills is a hilly upland area southeast of Dinsmore. There is a 70 m rise from the Rosetown and Goose Lake plains to general elevations of 670 to 700 m in the upland. Local highs reach 760 m. There is some surface drainage from the upland to the surrounding plains, especially to Luck Lake and the Anerley channel.

Native mixed-grass prairie vegetation is limited to steeply sloping hummocky morainal landscapes, where it is interspersed with cropland, and along coulees such as the Anerley channel. A variety of grasses are common on the uplands, with shrubs limited to more moist depressional areas.

A moderately to steeply sloping hummocky moraine with numerous glacial kettles is the most common landscape in this area. The associated soils are Dark Brown loams formed in glacial till.

Most of the Coteau Hills are cropland; however, appreciable areas of hilly land are used as rangeland or pasture. Cereals are the major crop. More than 40% of the cropland area is summerfallow.

M16. Chaplin Plain

The Chaplin plain is a mixture of small morainal uplands and glaciofluvial plains in the Old Wives, Chaplin, and Reed lakes area west of Moose Jaw. Elevations range from 730 to 770 m in some of the uplands but drop to below 700 m at the lakes and to 640 m at Thunder

Creek, on the north side of the area. Although the Wood River flows through the southern part of the area, very little surface drainage is provided by it. The northern extremities of the area drain through local creeks into Thunder Creek and the South Saskatchewan River.

Extensive areas of native mixed-grass prairie occur in association with steeply sloping hummocky morainal landscapes, sandy soils, and coulees and valley sides. In sandy areas, the poorly stabilized dunes are characterized by grasses, with creeping juniper and other shrubs on the more stable areas. Trembling aspen is common in areas where the water table is near the surface. A variety of grasses are common on the uplands of hummocky moraines, with shrubs limited to more moist depressional areas.

The hummocky morainal landscapes that dominate the area are generally steeply sloping. Brown loam soils formed in glacial till deposits are common on these landscapes. The glaciofluvial landscapes are also hummocky but more gently sloping. Sandy and gravelly Brown soils are most common in these areas. The highly saline Chaplin Lake and the associated salt mining operation is a dominant landscape feature in the area.

Most of the Chaplin plain is cropland; however, appreciable areas of hilly land and sandy and gravelly soils are rangeland and pasture. Cereals are the major crop. More than 40% of the cropland area is summerfallow. A PFRA community pasture represents some of the rangeland and pasture in the area.

M17. Swift Current Plateau

The Swift Current plateau is a relatively low-lying glaciated plateau in the vicinity of Swift Current. Elevations on the plateau range from 880 to 975 m. The dissected slopes drop from these elevations to 750 m on the plains below. There is an abundance of surface drainage in this area through numerous gullies that lead to Grassy, Russel, Notukeu, and Swiftcurrent creeks.

Native mixed-grass prairie is limited to gullied land, coulees, and valleys such as Swiftcurrent and Notukeu creeks.

This bedrock-controlled area has been glaciated and subsequently covered by a veneer of wind-blown silt (loess). Slopes on the plateau top are gentle, with frequent shallow gullies. Brown loam soils formed in loess and glacial till are most common on the plateau. The gullies deepen on the more steeply sloping plateau sides. Brown loam soils formed in glacial till occur in these areas.

Most of the Swift Current plateau is cropland; however, appreciable areas of gullied topography are rangeland and pasture. Cereals are the major crop, and more than 40% of the cropland area is summerfallow. A PFRA community pasture encompasses some of the rangeland and pasture in the area.

M18. Wood River Plain

The Wood River plain is a large plain that includes the north- and east-facing slopes to the Wood Mountain and Swift Current plateaus and the plain below. It extends from Cadillac to Assiniboia. Elevations drop sharply from highs of 820 to 850 m at the top of the slopes to 730 m at the base. The plain then slopes more gently to elevations of 640 m in the northeast part of the area. Numerous gullies that lead to the Wood River and Notukeu Creek provide surface drainage to much of the sloping lands, but there is little drainage development on much of the remaining land.

Native mixed-grass prairie is limited to steeply sloping hummocky morainal landscapes, where it is interspersed with cropland, and along the Wood River and Notukue Creek and numerous other coulees scattered throughout the area. A variety of grasses are common on the uplands, with shrubs limited to more moist depressional areas.

This area comprises four distinct landscapes. The sloping lands have a relatively thin mantle of glacial till covering the bedrock. Gullies are common on this gently to moderately sloping land. Abutting the sloping lands is a band of steeply sloping hummocky moraine with numerous glacial kettles. An undulating morainal landscape with long and gentle slopes is also common, as are nearly level glaciolacustrine plains. Except for local areas of clay glaciolacustrine deposits, all areas are loamy textured. Brown soils are associated with all landscapes.

Most of the Wood River plain is cropland; however, appreciable areas of hilly or gullied land are used as rangeland and pasture. Cereals are the major crop. More than 40% of the cropland area is summerfallow.

M19. Dirt Hills

The Dirt Hills is a hilly morainal upland representing one of the most prominent breaks between the Second Prairie Steppe to the east and the Third Prairie Steppe to the west. Elevations rise from 600 m on the plain below to 820 m in the hills. There is extensive drainage from the escarpment in the more southerly extension of the hills into Avonlea Creek and the Rouleau marsh. Further north and west the escarpment drains through Snowdys Coulee and Wilson and Sandy creeks to Thunder Creek and the Moose Jaw River.

Native mixed-grass prairie is limited to hummocky morainal landscapes, where it is interspersed with areas of cropland. A more continuous cover occurs in steeply sloping areas and along the Missouri Coteau escarpment. A variety of grasses are common on the uplands, with shrubs limited to more moist depressional areas.

Landscapes on the east-facing escarpment are moderately sloping hummocky moraine with frequent gullies in some parts. In the hills proper, steeply to very steeply sloping hummocky moraines with numerous glacial kettles are most common. In some parts, the moraine is comprised of a series of curvilinear ridges, representing ice-thrusting during glaciation. Dark Brown loam soils formed in glacial till are associated with all of these landscapes.

Most of the Dirt Hills is cropland; however extensive areas of hilly land are rangeland or pasture. Cereals are the major crop, with small amounts of forages. More than 40% of the cropland area is summerfallow.

M20. Coteau Lakes Upland

The Coteau Lakes upland is a hilly hummocky morainal area that extends from near Mossbank to the United States border, south of Minton. Elevations range from 730 to 760 m throughout most of the area, falling to 700 m at Lake of the Rivers in the west and 670 m at the Trossachs Plain in the east. With the exception of a few local creeks and coulees that drain to Lake of the Rivers, Willow Bunch Lake, and Big Muddy Lake, most drainage carries to a number of smaller lakes within the area.

Native mixed-grass prairie vegetation is limited to hummocky morainal landscapes, where it is interspersed with cropland. A more continuous cover occurs in steeply sloping areas and sandy soils, especially in PFRA community pastures. A variety of grasses are common on the uplands, with shrubs limited to more moist depressional areas.

The hummocky morainal landscapes that dominate the area are generally steeply to very steeply sloping, although they may be more gently sloping in some areas. Brown loam soils formed in glacial till deposits are common on these landscapes. Several large areas of glaciofluvial landscapes are also hummocky but more gently sloping. Sandy and gravelly Brown soils are most common in these areas. Glaciolacustrine plains with Brown clay soils occur locally north of Ogema and west of the Lake of the Rivers channel. The Lake of the Rivers, Willow Bunch Lake, and the Big Muddy Valley are prominent landscape features on the margin of the area. These valleys originated as a spillway that drained a glacial lake in the Old Wives Lake area southward to the Missouri River in the United States.

Most of the Coteau Lakes upland is cropland; however, extensive areas of hilly land are used as rangeland and pasture. Cereals are the major crop, and more than 40% of the cropland area is summerfallow. Several PFRA community pastures encompass some of the rangeland and pasture that occurs in the area.

M21. Lake Alma Upland

The Lake Alma upland is a hilly hummocky morainal area, representing the Missouri Coteau. It extends from Ceylon to the United States border. Elevations rise from 600 m at the base of the upland to 730 m in several hilly uplands. There is some drainage to Long Creek in The Gap and from several coulees along the escarpment; otherwise, surface drainage is limited to flow to local small lakes.

Native mixed-grass prairie is limited to hummocky morainal landscapes, where it is interspersed with cropland. A more continuous grassland cover occurs in steeply sloping areas and coulees on the Missouri Coteau escarpment. A variety of grasses are common on the uplands, with shrubs limited to more moist depressional areas.

The hummocky morainal landscapes that dominate the area are moderately sloping with frequent gullies on the eastern edge of the area. The moraines are more steeply sloping in the upper portion of the upland. Dark Brown loam soils formed in glacial till deposits are common on all of these landscapes.

Most of the Lake Alma upland is cropland. Cereals are the major crop and only slightly more than 30% of the cropland area is summerfallow. Pasture and rangelands are associated with local areas of hilly land.

M22. Wood Mountain Plateau

The Wood Mountain plateau is a thinly glaciated dissected plateau that lies along the United States border and extends from Coronach to Shaunavon. Elevation of the plateau approaches 1,000 m. This plateau is dissected to elevations of 800 to 850 m by an intense network of gullies and creeks. Most of the drainage is to the south, with Otter, Little Breed, Breed, and Daniel creeks draining the western part of the plateau into the Frenchman River. Further east, Bluff, MacEachern, Rock, Boggy, Morgan, Girard, North Beaver, and West Beaver creeks, Wood Coulee, and the West Poplar and East Poplar rivers drain the plateau to the Missouri River in the United States. There is a limited amount of drainage from the plateau to the Big Muddy Valley, which also drains southward to the Missouri River. Fife Lake and Twelve Mile Lake, which lie on the north flank of the plateau, receive some drainage from the plateau through Gollies and Wood Mountain creeks and a number of shorter gullies. Further west, the north flank of the plateau is drained to Old Wives Lake through Six Mile and Pinto creeks and the Wood River.

Extensive areas of native mixed-grass prairie occur in association with quartzite-covered plateaus and gullied lands. A variety of grasses are common on the uplands, with shrubs limited to more moist depressional areas.

The landscape of the upper portion of the area comprises small plateaus, with numerous, small gullies to break their surface. Quartzites and gravels of Tertiary age are common on the surface. The land surrounding the plateau is often strongly gullied while at other times a thin mantle of glacial till subdues the gullied surface. Bedrock is exposed in many gullies and valleys. Brown loam soils are common on the plateaus and more gentle slopes. Regosolic soils occur in the strongly gullied areas.

Most of the Wood Mountain plateau is rangeland, as gullied topography and gravelly soils severely limit the extent of cropland. Cereals are the major crop, with small amounts of forages. Nearly 40% of the cropland area is summerfallow. Several PFRA community pastures represent some of the rangeland and pasture in the area.

M23. Climax Plain

Located between the United States border and the Frenchman River, the Climax plain is a broad till plain that slopes gently eastward from 975 m at the base of the Wood Mountain upland and Old Man on His Back plateau, to 850 m at the Frenchman River. Eastbrook and Wrightville coulees and Nerada and several smaller creeks provide a limited amount of drainage from the highlands in the northern part of the area into the Frenchman River, whereas Mundell, Whitewater, and East Whitewater creeks and Cottonwood Coulee drain a considerable portion of the southern part of the area, with flow into the United States.

Native mixed-grass prairie is limited to hummocky morainal landscapes and Solonetzic soils, where it is interspersed with cropland. A more continuous cover occurs in steeply sloping areas and coulees, and especially in the several PFRA community pastures in the area. A variety of grasses are common on the uplands, with shrubs limited to more moist depressional areas and coulees.

Landscapes in the area are mostly very gently to gently undulating and gently rolling till plains. Gullies are common in many areas. The balance of the area is gently to moderately sloping hummocky moraine; in places, there are many glacial kettles. Brown loam soils prevail on the hummocky moraines while Brown Solonetzic and Brown soils are common on the undulating till plains.

Most of the Climax plain is cropland; however, extensive areas of Solonetzic soils and gullied land are used as rangeland and pasture. Cereals are the major crop, and nearly 50% of the cropland area is summerfallow. Several PFRA community pastures represent some of the rangeland and pasture in the area.

M24. Old Man on His Back Plateau

This area takes its name from a small plateau on the western side of the area, but the Boundary plateau near the United States border and another plateau against the Frenchman River are evidence of a once larger Tertiary plateau in the area. Otherwise, a hummocky moraine masks the bedrock surface. Elevations on the plateaus are 1,050 m, with much of the intervening area at 950 to 975 m. There is considerable surface drainage of Boundary plateau through Myndell and Coteau creeks and of Old Man on His Back plateau through Lyons and Rangeview creeks. The plateau in the extreme north drains into the Frenchman River. The hummocky moraine throughout the remainder of the area has little surface drainage.

Native mixed-grass prairie is limited to hummocky morainal landscapes — where it is interspersed with cropland — and to coulees. A more continuous grassland cover occurs in steeply sloping areas and especially in the PFRA community pasture. A variety of grasses are common on uplands, with shrubs limited to more moist depressional areas and coulees.

The landscape of the area is a strongly sloping hummocky moraine. It is strongly gullied in plateau areas; otherwise, glacial kettles are common. Brown loams formed in glacial till are the most common soils.

Most of the Old Man on His Back plateau area is rangeland, although appreciable areas of gentle slopes are cropped. Cereals are the major crop in these areas, and nearly 50% of the cropland area is summerfallow. A PFRA community pasture represents some of the rangeland and pasture in the area.

M25. Wild Horse Plain

The Wild Horse plain lies along the Alberta border between the Cypress Hills and the United States border. This plain slopes gently southward from 1,000 m at the base of the Cypress Hills upland to 850 m at the United States border. Lodge, Middle, MacRae, and Battle creeks all head near the Cypress upland and flow south into the United States.

Native mixed-grass prairie is limited to areas of strong Solonetzic soil development, especially in the many PFRA community pastures in the area, and to coulees. In the Solonetzic areas, the vegetation is characterized by salt-tolerant wheatgrasses, pincushion cactus, greasewood, and gumweed.

Except for a limited amount of hummocky moraine against the Cypress Hills, the landscape is an undulating till plain with numerous shallow gullies. The soils are mostly Brown Solonetzic clay loams formed in glacial till deposits.

Most of the Wild Horse plain is rangeland and pasture, with only small amounts of cropland. Cereals are the major crop in these areas, with small amounts of forages. Nearly 50% of the cropland area is summerfallow. Several PFRA community pastures encompass some of the rangeland and pasture in the area.

Cypress Upland Ecoregion

The Cypress Upland is a typical plateau with steeply sloping escarpments and numerous valleys and coulees that rises abruptly above the surrounding plains. It was formed during the Tertiary period from materials worn round on their long river journey from newly formed western mountains. The effect of the abrupt and significant rise in elevation is reflected in both the soils and the vegetation. At the base of the upland, mixed grasslands developed on Dark Brown soils are prevalent. With a rise in elevation, the vegetation changes to a submontane fescue prairie on the south-facing slopes, and finally at the upper elevations, to a mix of lodgepole pine, white spruce, and aspen, along with patches of fescue prairie. Black and Dark Gray soils are found on the top of the plateau. This is the smallest ecoregion in Saskatchewan, occupying only 0.5 million hectares or less than 1% of the province. It is only slightly altered by agricultural use.

PHYSIOGRAPHY. The Cypress upland is a dissected plateau with elevations that extend nearly 600 m above the surrounding plain. It comprises a series of benchlands, often referred to as the West, Centre, and East blocks, with gravel-capped plateau surfaces at 1,350 m in the west and 1,200 to 1,250 m further east. The plateaus are surrounded by strongly dissected landscapes with drainage to the south as part of the Missouri River basin and to the east as part of the Saskatchewan basin. Most of the north slope drains to Walsh flats, Maple Creek marsh, and other local basins on the plain below. Glacial deposits cover most of the slopes at lower elevations and extend up and into The Gap, which separates the West and Centre blocks at 1,080 to 1,140 m and as high as 1,250 m in some areas.

High elevations with associated cool and moist conditions promote the development of forest vegetation in the Cypress Hills.

GEOLOGY. The Cypress Hills stand in sharp contrast nearly 600 m above the flat-lying prairies that surround them. The hills owe their existence to their unique geology. A sequence of very coarse gravels were deposited during the middle to late Tertiary period (between 44 to 35 million years ago). These gravels were laid down in migrating braided river and stream systems, which formed a sheet-like capping over unconsolidated sands, silts, and clays of older Early Tertiary and Late Cretaceous formations. The coarse gravels formed an erosion-resistant armour that protected the underlying sediments. In adjacent areas where protective armour cap was not deposited or removed by erosion, the soft sediments were easily eroded prior to the last glacial advance. Any landform higher than 1,250 m above sea level stood above the glaciers in the last ice age. Geologists call such hills "nunataks," an Inuit term meaning island. The Cypress Hills were nunataks during the last ice age.

The Tertiary gravels contain hard, coarse, well-rounded quartzite and chert pebbles and cobbles. It is believed these materials were eroded from the front ranges of the Rocky Mountains located 300 to 400 km to the southwest in Montana. Along the way, the drainage systems also picked up and transported porphyritic rocks, such as trachyte, which are believed to have eroded from intrusive uplifts in the Bearpaw Mountains and the Sweet Grass Hills of northern Montana.

CLIMATE. The Cypress Upland Ecoregion has a subhumid to humid continental climate that is cooler and more moist than the surrounding Mixed Grassland Ecoregion. The mean annual daily temperature is 2.7°C. The mean July temperature is 16.0°C and the mean January temperature is -12.1°C. The mean annual precipitation is 450 mm, with 244 mm of rainfall occurring from May to September. The summers are short and warm, having a frost-free period of 52 days and a total of 1,288 degree days above 5°C.

LANDFORMS AND SOILS. There are a number of landforms in the Cypress upland that are unique to all but the Wood Mountain area of the province. There is an unglaciated bedrock surface that lies above 1,300 m in the West Block. It comprises two nearly level plateaus separated by a broad steep valleys formed in Tertiary times. These plateau remnants are capped by quartzite gravels and cobbles that are locally cemented into conglomerate. Glacial erratics are found on bedrock that forms the long, gentle slopes at 1,100 to 1,300 m on the south side of the Cypress upland, suggesting these areas were covered with ice during glaciation.

In some areas the bedrock surface has a cover of glacial drift formed as ground and hummocky moraine that masks the underlying bedrock surface. In other parts, such as on the north slope of the Cypress uplands, there are prominent hummocky moraines as well as glaciolacustrine deposits, which were formed in glacial lakes between the ice to the north and the uplands to the south.

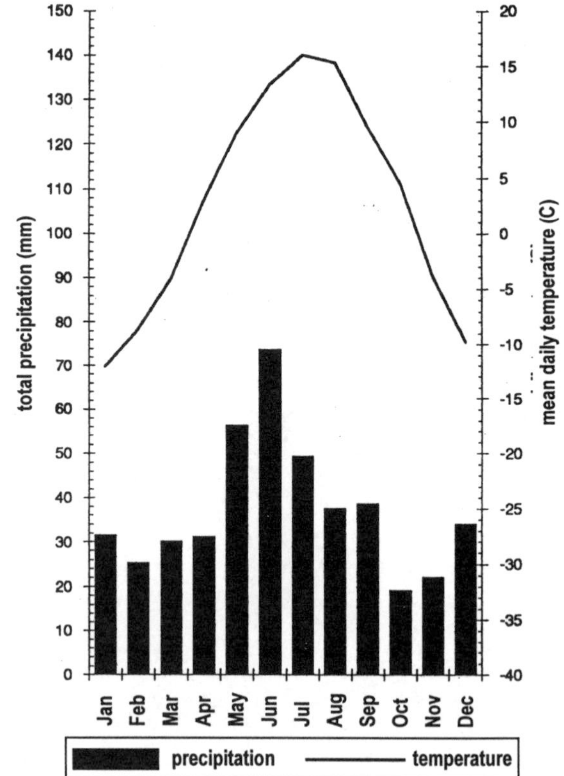

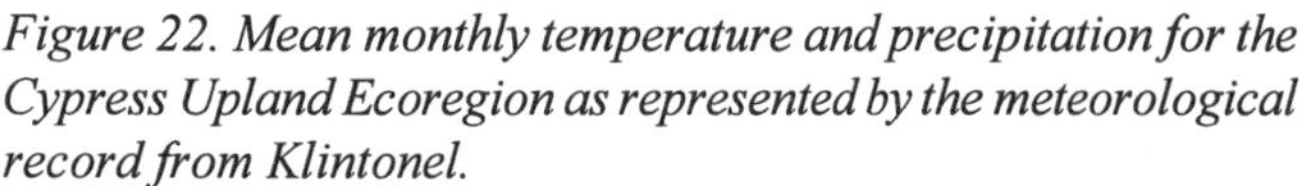

Figure 22. Mean monthly temperature and precipitation for the Cypress Upland Ecoregion as represented by the meteorological record from Klintonel.

Prairie crocus blooming in spring.

The south-facing slopes of the Cypress upland are dominated by Dark Brown soils under grassland vegetation, although Brown soils occur at lower elevations. Black soils are common on unglaciated fescue prairie-lodgepole pine covered plateaus that extend from the Centre Block to the Alberta border and under mixedgrass prairie in the East and Centre blocks. Dark Gray and Gray Luvisolic soils are found under white spruce and aspen forests on north-facing slopes.

GROUNDWATER. The Cypress Upland Ecoregion is essentially unglaciated; hence, aquifers are limited to those in the bedrock sands and gravels of the Eastend to Ravenscrag and the Cypress formations.

VEGETATION. The vegetation of the Cypress upland is composed of a mixture of prairie and montane species. The prairie vegetation is representative of the plains that surround the Cypress upland while the montane element is similar to vegetation of the Rocky Mountain foothills. There are eight major vegetation associations found in the Cypress upland.

A lodgepole pine woodland contains many remnants from a montane flora and forms the predominant forest type in the ecoregion. Montane species include lodgepole pine, bluebunch fescue, alpine bistort, lance-leaved spring-beauty, purple clematis, heart-leaved buttercup, western meadow-rue, shining-leaved meadow-sweet, northern Gairdner's squawroot, pinedrops, kitten-tails, yellow monkeyflower, heart-leaved arnica, and white hawkweed.

Lodgepole pine is so named because it has long straight trunks that were historically used for teepee poles. This association grows in drier areas at elevations above 1,400 m and extends from the Central Block in Saskatchewan to the western extremity of the upland. The lodgepole pine association is adapted to fire.

A white spruce forest is found on uplands in cooler and moister areas, such as north-facing slopes and near springs. It forms pure stands near wetlands, coulees, and creeks, but occurs in mixed stands with trembling aspen on well-drained soils. Tree densities are lower than the lodgepole pine woodlands. The white spruce woodland is an old growth type and can colonize areas that were once dominated by lodgepole pine. Vegetation under the canopy is abundant and stratified into two tiers. The understory tier is dominated by red-osier dogwood, willows, and low bush-cranberry. The forest floor consists mostly of the wild black currant and red baneberry with lower cover species such as bunchberry, twin-flower, pink wintergreen, ferns, and stiff club-moss. A few green-flowered bog-orchids and mosses may also be present, and lichens often grow on the branches of spruce trees.

Aspen woodlands occur in many habitats in the Cypress upland. They occur in patches below the lodgepole pine woodland on the north side of the plateau and on the surrounding grasslands. On the grasslands, they occur along moist creek beds while up on the plateau they are found in wetter depressions. Trembling aspen is found in pure stands or mixed with other deciduous trees such as balsam poplar, Manitoba maple, cottonwood, and white spruce. Understory species include willow, saskatoon, choke cherry, red-osier dogwood, pin cherry, northern gooseberry, and wild white geranium. Forest floor plants include western Canada violet and American wild strawberry.

There is a fescue prairie grassland on top of the western plateau. Plains rough fescue is the dominant grass with bluebunch fescue, timber oat grass, and bluegrass also present. Important shrubs and herbs include shrubby cinquefoil, prairie crocus, mountain shootingstar, silvery lupine and low larkspur, low goldenrod, and great-flowered gaillardia.

The mixedgrass prairie is found on the eastern part of the plateau and on dry south-facing slopes. The most common grasses are northern wheatgrass, needle-and-thread, western porcupine grass, blue grama grass, and various dryland sedges. Along slopes, creeping juniper, yellow umbrellaplant, narrow-petaled stonecrop, milk-vetches, purple prairie-clover and moss phlox are common associates. On overgrazed areas western wheatgrass, June grass, sand dropseed, silver sagebrush, and ball and prickly-pear cactus become more abundant. In dry exposed places prairie selaginella is found. Legumes are also common and include early yellow locoweed and purple prairie-clover.

Wetlands in the Cypress upland include plant associations that live in coulees and depressions with standing water, as well as those growing in areas near creeks, lakes, ponds, and spring-fed marshes. Along the waters edge, horsetail, common cattail, marsh reed grass, tall manna grass, bur-reed, bulrush, marsh skullcap, western water-hemlock, purple avens, and American speedwell are found. Partly or wholly submerged aquatic plants like slender naiad, yellow water crowfoot, pondweeds, and duckweeds are abundant in stagnant water. Yellow monkeyflower and mare's-tail are found along creeks and streams.

River valleys have distinctive flora. The Frenchman River Valley supports dense shrub growth that includes willow, red-osier dogwood, Wood's rose, white birch, and western snowberry, while Battle Creek consists of the lodgepole pine association. Prairie communities surround the rivers' edges and include aspen groves and sedge meadows.

The mule deer is distinguished from its white-tailed relative by long ears and a smaller rounded tail.

WILDLIFE. Because of the diversity of habitat, the Cypress upland supports a large variety of mammals. Pronghorn are the dominant ungulate on the grasslands, while mule and white-tailed deer are common in wooded coulees, and moose and elk inhabit the forested hills and valleys. Other important grassland species include Richardson's ground squirrel, thirteen-lined ground squirrel, northern pocket gopher, and white-tailed jack rabbit. Predators on these species include red fox and coyote. The striped skunk and badger are also present, but less common.

The woodlands provide food and shelter to small mammals such as porcupine and least chipmunk. Mule and white-tailed deer also use the woodland areas for cover and browse. Although not abundant, white-footed mouse, lynx, and bobcat also live here. In pine and spruce woodlands one finds the reintroduced (after a fire in 1886) red squirrel, as well as masked shrew, bushy-tailed woodrat, moose, and elk.

The brushland and wetland vegetation provides shelter

to mountain cottontail and the snowshoe hare. Along the rivers and streams live many of the fur-bearing mammals such as beaver, muskrat, mink, and least weasel.

Historically, bison herds grazed the plateau and surrounding plains; cougars, wolves, and black and grizzly bears lived in the woodlands.

A total of 246 bird species has been recorded for the Cypress upland. The common birds here are similar to those of the Boreal Plain Ecozone and the surrounding mixed grassland. The species richness during the winter is the highest in the province. Among the many species attracted to the wooded hills are sharp-shinned hawk, ruby-throated hummingbird, white-crowned sparrow, western tanager, ruffed grouse, blue jay, and white-breasted nuthatch. Prairie species that live in the fescue and mixed grasslands are killdeer, Baird's sparrow, savannah sparrow, chestnut-collared longspur, and willet. About half of the species observed in the Cypress upland breed there.

Similar to the montane vegetation, a few montane bird species also have breeding ranges in the Cypress upland. These include the yellow-rumped warbler, dark-eyed junco, and MacGillivray's warbler. Of further interest is the northern flicker that has two subspecies, the yellow-shafted and western red-shafted flicker, with breeding ranges that overlap. Because of this, interbreeding does occur, producing special hybrids. The rare (and once nearly extinct) trumpeter swan also nests on lakes in the Cypress upland. Its population has declined from a high of three pair to a single adult.

The fish species of the Cypress upland are unique to Saskatchewan and are dependent on the river system in which they occur. The fish species in the Missouri River drainage basin are at their northern distribution limit and include rock bass, stonecat, brassy minnow, brown and black bullhead, chestnut lamprey, tadpole madtom, channel catfish, bigmouth buffalo, and the western silvery minnow. One species, the mountain sucker, is at its eastern limit of distribution and is more common in Alberta. Brown and rainbow trout have been introduced to both the Frenchman River and Battle Creek. Fish found throughout the Cypress upland include northern pike, walleye, yellow perch, cisco, and slimy sculpin.

Common amphibians and reptiles in the woodlands and around the wetlands and rivers include the northern leopard frog and the tiger salamander. In addition the wandering garter snake and western plains garter snake are also known to occur in woodland and grassland associations.

Free-range cattle are a common sight in the Cypress Upland Ecoregion.

HUMAN ACTIVITY. The population of this ecoregion is approximately 2,000. The major community is Eastend, which is developing the tourist potential of a recent archaeological find, a *Tyrannosaurus rex*, one of only 12 known in the world. Physical conditions allow free-range livestock grazing and limited production of cereals on smoother lower slopes. Approximately 21% of the ecoregion is cultivated. Wildlife hunting, recreation, and nature activities are also important uses on rougher upper slopes. Cypress Hills Provincial Park occurs in this ecoregion.

Approximately 23% of the ecoregion is within some form of park or protected area, although a large part of that percentage is made up of PFRA community pastures, provincial pastures, and lands designated under the *Wildlife Habitat Protection Act*.

Landscape Areas

N1. Cypress Slope

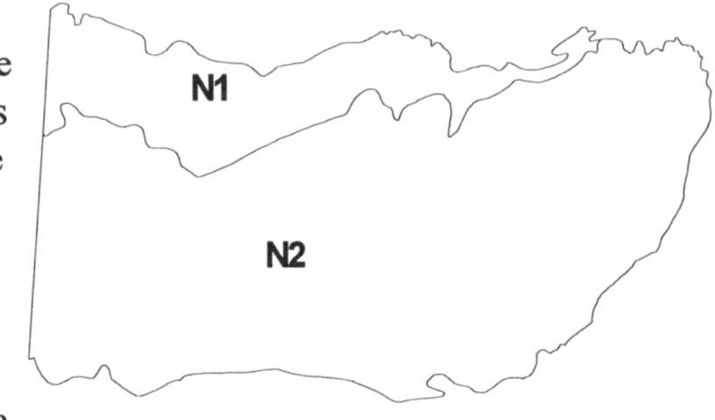

The Cypress slope is the morainal area on the north side of the Cypress Hills that lies below the Cypress escarpment. Elevations fall from 1,000 m at the base of the escarpment to 850 m at the margin of the plain below. Surface drainage is northward through Abbott, McCoy, Downie, Hay, Birch, Piapot, Fauquier, Shuard, and many other creeks and coulees.

The native vegetation of the sloping lands is dominated by patches of rough fescue and oat grass as the characteristic grassland species and lodgepole pine and trembling aspen as tree species. White spruce and some balsam poplar are common along ravines. Meadow-sweet and various grasses and herbs occur under the pine forests, while meadow-sweet and bluegrass are common under trembling aspen.

The steep to very steeply sloping hummocky morainal landscapes that dominate this area have been extensively gullied. Dark Brown loams formed in glacial till are the most common soils in the area.

Most of the Cypress slope is rangeland and pasture, although cropland does occur in areas with more gentle slopes. Cereals, including relatively large amounts of fall rye, are the major crop and there is a large amount of forages. Less than 30% of the cropland area is summerfallow.

N2. Cypress Hills

The Cypress Hills is a bedrock-controlled plateau representing a remnant of a former Tertiary surface. It includes benchlands at the top of the hills and the strongly dissected lands surrounding them. The benchlands can be considered in three blocks. The West Block, with two plateaus at 1,350 m, is surrounded by a strongly dissected plateau in the headwaters area of Battle Creek, with elevations dropping to 1,000 m. The Centre Block is somewhat lower, with elevations of 1,200 to 1,250 m on the upper parts. This area is dissected by Fairwell, Davis, Caton, and Conglomerate creeks, with elevations as low as 1,050 m. The Gap, separating the West and Centre blocks, is a steeply sloping hummocky moraine at 1,080 to 1,140 m. There are glacial kettles throughout this area except for the extremities on the north and south sides, which are gullied. The East Block is lower still, with elevations on the benchlands generally at 1,150 m and some as low as 1,000 m. The benchlands are surrounded by the Cypress escarpment, where elevations drop to 1,000 m. This escarpment is drained through Bone and Jones creeks leading to Swiftcurrent Creek in the eastern part and Conglomerate, Rose, Fairwell, Caton, Davis, and Adams creeks leading to the Frenchman River and Cypress Lake in the southern part. The northern escarpment is drained to various lakes in the plain below by Abbott, Gap, Fleming, Hay, Piapot, Bear, Shuard, and many other creeks.

The native vegetation of the level uplands is dominated by rough fescue and oat grass with shrubby cinquefoil as an abundant shrub and lodgepole pine as the characteristic tree species. Trembling aspen also occupy some of the dry uplands. White spruce and some balsam poplar are common along ravines. Meadow-sweet and various grasses and herbs occur under the pine forests, while meadow-sweet and bluegrass are common under aspen.

The landscapes in the area are dominantly undulating and, occasionally, hummocky morainal. The morainal surface, for the most part, has been altered by gullying, and only occasionally are glacial kettles present. The tops of some of the highest benches are relatively level. Here, the Tertiary surface appears at the surface, covered only by a very thin veneer of loess. Black loamy soils formed in loess and glacial till occur on the highest benches. Dark Brown loamy soils formed in glacial till are most common on the hummocky moraine and dissected morainal surfaces at lower elevations, except on the lower south side where Brown soils prevail.

Nearly all of this area is rangeland or pasture.

Conclusion

The Importance of an Ecosystem Perspective

How do we encourage a more integrated understanding of ecosystems? An ecosystem approach depends on the development of an ecosystem management framework in which sustainable development goals can be developed and pursued. Accepting the basic rationale of "thinking in terms of ecosystems" is a first step that must be followed by appropriate plans and actions. An ecosystem approach demands that specific problems are identified and priorities established, and that monitoring, research, and assessment are at adequate levels to allow management activities to work towards conservation goals.

Government department mandates that now restrict the potential range of actions of organizations must be widened. Jurisdictional boundaries should no longer restrict authorities to politically determined boundaries in assessing issues. Information exchange should encourage holistic assessments and decision making. The complexity of environmental and resource management challenges all levels of governments, special interest groups and stakeholders to work together towards an ecosystem approach which integrates skills, information, assessment and management.

But how is this broad ecosystem approach to be encouraged? How is a shared understanding of the social, economic, and environmental problems/concerns of Saskatchewan, Canada, and North America to be cultivated? How many major ecosystems are there in Saskatchewan, Canada, or North America? Which ecosystems do we share with Mexico and the United States or, indeed, with other continents? In what ecosystems do most people live? How diverse are northern and southern ecosystems? Questions like these are perplexing both in their scope and uncertainty. We know from our experience what some the answers are and, more importantly, how vital ecosystem information is becoming. A starting point to answering these questions has been the development of an ecological land classification system that encourages the integration and assessment of information.

Moving Towards an Ecosystem Approach

The need to make decisions on a broader and more inclusive basis has been demonstrated in dealing with international issues such as acid rain, Great Lakes pollution and water resource management, waterfowl conservation, and cod fisheries management. These issues have been of immediate concern to Canadians and Americans in particular. Many initiatives such as those of the Commission for Environmental Cooperation (CEC, 1994), the North American Waterfowl Management Plan, the North American State of the Environment Reporting and the North American Protected Areas Commission have recognized this requirement to look beyond any one jurisdiction to the larger continental and ecosystem setting.

In Saskatchewan there has been a shift to a cooperative approach to management between governments at all levels, along with non-government agencies, to measure and counter deleterious changes to the environment. In 1995, Saskatchewan was integral in helping to develop the Canadian Biodiversity Strategy. The strategy was completed by a federal-provincial-territorial working group along with a stakeholder advisory group. The plan involves a cooperative approach to maintaining the natural biological diversity through integrated resource management, interjurisdictional "species-at-risk" programs, and protection of representative areas.

In 1996, Saskatchewan Environment and Resource Management released an action plan to create a representative areas network. The network will consist of lands, selected to represent the natural ecological and biological diversity of the province and managed to protect that diversity. The action plan has identified key actions to achieve the goal of representing each of the province's ecoregions.

Continuing the Ecosystem Approach

Transcribing the value of the ecological approach through issues like acid rain, loss of Great Plains native grasslands, Great Lakes pollution and control, and biodiversity conservation provides useful lessons in reinforcing the relationships between people and their environment. From them we learn what relationships emerge when ecosystem components and structures are changed (consequence of removing forests, losing soils resources, changing water quality), ecosystem processes are altered (consequences of climatic and hydrological regimes), or ecosystem carrying capacities exceeded (consequences of over-harvesting). This ecological perspective and realization have been fundamental starting points for building an ecological framework for North America.

Oddly, terms like ecology, ecosystem and ecoregion are not always thought of as holistic concepts, nor are similar terms like natural region and forest region. No one owns these words but it is crucial that people understand how they are used by different groups and organizations. At times, these terms have been reduced to describing particular parts of the ecosphere. Ascribing ecology to the mere distribution of native animals/plants, to the extent of particular climatic regimes, to endemic species or to potential vegetation types is a contradictory venture for planning and management cases that require comprehensive information.

Current day issues and long term goals are embracing in their need for comprehensive and systems-based information. Where plant distribution maps, for example, were once important catalysts to encourage ecological thinking, they now tend to promote reductionist thought and actions. Plants, insects, wildlife, and people need to be more fully thought of as interacting/dependent organisms that are very dependent on the quality and character of their physical setting. What relationships (e.g. resource stocks, air purification) are there between trees and people, or between trees and soils/climate/habitat/land use, or between harvesting timber today and sustaining forests for tomorrow? A systems-wide notion of thinking needs to be practiced across a range of spatial (regional, country, continent) and temporal scales (now and in the future) to answer such a question.

The Next Steps

We have much to learn about ecosystems. While an ecosystem perspective is a logical and practical route for achieving sustainability goals, it has not been a working principle in most organizations and departments. Traditionally, it is the individual component parts of ecosystems (e.g. soils, water, wildlife, land use) that have been examined. However, research and management agencies are expanding their efforts to collect a broader range of information as well as work in cooperative partnerships with other resource agencies. The extension of these initiatives is strategic for environmental planning and management. For example, region-wide cooperation is needed for the conservation and protection of migratory species and for the solution of transboundary environmental issues such as pollutant dispersion.

Scientists will continue to refine their knowledge of the ecological regions of Saskatchewan. Based on that knowledge, there is a need to construct an ecosystem information base that allows analyses of issues relative to physical, biological, and human points of reference. For example, how do issues of agricultural sustainability on the prairies relate to issues of human health and biodiversity conservation? Answering such questions requires an interdisciplinary approach, one that integrates the skills of many different professionals and organizations and transcends traditional departmental mandates. Such a transdisciplinary integration process is complex, but it is the only way to approach the very involved issues confronting Saskatchewan today and into the future.

Appendix I: GEOLOGICAL TIME SCALE

Eon	Era	Period		Epoch	Absolute Age (Ma)	Age of	Events
Phanerozoic	Cenozoic	Quaternary		Holocene	0-2	Mammals	Humans
				Pleistocene			Scabland Floods
		Tertiary	Neogene	Pliocene	2-5		
				Miocene	5-24		Columbia Basalts
			Paleogene	Oligocene	24-37		
				Eocene	37-58		
				Paleocene	58-66		Extinction of Dinosaurs
	Mesozoic	Cretaceous			66-144	Reptiles	Flowering Plants
		Jurassic			144-208		First Birds & Mammals
		Triassic			208-245		First Dinosaurs
	Paleozoic	Permian			245-286	Amphibians	Extinction of Trilobites
		Carboniferous	Pennsylvanian		286-320		First Reptiles
			Mississippian		320-360		Large Primitive Trees
		Devonian			360-408	Fishes	First Amphibians
		Silurian			408-438		First Land Plants
		Ordovician			438-505	Invertebrates	First Fish
		Cambrian			505-545		First Shells, Trilobites
Proterozoic	Precambrian				545-2,500		First Multicelled Organisms
Archean					2,500-3,800		First One-celled Organisms
Hadean					3,800-4,600		Origin of the Earth

Appendix II: VERTEBRATE SPECIES LISTS

Following are lists of the common and scientific names of species referred to in this book.

MAMMALS

COMMON NAME	SCIENTIFIC NAME
Arctic Shrew	*Sorex arcticus*
Arctic Fox	*Alopex lagopus*
Badger	*Taxidea taxus*
Beaver	*Castor canadensis*
Big Brown Bat	*Eptesicus fuscus*
Bison	*Bos bison*
Black Bear	*Ursus americanus*
Bobcat	*Lynx rufus*
Bushy-tailed Woodrat	*Neotoma cinerea*
Caribou -Woodland - Barren-ground	*Rangifer tarandus*
Cougar	*Felis concolor*
Coyote	*Canis latrans*
Deer Mouse	*Peromyscus maniculatus*
Eastern Cottontail	*Sylvilagus floridanus*
Eastern Gray Squirrel	*Sciurus carolinensis*
Ermine, Short-tailed Weasel	*Mustela erminea*
Fisher	*Martes pennanti*
Fox squirrel	*Sciurus niger*
Franklin's Ground Squirrel	*Spermophilus franklinii*
Gray Wolf	*Canis lupus*
Grizzly Bear	*Ursus arctos*
Least Weasel	*Mustela nivalis*
Least Chipmunk	*Tamias minimus*
Little Brown Bat	*Myotis lucifugus*
Lynx	*Lynx canadensis*
Marten	*Martes americana*
Masked Shrew	*Sorex cinereus*
Meadow Jumping Mouse	*Zapus hudsonius*
Meadow Vole	*Microtus pennsylvanicus*
Mink	*Mustela vison*
Moose	*Alces alces*
Mountain Cottontail	*Sylvilagus nuttallii*
Mule Deer	*Odocoileus hemionus*
Muskrat	*Ondatra zibethicus*
Northern Grasshopper Mouse	*Onychomys leucogaster*
Northern Short-tailed Shrew	*Blarina brevicauda*
Northern Bog Lemming	*Synaptomys borealis*
Northern Flying Squirrel	*Glaucomys sabrinus*
Northern Pocket Gopher	*Thomomys talpoides*
Olive-backed Pocket Mouse	*Perognathus fasciatus*
Porcupine	*Erethizon dorsatum*
Prairie Vole	*Microtus ochrogaster*
Prairie Long-tailed Weasel	*Mustela frenata*
Pronghorn	*Antilocapra americana*
Pygmy Shrew	*Sorex hoyi*
Raccoon	*Procyon lotor*
Red-backed Vole	*Clethrionomys gapperi*
Red Fox	*Vulpes vulpes*
Red Squirrel	*Tamiasciurus hudsonicus*
Richardson's Ground Squirrel	*Spermophilus richardsonii*
River Otter	*Lutra canadensis*
Sagebrush Vole	*Lemmiscus curtatus*
Snowshoe Hare	*Lepus americanus*
Striped Skunk	*Mephitis mephitis*
Swift Fox	*Vulpes velox*
Thirteen-lined Ground Squirrel	*Spermophilus tridecemlineatus*
Elk	*Cervus elaphus*
White-tailed Jack Rabbit	*Lepus townsendii*
White-tailed Deer	*Odocoileus virginianus*
White-footed Mouse	*Peromyscus leucopus*
Wolverine	*Gulo gulo*
Woodchuck	*Marmota monax*
Yellow-cheeked or Taiga Vole	*Microtus xanthognathus*

AMPHIBIANS

COMMON NAME	SCIENTIFIC NAME
Boreal Chorus Frog	*Pseudacris triseriata*
Canadian Toad	*Bufo hemiophrys*
Great Plains Toad	*Bufo cognatus*
Northern Leopard Frog	*Rana pipiens*
Tiger Salamander	*Ambystoma tigrinum*
Wood Frog	*Rana sylvatica*

BIRDS

COMMON NAME	SCIENTIFIC NAME
Alder Flycatcher	*Empidonax alnorum*
American Redstart	*Setophaga ruticilla*
American Robin	*Turdus migratorius*
American Crow	*Corvus brachyrhynchos*
American Goldfinch	*Carduelis tristis*
American White Pelican	*Pelecanus erythrorhynchos*
American Tree Sparrow	*Spizella arborea*
American Coot	*Fulica americana*
Arctic Tern	*Sterna paradisaea*
Baird's Sparrow	*Ammodramus bairdii*
Bald Eagle	*Haliaeetus leucocephalus*
Barn Swallow	*Hirundo rustica*
Barred Owl	*Strix varia*
Belted Kingfisher	*Ceryle alcyon*
Black-capped Chickadee	*Parus atricapillus*
Black-and-white Warbler	*Mniotilta varia*
Black-billed Magpie	*Pica pica*
Black-billed Cuckoo	*Coccyzus erythropthalmus*
Black-crowned Night Heron	*Nycticorax nycticorax*
Black-throated Blue Warbler	*Dendroica caerulescens*
Blackpoll Warbler	*Dendroica striata*
Black Tern	*Chlidonias niger*
Blue Jay	*Cyanocitta cristata*
Blue-winged Teal	*Anas discors*
Bohemian Waxwing	*Bombycilla garrulus*
Boreal Chickadee	*Parus hudsonicus*
Brewer's Blackbird	*Euphagus cyanocephalus*
Broad-winged Hawk	*Buteo platypterus*
Brown-headed Cowbird	*Molothrus ater*
Bufflehead	*Bucephala albeola*
Burrowing Owl	*Speotyto cunicularia*
Canada Goose	*Branta canadensis*
Chestnut-collared Longspur	*Calcarius ornatus*
Chestnust-sided Warbler	*Dendroica pennsylvanica*
Chimney Swift	*Chaetura pelagica*
Chipping Sparrow	*Spizella passerina*
Clay-colored Sparrow	*Spizella pallida*
Common Raven	*Corvus corax*
Common Loon	*Gavia immer*
Common Redpoll	*Carduelis flammea*
Common Goldeneye	*Bucephala clangula*
Common Merganser	*Mergus merganser*
Common Yellow-throat	*Geothlypis trichas*
Dark-eyed Junco	*Junco hyemalis*
Double-crested Cormorant	*Phalacrocorax auritus*
Downy Woodpecker	*Picoides pubescens*
Eastern Wood-pewee	*Contopus virens*
Ferruginous Hawk	*Buteo regalis*
Fox Sparrow	*Passerella iliaca*
Franklin's Gull	*Larus pipixcan*
Golden Eagle	*Aquila chrysaetos*
Gray Jay	*Perisoreus canadensis*
Gray-cheeked Thrush	*Catharus minimus*
Great Blue Heron	*Ardea herodias*
Great Gray Owl	*Strix nebulosa*
Great Horned Owl	*Bubo virginianus*
Great Crested Flycatcher	*Myiarchus crinitus*
Greater Yellowlegs	*Tringa melanoleuca*
Green-winged Teal	*Anas crecca*
Gyrfalcon	*Falco rusticolus*
Hairy Woodpecker	*Picoides villosus*
Harris' Sparrow	*Zonotrichia querula*
Hermit Thrush	*Catharus guttatus*
Horned Grebe	*Podiceps auritus*
Horned Lark	*Eremophila alpestris*
House Sparrow	*Passer domesticus*
House Wren	*Troglodytes aedon*
Indigo Bunting	*Passerina cyanea*
Killdeer	*Charadrius vociferus*
Lazuli Bunting	*Passerina amoena*
Least Flycatcher	*Empidonax minimus*
Least Sandpiper	*Calidris minutilla*
Lesser Scaup	*Aythya affinis*
Long-billed Curlew	*Numenius americanus*
MacGillivray's Warbler	*Oporornis tolmiei*
Mallard	*Anas platyrhynchos*
Marbled Godwit	*Limosa fedoa*
McCown's Longspur	*Calcarius mccownii*
Mew Gull	*Larus canus*
Mourning Dove	*Zenaida macroura*
Mourning Warbler	*Oporornis philadelphia*
Nashville Warbler	*Vermivora ruficapilla*
Northern Flicker	*Colaptus auratus*
Northern Harrier	*Circus cyaneus*
Northern Waterthrush	*Seiurus noveboracensis*
Northern Shoveler	*Anas clypeata*
Olive-sided Flycatcher	*Contopus borealis*
Osprey	*Pandion haliaetus*
Ovenbird	*Seiurus aurocapillus*
Palm Warbler	*Dendroica palmarum*
Philadelphia Vireo	*Vireo philadelphicus*
Pileated Woodpecker	*Dryocopus pileatus*
Pine Grosbeak	*Pinicola enucleator*
Piping Plover	*Charadrius melodus*
Red-breasted Nuthatch	*Sitta canadensis*
Red-breasted Merganser	*Mergus serrator*
Red-tailed Hawk	*Buteo jamaicensis*
Red-necked Grebe	*Podiceps grisegena*
Red-necked Phalarope	*Phalaropus lobatus*
Red-throated Loon	*Gavia stellata*
Red-winged Blackbird	*Agelaius phoeniceus*
Red Crossbill	*Loxia curvirostra*
Ring-necked Duck	*Aythya collaris*
Ring-billed Gull	*Larus delawarensis*
Rock Ptarmigan	*Lagopus mutus*
Rock Dove	*Columba livia*

COMMON NAME	SCIENTIFIC NAME
Rose-breasted Grosbeak	*Pheucticus ludovicianus*
Ruby-throated Hummingbird	*Archilochus colubris*
Ruby-crowned Kinglet	*Regulus calendula*
Ruffed Grouse	*Bonasa umbellus*
Sandhill Crane	*Grus canadensis*
Savannah Sparrow	*Passerculus sandwichensis*
Semipalmated Plover	*Charadrius semipalmatus*
Sharp-tailed Grouse	*Tympanuchus phasianellus*
Sharp-shinned Hawk	*Accipiter striatus*
Short-eared Owl	*Asio flammeus*
Snow Bunting	*Plectrophenax nivalis*
Solitary Vireo	*Vireo solitarius*
Song Sparrow	*Melospiza melodia*
Sora	*Porzana carolina*
Sprague's Pipit	*Anthus spragueii*
Spruce Grouse	*Dendragapus canadensis*
Surf Scoter	*Melanitta perspicillata*
Swainson's hawk	*Buteo swainsoni*
Three-toed Woodpecker	*Picoides tridactylus*
Tree Swallow	*Tachycineta bicolor*

COMMON NAME	SCIENTIFIC NAME
Trumpeter Swan	*Cygnus buccinator*
Upland Sandpiper	*Bartramia longicauda*
Vesper Sparrow	*Pooecetes gramineus*
Warbling Vireo	*Vireo gilvus*
Western Tanager	*Piranga ludoviciana*
Western Meadowlark	*Sturnella neglecta*
Whip-poor-will	*Caprimulgus vociferus*
White-crowned Sparrow	*Zonotrichia leucophrys*
White-winged Crossbill	*Loxia leucoptera*
White-breasted Nuthatch	*Sitta carolinensis*
Willet	*Catoptrophorus semipalmatus*
Willow Ptarmigan	*Lagopus lagopus*
Wood Duck	*Aix sponsa*
Yellow-headed Blackbird	*Xanthocephalus xanthocephalus*
Yellow-rumped Warbler	*Dendroica coronata*
Yellow-bellied Sapsucker	*Sphyrapicus varius*
Yellow Warbler	*Dendroica petechia*
Yellow-throated Vireo	*Vireo flavifrons*

FISH

COMMON NAME	SCIENTIFIC NAME
Arctic Grayling	*Thymallus arcticus*
Bigmouth Buffalo	*Ictiobus cyprinellus*
Black Bullhead	*Ictalurus melas*
Brassy Minnow	*Hybognathus hankinsoni*
Brown Bullhead	*Ameiurus nebulosus*
Brown Trout	*Salmo trutta*
Burbot	*Lota lota*
Channel Catfish	*Ictalurus punctatus*
Chestnut Lamprey	*Ichthyomyzon castaneus*
Cisco	*Coregonus artedii*
Emerald Shiner	*Notropis atherinoides*
Fathead Minnow	*Pimephales promelas*
Goldeye	*Hiodon alosoides*
Lake Chub	*Couesius plumbeus*
Lake Whitefish	*Coregonus clupeaformis*
Lake Trout	*Salvelinus namaycush*
Lake Sturgeon	*Acipenser fulvescens*
Longnose Dace	*Rhinichthys cataractae*
Longnose Sucker	*Catostomus catostomus*
Mooneye	*Hiodon tergisus*

COMMON NAME	SCIENTIFIC NAME
Mountain Sucker	*Catostomus platyrhynchus*
Ninespine Stickleback	*Pungitius pungitius*
Northern Pike	*Esox lucius*
Rainbow Trout	*Oncorhynchus mykiss*
Rock Bass	*Ambloplites rupestris*
Sauger	*Stizostedion canadense*
Shorthead Redhorse	*Moxostoma macrolepidotum*
Shortjaw cisco	*Coregonus zenithicus*
Slimy Sculpin	*Cottus cognatus*
Smallmouth Bass	*Micropterus dolomieu*
Spoonhead Sculpin	*Cottus ricei*
Spottail Shiner	*Notropis hudsonius*
Stonecat	*Noturus flavus*
Tadpole Madtom	*Noturus gyrinus*
Trout-Perch	*Percopsis omiscomaycus*
Walleye	*Stizostedion vitreum*
Western Silvery Minnow	*Hybognathus argyritis*
White Sucker	*Catostomus commersoni*
Yellow Perch	*Perca flavescens*

REPTILES

COMMON NAME	SCIENTIFIC NAME
Bull Snake	*Pituophis melanoleucus*
Painted Turtle	*Chrysemys picta*
Plains Garter Snake	*Thamnophis radix*
Prairie Rattlesnake	*Crotalus viridis*
Red-sided Garter Snake	*Thamnophis sirtalis*
Redbelly Snake	*Storeria occipitomaculata*

COMMON NAME	SCIENTIFIC NAME
Short-horned Lizard	*Phrynosoma douglasi*
Smooth Green Snake	*Opheodrys vernalis*
Snapping Turtle	*Chelydra serpentina*
Wandering Garter Snake	*Thamnophis elegans*
Western Plains Garter Snake	*Thamnophis radix*
Western Hognose Snake	*Heterodon nasicus*

Appendix III: VASCULAR PLANT SPECIES LIST

Following are lists of the common and scientific names of species referred to in this book.

COMMON NAME	SCIENTIFIC NAME
Alkali Grass or Saltgrass	*Distichlis spicata*
Alpine Azalea	*Loiseleuria procumbens*
Alpine Bistort	*Polygonum viviparum*
American Elm	*Ulmus americana*
American Speedwell or American Brooklime	*Veronica americana*
American Wild Strawberry	*Fragaria virginiana*
Arctic Rock-cress	*Arabis arenicola*
Arum-leaved Arrowhead	*Sagittaria cuneata*
Awned Sedge	*Carex atherodes*
Awned Wheat Grass	*Elymus trachycaulus* ssp *subsecundus*
Ball Cactus	*Escobaria vivipara*
Balsam Fir	*Abies balsamea*
Balsam Poplar	*Populus balsamifera*
Baltic Rush	*Juncus balticus*
Bastard Toadflax	*Comandra umbellata*
Beaked Hazelnut	*Corylus cornuta*
Beaked Sedge	*Carex rostrata*
Beaked Willow	*Salix bebbiana*
Bearberry	*Arctostaphylos uva-ursi*
Big Bluestem	*Andropogon gerardii*
Bishop's-cap	*Mitella nuda*
Black Spruce	*Picea mariana*
Blue Grama Grass	*Bouteloua gracilis*
Bluebunch Fescue or Idaho Fescue	*Festuca idahoensis*
Bluejoint	*Calamagrostis canadensis*
Bog Cranberry	*Vaccinium oxycoccos* var. *intermedium*
Bog Laurel	*Kalmia polifolia*
Bristly black currant	*Ribes lacustre*
Brown-eyed Susan or Great-flowered Gaillardia	*Gaillardia aristata*
Buck-bean	*Menyanthes trifoliata*
Buffaloberry, Thorny	*Shepherdia argentea*
Buffaloberry, Canada	*Shepherdia canadensis*
Bunchberry	*Cornus canadensis*
Bur Oak	*Quercus macrocarpa*
Bush honeysuckle	*Diervilla lonicera*
Canada blueberry	*Vaccinium myrtilloides*
Canada Wild Rye	*Elymus canadensis*
Canadian Rice Grass	*Oryzopsis canadensis*
Choke cherry	*Prunus virginiana var melanocarpa*
Close-sheathed Cotton-grass	*Eriophorum brachyantherum*
Cloudberry	*Rubus chamaemorus*
Cottonwood or Western Cottonwood	*Populus deltoides*
Common Bladderwort or Greater Bladderwort	*Utricularia vulgaris*
Common Cattail	*Typha latifolia*
Common horsetail	*Equisetum arvense*
Common Oak fern	*Gymnocarpium dryopteris*
Cream-colored Vetchling	*Lathyrus ochroleucus*
Creeping Juniper	*Juniperus horizontalis*
Creeping Spike-rush	*Eleocharis palustris*
Crocus Anemone	*Pulsatilla patens*
Dewberry	*Rubus pubescens*
Dwarf Birch	*Betula pumila* var. *glandulifera*
Early Blue Violet	*Viola adunca*
False Asphodel	*Tofieldia glutinosa*
Felt-leaved Willow	*Salix silicicola*
Field Chickweed	*Cerastium arvense*
Fireweed	*Epilobium angustifolium*
Flat-leaved Bladderwort	*Utricularia intermedia*
Fluccose Tansy	*Tanacetum huronense* var. *floccosum*
Fowl Bluegrass	*Poa palustris*
Foxtail Barley/Wild Barley	*Hordeum jubatum*
Fringed Loosestrife	*Lysimachia ciliata*
Giant Bur-reed	*Sparganium eurycarpum*
Giant Reed Grass	*Phragmites australis*
Greasewood	*Sarcobatus vermiculatus*
Great bulrush	*Scirpus tabernaemontani*
Green Alder	*Alnus viridis*
Green Ash	*Fraxinus pennsylvanica*
Green-flowered Bog-orchid	*Platenthera hyperborea*
Green-fruited Bur-reed	*Sparganium chlorocarpum*
Ground Cedar	*Lycopodium camplanatum*
Ground Juniper or Common Juniper	*Juniperus communis*
Gumweed	*Grindelia squarrosa*
Hairy-fruited Sedge	*Carex lasiocarpa*
Hairy Golden-Aster	*Heterotheca villosa*
Hairy Wild Rye	*Elymus innovatus*
Harebell	*Campanula rotundifolia*
Hay Sedge	*Carex siccata* or *Carex foenea* (var. *foenea*)
Heart-leaved Arnica	*Arnica cordifolia*
Heart-leaved Buttercup	*Ranunculus cardiophyllus*
High bush-cranberry	*Viburnum opulus*
Hoary sage brush	*Artemisia cana*
Hooker's Oat Grass	*Helictotrichon hookeri*
Horned Pondweed	*Zannichellia palustris*
Indian Rice Grass	*Oryzopsis hymenoides*
Inland Sea Thrift or Athabasca Thrift	*Armeria maritima* ssp *interior*
Jack Pine	*Pinus banksiana*
June Grass	*Koeleria macrantha*
Kentucky Blue Grass	*Poa pratensis*
Kitten-tails	*Besseya wyomingensis*
Labrador Tea	*Ledum palustre*
Lance-leaved Spring-beauty	*Claytonia lanceolata*
Lance-leaved Stonecrop	*Sedum lanceolatum*

COMMON NAME	SCIENTIFIC NAME
Leather-leaf	*Chamaedaphne calyculata*
Lesser Duckweed or Common Duckweed	*Lemna minor*
Little Bluestem	*Schizachyrium scoparium*
Lodgepole Pine	*Pinus contorta*
Low Bush-cranberry or Mooseberry	*Viburnum edule*
Low Goldenrod	*Solidago missouriensis*
Low Larkspur	*Delphinium bicolor*
Low Sedge	*Carex eleocharis*
Mackenzie Hairgrass	*Deschampsia mackenzieana*
Manitoba Maple	*Acer negundo*
Mare's-tail	*Hippuris vulgaris*
Marsh Cinquefoil	*Comarum palustre*
Marsh Reed Grass/Bluejoint	*Calamagrostis canadensis*
Marsh Skullcap	*Scutellaria galericulata*
Marshmarigold	*Caltha palustris*
Meadow-sweet or Narrow-leaved Meadowsweet	*Spiraea alba*
Moss Campion	*Silene acaulis* var. *exscapa*
Moss Phlox	*Phlox hoodii*
Mountain Maple	*Acer spicatum*
Mountain Shootingstar	*Dodecatheon conjugens*
Mud Sedge	*Carex limosa*
Narrow-leaved Labrador Tea	*Ledum palustre* ssp *decumbens*
Narrow-petaled Stonecrop	*Sedum stenopetalum*
Narrow Reed Grass	*Calamagrostis stricta*
Needle-and-Thread or Spear Grass	*Stipa comata*
Northern Awnless Brome	*Bromus pumpellianus*
Northern Bedstraw	*Galium boreale*
Northern Beech-fern	*Phegopteris connectilis*
Northern Bog Sedge	*Carex gynocrates*
Northern Comandra	*Geocaulon lividum*
Northern Gairdner's Squawroot	*Perideridia gairdneri* ssp *borealis*
Northern Gooseberry	*Ribes oxyacanthoides*
Northern Grass-of-Parnassus	*Parnassia palustris*
Northern Reed Grass	*Calamagrostis stricta* ssp *inexpansa*
Northern Twayblade	*Listera borealis*
Northern Wheatgrass	*Elymus lanceolatus* ssp *lanceolatus*
Northern Wormwood	*Artemisia campestris* ssp *borealis*
Nuttall's Salt-meadow Grass or Nuttall's Alkali Grass	*Puccinellia nuttalliana*
Pale laurel	*Kalmia polifolia*
Palmate-leaved coltsfoot	*Petasites palmatus*
Pasture Sage	*Artemisia frigida*
Pin Cherry	*Prunus pensylvanica*
Pinedrops	*Pterospora andromedea*
Pink Wintergreen	*Pyrola asarifolia*
Plains Rough Fescue	*Festuca hallii*
Plains Wormwood	*Artemisia campestris*

COMMON NAME	SCIENTIFIC NAME
Poison Ivy	*Toxicodendron rydbergii*
Porcupine Grass	*Stipa spartea*
Prairie Cord Grass	*Spartina pectinata*
Prairie Crocus	*Pulsatilla patens*
Prairie Rose	*Rosa arkansana*
Prairie Sage	*Artemisia ludoviciana*
Prairie Selaginella or Little Clubmoss	*Selaginella densa*
Prairie Sunflower	*Helianthus couplandii*
Prickly-pear Cactus	*Opuntia polyacantha*
Prickly Rose	*Rosa acicularis*
Proliferous Red Fescue	*Festuca rubra* var *prolifera*
Purple Avens	*Geum rivale*
Purple Clematis	*Clematis occidentalis*
Purple Qat Grass	*Schizachne purpurascens*
Purple Prairie-clover	*Dalea purpurea*
Purple Reed Grass	*Calamagrostis purpurascens*
Rattlesnake Plantain	*Goodyera oblongifolia*
Red Baneberrry	*Actaea rubra*
Red Currant	*Ribes triste*
Red Elderberry	*Sambucus racemosa*
Red Samphire	*Salicornia rubra*
Red-osier Dogwood	*Cornus sericea*
Reed Canary Grass	*Phalaris arundinacea*
Reindeer Moss	*Cladina rangiferina*
Richardson's Needle Grass	*Stipa richardsonii*
Richardson's Pondweed	*Potamogeton richardsonii*
River Alder	*Alnus incana* ssp *tenuifolia*
Round-leaved Hawthorn	*Crataegus rotundifolia*
Round-leaved Sundew	*Drosera rotundifolia*
Sago Pondweed	*Potamogeton pectinatus*
Saltgrass or Alkali Grass	*Distichlis spicata*
Sand Dropseed	*Sporobolus cryptandrus*
Sand Grass	*Calamovilfa longifolia*
Sand Heather	*Hudsonia tomentosa*
Saskatoon	*Amelanchier alnifolia*
Schreber's Moss/Feather Moss	*Pleurozium schreberi*
Seaside Arrow-grass	*Triglochin maritima*
Sea Lime Grass	*Leymus mollis*
Shining-leaved Meadow-sweet	*Spiraea betulifolia* var. *lucida*
Showy Aster	*Aster conspicuus*
Shrubby Cinquefoil	*Pentaphylloides floribunda*
Silver Sagebrush or Hoary Sagebush	*Artemisia cana*
Silvery Lupine	*Lupinus argenteus*
Skeletonweed	*Lygodesmia juncea*
Skunk Currant	*Ribes glandulosum*
Slender Arrow-grass	*Triglochin palustre*
Slender Naiad	*Najas flexilis*
Slender Wheat Grass	*Elymus trachycaulus* ssp *trachycaulus*
Small Bedstraw	*Galium trifidum*
Small-leaved Pussy-toes	*Antennaria microphylla*
Smooth Aster	*Aster laevis*
Smooth Brome	*Bromus inermis*

COMMON NAME	SCIENTIFIC NAME
Smooth Cliff-brake	*Pellaea glabella*
Smooth Woodsia	*Woodsia glabella*
Spangletop	*Scolochloa festucacea*
Sphagnum Moss/Peat Moss	*Sphagnum*
Spike-leaved Water-milfoil	*Myriophyllum spicatum*
Spike-rush	*Eleocharis*
Starflower	*Trientalis borealis*
Stiff Club-moss	*Lycopodium annotinum*
Sun-loving Sedge	*Carex pensylvanica*
Swamp Birch	*Betula pumila* var. *glandulifera*
Swamp Gooseberry	*Ribes Lacustre*
Swamp Horsetail	*Equisetum fluviatile*
Sweet Gale	*Myrica gale*
Tall Cotton-grass	*Eriophorum angustifolium*
Tall Lungwort	*Mertensia paniculata*
Tall Manna Grass	*Glyceria grandis*
Tamarack or Larch	*Larix laricina*
Three-leaved Solomon's-seal	*Maianthemum trifolium*
Two-leaved Solomon's-seal	*Maianthemum canadense var. interius*
Timber Oat Grass	*Danthonia intermedia*
Trembling Aspen	*Populus tremuloides*
Tufted Bulrush	*Scirpus cespitosus*
Twinflower	*Linnaea borealis*
Two-stamened Sedge	*Carex diandra*
Tyrrell's Willow	*Salix planifolia* ssp *tyrrellii*
Veiny Meadow Rue	*Thalictrum venulosum*
Vine-leaved Coltsfoot	*Petasites vitifolius*
Water Arum or Wild Calla	*Calla palustris*
Water Crowfoot - white	*Ranunculus aquatilis*
- yellow	*Ranunculus gmelinii*
Water Sedge	*Carex aquatilis*
Water Smartweed	*Polygonum amphibium*

COMMON NAME	SCIENTIFIC NAME
Water-parsnip	*Sium suave*
Western Canada Violet	*Viola canadensis* var *rugulosa*
Western Meadow-rue	*Thalictrum occidentale*
Western Mountain Ash	*Sorbus americana*
Western Porcupine Grass	*Stipa curtiseta*
Western Sea-blite	*Sueda maritima*
Western Snowberrry	*Symphoricarpos occidentalis*
Western Water-hemlock	*Cicuta maculata*
Western Wheatgrass	*Pascopyrum smithii*
White Birch	*Betula papyrifera*
White Hawkweed	*Hieracium albiflorum*
White-grained Mountain Rice Grass	*Oryzopsis asperifolia*
White Prairie Aster	*Aster falcatus*
White Spruce	*Picea glauca*
Widgeon-grass	*Ruppia maritima*
Wild Bergamot	*Monarda fistulosa*
Wild Black Currant	*Ribes americanum*
Wild Calla or Water Arum	*Calla palustris*
Wild Mint	*Mentha arvensis*
Wild Peavine	*Lathyrus venosus*
Wild Red Raspberry	*Rubus idaeus*
Wild Rice or Annual Wild Rice	*Zizania aquatica*
Wild Sarsaparilla	*Aralia nudicaulis*
Wild White Geranium	*Geranium richardsonii*
Wolf-willow	*Elaeagnus commutata*
Woolly sedge	*Carex lanuginosa*
Wood's Rose	*Rosa woodsii*
Yarrow	*Achillea millefolium*
Yellow Locoweed - late	*Oxytropis campestris*
- early	*Oxytropis sericea*
Yellow Monkeyflower	*Mimulus guttatus*
Yellow Umbrellaplant	*Eriogonum flavum*

Glossary

abiotic Devoid of life; non-living.

alluvial Pertaining to or composed of alluvium, or deposited by a stream or running water.

alluvium A general term for clay, silt sand, gravel, or similar unconsolidated material deposited during comparatively recent geologic time by a stream or other body of running water as a sorted or semi-sorted sediment in the bed of the stream or on its flood plain or delta.

aquifer A body of rock that contains sufficient saturated permeable material to conduct groundwater and to yield economically significant quantities of groundwater to wells and springs.

aquitard Groundwater system where soil materials may be saturated but the water is slow to move and difficult to extract.

arctic climate Conditions that support the development of treeless vegetation, with tundra or polar deserts.

basal aquifer Aquifers situated above Precambrian basement rocks and usually confined by thick Cretaceous shale aquitards.

base metal Any of the more common and chemically active metals, e.g. lead, copper.

basement rocks A complex of undifferentiated rocks that underlies the sedimentary rocks and deposits in an area. In Saskatchewan, the rocks of the complex are igneous and metamorphic and of Precambrian age.

bedrock A general term for the rock, usually solid, that underlies soil or other unconsolidated, superficial material.

bedrock aquifer Water-bearing bedrock.

bedrock surface The top of the uppermost layer of usually solid rock. It may occur on the surface or be buried beneath glacial and other unconsolidated material.

bentonite A form of clay, most forms possessing the ability to swell significantly when moistened. Natural deposits are mined for use as drilling mud and sealants.

biomass Any quantitative estimate of the total mass of organisms comprising all or part of a population or any other specified unit. Measured as volume, mass, or energy.

biotic Pertaining to life or living organisms; caused by, produced by or comprising living organisms.

boreal climate Environmental conditions that support the development of closed-canopied forests of conifer or mixed conifer-hardwood.

bowl bogs A bog, developed in a topographic depression, receiving mineralized water. This water is not reached by plant roots owing to peat accumulations, except near the margins of the bog.

calcareous Rich in calcium salts; pertaining to limestone or chalk.

carbonate CO_3, carbon trioxide ion.

Carswell meteorite impact structure Site of a large meteor impact located in the Athabasca Basin.

classification, soil Soils are classified using the Canadian Soil Classification System. The taxonomic units used in this book are:

Brunisolic Soils chiefly occurring on sandy deposits in the boreal forest region having brown to reddish-brown subsurface horizons that lack sufficient accumulations of amorphous iron oxides and organic matter to qualify as Podzolic soils. Eutric Brunisols are neutral to slightly alkaline; Dystric Brunisols are acid in reaction; and gleyed Brunisols are imperfectly drained.

Chernozemic Soils formed under grasses and forbs, or under grassland-forest transition vegetation. The soils have a dark colored surface, and subsurface horizons that are calcareous or of high base status. Brown soils occur in the sub-arid to semiarid grassland region and have a brown surface horizon; Dark Brown soils occur in the semiarid grassland region and have a dark brown surface horizon; Black soils occur in the subhumid aspen parkland region and have a black surface horizon; Dark Gray soils occur in the sub-humid grassland-forest transition and have a dark gray, partially eluviated surface horizon.

Cryosolic Mineral or organic soils that have perennially frozen material within one metre of the surface. Most Cryosols in Saskatchewan are Organocryosols.

Gleysolic Mineral soils formed under wet conditions but peaty gleysols have a layer of peat over the mineral soil.

Luvisolic Soils developed under forest that have a gray, eluviated surface and a subsurface where silicate clays that have been leached from above accumulate.

Organic Soils that have developed chiefly from organic deposits. They are usually saturated for most of the year, but some are only saturated for a few months.

Regosolic Weakly developed soils usually associated with recent deposits or eroded surfaces.

Solonetzic Soils developed under grass or grass-forest vegetation in semiarid to sub-humid climates. They are characterized by a stained, brownish subsurface layer and saline subsoils.

climax vegetation Community of plants the composition of which is more or less stable, in equilibrium with existing environmental conditions.

colluvial Pertaining to material transport to a site by gravity, as in rocks at the base of a slope.

coniferous Evergreen shrubs and trees characterized by needle-shaped leaves, cones and a resinous wood.

continental climate The climate of the interior of a continent, characterized by seasonal temperature extremes, and by the occurrence of maximum and minimum temperatures soon after summer and winter solstice, respectively.

cordillera An entire mountain system, including all subordinate ranges, interior plateaux and basins.

coulee A drainage course created by erosive forces of water flow from glaciers or surface runoff.

crystalline rock A term designating an igneous rock or a metamorphic rock, as opposed to a sedimentary rock.

deciduous Plants that shed their leaves or needles at a particular season, usually autumn.

delta A low, nearly flat alluvial tract of land. Generally deposited at or near the mouth of a river, commonly forming a triangular or fan-shaped plain of considerable area enclosed and crossed by many distributaries of the main river.

dendritic drainage A non-systematic or treelike (branching) pattern of valleys extending in many directions in a region, usually on rocks of uniform resistance.

diversity A measure of the number of species and their relative abundance.

divide The line of separation, or the ridge, summit, or narrow tract of high ground, marking the boundary between two adjacent drainage basins, or dividing the surface waters that flow naturally in one direction from those hat flow in the opposite direction.

dolomite A sedimentary rock comprised of calcium carbonate and magnesium.

drainage classes A group of soils defined as having a specific range in relative wetness under natural conditions as it pertains to wetness due to a water table under conditions similar to those under which the soil developed. The classes include:

rapidly drained The soil moisture content seldom exceeds field capacity; commonly of coarse texture or on steep slopes.

well-drained The soil moisture content does not normally exceed field capacity for a significant part of the year.

moderately well-drained The soil moisture in excess of field capacity remains for a small but significant part of the year.

imperfectly drained The soil moisture in excess of field capacity remains in lower parts of the soil for moderately long periods of the year.

poorly drained The soil moisture in excess of field capacity remains in all parts of the soil for a large part of the year.

very poorly drained Free water remains at or near the surface for a large part of the year.

drift See glacial drift.

drumlin A low, smoothly rounded, elongated and oval hill, mound or ridge composed of compact glacial till, built under the margin of the ice, and shaped by its flow, or carved out of an older moraine by readvancing ice; its longer axis is parallel to the direction of movement of the ice. It usually has a blunt nose pointing in the direction from which the ice approached, and a gentler slope tapering in the other direction. From the Scottish "drum," a long narrow ridge.

dune A low mound, ridge, bank, or hill of loose windblown granular material (usually sand), either bare or covered with vegetation, capable of movement from place to place, but always retaining its own characteristic shape.

ecosystem A community of organisms, interacting with one another, plus the environment in which they live and with which they also interact.

endemic Restricted to a particular region, and occurring nowhere else in the world.

eolian Pertaining to the action or effect of the wind (aeolian).

ericaceous Belonging to the heath genus *Erica* or its family *Ericaceae*.

erratics Rock fragments that are transported into an area from the outside, found either incorporated into the sediment or lying free; glacial erratics.

erosional unconformity An interruption in the geological record where uplift and erosion have resulted in loss of the previously formed record so that a rock unit is overlain by another that is not next in stratigraphic succession.

escarpment A long cliff or steep slope that separates two levels of gently sloping land surfaces, produced by erosion and faulting.

esker A long, low, narrow, sinuous, steep-side ridge or mound composed of sand and gravel that was deposited by a stream flowing in a tunnel beneath or within a glacier and left behind when the ice melted. From the Irish eiscir, 'ridge.'

eutrophication The process by which waters attain concentrations of nutrients that are optimal for plant or animal growth.

evapotranspiration The actual total loss of water by evaporation from soil and from water bodies, and transpiration from vegetation over a given area with time.

even-aged Generally referring to a population comprised of individuals of similar age class.

exposure A continuous area in which a rock formation or geologic structure is visible, either naturally or artificially, and is unobscured by soil, vegetation, water, or the works of man. (*Synonym* outcrop).

fault A fracture or zone of fractures along which there has been relative movement of the sides parallel to the fracture.

felsenmere A flat or gently sloping area covered with a continuous veneer of large angular blocks of rock derived from well-jointed underlying bedrock by intensive frost action.

fen A eutrophic mire, with a winter water table at ground level or above, usually dominated by herbaceous grasses.

field capacity The moisture content of a soil 2 to 3 days after the soil has been saturated and free drainage has practically ceased.

filamentous Comprised of thread-like structures.

fluting The formation by glacial action of large, smooth, deep, gutter-like channels or furrows on the stoss side of a rocky hill obstructing the advance of a glacier.

forage The leaves and stems of crops harvested as hay for animal feed. These crops are often perennial, e.g., alfalfa, brome grass, crested wheat .

forbs Broad-leaved herbaceous plants.

frost boil A low mound developed by local differential frost heaving at a place most favourable for the formation of segregated ice and accompanied by an absence of insulating cover of vegetation.

glacial drift A general term for material transported by glaciers or icebergs and deposited directly on land or in the sea.

glacial erosion The grinding, plucking, scouring, gouging, grooving, scratching and polishing effected by the movement of glacier ice armed with rock fragments frozen into it, together with the erosive action of meltwater streams.

glacial spillway The channel or watercourse formed by the erosive forces of water draining a glacial lake.

glacial till Unsorted and unstratified drift, generally unconsolidated, deposited directly by and underneath a glacier without subsequent reworking by water from the glacier, and consisting of a heterogeneous mixture of clay, silt, sand, gravels and boulders varying widely in size and shape.

glaciofluvial Pertaining to the meltwater streams flowing from the wasting glacier ice and especially to the deposits and landforms produced by such streams.

glaciolacustrine Pertaining to, derived from, or deposited in glacial lakes; especially said of the deposits and landforms composed of suspended material brought by meltwater streams flowing into lakes bordering the glacier but also including lakes lying entirely on glacial ice and due to differential melting.

graminoids Members of the grass family, or plants resembling grasses.

granite gneiss A metamorphosed granite.

grasses Plants that have rounded and hollow jointed stems, narrow sheathing leaves, flowers borne in spikes or panicles, and hard, grain-like seeds.

ground moraine The rock debris dragged along, in or beneath a glacier or ice sheet; also, this material after it has been deposited or released from the ice during ablation, to form an extensive, fairly even, thin layer of till, having a gently rolling surface.

groundwater That part of the subsurface water that is the zone of saturation, including underground streams.

herb Plant with no persistent parts above ground, as distinct from shrubs and trees.

herbivory Feeding on plants, plant parts.

hummocky moraine An area of knob-and-kettle topography that may have been formed either along a live-ice front or around masses of stagnant ice.

ice scour The process of scraping of land or sediments and associated plants by the movement of glaciers, or ice on rivers or lakes.

igneous Pertaining to rocks that are formed by the solidification of molten magma.

inter-till aquifer An aquifer situated between two glacial till units.

kame A long, low, steep-sided hill, mound, knob, hummock, or short irregular ridge composed chiefly of poorly sorted and stratified sand and gravel deposited by a sub-glacial stream as an alluvial fan or delta against or upon the margin of a melting glacier.

kettle A steep-sided, usually basin- or bowl-shaped hole or depression without surface drainage in glacial drift deposits, often containing a lake or other wetland, and believed to have formed by the melting of a large, detached block of stagnant ice that had been wholly or partly buried in the glacial drift.

lacustrine Pertaining to lakes, ponds, or other relatively static waters.

lag The large rocks and boulders that remain in place after erosion has removed the smaller, lighter materials.

leaching The removal of the soluble constituents of a rock, soil, or ore by the action of percolating waters.

lichens Flowerless plants composed of fungi and algae in symbiotic union, commonly growing in flat greenish gray, yellowish, or blackish patches on rocks, trees, etc.

limestone A sedimentary rock consisting chiefly of calcium carbonate, primarily in the form of the mineral calcite.

loess A homogeneous, commonly non-stratified, porous, friable, unconsolidated, usually highly calcareous blanket deposit, composed chiefly of materials ranging in size from clay to fine sand.

mantle The soils and sediment formations that overlay bedrock.

marl deposits A sediment consisting of clay and carbonate of lime.

marsh A wet or periodically wet area, with aquatic or grass-like vegetation and no peat formation.

meltwater channel The watercourse followed by water flowing from melting glaciers.

metamorphic rock A rock derived from pre-existing rocks by mineralogical, chemical, and structural changes, essentially in the solid state, in response to marked changes in temperature, pressure, shearing stress, and chemical environment at depth in the earth's crust.

montane Pertaining to mountainous regions; usually the cool, moist, upland habitat below the tree line, dominated by evergreen trees.

moraine A mound, ridge, or other distinct accumulation of unsorted, unstratified glacial drift, predominantly till, deposited chiefly by direct action of glacier ice in a variety of topographic landforms that are independent of control by the surface on which the drift lies.

mudstone A hard mud having the texture and composition but lacking the fine lamination of shale; approximately equal proportions of clay and silt.

nunataks An isolated knob, hill, ridge, or peak that projects above a glacier and is completely surrounded by ice.

oilseed A crop that produces seeds containing a high percentage of oil. The oil can be economically extracted for food or industrial uses, e.g., canola, flax.

open-crowned Pertaining to the generally open canopy of woodlands.

open-water zone The deeper areas (depth >1 m) of a water body where shoreline plants are incapable of growing.

outcrop The part of the geologic formation or structure that appears at the earth's surface. (*Synonym:* exposure).

outliers Portions of an ecoregion which are geographically separated from the main portion of the ecoregion.

outwash Stratified sand or gravel removed or "washed out" from a glacier by meltwater streams and deposited in front of or beyond the margin of an active glacier.

overburden The loose soil, silt, sand, gravel, or other unconsolidated material overlying bedrock.

oxbow Loop-shaped meanders of streams, some of which may have become cut off from the flow of water.

palsas Irregular to sub-rounded peat domes that can rise eight feet or more above the surround organic terrain. It is formed when accumulating peat and developed plant cover insulate the frozen layer and allow it to increase in volume. The vegetation on the palsa is usually black spruce, or white birch, but the surrounding area is dominated by sedge-grass vegetation. An open "lead" of water is often found at the base of the palsa. As the frozen layer thickens, and thus the height of the palsa increases, it becomes unstable, and cracks form in the top of the dome, the sides slump, breaking the insulating layer, changing the energy balance and causing the frozen lens to melt and eventually collapse completely leaving a small pool of water. A sedge meadow forms initially, and trees invade very slowly. This results in a nearly circular, treeless patch of meadow in the treed bog, known as a "palsa scar." They indicate relatively recent disappearance of discontinuous permafrost from organic terrain.

passerine Perching birds which feed mainly upon seeds and/or insects (e.g., sparrows, larks).

peat An unconsolidated deposit of raw to well-decomposed plant remains of a water saturated environment such as a bog or fen, and of persistently high moisture content.

peneplain A low, nearly featureless, and gently undulating or almost planar land surface of considerable area which presumably has been reduced by the process of long-continued sub-aerial erosion.

permafrost Any soil, subsoil, or other surficial deposit occurring in arctic or subarctic regions at a variable depth below the earth's surface in which a temperature below freezing has existed for a long time (from two to thousands of years).

PFRA community pastures Marginal agricultural lands managed by Agriculture and Agri-Food Canada. They accommodate sustainable grazing practices and other compatible land uses, such as wildlife habitat, recreation, mineral extraction, and preservation of archaeological sites.

phytoplankton Species of plants that exist in suspension in water (or air) with little or no capability of movement independent of that of the suspending medium. In aquatic environments, these are typically represented by microscopic algae such as diatoms and desmids.

plutonic rock A rock formed at considerable depth by crystallization of magma. It is characteristically a medium to coarse grained rock (e.g., granite).

polygonally patterned A form of patterned ground marked by polygonal or polygonal-like arrangements of rock, soil, and vegetation, produced on a level or gently sloping surface by frost action.

pothole Small (less than two hectares), shallow, semi-permanent ponds, which were formed in glacial deposits during the melting of the glaciers.

predation The consumption of one animal (the prey) by another (the predator); also refers to the consumption of plants by animals, or the partial consumption of a large prey organism by a smaller predator.

protected area Designated provincial Crown lands under the Parks Act, or similar legislation, which protect and preserve site-specific cultural (e.g., archaeological, historical, paleontological) and natural areas of provincial significance.

provincial community pastures Large blocks of provincial Crown land that have been assembled to provide supplemental grazing for livestock producers and to maintain marginal agricultural lands in permanent cover. These lands are managed to accommodate complementary multiple uses, such as wildlife habitat, recreation, heritage interests, and mineral activities.

provincial historic sites Small parcels of Crown land that contain prehistoric or historic resources of provincial significance.

provincial parks Parcels of Crown land that protect heritage resources within Saskatchewan. Provincial parks are designated in four categories: historic parks, natural environment parks, recreation parks, wilderness parks.

pulse A legume plant that produces edible seeds. The plant obtains nitrogen from the air by way of a symbiotic relationship between its roots and Rhizobium bacteria, e.g., peas, beans, lentils.

rangeland Extensive areas of grasslands that are used and managed as habitat and food supply for free-roaming livestock such as cattle, sheep, horses, and bison.

raptor Birds of prey such as owls, hawks, and eagles.

reaction The degree of acidity or alkalinity (of a soil), usually expressed as a pH value.

relief (a) A term used loosely for the actual physical shape, configuration, or general unevenness of a part of the earth's surface, considered with reference to variations of height and slope or to irregularities of the land surface; the elevations or differences in elevation, considered collectively, of a land surface.

(b) The difference in elevation between the hilltops or mountains and lowlands or valleys of a given region. A region showing a great variation in elevation has "high relief," and one showing little variation has "low relief."

regeneration Restoration by an organism of tissues or organs that have been removed.

regional parks Areas that provide outdoor recreational opportunities in relatively close proximity to small communities and rural areas on a regional basis throughout the province.

richness A measure of the absolute number of species in an assemblage.

riparian systems The portion of the vegetated land adjacent to water bodies which interacts with the aquatic environment with respect to biological, chemical, and physical features.

root zone The portion of the soil profile and area beneath a plant which contains the majority of actively growing plant roots.

sandstone A rock comprised of an abundance of sand-size particles set in a matrix of finer materials and more or less firmly united by cementing materials.

scarpment A steep slope of a hill, valley, or escarpment.

schistose Foliated structure in crystalline rocks due to the parallel, planar arrangement of the platy mineral grains.

seed-banking species Plant species which produce seeds that can remain dormant for many years until conditions become favorable for germination.

serotinous Produced, blossoming, or developing late in the season.

shale A fine-grained, hard, sedimentary rock formed by the consolidation of clay, silt, or mud, and characterized by a laminated structure and a composition with an appreciable content of clay minerals.

shrubs A woody perennial plant of low stature, characterized by persistent stems and branches springing from the base.

slake To combine chemically with water, such as with some shales which become soft and highly plastic when moist.

species diversity See diversity.

species richness See richness.

staging area An area used by migratory wildlife (particularly waterfowl and shorebirds) for resting and flock/herd assembly prior to migration.

still-stand A location where the progressing edge of a glacier remains at a fixed location as melting rate is offset by advancement of the ice. A long, narrow moraine may be left along this location after the glacier recedes.

strandline The ephemeral line or level at which a body of standing water, as a lake, meets the land; the shoreline.

striation A superficial scratch on a rock surface by a geological agent such as glaciers and usually occurring as one of a series of parallel lines.

subarctic climate Environmental conditions that support the development of open-canopied coniferous woodlands, with tundra patches.

successional series The various plant communities that occur in the same area as vegetation develops.

sucker An underground shoot arising adventitiously from the base of the stem or from the roots, and emerging to form a new plant.

surficial aquifer An aquifer that is present at the surface.

summerfallow Land that is not seeded to crop, but rather is tilled several times during the summer to control weeds, conserve soil moisture, and break down crop residues from the previous year.

thermokarst Karst-like topographic features produced in a permafrost region by the local melting of ground ice and the subsequent settling of the ground.

till See glacial till.

till plain An extensive area with a flat to undulating surface, underlain by till, which is commonly covered by ground moraine.

topographic relief The elevations or differences in elevation, considered collectively, of a land surface.

transpiration Loss of water vapour from an organism through a membrane or through pores.

trellis drainage A drainage pattern characterized by parallel main streams intersected at or near at right angles by their tributaries which in turn are fed by elongated secondary tributaries parallel to the main streams, resembling in plan the stems of a vine or trellis.

tundra A treeless, level, or gently undulating plain characteristic of arctic or subarctic regions. It usually has a marshy surface that supports a growth of mosses, lichens, and numerous low shrubs, and underlain by a dark, mucky soil and permafrost.

turbid Cloudy; opaque with suspended matter.

underfit streams A misfit stream that appears to be too small to have eroded the valley in which it flows.

understory That portion of the trees or other vegetation in a forest stand below the main canopy level.

varved Having a banded sediment layer deposited in a lake in a single year. Sediment having a paler, coarser layer deposited in spring and summer and a darker layer deposited in autumn and winter.

volcanic rock A generally finely crystalline or glassy igneous rock resulting from volcanic action at or near the surface, either ejected explosively or extruded as lava.

watershed An elevated boundary area separating tributaries that drain into different river systems.

References

Abouguendia, Z.M. (ed.). 1981. *Athabasca Sand Dunes in Saskatchewan.* Mackenzie River Basin Study Report Supplement No. 7. Mackenzie River Basin Committee. 329pp.+ appendices.

Abouguendia, Z.M., R.C. Godwin and D.J. Richert. 1979. Botanical investigations along the proposed Key Lake Road. Final Report. Saskatchewan Research Council Report No. C79-20.

Acton, D.F., G.A. Padbury and J.A. Shields. 1990. *Soil Landscapes of Canada – Saskatchewan.* Land Resource Research Centre, Research Branch, Agriculture Canada, Ottawa, Ontario, Canada. Publication 5243/B.

Agriculture Canada Expert Committee on Soil Survey. 1987. *The Canadian system of soil classification.* 2nd ed. Agric. Can. Publ. 1646. 164pp.

Argus, G.W. 1964. Plant collections from Carswell Lake and Beartooth Island northwestern Saskatchewan, Canada. *Canadian Field-Naturalist* 78:139-149.

Argus, G.W. 1966. Botanical investigations in northwestern Saskatchewan: the subarctic Patterson-Hasbala Lakes region. *Canadian Field-Naturalist* 80:119-143.

Atmospheric Environment Service. 1994. Canadian monthly climate data and 1961-1990 normals, 1994 release. CD-ROM. Environment Canada, Ottawa, Ont.

Atton, F.M. 1969. Fish, amphibians and reptiles. Pages 83-84 in J.H. Richards and K.I. Fung (eds.) *Atlas of Saskatchewan.* University of Saskatchewan, Saskatoon, Sask.

Banfield, A.W.F. 1974. *The mammals of Canada.* National Museum of Natural Science, National Museums of Canada, Ottawa, Ont. University of Toronto Press, Toronto, Ont. 438pp.

Beckingham, J.D., D.G. Nielsen and V.A. Toransky.1996. Field guide to ecosites of the mid-boreal ecoregions of Saskatchewan. Canadian Forestry Service, Special Report #6. UBC Press, Vancouver, B.C.

Bird, R.D. 1961. *Ecology of the aspen parkland of western Canada.* Research Branch, Canada Department of Agriculture, Ottawa, Ont. Publication 1066. 155pp.

Bradley, S.W., J.S. Rowe and C. Tarnocai. 1982. *An ecological land survey of the Lockhart River map area, Northwest Territories.* Lands Directorate, Environment Canada, Ottawa, Ont. Ecological Land Classification Series, No. 16. 152pp.

Brown, R.J.E. 1965. Permafrost investigations in Saskatchewan and Manitoba. National Research Council, Division of Building Research, Ottawa, Ont. Technical Paper No.193, 73pp.

Brown, R.J.E. 1967. Permafrost in Canada. Map 1246A. Geological Survey of Canada, Energy, Mines and Resources, Ottawa, Ont.

Budd, A.C. and K.F. Best. 1969. *Wild plants of the Canadian Prairies.* Research Branch, Agriculture Canada, Ottawa, Ont. Publ. No. 983, 519pp.

Canada Soil Inventory. 1988. Soil landscapes of Canada (Saskatchewan). Land Resource Research Centre, Research Branch, Agriculture Canada, Ottawa, Ont. LRRC Contribution No. 87-45. Provincial map at 1:1 million scale.

Carroll, S.B. and L.C. Bliss. 1982. Jack pine-lichen woodland on sandy soils in northern Saskatchewan and northeastern Alberta. *Can. J. Bot.*60:2270-2282.

Clayton, L. and S.R. Moran. 1974. A glacial process-form model. Pages 89-119 in D.R. Coates, (ed.) *Glacial geomorphology.* George Allen & Unwin, Boston.

Commission for Environmental Cooperation. 1997. Ecological Regions of North America – Toward a Common Perspective. Commission for Environmental Cooperation, Montreal, Quebec, Canada.

Cook, F.R. 1966. A guide to the amphibians and reptiles of Saskatchewan. Sask. Museum of Natural History, Regina, Sask. Popular Series No. 13. 40pp.

Coupland, R.T. 1992. Mixed prairie. Pages 151-182 in R.T. Coupland (ed.) *Ecosystems of the World 8A. Natural grasslands.* Elsevier, New York.

Dirschl, H.J. and D.L. Dabbs. 1969. A contribution to the flora of the Saskatchewan River Delta. *Canadian Field-Naturalist* 83:212-228.

Dodd, J.D. and R.T. Coupland. 1966. Vegetation of saline areas in Saskatchewan. *Ecology* 47:958-968.

Ecological Stratification Working Group. 1995. A national ecological framework for Canada. Agriculture and Agri-Food Canada, Research Branch, Centre for Land and Biological Resources Research and Environment Canada, State of the Environment Directorate, Ecozone Analysis Branch, Ottawa/Hull. Report and national map at 1:7.5 million scale.

Ecological Stratification Working Group. 1996. A National Ecological Framework for Canada. Centre for Land and Biological Resources Research, Research Branch, Agriculture and Agri-Food Canada, State of the Environment Directorate, Environmental Conservation Service, Environment Canada. Ottawa, Ontario, Canada.

Ecoregions of Saskatchewan CD-ROM Committee. 1998. Ecoregions of Saskatchewan CD-ROM. Saskatchewan Education, Regina, Saskatchewan.

Ecoregions Working Group. 1989. *Ecoclimatic regions of Canada.* Canadian Wildlife Service, Environment Canada. Ecological Land Classification Series No. 23. 117pp. + national map.

Erskine, A.J. 1977. Birds in boreal Canada: communities, densities, and adaptations. Canadian Wildlife Service, Report series #41:1-73.

Gauthier, D.A. and D. Henry. 1989. Misunderstanding the prairies. In: *Endangered Spaces – the Future for Canada's Wilderness.* M. Hummel (editor), Key Porter Books Limited, Toronto, Ontario, Canada.

Hammer, U.T, R.C. Haynes, J.M. Heseltine and S.M. Swanson. 1975. The saline lakes of Saskatchewan. *Verh. Internat. Verein. Limnol.* 19:589-598.

Hammer, U.T and R.C. Haynes. 1978. The saline lakes of Saskatchewan. II. Locale, hydrography, and other physical aspects. *Int. Revue ges. Hydrobiol.* 63:179-203.

Harms, V.L. 1974. Botanical studies in the boreal forest along the Green Lake-La Loche Road, northwestern Saskatchewan. *Musk Ox* 14:37-54.

Harris, W.C., A. Kabzems, A.L. Kosowan, G.A. Padbury and J.S. Rowe. 1983. Ecological regions of Saskatchewan. Forestry Division, Sask. Parks and Renewable Resources. Technical Bulletin No.10. 57pp. + provincial map at 1:2.5 million scale.

Hart, R.T and R.R. Stewart. 1981. Terrestrial wildlife habitat of the Cypress Hill (72F) map area, Saskatchewan. Sask. Tourism and Renewable Resources. Wildlife Tech. Rep. 81-7.

Juurand, P. 1974. Description and analysis of scenic resources along the Churchill, Sturgeon-Weir and Clearwater Rivers. Planning, National Parks Branch, Parks Canada. 19pp.

Kabzems, A., A.L. Kosowan and W.C. Harris. 1986. Mixedwood section in an ecological perspective, Saskatchewan. Sask. Parks and Renewable Resources, Forestry Division, Technical Bulletin No. 8. 2nd. ed. 118pp.+ forest inventory map at 1:1 million scale.

Kessel, B., S.M. Murphy and L.J. Vining. 1984 Waterfowl populations and limnologic characteristics of taiga ponds. *J. Wildlife Management* 48:1156- .

Klassen, R.W. 1991. Surficial geology and drift thickness, Cypress Lake, Saskatchewan. Geological Survey of Canada, Map 1766A, scale 1:250,000.

Korol, J. 1995. Riparian forest communities in the southern boreal region of central Saskatchewan. Prince Albert Model Forest Report, Prince Albert, Sask. 129pp.

Kupsch, W.O. 1975. The Churchill-Reindeer Rivers area: evolution of its landscape. *Musk Ox* 15:10-29.

Larson, J.A. 1989. The northern forest border in Canada and Alaska: biotic communities and ecological relationships. Springer-Verlag, New York. 255pp.

Looman, J. 1986. The vegetation of the Canadian prairie provinces: III. Aquatic and semi-aquatic vegetation: aquatic plant communities. *Phytocoenologia* 14:19-54.

Looman, J. 1987. The vegetation of the Canadian prairie provinces: IV. The woody vegetation: deciduous woods and forests. *Phytocoenologia* 15:51-84.

Looman, J. and K.F. Best. 1979. *Budd's Flora of the Canadian prairie provinces.* Agriculture Canada, Research Branch, Ottawa, Ont. Publication No.1662. 863pp.

Macdonald, R. and P. Broughton (compilers). 1980. Geological map of Saskatchewan, provisional edition. Sask. Mineral Resources. Provincial map at 1:1 million scale.

Mendis, A.S. 1956. A limnological comparison of four lakes in central Saskatchewan. Dept. Natural Resources, Fisheries Branch, Report No.2, Prince Albert, Sask. 23pp.

Moss, E.H. 1974. *Flora of Alberta.* University of Toronto Press, Toronto, Ont. 546pp.

Moss, H.C. 1965. Guide to understanding Saskatchewan soils. Ext. Publ. 175. University of Saskatchewan, Saskatoon, Sask. 79pp.

Newsome, R. and R.L. Dix 1968. The forests of the Cypress Hills, Alberta and Saskatchewan, Canada. *American Midland Naturalist* 80:118-185.

Padbury, G.A., W.K. Head and W.E. Souster. 1978. *Biophysical resource inventory of the Prince Albert National Park, Saskatchewan.* Saskatchewan Institute of Pedology Publication S185. University of Saskatchewan, Saskatoon, Sask. 526pp.

Padbury, G.A. and D.F. Acton. 1994. Ecoregions of Saskatchewan. Minister of Supply and Services Canada and Saskatchewan Property Management Corporation, Ottawa/ Regina. Provincial map at 1:2.5 million scale.

Paterson, D.F. 1973. Geology of Saskatchewan. Saskatchewan Mineral Resources. Poster.

PCAP Committee. 1998. Saskatchewan Prairie Conservation Action Plan. Canadian Plains Research Center, University of Regina, Regina, Saskatchewan, Canada. Http://www.cprc.uregina.ca

Pupp, Christian, Harm Maathuis and Gary Grove. 1991. Groundwater quality in Saskatchewan: hyrogeology, quality concerns, management. Environment Canada, National Hydrology Research Institute, Saskatoon, Sask. 66pp.

Rawson, D.S. 1960. Five lakes on the Churchill River near Stanley, Saskatchewan. Department of Natural Resources, Fisheries Branch, Prince Albert, Sask. Fisheries Report No. 5, 38pp.

Rawson, D.S. 1957. Limnology and fisheries of five lakes in the Upper Churchill Drainage, Saskatchewan Department of Natural Resources, Fisheries Branch, Prince Albert, Sask. Report No. 3, 61pp.

Rawson, D.S. and J.E. Moore. 1944. The saline lakes of Saskatchewan. *Can. J. Res.* 22:141-201.

Richards, J.H. and K.I. Fung. 1969. *Atlas of Saskatchewan.* University of Saskatchewan, Saskatoon, Sask. 236pp.

Ripley, E.A. 1992. Grassland climate. Pages 7-24 in Robert T. Coupland (ed.) *Ecosystems of the World 8A. Natural Grasslands, Introduction and Western Hemisphere.* Elsevier, New York.

Ritchie, J.C. 1956. The vegetation of northern Manitoba. I. Studies in the southern spruce forest zone. *Can. J. Botany* 34:523-561.

Rowe, J.S. 1972. *Forest regions of Canada.* Department of the Environment, Canadian Forestry Service. Publication No. 1300. 172 pp.

Rowe, J.S. 1983. *Landscapes: a guide to the landforms and ecology of southern Saskatchewan.* Reference Manual. Sask. Environment, Regina, Sask. 101pp.

Rowe, J.S. 1984. Lichen woodland in northern Canada. Pages 225-237 in R. Olson, R. Hastings, and F. Geddes (eds.) *Northern ecology and resource management.* University of Alberta Press, Edmonton, Alta.

Roy, J.F. 1996. *Birds of the Elbow.* Special Publ. No. 21, Sask. Natural History Society, Regina, Sask. 325pp.

Rump, P.C. and Kent Harper. 1980. *Land use in Saskatchewan.* 2nd. ed. Policy, Planning and Research Branch, Sask. Environment, Regina, Sask. 185pp.

Saskatchewan Geological Survey. 1994. Geology and mineral resources of Saskatchewan. Sask. Energy and Mines, Misc. Rep. 94-6, 99pp.

__________ .1990. Mineral resource map of Saskatchewan. Sask. Energy and Mines, 1990 edition.

Sauchyn, David J. (ed.) 1993. *Quaternary and Late Tertiary landscapes of southwestern Saskatchewan and adjacent areas.* Canadian Plains Research Center, University of Regina, Regina, Sask. 114pp.

Schreiner, B.T. 1984. Quaternary geology of the Precambrian Shield, Saskatchewan. Sask. Energy and Mines, Rep. 221. Regina. 106pp. + map.

__________. 1986. Quaternary Geology as a Guide to Mineral Exploration in the Southeastern Shield Saskatchewan. Sask. Energy Mines, Open File Report 86-5, 39pp.

Scott, W.B. and E.J. Crossman. 1973. *Freshwater fishes of Canada.* Fisheries Research Board of Canada, Bulletin 184, Department of Environment, Ottawa, Ont. 965pp.

Secoy, D.M. and T.K. Vincent. 1976. Part I. Distribution and population status of Saskatchewan's amphibians and reptiles. Sask. Parks and Renewable Resources, Wildlife Branch, Regina, Sask.

Simpson, M.A. (compiler) 1997. Surficial geology map of Saskatchewan. Sask. Energy Mines/Sask. Research Council. 1:1 million scale map.

Sloan, C.E. 1972. Check Ref.Txt file

Smith, A.R. 1996. *Atlas of Saskatchewan birds.* Sask. Natural History Society, Regina, Sask. Special Publication No. 22. 456pp.

Smith, D.C. 1978. The Athabasca sand dunes: a physical inventory. Indian and Northern Affairs, National Parks Branch, Ottawa, Ont.

Stewart, R.E. and H.A. Kantrud. 1971. Classification of natural ponds and lakes in the glaciated prairie region. U.S. Bureau of Sport Fisheries and Wildlife, Resource Publication 92. 57pp.

Stokes, D. and L. Stokes. 1996. *Stokes field guide to birds, western region.* Little, Brown and Company, Toronto, Ont.

Storer, J. 1989. *Geological History of Saskatchewan.* Royal Sask. Museum, Regina, Sask. 91pp.

Wiken, E. 1966. Ecosystems: frameworks for thought. *World Conservation* 27(1). Gland, Switzerland. CH-1196.

Wiken, E. 1996. Terrestrial and Marine Ecozones of Canada. Ottawa, Environment Canada.

Wiken, E.B., D.A. Gauthier, I. Marshall, K. Lawton and H. Hirvonen. 1996. A perspective on Canada's ecosystems: an overview of the terrestrial and marine ecozones. Canadian Council on Ecological Areas, Occasional Paper Number 14, Ottawa, Ontario, Canada. Http://www.cprc.uregina.ca/ccea

Wolfe, S.A., D.J. Huntley and J. Ollerhead. 1995. Recent and late Holocene sand dune activity in southwestern Saskatchewan. Pages 131-140 in *Current research 1995-B*. Geological Survey of Canada. Ottawa, Ont.

Zoltai, S.C. 1972. Palsas and peat plateaus in central Manitoba and Saskatchewan. *Can. J. For. Res.* 2:291-302.